THE
SETTLING
OF
NORTH AMERICA

THE ATLAS OF THE GREAT MIGRATIONS INTO NORTH
AMERICA FROM THE ICE AGE TO THE PRESENT

EDITED BY
HELEN HORNBECK TANNER

ASSOCIATE EDITORS:

JANICE REIFF JOHN H. LONG

DIRK HOERDER HENRY F. DOBYNS

MACMILLAN • USA

MACMILLAN
A Simon & Schuster Macmillan Company
1633 Broadway
New York, NY 10019-6785

Library of Congress Cataloging–in–Publication Data

The settling of North America : the atlas of the great migrations into
    North America from the Ice Age to present.
          p.   cm.
      Includes index.
      1. North America—Emigration and immigration—History—Maps.
    2. Immigrations—North America—History—Maps.
      G1106.E27S4   1995 <G&M>   95–37756
      304.8'097'022—dc20   CIP
                                                   MAP

ISBN 0–02–616272–5

Printed in Great Britain by
Bath Press Limited, Avon, England.

Design, artwork and typesetting by
Swanston Publishing Limited, Derby, England.

10   9   8   7   6   5   4   3   2   1

DESIGN: Malcolm Swanston and Ralph Orme

EDITORIAL: Chris Schüler and Rhonda Carrier

ILLUSTRATION: Ralph Orme

INDEXING: Barry Haslam and Jean Cox

MAPS DESIGNED AND CREATED BY: Andrea Fairbrass, Peter Gamble, Elsa Gibert,
Elizabeth Hudson, Isabelle Lewis, David McCutcheon, Ralph Orme, Kevin Panton,
Nick Whetton and Malcolm Swanston

PICTURE RESEARCH: Charlotte Taylor

TYPESETTING: Jeanne Arnold

CONTRIBUTORS

EDITOR

HELEN HORNBECK TANNER, Senior Research Fellow, The Newberry Library, Chicago, has written in the fields of Indian and colonial history. As editor of the *Atlas of Great Lakes Indian History* (University of Oklahoma Press, 1986), she received the 1988 Erminie Wheeler-Voegelin Award from the American Society for Ethnohistory. Her other publications include *Zéspedes in East Florida* (1963 and 1989) and *The Ojibwa* (1991). *(Pages 22, 52, 68, 90, 126, 154, 176, 194.)*

ASSOCIATE EDITORS

HENRY F. DOBYNS is the author of *Their Numbers Become Thinned* (1983) and *Native American Historical Demography: A Critical Bibliography* (1976). His continuing research interests are in demography and the Spanish colonial frontier. *(Pages 24, 26, 28, 30, 42, 44, 74, 76)*

DIRK HOERDER teaches North American social history at the University of Bremen, Germany. His publications include *"Struggle a Hard Battle:" Essays on Working-Class Immigrants* (DeKalb: Northern Illinois University Press, 1986), *Labor Migration in the Atlantic Economies: The European and North American Working Classes During the Period of Industrialization* (Westport: Greenwood Press, 1985). *(Pages 94, 112, 114, 116, 118, 120, 124, 128, 130, 132.)*

JOHN H. LONG is editor of the *Atlas of Historical County Boundaries*, a project of the Newberry Library, Chicago. He was assistant editor of the *Atlas of Early American History: The Revolutionary Era, 1760–1790* (1976). *(Pages 66, 70, 72, 88, 92, 96, 98, 100.)*

JANICE REIFF, Assistant Professor of History at the University of California – Los Angeles, is completing a book entitled *Manufacturing Communities: Pullman Workers and their Towns, 1880–1891*. She is the author of *Structuring the Past: The Use of Computers in History* (1991). *(Pages 134, 146, 148, 150, 152, 154, 180, 188.)*

CONTRIBUTORS

JOHN S. AUBREY, Ayer Librarian at The Newberry Library, Chicago, has special research interests in U.S. History and American Indian Studies. *(Page 152.)*

BERNARD BAILYN is Adams University Professor Emeritus and James Duncan Phillips Professor of Early American History Emeritus at Harvard University. He has received the Pulitzer Prize for two publications, *Ideological Origins of the American Revolution* (1968) and *Voyagers to the West* (1987). He serves as Director of the International Seminar on the History of the Atlantic World. *(Page 46.)*

DAVID BUISSERET, Professor of History at the University of Texas at Arlington, is a specialist in French history and the history of cartography. Since 1982 he has been editor of *Terrae Incognitae*, the journal of the Society for the History of Discoveries. *(Page 48.)*

CHRISTIANE HARZIG is a Fellow at the University of Bremen, Germany, where she is investigating multiculturalism in a multinational perspective. *(Page 132.)*

SUSAN KLING is a graduate student at the University of California – Los Angeles, doing research on women and public space in 19th-century British cities. *(Page 166.)*

JERRY LEWIS, a member of the Citizen Band Potawatomi, is Cultural Diversity Director at South Suburban College and teaches workshops on American Indian history at Governors State University in Chicago. *(Pages 90, 168, 194.)*

PATRICK MANNING is Professor of History and of African-American Studies at Northeastern University, Boston. He is the author of *Slavery and African Life* (Cambridge University Press, 1990) *(Pages 50, 54.)*

ROBERT C. OSTERGREN is a historical geographer specializing in American immigration and ethnicity. He is the author of a book on Swedish immigration to the upper Mid-West 1835–1915: *A Community Transplanted* (1988), for which he received the Theodore Saloutos Memorial Book Award in Immigration History. He is currently Professor of Geography at the University of Wisconsin–Madison. *(Page 118.)*

GABRIELE SCARDELLATO is Head of Research Programmes at the Multicultural History Society of Ontario. A specialist in immigration history, he is the author of *Within Our Temple: A History of the Order of the Sons of Italy in Ontario* (1995). *(Page 122.)*

CHRIS SCHÜLER is a freelance writer and editor. He has edited *The Atlas of North American Exploration*, by Glyndwr Williams and William H. Goetzmann (Prentice Hall, 1992), and holds a Diploma in Field Archaeology from London University. *(Pages 156, 174.)*

OMAR S. VALERIO-JIMÉNEZ is a doctoral candidate in history at the University of California – Los Angeles, doing research on the culture of the Mexican-American border regions. *(Pages 170, 172.)*

ADAM WALASZEK, Professor of History and Director of the Polonia Institute of the Jagiellonian University, Krakow. Translated titles of his major studies are: *Return Migration from the United States to Poland After World War I* (1983) and *Polish Workers, Work, and the Labor Movement in the United States of America, 1880–1922* (1988).

FOREWORD

The aim of this atlas is to tell the story of the settling of North America, from the first bands of hunters to cross from Siberia, to the great waves of immigrants fleeing poverty, persecution, or warfare in the 19th and 20th centuries. It follows the fortunes and experiences of the new settlers. It shows what these waves of settlers have in common: the pressure to flee their "old country," the lure of a new and better life, the struggle to survive in a challenging and often hostile environment. It also shows that they did not leave everything behind, bringing their own different cultures and lifestyles to their new home.

This dramatic story, involving the movement of large numbers of people over great distances, is ideally suited to presentation in cartographic form. A sequence of maps can show the additions of new populations into North America layer by layer with a directness that would be impossible in any other format. Populations are made up of individuals and families, so while some maps deal with large-scale movements of people, others focus on quite small, specific groups. In addition, some maps are complemented by portraits and extracts from letters, diaries, poems, and songs, to emphasize the experiences of individuals who were a part of the migration process.

With people uppermost in mind, political boundaries are of secondary importance; in fact they frequently become blurred in the lives of people who live in frontier zones. On most of the maps dealing with the earlier periods, modern international and state boundaries are shown in pale gray to assist the reader in identifying locations without distracting from the historical situation. The southern limit of North America varies according to the subject and period, but is definitely south of the present U. S.–Mexican border. The northern extent of the atlas is also variable, although Northern Canada gets little special attention for the simple reason that so few people live there.

The atlas is divided chronologically into eight parts, each of which reflects a distinct era in migration history. No field of human activity ever fits quite that conveniently into neat divisions, however, so inevitably there are overlaps. The beginning of the story remains the most controversial. The date of the first migration from Siberia into North America is hotly contested, and new archaeological finds mean that dates are constantly being revised. The maps covering the earliest millennia are widely-spaced in time; it seems that people's lives changed very slowly then, and very little data is available. About four or five thousand years ago, population movements and technological innovations spurred more rapid change in the way some of the people lived, and in the groups they formed, and the maps follow one another at shorter time intervals.

The arrival of Europeans in the 16th century greatly increased the pace of population change. The maps in this part of the atlas trace the impact of the main colonial powers—Spain, England, and France—on the North American population. They also show the continued presence of the Indian people and their interaction with the European settlers; one map in Part II shows for the first time the Indian communities that existed close to the English settlements along the Atlantic coast in the 17th century. (The term "Native American" is not used because it seems artificial and inaccurate to most Indians.) The forced migration of Africans to North America is covered in detail, highlighting the connections between particular areas of Africa and destinations in North America. One map focuses on the presence of specific West African traditions in Louisiana and the way in which they blended with French, Spanish, and Indian lifeways to create the distinctive culture of that state.

The great 19th-century migrations from Europe are covered in detail, with maps highlighting the development of distinctive communities in different regions of North America, such as the strong German and Scandinavian presence in the Midwest or the Ukrainian settlements of the southern Canadian prairies. City maps focus on immigrant communities in cities such as Chicago, Milwaukee, and Cleveland. The internal migrations of the period are also shown, including the westward movement of settlers to Oregon, Utah, and California, and the relocation of Indians that this movement caused. The 20th century is strongly represented in the final chapters. The city plays a dominant role in the life and expectations of recent immigrants, and the atlas aims to provide the newest ethnic portraits of contemporary North American cities. Today's new arrivals from South Asia, the Pacific Rim, and Latin America are covered in detail, as is the flight from rust-belt to sun-belt and the survival, after 400 years of settlement from overseas, of America's first peoples.

Each part begins with a timeline, which aims to put the waves of migration into a framework of world history. Events which caused people to migrate to North America—such as the fall of South Vietnam in 1975—feature prominently. So do events such as Cromwell's massacre of Irish Catholics at Drogheda and Wexford in 1649, which, though they were not direct causes of emigration to North America, form an important chapter in a history that eventually brought people to North America in large numbers.

A work of this scope spans a vast range of special fields. As a result, the editorial team is composed of anthropologists and historians working in many different areas, including colonial, social, immigration, Indian, and Latin American history. They form an international network extending through Canada, England, Germany, Poland, and across the U. S. We are indebted to the many published works which have mapped population movements in certain areas during limited periods of time. Because this is the first attempt to provide a complete cartographic overview of the settling of North America in one volume, however, much original research was required. The recent past is the least understood, and the attempt to translate the latest census data into map form proved especially challenging. Creating this atlas has been a mind-expanding experience.

Helen Hornbeck Tanner,
Beulah, Michigan, August 1995

CONTENTS

PART I:
THE FIRST
AMERICANS

Introduction
by Henry F. Dobyns

The first settlers of North America walked across the dry land that connected Alaska to Siberia when the water level was much lower than it is today. Spreading out through the empty continent, their descendants adapted to the varied environments they found. They domesticated plants, built towns and villages, and traded rare commodities across vast distances. Some remained nomadic hunter-gatherers, while others lived in powerful city-states centered on great temple mounds; some built sturdy cedar-plank houses, others dwelt in multi-story pueblos built of stone or adobe, growing corn on terraces watered by irrigation channels.

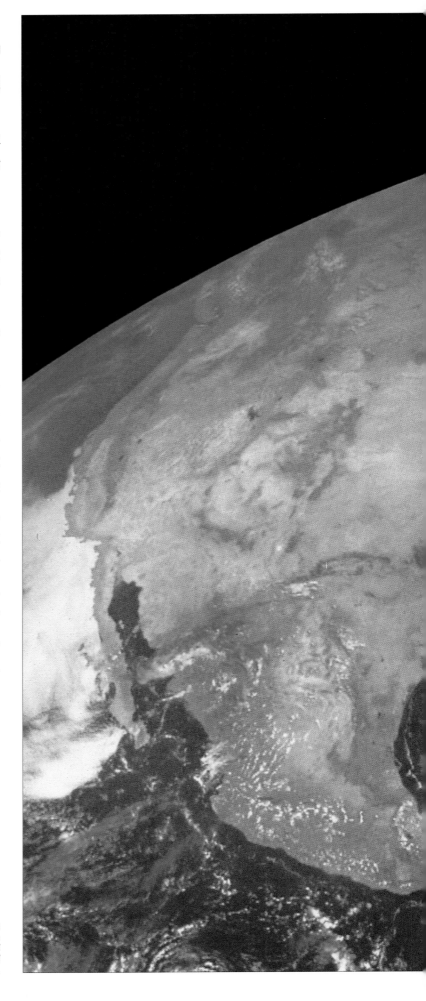

Right: the North American continent, seen from an orbiting satellite. After crossing from Siberia, the first humans probably moved south along the west coast, moving inland and spreading out as the glaciers retreated.

For many thousands of years after modern man, *Homo sapiens*, first appeared in the Old World, the American continent remained empty of human life. It was first colonized by a relatively small group who crossed from Asia during the last Ice Age. At this time, so much water was locked up in the ice that the sea level had fallen to the point where Siberia and Alaska were connected by dry land, allowing the first colonists to amble east into North America, probably in pursuit of animal herds. What remains uncertain is precisely when this happened. There seem to have been so few original Americans that they left no direct evidence of their passage, such as a trail. Any other evidence, such as stone tools, would have been covered by the rising sea as the ice melted. The only way to estimate when they arrived is by reconstructing the advances and retreats of the glaciers, and the related rise and fall of the sea level, to establish when the crossing could have been possible.

Above: a modern Inuit village on Little Diomede Island, Alaska, the point where the Asian and American continents almost meet; Great Diomede Island, just a few hundred yards across the Bering Straits, is in Russia. During the last Ice Age, when the sea level was lower than it is today, the first settlers of North America walked across the straits.

Once the first hunters had arrived in North America, both they and the large Ice Age mammals they hunted would have found their passage blocked by the barren glaciers which covered the northern part of the continent. They could only have migrated south during those relatively brief periods when conditions allowed. Recent studies indicate that the ice began to melt, causing a rapid rise in sea level, between 15,000 and 12,000 years ago. There is, however, evidence suggesting that humans were living south of the glaciated portions of North America thousands of years before this thaw. Meadowcroft Rockshelter near Pittsburgh, Pennsylvania was home to some of the earliest Americans. Experts have argued over the age of the trash they left for nearly two decades, but it seems that the ancestors of these people must have crossed Beringia about 22,500 years ago.

The route the earliest colonizers took is also uncertain. The ice sheet covering the North American continent eventually divided into an eastern (Laurentide) glacier and a western (Cordilleran) ice cap, leaving a plains corridor between. Some experts believe that the first Americans, and the big game they hunted, moved rapidly south through this corridor. Others argue that the corridor consisted mainly of frozen lakes, devoid of life, and was too inhospitable for migration. Instead, they hold that the first colonists migrated south along the Pacific coast while sea level was still much lower than it is today. The maritime climate kept coastal areas free of ice, except for mountain glaciers which could be crossed quickly. Again, the ocean has covered any direct evidence of their passing, although recent discoveries of bear remains in coastal caves back up this view.

Convincing evidence for the Pacific coast route is also provided by the analysis of Indian languages. Languages multiply over time, as people split into separate groups and evolve their own ways of speaking. The more languages that have developed in a region, therefore, the longer it has been inhabited. Since there are more Indian languages spoken along the Pacific coast than anywhere else in North America, people probably colonized that coast before expanding inland. Linguistic analysis also shows that Indians have lived in the southern parts of North America, which were never covered by glaciers, much longer than in areas which were once glaciated. This suggests that, after moving down the Pacific coast, the early Indians spread out across the south long before the end of the Ice Age, between 15 and 12 thousand years ago. Only when the glaciers melted did they move into the northern regions.

The early hunters

As they spread out across the continent, the early colonists adapted a number of different lifeways according to the environments in which they found themselves. From the beginning, they used stone tools, but these were relatively simple and not adapted to specific tasks. They worked wood much better; early Indians killed a giant land tortoise in Florida more than 13,000 years ago, using a wooden stake as their weapon. Later Indians learned to chip stone tools and projectile points for specific tasks. About 11,000 years ago, one group devised a very distinctive long spear point designed to kill mammoths. Known as "Clovis-fluted" from the site on the high plains where the first example was found with bison bones, the spear point was elegantly chipped from both edges and then from the base of both faces. This fluting probably enabled the highly skilled flint knappers to tie their points to long wooden spears so that they stayed in place when thrust into tough mammoth hide. Hunters using these spear points appear to have hunted the North

Above: the Inuit of the Canadian and Alaskan Arctic have adapted modern technology to their traditional lifeways, using motorized snow sleds for transport. Butane lamps have replaced whale oil as the principal source of lighting for their igloos. The photograph was taken at Baker Lake, Northwest Territories, Canada.

kits. The inhabitants of the Fraser–Columbia River Plateau, for instance, used a common set of stone tools with local variations, as did the peoples in the Rocky Mountains, the Great Basin, and the Basin and Mountain Range areas to the south. The diet of the latter included a large quantity of migratory waterfowl, probably caught in nets when visiting shallow lakes. These peoples relied on the *atl-atl* or dart-thrower, since the bow and arrow did not reach them until about AD 700. A distinctive stone dart point—called "Gypsum point" after the cave where examples were first excavated—was widely used by these hunters, although they also employed other dart points for different kinds of game.

Along the Atlantic coast from Newfoundland to Boston Harbor, people relied heavily on marine resources. Because they covered the bodies of their dead with red pigment, they became known as the "Red Paint" peoples. Natives of the Great Lakes area who quarried shallow copper deposits and used stone tools to cold-hammer the metal into sheets and other forms are known as the "Old Copper" peoples. Technological innovation also occurred in southern North America. The traditional Indian sexual division of labor suggests that women used the ancient milling stones discovered in the eroding banks of modern gullies in the southwestern Sonoran Desert. The peoples of northern Florida began to produce ceramic vessels around 2000 BC. Women probably made these pots, and they certainly changed the nature of women's chores and became indispensable for storing and cooking cultivated foods. Boiling food in pots was more efficient than the previous method of heating stones in a fire, then using wooden tongs to drop them into a basket or stone pot to heat food, fishing them out when they had cooled, and repeating the task until the food was done. The people who left the puzzling physical residues of the way of life sometimes called the "Poverty Point Anomaly" carried on cooking with fired clay balls, since they had no stones, from 1300 to 200 BC. More than 2200 Poverty Point type sites, some of which include the earliest earth mounds, are known in the lower Mississippi valley.

American mammoth to extinction, although a severe drought 11,000–10,000 years ago may have played a greater role in this, as it killed many of the plants on which mammoths fed.

All those areas of North America's Arctic coast that would ever be occupied were colonized between 2160 and 1860 BC. As early as 4000 BC, an Aleutian Island tradition existed on Anangula Island; by 3000 BC, Aleutian islanders had developed stone lamps, barbed stone harpoon heads, and chipped slate knives. On Kodiak Island, polished slate, rocker knives, lance heads, stone lamps, and barbed bone harpoon heads were used. By 2000 BC, the people of the region had established a way of life based on fishing and hunting sea mammals. It changed very little for almost 4000 years, until Cold War establishments invaded the Arctic after World War II. The Inuit then began to mechanize their economy with internal-combustion powered snow sleds.

Further south, on the northwest coast of modern Alaska and British Columbia, the culture of the present-day native inhabitants was already emerging by 2000 BC, although there is insufficient evidence to show how far it spread. Living by hunting, fishing, and gathering, these people developed several distinctive regional stone tool

The spread of horticulture

It is not clear how long ago gatherers of wild plant foods from the Mississippi River valley began to select those seeds which were most useful. By approximately 1500 BC, they had partially domesticated between four and eight genera of native plants. These are classed as "cultivars" because, although altered by human selection, they could still propagate themselves without assistance. The most important cultivars in the Mississippi River basin were the sunflower (*Helianthus annus*), the sumpweed or marsh elder (*Iva annus macrocarpa*), the giant ragweed

(*Ambrosia trifidia*), the maygrass (*Phalaris caroliniana*), the pigweed (*Amaranthus*), the knotweed (*Polygonum*), the lambsquarter or goosefoot (*Chenopodium*), and the "little barley." A plant that has been modified to the point where it can survive only with human assistance is called a "cultigen." The sunflower is grown today in many parts of the world as a true cultigen, as are *Amaranthus* and *Chenopodium,* which are still grown as high altitude crops in the Andes. These cultigens are part of the Indian legacy of domesticated food plants to the world.

The energy provided by seed cultivars helped people in what is now Ohio to carry the many baskets full of earth needed to construct burial mounds. Scholars call these pioneer mound-makers the Adena culture. The earliest

Left: corn was widely grown throughout North America. Deliberate selection gradually modified tiny wild corn to produce the plump cobs we know today. Indian corn is usually multicolored, with red and blue grains as well as the more familiar yellow.

Right: this computerized map, produced by the Arkansas Archaeological Survey, shows 21,700 sites in the state. All date from before 1800, and nearly all are pre-European. Although they were not all occupied simultaneously, they show how thoroughly North America was settled over the millenia before the arrival of Europeans.

remains of their distinctive way of life date back to 700 BC. In some areas it continued in some areas until about AD 400, while in others the "Hopewell" way of life evolved in the 2nd or 1st century BC, and spread widely through the Mississippi River basin. Hopewell mounds characteristically take the form of earthen effigies of animals, especially reptiles. Horticultural evidence has not survived at many sites, but enough is now known to suggest that domesticated plants provided much of the Hopewell diet.

The main Indian legacy of domesticated plants consists of maize, beans, squash, tomato, potato, sweet potato, *yuca* or *cassava*, and cotton. All except the potato, which was domesticated in the Andes, were domesticated within the tropical zone, as were many other plants which never spread beyond the tropics. Maize reached the North American peoples no later than AD 10; maize, beans, and squash spread to native peoples in arid present-day

Arizona and New Mexico a few centuries later. In this environment, plant cultivators could not depend on rainfall like the inhabitants of the future Corn Belt, and had to irrigate their crops with river or spring water. They also domesticated additional plants; basket-making irrigator women, for example, selected seeds from the longest black Devil's Claw *(Proboscidium parviflora)* pods until the plant produced 16- to 18-inch pods.

Tropical food plants also fueled the development of the distinctive Pueblo way of life on the Colorado Plateau. Speakers of six languages learned to cultivate crops and to construct multi-story, multi-family community structures called "pueblos" by AD 900. Marginal peoples such as the Goshute in the Great Basin relied on *Amaranthus*, but lacked the other cultigens. The ancestors of South

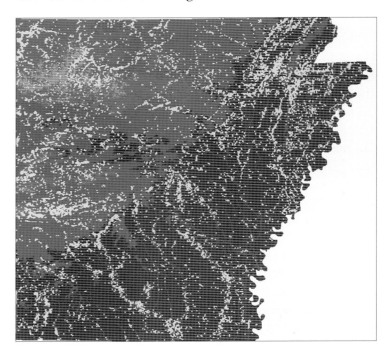

Florida's Calusa people cultivated a different basic tropical American cultigen called *yuca* or *cassava*. The original plant must have reached Florida aboard a canoe northbound from Cuba. The ancestors of the Calusa also planted and tended chirimoya trees and harvested dates from the Florida palmetto.

Trade

The distribution of tropical cultigens in North America implies that Indians traded seeds and cuttings. Northerners must have exchanged something with southerners to obtain those seeds and cuttings. By about 1400, almost every Indian group was trading in foods, fabrics, feathers, pelts, or precious stones. Certain long-distance trade routes defined zones of dynamic human relations; the outstanding example was the sea-going canoe route between Siberia and the mouth of the Columbia River. In

Right: Nootka Village at Friendly Cove on Vancouver Island, painted by John Webber, who accompanied Captain Cook on his 1778 voyage to the region. The plank houses of the northwest coast were the largest family dwellings in North America. In the center is one of the ocean-going canoes which the Nootka used for fishing, hunting marine mammals, and to trade up and down the coast. The craft on the right is Cook's ship's boat.

their dangerous subarctic environment, the Inuit along the Siberia–Kodiak Island reach remained culturally conservative, but the Indian peoples of the Northwestern Coast from the Tlingit to the Chinook on the lower Columbia River shared a distinctive way of life based on maritime food resources. These peoples lived in cedar plank houses, which were the largest family dwellings on the continent, and their sea-going canoes matched or exceeded in size any dugouts elsewhere on the continent. They exchanged a distinctive set of valuable commodities: Asian iron; ceremonial robes made of mountain goat hair, cedar bark, and dog-hair; nephrite adze blades and hafted "slave-killer" spikes; basket hats; big-horn sheep horn spoons and ladles; and human slaves. Many of these peoples exported fish and whale oil to continental partners in exchange for pelts, horns, and slaves. This trade spread the influence of the coastal peoples, if not their entire way of life, to those living inland. The Chinook imported continental commodities via a major trade center at the Dalles, on the Columbia River near present-day Portland, Oregon. Spearers from numerous peoples congregated at the falls there to feast during salmon runs. The Wishram and Wasco dried and powdered tons of salmon for export up- and downstream, and the trade center attracted traders bearing goods from the entire Columbia–Snake River system, including slaves. Slave-hunters drove captives from as far south as the Atseguwai and Modoc in northern California to the Wishram–Wasco trade fair. There Chinook traders acquired them for the northwest coast market.

Far up the Snake River in Wyoming, Shoshonean-speaking traders balanced the commodity demands of the Northwestern Coast with the demands of horticultural Mandans living in the middle Missouri River valley. The Mandans also ran a trading center, dealing with the western Crow, Crees from the north, the southern Arikara, and the eastern Dakota. Between 1400 and 1500 the Dakota, living around the wild rice-rich lakes of northern Minnesota, may have had direct access to Lake Superior. At most they had to deal with a single set of middlemen between them and the lake canoe routes. Commodity exchange may, therefore, have been transcontinental. This is not to say that any specific commodity was carried from coast to coast, simply that internal trade routes extended from the Pacific Ocean to the Atlantic.

As Europeans in search of North American furs quickly discovered, Indian traders already plied the waters of the St Lawrence River and Great Lakes in birch-bark canoes, dealing in pelts, maize, flint, basketry, ceramic pots, marine shells, copper, and other commodities. They carried their light canoes from one waterway to another, a practice the French fur-seekers called *portage*. This allowed them to travel not only on the Lakes and the St Lawrence, but also along the Saguenay, Ottawa, Saskatchewan, Ohio, and Mississippi rivers, and their tributaries. A complex network of canoe routes linked trading partners, some of whom lived at great distances from one another. Hurons from the eastern shore of Lake Huron, for example, traded with Winnebagos upstream from Green Bay on Lake Michigan.

Southeastern North America is also well endowed with rivers navigable by canoe, but because Europeans did not penetrate that region by canoe as they did farther north, Indian river transport there went largely unreported. When the survivors of de Soto's ill-fated Spanish expedition floated down the Mississippi in 1543, they had to fight off veritable canoe navies launched by the major powers along the river. The existence of such navies raises the question of whether powerful mini-states prohibited trade beyond their borders. Yet physical remains of such commodities as copper ritual objects, marine shells, ceramic vessels, and galena show that the region's mini-states did exchange some items over long distances. If canoe crews did not transport valuable commodities, overland traders and ruler-to-ruler expeditions did.

Many southwestern North American peoples were linked to tropical product suppliers in Mesoamerica. Pueblo peoples imported live parrots and macaws as well as their feathers from the tropics in exchange for blue opals and turquoise. They traded for seal skins, abalone (*Haliotis*), and *Olivella* shells from the Pacific coast; one use of strung *Olivella* was as a medium of exchange. Pueblo imports from Great Plains hunter-traders included bison robes and bison hide shields, chamois skins, buck and doe skins, and big game jerky. To the west of the pueblos, the northeastern Pai took products from the Pacific coast as well as sun-dried *Agave* pulp, locally quarried red hematite, and perfect buckskins for ritual purposes to their Hopi trading partners. At various times, potters at different pueblos specialized in making pots to export.

People traded many perishable commodities that left no physical residues to be excavated. On the frontiers of maize cultivation—Georgian Bay, the Colorado and Missouri rivers—Huron, Panya, and Mandan traders exchanged maize for meat, animal pelts, and sea shells. Some traders carried shells great distances. Canadian Cree imported conch (sea snail) shells from the Florida Keys. Other Canadians imported the bills of ivory-billed woodpeckers.

A populous continent

By 1515, the number of Americans had increased dramatically; estimates of the population range from one million to 18 million. As the population grew, it split into numerous ethnic groups speaking more or less distinctive languages. By the early 16th century there were many distinctive lifestyles. Within each region, similar lifestyles reflected a common cultural heritage. Geography did not entirely determine human cultural patterns: regions with a common cultural heritage often crossed natural divides. Indeed, the limitations of some natural environments appear to have stimulated people to make them habitable.

Arctic Aleuts and Inuit had a different ancestry from Indians. They arrived in North America much later, paddling skin-covered boats across the Bering Strait and along the Arctic coast in around 2000 BC. They exploited marine mammals and fish with highly specialized tools, weapons, and water craft, and wore fur and waterfowl clothing that protected them against extreme temperatures. Inuit houses differed from Indian houses, in that they used driftwood supported by rafters of whale bone. In the depths of winter, Inuit cut blocks of ice or packed snow and stacked these in a dome called an igloo. Subarctic Indians relied heavily on fresh water fish and large game mammals, and also dressed warmly. They fashioned conical winter lodges consisting of 30-40 long poles tied together at the top. When they were on the move they improvised brush shelters.

Some trading peoples, including Jumanos and the ancestors of the Apaches, undertook long journeys across the Great Plains, from the Rio Grande to the western tributaries of the Mississippi, with pack dogs hauling travois laden with skin tipis which could be quickly raised and lowered. The Mandans inhabiting the northwestern limit of horticulture in the Middle Missouri River region lived in earth-covered lodges like Caddoan-speaking horticulturalists on the eastern edge of the Prairie Plains. Stout oak or cottonwood posts supported the heavy roofs consisting of up to 100 rafters resting on joists connecting four central posts and 12 wall posts in a circle.

Horticultural villagers who harvested wild rice and large quantities of fish and eels lived around the Great Lakes and along the St Lawrence River. They covered their houses with birch bark so that they shed water. In the Laurentian region, Iroquoian-speaking peoples built "long houses" with partitioned compartments for families, a style shared by some Algonquian tribes. Other Algonquian-speakers made circular wigwams consisting of either walls of cattail mats protected by a birch-bark roof, or entirely of birch bark scrolls. Elsewhere, horticultural townspeople were drawn to rivers providing fish, shellfish, and waterfowl. In the Mississippi River Basin

Right: a Indian family from the area of today's North Carolina, painted by John White, governor of the first, short-lived English settlement in the region. The peoples who lived along the tidewater estuaries of the Atlantic coast fished and farmed intensively. White has shown the man holding a bow and arrow, in the foreground he has shown potatoes and corn, two crops that would have been new to him, and which became Native America's most important contribution to world food resources.

and along the major streams which drain into the Gulf of Mexico, they expended great energy building temple mounds and pyramids. These formed the centerpieces of populous cities of wattle-and-daub houses. The Atlantic seaboard from southern Maine to Georgia was densely populated by people who began raising corn a few centuries later than the Ohio Valley farmers. The coastal people farmed, but continued to depend heavily on fishing along the tidewater estuaries. They lived in orderly villages and built more or less circular wigwams. At the southern tip of Florida, the Calusa lifeway more closely resembled that of Caribbean islanders and Amazon basin peoples than those of other North Americans. The semitropical climate required little protective housing other than storehouses.

Hunters and gatherers lived in hamlets—which the Spanish labeled *rancherías*—across a huge territory from the California Coast Range through the Western mountainous region to the Great Plains. The typical dwelling in these hamlets was the *wickiup*, built from a framework of tree branches thatched with grass in the south or covered with mats made of native hemp or dogbane in the north. In the Little Colorado River and Río Grande valleys, people lived in small towns of multi-family, multi-story buildings, and irrigated their crops. These communities are known as pueblos, from the Spanish word for village. Northern pueblos were built of stone masonry and occasionally of earth, while southern pueblo dwellers generally built their town walls from adobe (moist clay mixed with vegetable fibers laid up in courses). Pueblos had solid ground floor exterior walls for security; the doors are all in the upper stories, and people entered and left by ladders.

Ranchería dwellers in the central Great Basin, on the Colorado Plateau north and south of the Grand Canyon, on the California and Sonoran deserts and Mexico's central plateau also practiced irrigation. The Owens Valley Paiutes made up one horticultural outpost in California's Sierra Nevada, domesticating and irrigating local plant species. Northern irrigators lived in wickiups like their hunter-gatherer neighbors, while western irrigators lived in multi-family, semi-subterranean structures covered by earth, the heavy roofs of which were supported by cottonwood posts. Southern irrigators lived in either earth-covered wickiups in pits, or wattle-and-daub houses. After about 1200, when communities seem to have begun fighting over scarce food resources, those crowded in the riverine oases built multi-story, stronghold storehouses with adobe walls.

The cultural dynamics that formed these distinctive lifeways appear to have bypassed two coastal zones, whose inhabitants were culturally conservative. The peoples of the Baja California peninsula and part of the Upper California coast could exploit marine resources. The Chumash people at the northern tip of this region were unusually dynamic, developing their distinctive sea-going canoes apparently quite independently of the distant peoples of the Northwest. The Chumash were so efficient in exploiting marine food resources as well as continental vegetable foods that their population reached a density unequaled on the Pacific coast between Mesoamerica and the northwest coast. Inhabitants of the coast of the Gulf of Mexico between the Mississippi River valley and Mesoamerica and of a considerable region extending inland into southern Texas and northeastern Mexico, were also cultural conservatives. Despite being neighbors of horticultural peoples to the south and east, they remained hunter-gatherers.

Right: most pueblos had one or more kivas *(sunken chambers), where religious rites would be enacted and sacred objects were kept. The interior of the kiva would usually be decorated with frescoes; this one comes from Kuaua Pueblo, one of the Tiguex group in New Mexico, and dates from around AD 1500*

Far right: the typical dwelling of the Southwest was the pueblo, a multi-story, multi-family building of stone or adobe. After about AD 1300, when the Navajo began to migrate into the region, pueblos tended to be constructed in defensible locations; this one, at Puye, New Mexico, sits atop a cliff-face.

TIMELINE
EARLIEST TIMES–AD 1515

NORTH AMERICA	THE CARIBBEAN, CENTRAL & S. AMERICA	EUROPE, AFRICA, & ASIA
		c. 4 million BC Earliest hominid remains (in Africa); Lower Palaeolithic era
		c. 1.8 million BC First large-brained hominid (*Homo habilis*) at Olduvai Gorge. Simple stone chopping tools
		c. 1.5 million–200,000 BC *Homo erectus*. Well-crafted stone handaxes all over Africa, Asia, and Europe
c. 30–25,000 BC Hunters begin to cross dry land between Siberia and America		*c.* 200,000 Modern humans (*Homo sapiens*) develop
c. 14,000 BC Last ice age recedes		*c.* 20,000–8000 BC Mesolithic hunter-gatherers
c. 13,000 Bluefish Cave occupied–earlier occupation site in the Yukon and Alaska region		
c. 13,500 First secure traces of human occupation in North America at Meadowcroft Rockshelter		
c. 11,000 Clovis spear point perfected		
c. 10,000 North American ice-sheets retreat and settlements become more abundant. Paleo-Indian stage in North America. Nomadic big-game hunters using first Clovis and later Folsom stone projective points		
		8000–2000 Late Neolithic. Pottery appears
c. 7000 Na-Dine Athapascans migrate from Asia to northwest Canada. Semi-permanent settlements emerge in North America. Increasing use of plant foods in diet.	*c.* 5000 First cultivation of maize in Tehuacán Valley, Central Mexico	
c. 4500 First mounds built along lower Mississippi		
c. 3000 Aleut and Inuit migrate from Siberia. First copper forging in North America. New people move into upper Great Lakes and Tennessee Valley, N.Y.		3100 Dynastic state emerges in Egypt
c. 2500 First pottery in North America in coastal Georgia and Florida	*c.* 2500 Ceramics in use in Mesoamerica	*c.* 2500 Great Pyramids built in Egypt. Urban civilization of Indus valley
		2000 Minoan Crete. Stonehenge, England
c. 2000 Many peoples engage in agriculture		
c. 1500 Poverty Point settlement. Settled villagers	*c.* 1500 Highland Olmec settlement at Chalcatzingo	*c.* 1500 Rice domesticated in Africa
c. 1000 Adena culture in eastern woodlands	*c.* 1200 Olmec civilization in Mexico	
	c. 900 La Venta principal Olmec center	
		c. 550 Persian empire of Cyrus the Great
		525 Persians conquer Egypt
	c. 500 Early Zapotec culture emerges at Monte Albán, Mexico	490–79 War between Persia and Greek states
		486 Death of Buddha
		479 Death of Confucius
		431–404 Peloponnesian War between Athens and Sparta
c. 310 Hopewell culture in eastern woodlands		334–29 Alexander the Great conquers Persian empire
		264–146 Wars between Rome and Carthage for domination of Mediterranean
		221–206 China united under Quin dynasty
		202 Han dynasty established in China
c. AD 1 Pacific Northwest cultures emerge		AD 29 Jesus Christ crucified
	AD 50 City of Teotihuacan, Central Mexico, laid out on a regular grid plan. Construction of Pyramid of the Sun–largest structure in the Americas before advent of the Europeans	70 Romans sack Jerusalem
100 Mogollon-Hohokam cultures emerge in southwest		

NORTH AMERICA	THE CARIBBEAN, CENTRAL & S. AMERICA	EUROPE, AFRICA, & ASIA
	c. 200–700 Classic Zapotec culture at Monte Albán	220 Fall of Han dynasty in China
		304 Huns invade China
	c. 300 Classic Maya civilization develops in Yucatán lowlands of southern Mexico	379 Buddhism becomes state religion in China
		410 Visigoths sack Rome
		c. 425–500 Angles and Saxons settle Britain
		476 End of Roman Empire in Western Europe
	c. 500 City of Teotihuacan, Central Mexico, has 200,000 inhabitants	622 Flight of Mahomet from Mecca to Medina begins Muslim era
		636–42 Muslims conquer Syria, Persia, and Egypt
c. 700 Bow and arrow introduced from Asia by Inuit		711 Muslims begin conquest of Spain
		800 Charlemagne crowned emperor in Rome
c. 800 Mogollon people begin making Mibres pottery. First use of bow and arrow in Mississippi Valley		c. 862 Norse warriors ("Rus") establish first Russian state at Novgorod
		863 Byzantine missionaries Cyril and Methodius convert Slavs and devise Russian alphabet
c. 950 Chaco Pueblos flourish in Southwest	c. 900 Classic Maya states collapse. Toltecs rise to power in Central Mexico; Postclassic Maya in Yucatan; beginning of Chimú empire in Peru	
986 Norse settle in Greenland		
c.1000 Short-lived Norse settlement in Newfoundland		
c. 1050 Mississippian ritual and trade center of Cahokia (Illinois) has 10,000 inhabitants. Anasazi of Southwest move to well-defended settlements such as Pueblo Bonito in Chaco Canyon		1066 Normans conquer England
		1071 Seljuks ("the first Turks") defeat Byzantines at Manzikert and settle in Asia Minor
		1095 Crusaders persecute Jews in Europe
c.1100 Cliff Palace, Mesa Verde built. Thule Inuit expand eastward from Siberia to Greenland		1099 First Crusade captures Jerusalem
		1187 Saladin retakes Jersualem for Islam
c.1200 Moundsville, Alabama built	c.1170 Toltec state collapses	
	c.1200 Aztecs occupy Valley of Mexico	1211–39 Mongols conquer Northern China, Central Asia, and parts of Russia
	c.1250 Beginning of Inca empire in Peru	1337 Outbreak of Hundred Years War between England and France
1341 Inuit occupy Norse Western Settlement in Greenland	1345 Aztecs colonize central Mexico, founding capital Tenochtitlán at site of modern Mexico City	1346–48 Black Death (bubonic plague) reduces Europe's population by a third
c. 1350 Anasazi pueblos abandoned		1380–1402 Mongols invade Central Asia, India, and Turkey
c. 1380 Inuit occupy Norse Middle Settlement in Greenland		1386 Union of Poland and Lithuania; Lithuania becomes Christian
	1428 Aztec Empire formed	
	1440–68 Reign of Aztec ruler, Moctezuma	
c. 1450 Middle Mississippian towns suffer population collapse		1453 Ottoman Turks capture Constantinople (Istanbul). End of Hundred Years War
c.1480 Last Norse Greenland colony dies out	c.1470 Incas absorb Chimú empire	1492 Spanish capture Granada from Muslims. Jews expelled from Spain
	1492 Columbus arrives in Caribbean	
	1493 First Spanish settlement in the New World founded at Hispaniola	1494 Treaty of Tordesillas divides world between Spain and Portugal
1497 John Cabot, sailing for the English, lands in Newfoundland		1497 Vasco da Gama reaches India
		1508 Spanish conquer Canary Islands
1513 Ponce de Léon claims Florida for Spain	1510 First African slaves transported to the Americas	

HUMANIZING THE CONTINENT
THE FIRST MIGRATIONS INTO AMERICA, c.16,000–10,000 BP

The first humans to settle in the American continent were small bands of hunters who crossed from Asia towards the end of the last ice age.

Above: two early American hunters with back packs, skin clothing and spears in hand, trudge across the sub-glacial tundra in search of the wooly mammoth that feeds and clothes them. Mammoths were found across a wide area of the North American west, and the remains of mammoths killed by prehistoric hunters have been found as far south as Valsequila in southern Mexico.

That much we know; where they came from, and which route they took, is less certain. During the ice age, the sea level was lower than it is today because so much water was locked up in the ice. Siberia and Alaska were connected by a land bridge (known as Beringia), and the first pioneers may have walked across it. There is evidence that Siberia was inhabited as early as 35,000 BP. Once the human pioneers had crossed into North America, they would most probably have traveled south along the ice-free thin strip of Pacific coastline. South of the continental ice sheet, the higher peaks of the Rocky Mountains were also covered with ice. Probably the first opening through which the pioneers could have traveled east was the Columbia-Snake river system—but under ice age conditions, these rivers may well have carried such a volume of water that people could not climb through the canyons. Once they reached present-day southern California, they could turn eastward without encountering mountain ice sheets or uncrossable canyons. What is now southern Californian and Sonoran Desert would then have been well watered and clothed in vegetation supporting now extinct game animals including the wooly mammoth.

From there, they spread out across the continent. The earliest trash in the Meadowcroft rockshelter in Pennsylvania has been dated as more than 16,000 years old; if this is accurate, humans had reached the southern edge of the Laurentide ice sheet by then. The pioneers at Meadowcroft had surely left relatives along their backtrail from present-day southern Arizona. Some of those settlers seem to have perfected their flint-knapping skills and around 11,000 BP invented the Clovis-fluted spear

points intended to slay mammoths. Hunters using Clovis points appear to have been few in number, but hunting success may have generated rapid population growth. Such hunters ranged widely over the high plains and east to Wisconsin. The Clovis-fluted spear point persisted among hunters east of the Mississippi River for several millennia, but was replaced on the plains about 10,000 BP. Other hunters reached the Florida peninsula, where they adapted to the distinctive local wildlife and landscape. At the Little Salt Spring site in west central Florida, along with mammoth bones, the remains of ground sloths and giant land turtles—killed by a wooden stake—have been found and dated to 13,450 BP. Charcoal found nearby has been dated to 12,100 BP.

Below: Meadowcroft Rockshelter near Pittsburgh sheltered early American hunters some 16,000 years ago.

The Clovis point (above), named after the site in New Mexico where it was first found, is a finely-flaked spearhead, and was used from around 11,000 BP to hunt large mammals such as the wooly mammoth. After these became extinct it was superseded by the lighter Folsom point (far right), which has been found with the skeletons of long-horned bison.

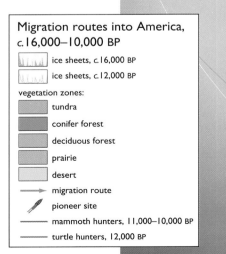

Migration routes into America, c.16,000–10,000 BP

- ice sheets, c.16,000 BP
- ice sheets, c.12,000 BP

vegetation zones:
- tundra
- conifer forest
- deciduous forest
- prairie
- desert
- migration route
- pioneer site
- mammoth hunters, 11,000–10,000 BP
- turtle hunters, 12,000 BP

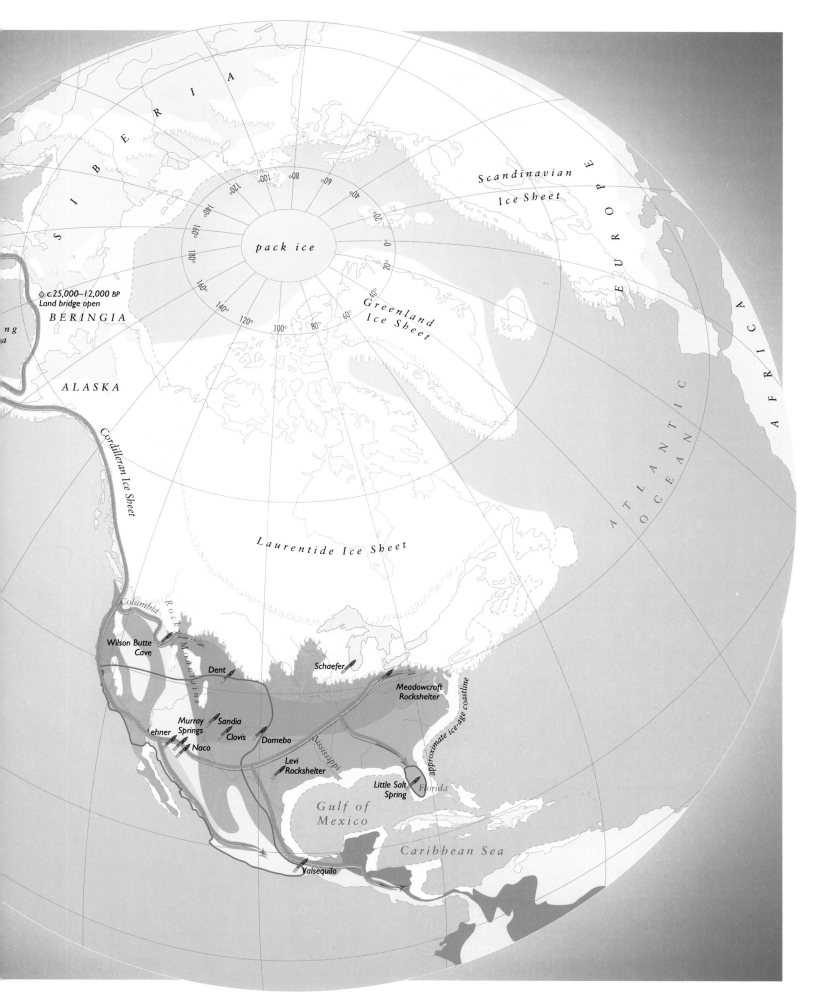

SIBERIA

Scandinavian
Ice Sheet

EUROPE

pack ice

◇ c.25,000–12,000 BP
Land bridge open

BERINGIA

AFRICA

ALASKA

Greenland
Ice Sheet

Cordilleran Ice Sheet

ATLANTIC
OCEAN

Laurentide Ice Sheet

Columbia

Rocky Mountains

Wilson Butte
Cave

Dent

Schaefer

Meadowcroft
Rockshelter

approximate ice-age coastline

Murray
Springs

Sandia

Lehner

Clovis

Naco

Domebo

Mississippi

Levi
Rockshelter

Little Salt
Spring

Florida

Gulf of
Mexico

Caribbean Sea

Valsequilo

PEOPLE AND LANDSCAPES
WAYS OF LIFE IN NORTH AMERICA, *c.* 2000 BC

By 2000 BC, Indians knew every habitable part of North America. Making complete use of wildlife, water, trees, and plants, these peoples devised a wide range of lifeways.

For all people, securing food and shelter demanded at least short seasonal excursions to fishing sites or berry patches. The caribou and bison hunters might spend five months on expeditions ranging over several hundred miles. Every group had a base in some recognized homeland. Permanent villages were established on the Pacific coast, where year-round fishing resources were available. Vital to their lifestyle were the gigantic red cedars which they used to build ocean-going canoes and plank houses.

The most visible results of organized communal activity were the mounds built by the societies of the lower Mississippi, which reached their peak at Poverty Point (> *below*). The first pottery in North America, dating from around 2500 BC, was made by people living along the St Johns River and Indian River districts of Eastern Florida, as well as in the Savannah River region of Georgia. At first, the fiber they used to temper their clay did not produce very strong vessels, but ceramic pots were the cooking and food storage technology of the future, and later potters learned to temper their clay with broken shells and sand or crushed rock.

Further up the Atlantic coast and interior of the eastern U.S. and Canada, Indian people all followed the annual round of seasonal hunting, moving to river or oceanside locations in the summer and returning to sheltered places in the winter. On the northern coast of Maine and Newfoundland, seafaring people hunted whales and subsisted on the resources of island and coastal areas. They had a distinctive burial custom, placing large quantities of red ochre in graves. Red ochre was highly prized throughout much of the St Lawrence River valley as well as in the Great Lakes region, where fishing was also vital to sustaining life.

Copper was mined in pits all around Lake Superior, the most notable location being present Isle Royale in the northwestern waters. Forging copper for axes and knives began around 3000 BC. Tools and ornaments were much used in the Green Bay area of northeastern Wisconsin, where large numbers of people lived. Similar implements of slate and other kinds of rock were fashioned east of the Great Lakes. Beads and bracelets were traded east to New York, west to Saskatchewan and south through the Mississippi valley to the Gulf Coast. Buffalo hunting dominated the lifeways of the people living on the plains west of the Mississippi River. In a region unsuitable to canoe travel, overland transport was handled by domesticated dogs dragging a travois made of a triangular pole frame. Everyone did a lot of long-distance walking.

Although people adjusted to the separate localities in North America, the population was not static. There were two last waves of migration from Asia. Around 7000 BC the Na-Dine Athapascans, whose language is linked to the Sino-Tibetan family, crossed into northwest Canada. A warm period, beginning around 5000 BC, allowed the Inuit to spread across the Arctic regions of Canada. It also made the southern plains almost intolerable. People moved north or west from the Great Basin to California's Sacramento River valley. Others shifted east into the Mississippi valley. Those who remained lived at lower altitudes for part of the year, moving higher into the mountains when the heat became excessive. The story of their existence over thousands of years is preserved in caves and rockshelters. The warming forced people in the plains to take refuge near springs which provided water when rivers and lakes dried up. Volcanic eruptions and earthquakes also caused people to move. The maturing of forest lands and the amelioration of the northern climate may have been the reason why, around 3000 BC, people moved north into the upper Great Lakes and the Genessee valley of New York.

For the most part, however, the same general way of life continued for thousands of years. People observed the changing positions of the sun, moon, and stars. On the northern plains they built "medicine wheels" of stones on the ground, the spokes aligned to record the summer solstice and keep track of a yearly calendar. Throughout the continent, people handed down to their children beliefs about a Creator of great power, the spirits that connected with that power, and the future life of souls when life on earth was over.

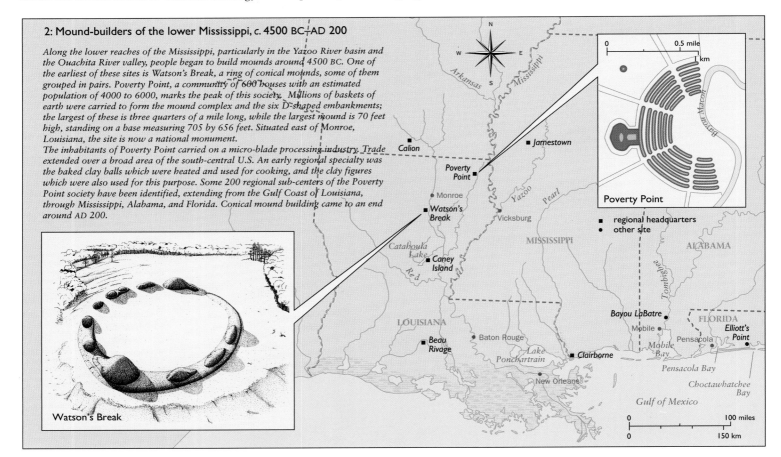

2: Mound-builders of the lower Mississippi, c. 4500 BC–AD 200

Along the lower reaches of the Mississippi, particularly in the Yazoo River basin and the Ouachita River valley, people began to build mounds around 4500 BC. One of the earliest of these sites is Watson's Break, a ring of conical mounds, some of them grouped in pairs. Poverty Point, a community of 600 houses with an estimated population of 4000 to 6000, marks the peak of this society. Millions of baskets of earth were carried to form the mound complex and the six D-shaped embankments; the largest of these is three quarters of a mile long, while the largest mound is 70 feet high, standing on a base measuring 705 by 656 feet. Situated east of Monroe, Louisiana, the site is now a national monument.

The inhabitants of Poverty Point carried on a micro-blade processing industry. Trade extended over a broad area of the south-central U.S. An early regional specialty was the baked clay balls which were heated and used for cooking, and the clay figures which were also used for this purpose. Some 200 regional sub-centers of the Poverty Point society have been identified, extending from the Gulf Coast of Louisiana, through Mississippi, Alabama, and Florida. Conical mound building came to an end around AD 200.

Poverty Point

- ■ regional headquarters
- ● other site

Watson's Break

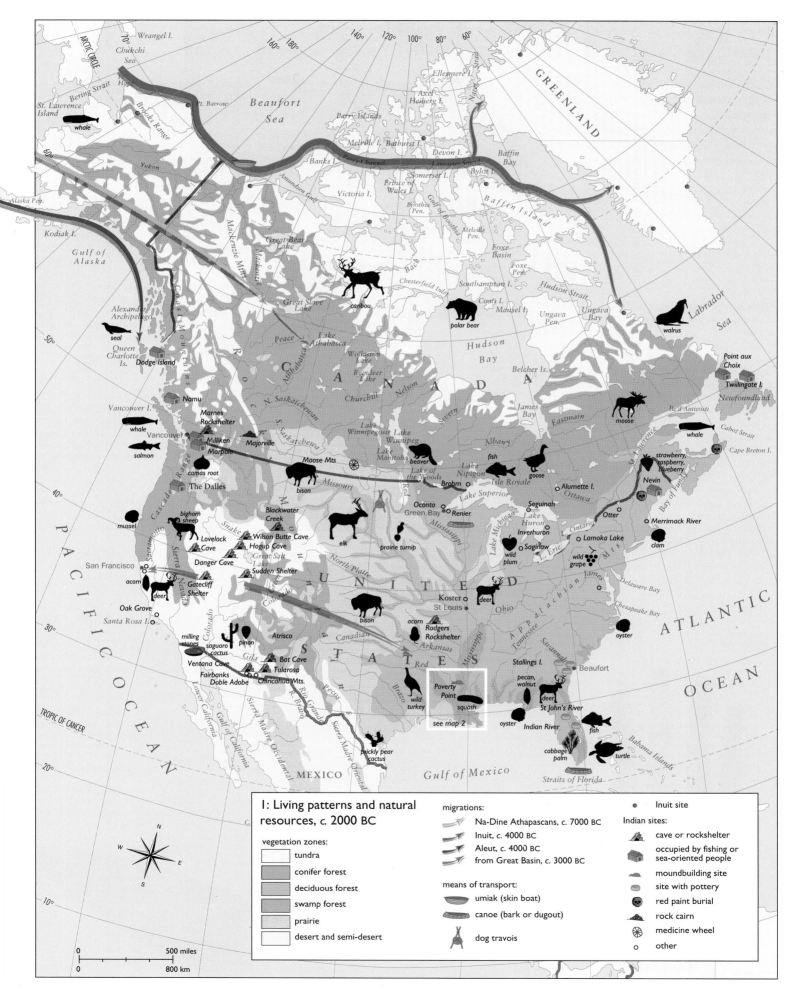

1: Living patterns and natural resources, c. 2000 BC

vegetation zones:
- tundra
- conifer forest
- deciduous forest
- swamp forest
- prairie
- desert and semi-desert

migrations:
- Na-Dine Athapascans, c. 7000 BC
- Inuit, c. 4000 BC
- Aleut, c. 4000 BC
- from Great Basin, c. 3000 BC

means of transport:
- umiak (skin boat)
- canoe (bark or dugout)
- dog travois

- Inuit site

Indian sites:
- cave or rockshelter
- occupied by fishing or sea-oriented people
- moundbuilding site
- site with pottery
- red paint burial
- rock cairn
- medicine wheel
- other

0 — 500 miles
0 — 800 km

EARTHWORKS AND EFFIGIES
THE ADENA-HOPEWELL MOUND-BUILDERS, *c.* 700 BC–AD 400

When Native American peoples of the eastern woodlands began to manipulate wild plants by deliberate selection, the improvement in their diet allowed them to channel their energies into building elaborate ceremonial earthworks.

As Native American populations grew in size and split into numerous ethnic groups, they continued to achieve a satisfactory standard of living without laboring unduly. Inhabitants of the Mississippi valley who gathered wild plant foods turned themselves into horticultural innovators some unknown centuries ago. Observant wild seed gatherers, probably women, evidently preferred the largest seeds that they could find. (The larger the seed, the fewer had to be collected for a given quantity of food.) By approximately 1500 BC, they had altered several types of native plant to cultivars—plants bred for certain traits, but which could still propagate themselves without human intervention. Among them were the sunflower, marsh elder, giant ragweed, maygrass, pigweed, knotweed, goosefoot and little barley.

In addition, cultigens—plants which have been modified to the extent that they depend on human intervention to reproduce—were already in use among the peoples of Mesoamerica. The earliest of these, squash, spread across southern North America later, and advanced northwards as far as the Great Lakes by around AD 100, but was not important as a basic food until later. Maize, too, was introduced from Mesoamerica during this period, but the strains were not yet sufficiently resistant to frost to make a major contribution to the North American diet.

Below: this human hand, cut from a sheet of mica from the Appalachian Mountains, was found in Ohio. The hand was a powerful religious symbol throughout the eastern woodlands, and appears frequently in Hopewell burials.

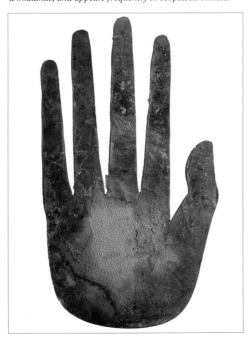

Above: the Hopewell peoples built mounds both as burials and in the form of elaborate effigies. These often took the shape of a bird or reptile, like this Serpent Mound in Ohio. At the top right of the picture is the serpent's head, swallowing an egg-like object which may represent the sun. The mound is about 4 feet high and 15 to 20 feet across; uncoiled, the snake would be 1330 feet long.

These agricultural developments meant that food surpluses could be created; no longer did all the people have to spend much of their time hunting and gathering. About 700 BC, some of them began working hard for at least short periods, moving large amounts of earth to construct burial mounds in the Ohio River valley. Prehistorians refer to this culture as Adena. The mounds, some of them up to 300 feet in diameter, were often circular, though squares, pentagons and irregular shapes which follow the natural landforms are also found. The burials were sometimes enclosed in a log chamber at the heart of the mound. The deceased were surrounded by grave goods including carved stone tablets and pipes for smoking tobacco.

By perhaps 100 BC, mound building and horticulture had spread to the inhabitants of most of the eastern part of the future U.S., west of the Appalachians. They developed a sophisticated culture, known as Hopewellian. Their mounds were larger than those of the Adena people, some of them more than 1500 feet in diameter, and could take elaborate geometrical shapes. Perhaps the most famous is the Serpent Mound in Ohio, although it is not typical and cannot be dated with any certainty. Most Adena earthworks were burial mounds. The wealth of grave goods—including effigies cut from sheet mica or beaten copper—in these burials suggests that Hopewell societies were strongly hierarchical, and that the deceased were high-ranking individuals. The Hopewell people, centered in southern Ohio for 500 years, carried on a long-distance trade in key commodities. Among these were chert and obsidian for making sharp stone tools and implements, galena for decoration, Gulf of Mexico marine shells for ceremonial trumpets, ornate breastplates, cups, and other utensils, natural copper from Lake Superior, mica, quartz crystals, and chlorite.

Some time after about AD 400, the Hopewellian culture went into decline. There was to be one last flourishing, however, way out to the northwest. In Wisconsin and Iowa, earthworks began to be constructed in the shape of animal effigies some time around AD 700. There are bird mounds with wingspans of up to 570 feet, a panther mound, a lizard mound and even a man mound. The fact that the style is confined to this remote region, and the absence of grave goods, suggest that the trade in exotic materials which connected the different Hopewellian societies had come to an end. By this time, the center of innovation in moving labor to construct artificial mounds had shifted to the Mississippi valley (> *pages 26–7*).

Below right: reptiles and birds clearly held great religious significance for the Hopewellian peoples, and their effigies, of copper or mica, are frequently found among the grave goods in burial mounds. This raven from Ohio is cut from a sheet of copper; the eye is pearl.

Below: Hopewell societies traded goods over vast distances. This knife, found in Ohio, is made from clear quartz from Arkansas, more than 600 miles away.

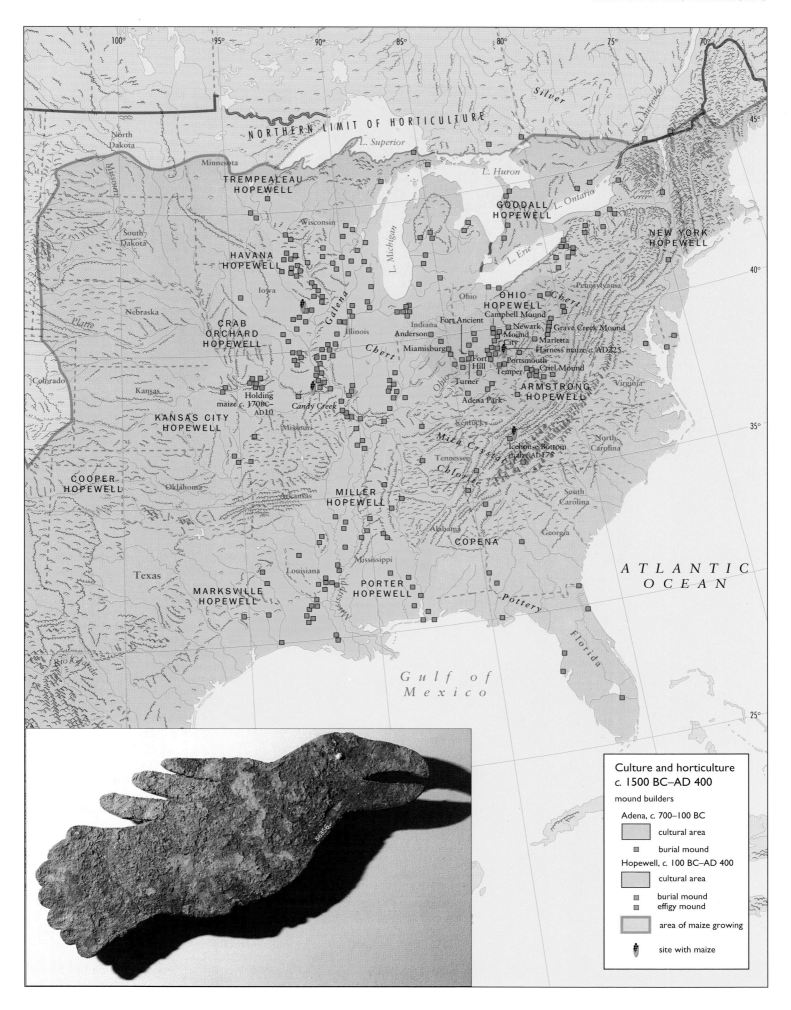

NORTHERN LIMIT OF HORTICULTURE

TREMPEALEAU
HOPEWELL

GOODALL
HOPEWELL

NEW YORK
HOPEWELL

HAVANA
HOPEWELL

OHIO
HOPEWELL
Campbell Mound
Newark   Grave Creek Mound
Mound   Marietta
City   Harness maize c. AD225
Portsmouth
Fort   Criel Mound
Temper

CRAB
ORCHARD
HOPEWELL

Fort Ancient
Anderson
Miamisburg

Turner
Adena Park

ARMSTRONG
HOPEWELL

maize c. 170BC–
AD10
Holding
Candy Creek

KANSAS CITY
HOPEWELL

Icehouse Bottom
maize AD175

COOPER
HOPEWELL

MILLER
HOPEWELL

COPENA

MARKSVILLE
HOPEWELL

PORTER
HOPEWELL

ATLANTIC
OCEAN

Gulf of
Mexico

North Dakota
Minnesota
L. Superior
L. Huron
L. Ontario
L. Erie
L. Michigan
Wisconsin
Iowa
Nebraska
Illinois
Indiana
Ohio
Pennsylvania
Virginia
Kansas
Missouri
Kentucky
Tennessee
North Carolina
South Carolina
Oklahoma
Arkansas
Colorado
Texas
Louisiana
Mississippi
Alabama
Georgia
Florida
South Dakota
Silver
Galena
Chert
Chert
Mica Crystal
Chlorite
Pottery
Rio Grande
Platte
Missouri
Ohio

Culture and horticulture
c. 1500 BC–AD 400

mound builders

Adena, *c.* 700–100 BC

☐ cultural area

◼ burial mound

Hopewell, *c.* 100 BC–AD 400

☐ cultural area

◼ burial mound
◼ effigy mound

☐ area of maize growing

⚑ site with maize

CHIEFDOMS AND TEMPLE MOUNDS
TOWNSPEOPLE OF THE MISSISSIPPI AND SOUTHWEST, AD 900–1450

Improvements in agriculture towards the end of the first millennium led to the growth of urban cultures throughout the Mississippi basin and in the Southwest.

Some time around AD 700, North American peoples began using the hoe, which greatly increased agricultural productivity. At around the same time, the use of the Asiatic bow and arrow became widespread, making hunters more efficient and altering the nature of warfare. Some 200 years later, beans were introduced to North America from Mexico. This high-protein food reduced the need for hunting for meat, freeing more people for construction work. The development of more frost-resistant strains of corn, and the full use of the great trio of native plants—corn, beans, and squash—increased storable food resources.

In the Ohio valley the Fort Ancient culture developed. Less confident and secure than their Hopewellian ancestors, these people concentrated on building earthwork defenses. Horticultural townspeople settled by rivers that provided fish, shellfish, and waterfowl. Throughout the Mississippi basin and along major streams draining into the Gulf of Mexico, they built large pyramidal mounds to support temples and raise the houses of the nobles above those of the populace. These structures were similar to those of the Toltecs and the Mayas in Mexico except that, in a region of soft alluvial soils, they were built of earth and topped with buildings of wattle and daub rather than stone. They formed the nuclei of sizeable towns, often enclosed by a wooden

Left: the pueblo at Cliff Palace, Mesa Verde, perched in a niche in a sheer Colorado cliff-face. The stone dwellings were built around AD 1150, and had been abandoned by 1450. In the foreground is a round kiva; the large number of these religious buildings at Cliff Palace suggests that it may have served as a ceremonial center for the surrounding area.

palisade, beyond which lay the cultivated areas that produced crops to support the urban population.

There were several regional variants of the basic Mississippian culture. The Middle Mississippian occupied a large area centered on the confluence of the Mississippi and Missouri rivers. Here, just outside present-day East St Louis, was the great city of Cahokia; at its peak between around 1050 and 1250, it may have had as many as 10,000 inhabitants. Another great Middle Mississippian center was Moundville in present-day Alabama. Outlying

settlements extended as far north as Aztalan in Wisconsin. By the time Europeans arrived, the population of the central area had declined considerably, and Cahokia was abandoned except for a small number of squatters.

The South Appalachian statelets were still functioning when Spanish explorers reached them in the 16th century, but rapidly succumbed to diseases the newcomers brought with them. The Caddoans of the Red River region, famous for their pottery, were still using their temple mounds in the late 17th century. The last of the Mississippian cultures, the Plaquemine, survived among the Natchez until 1735, when their Grand Village was destroyed by the French after an unsuccessful insurrection (> *pages 48–9*).

In the arid environment of the Southwest, plant cultivators could not depend on rainfall, and had to irrigate their crops with river or spring water. In the Southwest, maize cultivation gave rise to a distinctive group of cultures, the ancestors of the Pueblos which still exist today. The Hohokam—the name means "ancestors" in Piman—constructed extensive irrigation canals to grow maize in arid, near desert conditions. They built multi-story store-house redoubts and ceremonial ball courts similar to those used in the ritual games of Mesoamerica. The Anasazi, or ancestral Pueblos, and Mogollon built *kivas*—sunken chambers where sacred objects would be kept and religious rites enacted.

The northern Pueblo Indians typically constructed stone masonry walls, although some made earth walls. In the southern pueblos, town walls were typically built from adobe—moist clay mixed with vegetable fibers laid up in courses. Defensive pueblos had solid ground floor exterior walls; people entered and left by ladders. The bones of parrots and military macaws buried under room floors are evidence of the influence of Mesoamerica on the developing Pueblo peoples of the Southwest. Pueblo folk began importing macaws no later than AD 900; they still do.

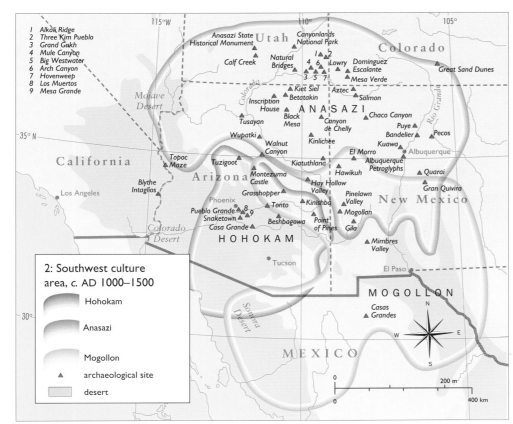

1 Alkali Ridge
2 Three Kin Pueblo
3 Grand Gulch
4 Mule Canyon
5 Big Westwater
6 Arch Canyon
7 Hovenweep
8 Los Muertos
9 Mesa Grande

2: Southwest culture area, c. AD 1000–1500

Hohokam

Anasazi

Mogollon

▲ archaeological site

☐ desert

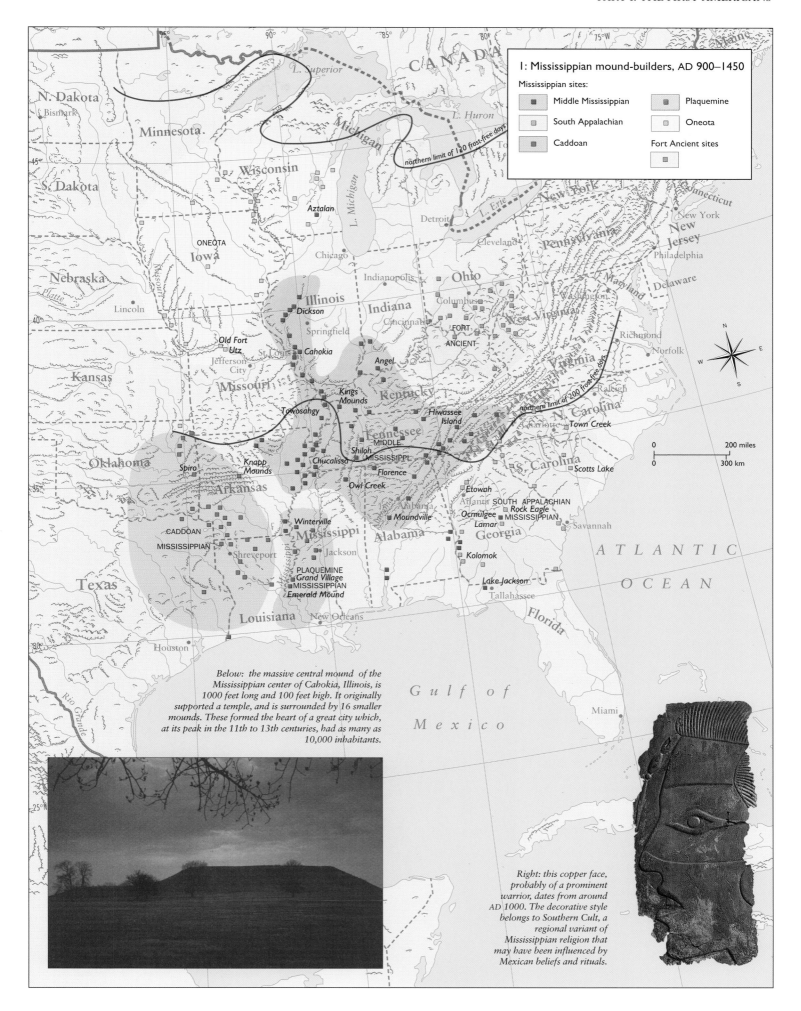

1: Mississippian mound-builders, AD 900–1450

Mississippian sites:

- ■ Middle Mississippian
- □ South Appalachian
- ■ Caddoan
- ■ Plaquemine
- □ Oneota

Fort Ancient sites

- ■

Below: the massive central mound of the Mississippian center of Cahokia, Illinois, is 1000 feet long and 100 feet high. It originally supported a temple, and is surrounded by 16 smaller mounds. These formed the heart of a great city which, at its peak in the 11th to 13th centuries, had as many as 10,000 inhabitants.

Right: this copper face, probably of a prominent warrior, dates from around AD 1000. The decorative style belongs to Southern Cult, a regional variant of Mississippian religion that may have been influenced by Mexican beliefs and rituals.

27

POTTERY, COPPER, AND SHELLS
NATIVE AMERICAN AND NORSE TRADERS, *c.* AD 1000–1450

The native peoples of every part of North America developed specialized crafts and resources, which they traded with near neighbors and more distant allies, forming a network that covered the entire continent.

The major trade routes of North America were the waterways, supplemented by footpaths through river valleys, across portages and mountain passes, and along ridges and bluffs of rugged terrain. The largest communication system covered the Mississippi River valley, embracing all the territory between the Appalachian Mountains and the Rockies. Indian traders traveled long distances to meet at trade gatherings. These were often held at a special time of the year at established centers, although the Shoshone rendezvous shifted from year to year. The centers had to have the resources to feed large numbers of people. At the Dalles on the Columbia River in Washington, salmon runs provided thousands of pounds of smoked and dried fish. Abundant whitefish at Sault Ste-Marie often fed 3000 people gathered for trading, religious ceremonies, and social events. Corn, beans and squash grown in the agricultural communities of Arizona and New Mexico fed the visitors who came to the important pueblo and ranchería centers. The corn-raising Mandan on the upper Missouri River traded their surplus harvest with Canadian Cree for skins and furs. In addition to the major routes and centers, every regional population cluster had its local network. In times of warfare, trade was curtailed, and unused paths filled with brambles.

Exotic goods, particularly lightweight items such as pigments for body paint, were a specialty of the long distance trade. Thin sheets of pounded copper were carried south from the Copper River country of Canada and the Lake Superior district. Shells, used as "money" by people living on both the Atlantic and Pacific coasts, were probably the most universally exchanged commodities. As late as the 19th century, a large conch shell from the Gulf of Mexico became a horn to assemble people in northern Michigan.

Beaks of the ivory-billed woodpecker were traded from Florida to the St Lawrence River Iroquois people to adorn ceremonial headgear. Feathers from Mexico contributed to the beauty of cloaks worn by nobility of southern chiefdoms. Cotton cloth, woven in the pueblos, and doe skins were traded for fine wearing apparel, along with pottery and baskets. A rare pelt from the northwest Pacific coast was a prized gift in the southwest desert country. The largest trade items were seagoing red cedar canoes, a specialty of the Haida of the Queen Charlotte Islands, and the birch-bark canoes made by the Ojibwa of the upper Great Lakes. The Northwest coast also traded in human slaves, captured in raids against small tribes in northern California and Oregon. Oil processed from sea mammals was also a regional specialty. Florida Indians paddled dugouts along the Keys to Cuba, carrying bear

Above: A Mississippian culture (Southern cult) figure made around 1000 AD in embossed copper depicts a warrior in the guise of a falcon, a symbol of power. He holds a war club in one hand and what appears to be a severed head in the other.

oil and cardinal feathers; this trade route lasted until the mid-19th century.

The first tentative European settlement, in the far northeast of the continent, was also a search for resources and trade goods. The Norse who came from Iceland to found three settlements in Greenland around the end of the 10th century were primarily looking for new pastures for their sheep and cattle, but they were also hunters and traders. They exported furs and walrus ivory to Europe, and traded with the Inuit as far north as Ellesmere Island. They regularly visited the area they called Markland (almost certainly Labrador) to gather timber. Their sagas record that they founded a settlement in a temperate area they named Vinland, after the wild grapes that grew there. The remains of a Norse settlement have been found at L'Anse Aux Meadows in Newfoundland; the handful of buildings, occupied for little more than 20 years round the year 1000, would have housed some 90 people. Spindle whorls attest that there were women among them, while butternuts, which do not grow this far north, suggest that they traded with Indians to the south.

The Greenland settlements survived until the 15th century, but after 1300 the worsening climate gradually made life harder. It also extended the habitat of the Thule Inuit, who began to migrate south, driving out the settlers. A European ship called at the Eastern Settlement in 1540 and found it deserted. The dead had all been buried save for the last man, whose corpse, wearing European-style clothes of the later 15th century, lay in the ruins of his farmhouse.

Above: originating in the Hohokam culture area (Arizona-New Mexico), this long necklace made from drilled shell and stone beads was used as trade goods. These found their way as far as the southern shores of the Great Lakes in the east and Vancouver Island in the north. They were also prized as personal decoration, lending the wearer increased social significance.

Left: feathers from a variety of brightly-plumaged wild birds were valued trade goods, some imported from Mexico and the Caribbean were particularly prized.

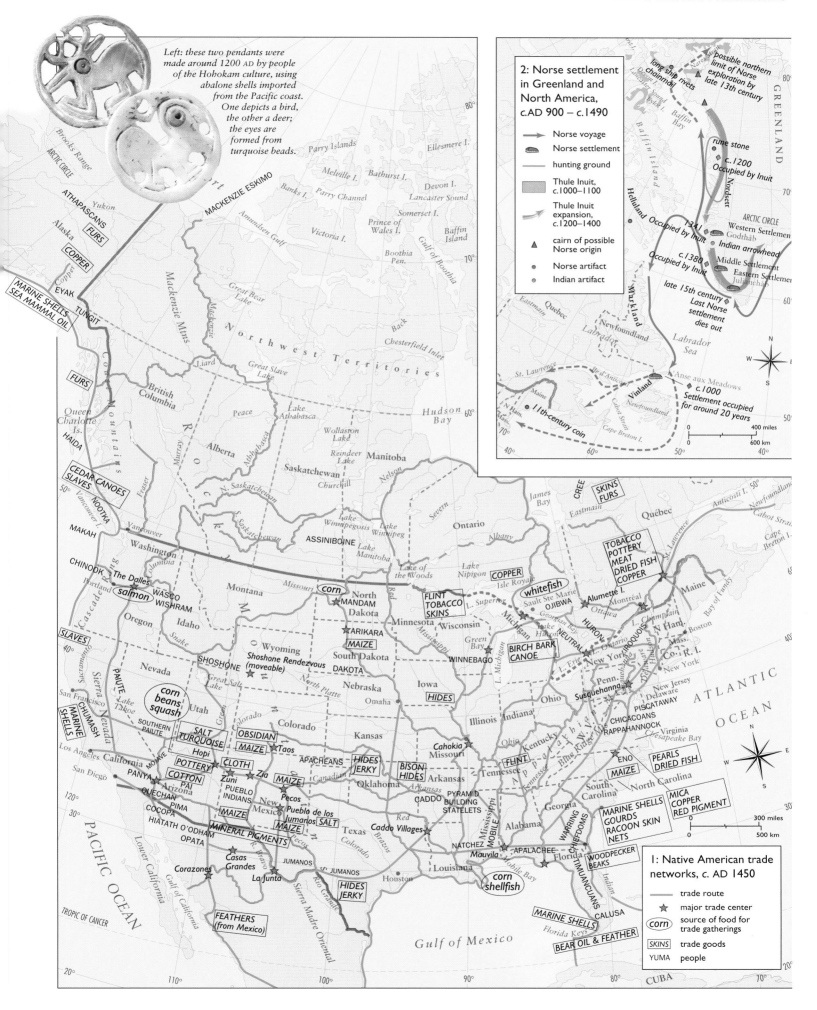

Left: these two pendants were made around 1200 AD by people of the Hohokam culture, using abalone shells imported from the Pacific coast. One depicts a bird, the other a deer; the eyes are formed from turquoise beads.

2: Norse settlement in Greenland and North America, c.AD 900 – c.1490

→ Norse voyage
⬛ Norse settlement
— hunting ground
▨ Thule Inuit, c.1000–1100
⬗ Thule Inuit expansion, c.1200–1400
▲ cairn of possible Norse origin
● Norse artifact
● Indian artifact

GREENLAND

long ship chainmail
possible northern limit of Norse exploration by late 13th century

rune stone
c.1200
Occupied by Inuit

Western Settlement
Godthåb

Indian arrowhead

c.1380
Occupied by Inuit

Middle Settlement
Eastern Settlement
Julianehåb

late 15th century
Last Norse settlement dies out

Markland

Helluland Occupied by Inuit

Occupied by Inuit

Nordseti

ARCTIC CIRCLE

Labrador Sea

Quebec
Eastmain
Labrador
Newfoundland

Maine
St. Lawrence
Île d'Anticosti
N.Ham.
Mass.

L'Anse aux Meadows
c.1000
Settlement occupied for around 20 years

Vinland
Cape Breton I.
Cabot Strait

11th-century coin

0   400 miles
0   600 km

Native American trade networks, c. AD 1450

ATHAPASCANS
FURS
COPPER

MARINE SHELLS
SEA MAMMAL OIL

EYAK
TUNGIT
MACKENZIE ESKIMO

Brooks Range
ARCTIC CIRCLE
Alaska
Yukon

FURS

Queen Charlotte Is.
HAIDA

CEDAR CANOES
SLAVES

British Columbia

NOOTHA
MAKAH

CHINOOK
The Dalles
salmon
WASCO
WISHRAM

SLAVES

Portland
Washington
Oregon
Idaho

Vancouver I.
Vancouver

Northwest Territories

Parry Islands
Ellesmere I.

Melville I. Bathurst I.
Devon I.
Banks I. Parry Channel Lancaster Sound
Prince of Wales I.
Somerset I.
Victoria I. Boothia Pen. Baffin Island
Amundsen Gulf Gulf of Boothia

Great Bear Lake
Mackenzie Mtns
Back
Chesterfield Inlet
Great Slave Lake
Liard
Peace
Lake Athabasca
Wollaston Lake
Reindeer Lake
Alberta
Saskatchewan
Manitoba
N. Saskatchewan
Churchill
Nelson
Hudson Bay

James Bay
CREE
SKINS
FURS

Ontario
Severn
Albany
Eastmain
Québec
Anticosti I.
Cabot Strait
Cape Breton I.

TOBACCO
POTTERY
MEAT
DRIED FISH
COPPER

Montana
North Dakota
corn
MANDAM
ARIKARA
MAIZE

South Dakota
DAKOTA

Wyoming
Shoshone Rendezvous (moveable)
SHOSHONE

Nevada
PAIUTE
SOUTHERN PAIUTE

Great Salt Lake
Utah
Colorado

corn beans squash

MARINE SHELLS
CHUMASH

Sierra Nevada
San Francisco
Sacramento
Lake Takoe

California
Los Angeles
San Diego

SALT
TURQUOISE
Hopi
POTTERY
COTTON
Zuni
CLOTH
Zia
MAIZE

PANYA
QUECHAN
COCOPA
PIMA
HIATATH O'ODHAM
OPATA

MOJAVE
PAI
Arizona

OBSIDIAN
MAIZE
Taos
Pecos
Pueblo de los Jumanos
SALT
MAIZE

New Mexico
MAIZE
Pueblo Indians

MINERAL PIGMENTS

Casas Grandes
Corazones
La Junta
JUMANOS
JUMANOS

FEATHERS (from Mexico)

Sierra Madre Oriental

Rio Grande

Red
Colorado
Brazos
Pecos

Texas

HIDES
JERKY

Oklahoma
APACHEANS

BISON
HIDES
Arkansas

FLINT

CADDO
PYRAMID BUILDING STATELETS
Caddo Villages

HIDES
JERKY

Houston

corn shellfish

Louisiana

Minnesota
Wisconsin
Lake Superior
Isle Royale
COPPER
Sault Ste Marie
OJIBWA
whitefish

FLINT
TOBACCO
SKINS

Iowa
Nebraska
North Platte
Omaha
HIDES

Kansas
Missouri

Cahokia

Illinois Indiana Ohio Kentucky
FLINT
Tennessee

Mississippi
Alabama
Georgia

NATCHEZ
Mauvila
MOBILE
Mobile Bay

APALACHEE
Florida

WARRING CHIEFDOMS

MARINE SHELLS
GOURDS
RACOON SKIN
NETS

WOODPECKER BEAKS

TIMUCUANS

MARINE SHELLS

BEAR OIL & FEATHER

Florida Keys

CUBA
Gulf of Mexico

Lake Winnipegosis
Lake Manitoba
Lake Winnipeg
Lake of the Woods
ASSINIBOINE
Lake Nipigon

Michigan
Green Bay
WINNEBAGO
L. Michigan

Lake Huron
Georgian Bay
L. Ontario
NEUTRAL
HURON
Alumette I.
Ottawa
Montréal
IROQUOIS
N.York
New York
L. Erie
Penn.
Susquehanna
New Jersey
Delaware
PISCATAWAY
CHICACOANS
RAPPAHANNOCK
Virginia
Chesapeake Bay

BIRCH BARK CANOE

N.Ham.
Mass.
Boston
Conn.
R.I.
L. Champlain

Maine
Bay of Fundy

ATLANTIC OCEAN

ENO
Virginia
North Carolina
MAIZE
South Carolina

PEARLS
DRIED FISH

MICA
COPPER
RED PIGMENT

Blue Ridge
Appalachians

0   300 miles
0   500 km

1: Native American trade networks, c. AD 1450

— trade route
★ major trade center
🔵 corn   source of food for trade gatherings
▢ SKINS   trade goods
YUMA   people

PACIFIC OCEAN
TROPIC OF CANCER

ARCTIC CIRCLE
Brooks Range

BEFORE THE INVASION

NORTH AMERICA, c. 1515

North America on the eve of the European invasion was a mosaic of distinctive peoples. Some were nomadic hunter-gatherers, others farmed intensively and lived in populous towns.

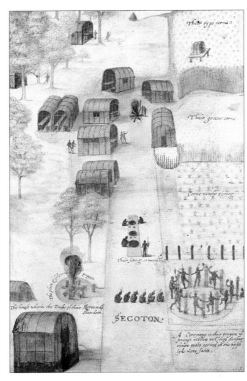

The most densely populated area of North America was probably the Atlantic seaboard from southern Maine to North Carolina. The region was mostly inhabited by Algonquian-speaking peoples. They settled and farmed along the tidal estuaries, stretching inland as far as the Appalachian fall line, combining intensive horticulture with efficient big and small game hunting and fishing. Native peoples along the St Lawrence River and around the Great Lakes lived by harvesting wild rice, fishing, big game hunting, and intensive horticulture. They paddled birch-bark canoes across lakes, up and down rivers, and portaged from one waterway to another to hunt, to fish, and to trade with peaceful partners or war with distant enemies.

By 1515 the focus of the Mississippian chiefdoms (> *pages 26–7*) had shifted south towards the Gulf of Mexico. These statelets were densely populated and mutually antagonistic. Their rulers exercised absolute power over hierarchically organized populations in large capitals with ceremonial plazas and, in many instances, multiple pyramid mounds. They also controlled a number of subservient towns which also had mounds, hamlets, and gardensteads. The towns were surrounded by fields where crops such as maize were grown, and were usually sited on rivers which provided both a means of transport and a supply of fish, mollusks, and crustaceans. We do not know what languages were spoken in the various statelets. The Indian names of those which were visited by Spaniards in the 16th century are known from the expedition chronicles; others can only be identified by their modern archeological site name. Florida was also populated by mound builders, but they were a culturally distinct group of peoples hunting alligators, manatees, conch, and other marine, river, and lake animals not available farther north. Some cultivated tropical trees such as the chirimoya, and tropical roots such as manioc.

The Mandan and various Caddoan-speaking groups cultivated fields along the Missouri River and other western tributaries of the Mississippi. They seasonally hunted bison, elk, antelope, and deer on the Great Plains. Very few people lived on the Plains in 1515. Only later did a number of groups move into this vacant environmental niche after they acquired, or in order to acquire, horses brought to the Americas by Spanish colonists (> *pages 74–5*). Mobile trading peoples carried commodities between the riverine horticultural towns, the Northwest coast and the pueblo towns. Scores of peoples lived in multi-storied stone or adobe pueblos (> *pages 26–7*). They grew maize, beans, and squash, which they irrigated with diverted river flows. To the west and southwest of the pueblos were the *rancherías*. These villages were similar to pueblos, but the houses were scattered rather than centralized. The inhabitants domesticated local

Above: the tidal estuaries along the Atlantic seaboard were densely settled by Indians living in agricultural villages. Secoton, pictured in this 1587 watercolor by John White, governor of the short-lived English colony at Roanoke, was situated near Chesapeake Bay. To the right are fields of maize in three stages of growth

plants and practiced irrigation. A few peripheral rancherían peoples relied more on hunting, fishing, and wild plant food collecting, but the people of the rancherian heartland were dynamic cultural innovators who manipulated the environment to ensure a reliable food supply.

Another dynamic zone of innovation extended from southern Alaska to the Columbia River, expanding up the major rivers. Sea-going canoes traded iron, pelts, copper, dried fish, fish oil, dentalium shells, and human slaves. Trade fostered cultural conformity along the main routes and, with slave raiding, made an important impact on many peoples living on the edges of this zone. Beyond these areas were peoples whose lifeways had changed little since 2000 BC: the Aleuts and Inuit in the Arctic, the Athapascan-speaking and other peoples of the Subarctic zone, the non-horticultural rancherians, and the folk of the Texas coast and Baja California. They lived much as their ancestors had three and a half millennia earlier, exploiting whatever food resources their marine, desert, and mountain habitats could provide.

Right: the beautiful pottery known as Mimbres was produced to an exceptional technical standard by Mogollon people (> page 26) and their pueblo-dwelling descendants from the 8th–16th centuries. Decorated with human and animal figures, these pots were used as burial offerings; like votive offerings from cultures of all periods the world over, they were ritually broken, usually by having a hole pierced through their base.

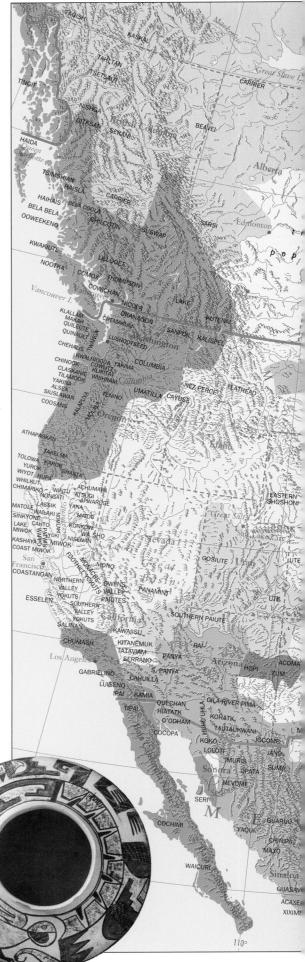

CHIPEWYAN

Athabasca

Hudson Bay

LABRADOR
ESKIMO

NASKAPI

CREE
(LATER
WEST
CREE)

Saskatchewan

Manitoba

Belcher Is.

ethnicity unknown

C   A   N   A   D   A

James
Bay

Quebec   MONTAGNAIS

Newfoundland

BEOTHUK
Newfoundland

Grand Banks

L. Winnipegosis

Saskatoon

Ontario

EAST CREE

New
Brunswick

Nova Scotia

L. Manitoba

Regina

Winnipeg

CREE

Halifax
MICMAC

ASSINIBOINE

L. of the Wood

MALISEET
PASSAMAQUODDY

BLACKFEET

GROS VENTRE
ARAPAHO

Rainy L.

Isle Royale

OJIBWA

ALGONQUIN

Maine
EASTERN
ABENAKI

LAURENTIAN

MANDAN

Montana

North Dakota

Minnesota

FOX

Lake Superior

Grand I.

Sault Ste Marie

MENOMINI

Georgian Bay

HURON

PETUN

WESTERN ABENAKI

PENACOOK
NIPMUCK
MASSACHUSETT

Massachusetts

POKANOKET

CROW
HIDATSA

DAKOTA

KICKAPOO

Wisconsin

OTTAWA

Toronto

WENRO

L. Ontario

MOHAWK
ONONDAGA
ONEIDA

New York

MAHICAN

ARIKARA

South Dakota

MASCOUTER

St Paul
Minneapolis

Michigan

L. Simcoe

Detroit

NEUTRAL

CAYUGA

SENECA

CONN. R.I.

KIOWA

WINNEBAGO

SAUK

Chicago

ERIE

Pennsylvania

New Jersey

LENAPE

UNAMI

Nebraska

PAWNEE

IOWA

Iowa

Illinois

Indiana

Ohio

Maryland   Delaware

Delaware Bay

ATLANTIC

Indianapolis

Cincinnati

West
Virginia

CONESTOGA

MONACAN

PATUXENT   NANTICOKE

ASSATEAGUE
POCOMOKE

Chesapeake Bay

OCEAN

Denver

Colorado

Kansas

Kansas City

Missouri

St Louis

Cahokia

Kentucky

Virginia

NOTTAWAY

PROTO-POWHATAN

N

WICHITA

Arkansas

Hiwasee
Island
Chiaha

Chisca

Guaquili

NOTTAWAY

MEHERRIN

NEUSIOK

TUSCARORA

WEAPEMEOC
ROANOKE

North Carolina

W   E

Campbell

Coste

Xuala

Chalaque

Ilapi

Cofitachequi

Hymahi

S

0   300 miles

APAQHEANS

Upper Nodena
Pecan Point
Pacaha

Tenn.

Talise

Bradley

Talise

Itaba

Etowah

Ocute

Ichisi

South
Carolina

YAMASEE

0   500 km

Oklahoma

Coligua

Quipana

Clarksdale

Casqui Parkin

Quizquiz

Ulibahali

Dundee

Chucalissa

Spiro

Tula

Autiamque

Anilco

Chicaza

Tuasi

Apalatya

Talisi

Toa

Georgia

CADDOAN

Chaguate

Aguacay

Winterville

Guachoya

Aminoya

Moundville

Alabama

Lainar

PROTO-CUSABO

CASCANGE-ICATUI
TACATACURU

Amaye

Dallas

Nagatex

Aquixo

Aays

Nondacao

Socatino

Big Eddy

Belcher

White

Mississippi

Mabilas

Atahachi

White

Capachequi

Kolomoki

Florida

Apalachee

Napituca

Aguacaleyquen

SATURIWA

Guasco

Emerald

Achuse

Fl. Walton
Beach

YUSTECA

Malapaz

POTANO

AGUA DULCE

Texas

Hasinai
Saunders

Louisiana

New Orleans

Mobile Bay

APALACHE

Ocale

OCALE

Urripacoxi

TOCOBAGA

ACUERA

TONKAWA

ATAPAKA

CHITIMACHA

Uzita

MOCOZO

AIS

ILMANO

KARANKAWA

CALUSA

CONCHO

TEKESTA

Miami

Uzita

Coahuila

COAHUILTECO

Key Marco

Florida Keys

Nuevo
León

CHIHUAHUA

TOBOSO

ME   X   I   C   O

Gulf of Mexico

CUBA

ZACATEC

Monterrey

HUICHOL

CAZCAN

San Luis
Potosí

Ways of life in North America, AD 1515

- Arctic hunter-gatherers
- Subarctic hunter-fisher-gatherers
- Northwest coast marine economy
- Plains hunter-gatherers
- Plains horticulturalists
- non-horticultural rancherian peoples
- rancherian peoples with low-intensity horticulture
- rancherian peoples with intensive horticulture
- pueblos with intensive horticulture
- seacoast foragers
- marginal horticultural hunters
- river-based horticultural chiefdoms
- orchard-growing alligator hunters
- tidewater horticulturalists
- fishers and wild rice gatherers

▲ town with temple mound

31

PART II: EUROPEANS AND AFRICANS ARRIVE

Introduction
by Helen Hornbeck Tanner

The 17th century saw the flourishing of many new communities along the Atlantic coast, as Europeans arrived on the continent after centuries of occasional encounters between explorers and North American inhabitants. Initial short-lived attempts to establish settlements finally succeeded with the development of a tobacco-growing region, and farming and trading centers. European settlers were generally intolerant of native beliefs and customs, and considered the original inhabitants to be savages and pagans. The expansion of the plantation system spurred economic growth but resulted in the enslavement of thousands of Indians and imported Africans, creating inter-racial hostilities

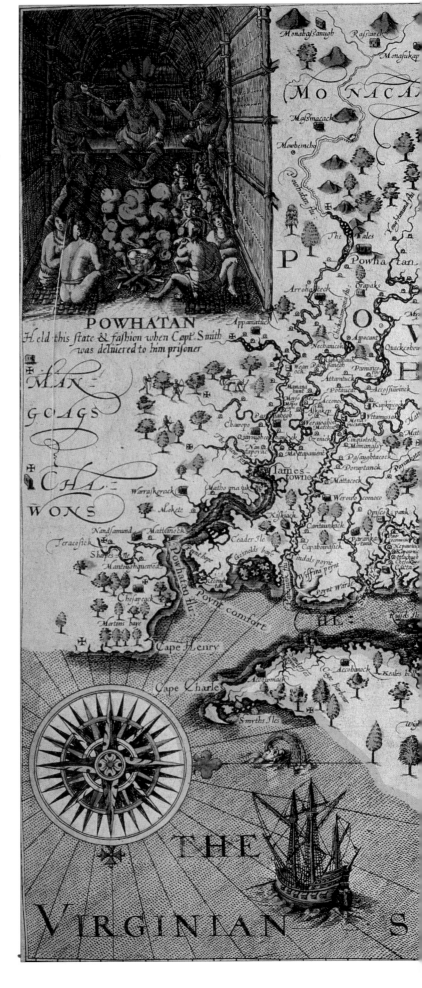

Right: a map of Virginia drawn in 1622 by John Smith, including in the top left corner Captain Smith's depiction of his earlier capture by Powhatan. As increasing numbers of colonialists endeavoured to push back the frontier, Indian tribes began to resist, sacking missions and launching often murderous attacks on settlers

The original people inhabiting North America had sporadic encounters with Europeans for hundreds of years before these outsiders came as colonists and began to take over land on Chesapeake Bay in 1607. Trading was the experience that first brought Indians into contact with Europeans, but the early traders were transients. By AD 1000, the Norse carried on a hazardous trade on the North Atlantic coast with "Skraelings," who knew that they should toss packages of skins over the walls of the trading fort to receive treasured strips of crimson cloth. The hostility of the native peoples apparently ended trade, though a Norse base existed briefly on the tip of Newfoundland. Subsequent contacts for a long period chiefly concerned Eskimo (Inuit) fishermen, although the Micmac and Maliseet also became involved. They were frequently in contact with Basque whalers, who were soon followed by fishing vessels from other north European ports. In addition to whaling, the cod fishery probably attracted a thousand boats a year. The main geographic focus for all this activity was the Labrador coast, and the straits of Belle Isle between Labrador and Newfoundland, on the northeast edge of future settlement areas in North America.

European exploration was the second type of activity that preceded actual settlements, Going upriver beyond the Gulf of St Lawrence, Jacques Cartier located sites for future French settlement in 1535. French, Italian, Spanish, and English captains sailed along both the Atlantic and Pacific coasts on exploratory voyages during the 16th century, making occasional landfalls, usually with exchanges of gifts. Europeans were initially received hospitably by Indian people, who admired their metal axes, knives, and swords. But gracious receptions ceased after a number of Indians were seized and transported to Europe to be displayed as curiosities in royal courts. Some lived to return with firsthand reports of the peculiar customs of "overseas people," but most succumbed to strange diets and disease.

Exploration and conquests were combined in the southern approach to North America carried out by the Spanish. They brought with them the military experience and religious zeal that had accumulated during centuries of battling to drive out the Muslim Arabs and recreate a totally Christian Spain. Cortez' conquest of Mexico in 1521 brought disease with the armies, and the consequent destruction of an estimated 90 percent of the population of the densely inhabited central valley of Mexico before the end of the century. Equally disastrous were subsequent expeditions through the southern regions of the present U. S. in search of other cities of gold that might rival Tenochtitlan, the fabled capital of the Aztecs. Survivors of the highly organized chiefdoms had to devise new societies and ways of life, and became the tribal groups encountered by English traders reaching the trans-Appalachian regions in the late 17th century.

The first European attempts at colonization were all short-lived. Best known is the Roanoke colony established on an island in Albemarle Sound off North Carolina in 1585, with support expeditions during the next two years. The few hundred men, women, and children completely disappeared before a delayed rescue mission arrived from England in 1591. The first success in founding a community was by the Spaniards, who acquired the site of St. Augustine, Florida, in 1565 after ousting the French Huguenots who had been there for the two previous years. The little town is the oldest European settlement in America north of the Rio Grande. On the other hand, St. Augustine never became a center for population expansion. With a massive stone fort, it was chiefly a military outpost of Cuba for the defense of the silver fleet following the Gulf Stream shipping lane that flows northward along the Florida coast before striking east toward Europe. St. Augustine was also a base for an extensive chain of Indian missions that extended across the Florida peninsula to Apalachee Bay and into present-day Georgia. Spain's other early base in North America was Santa Fé in present-day New Mexico, which was established in 1598 on the northern frontier of New Spain.

Long-range colonization projects in North America were initiated also by the English, French, and Dutch. Many different kinds of people came to the east coast of North America under the auspices of the three western European countries, and their ventures all started about the same time. Of the two English colonies, one started in

Below: a 16th-century Mexican manuscript shows a Spanish mass in the course of which converted Mexicans receive communion from Lienzo de Maxacala. Spanish explorer Bernal Díaz had defined the Spanish mission in the New World as being "to serve God...to give light to those in darkness and also to get rich."

yemoquayated que tlatoque

Above left and right: two armed and fearsome figures portrayed in the Codex Canadiensis, *clothed in extravagant garb and smoking enormous pipes. Codices were the earliest form of books, replacing the scrolls and wax tablets of earlier times*

Virginia in 1607, though settlement floundered until the 1620s, and the second began in Massachusetts in 1620. The French settlement at Québec began in 1608, and the Dutch settlement on the Hudson River began in 1624. In Virginia, the Jamestown settlement began with only 107 men located on a swampy peninsula upstream on the James River. The variety of colonists sent to Jamestown included Italian-trained glassblowers, French artisans skilled in silk production (sent there in the hope that mulberry trees and silk worms could produce the raw material), gentlemen dandys without any practical skills, and some families. A large proportion of the colonists to Virginia were indentured servants who would have to work off the price of their transatlantic passage in order to gain their freedom. Many had been homeless vagrants in England, and the chance to own land after seven years of hard labor made the overseas voyage seem attractive. Yet the 80 percent death rate for the 8000–9000 people who arrrived between 1610 and 1622 made early Virginia a true challenge to survival.

Reorganized in 1624, the colony finally found a road to success in tobacco culture, which created an elite of plantation owners with large landholdings. Along the way were wars with the leaders of Powhatan's paramount chiefdom, the Indian power on the west shore of Chesapeake Bay, which had a regional population of perhaps 20,000 which far outnumbered the first tenuous white settlements. The arrival of strangers was probably no surprise to Powhatan; he was aware of the periodic voyages of ships in North American waters reported through Indian information channels, and he regularly sent out emissaries to the northeast Atlantic coast, as well as to the Gulf of Mexico, to bring back news of any local events. Confronted with the English in their home country, his people felt growing resentment.

But the English had guns, and each war ended with the English acquiring more Indian land. In addition to quelling Indian opposition, by 1675 the governor faced an uprising in the west country known as Bacon's Rebellion. Nathanial Bacon's followers were mostly former indentured servants lacking land but eager to acquire lands preserved for the Indians by the longtime governor, who had promised to reserve backcountry territory for them. The Indians were his customers and clients in the

Indian trade, and their shoreline village sites had been taken over by English planters.

Events in Virginia reinforce the idea that the arrival of the English was really an "invasion." The military character of English colonization is often explained by pointing out that the English had previously invaded Ireland, devastating the country in the later part of the 16th century. To justify their conquest, the English categorized the largely Catholic inhabitants as "brutish savages" and confined them to reservations in order to take over the lands. The English did not approve of blending with other contingents of humankind, preferring to isolate themselves from any potentially modifying influence and preserve their own way of life.

The mild climate of the Chesapeake Bay drew other English colonial projects. Maryland was originally intended as refuge for Catholic families, but many Protestants were admitted in order to populate the region. Indians sold land to the proprietors to secure guns and supplies for warfare against their enemies. Maryland, too, became a tobacco growing region, but many people had to toil ceaselessly in order to survive, and the first generations were often forced to live in great privation and squalor.

The second region where the English established a foothold in North America was Plymouth on Cape Cod Bay, where Pilgrims landed in 1620 and barely survived the first winter. Their unambitious goal was to live a simple life away from the corruption that had surrounded them in England and the Netherlands. More strident were the Puritans, who began arriving at Massachusetts Bay in 1630. They brought 18,000 colonists to the "New England" by 1642. Although the initial death rate was as high as in other infant colonies, the Puritans prospered and spread out around Boston. For a time they remained a minority in the regional population, despite the introduction of disease. Southern New England probably had at least 125,000 Indian people in 1600, but this number was severely reduced by a respiratory epidemic in 1616, followed by smallpox in 1633. Vacated villages provided land for incoming colonists, who considered the smallpox scourge an "act of God."

The Puritans were a distinctive people, unique among colonizing groups for their religious zeal, belief in hard work and education, and their regimented lives. Leaders in the society were university-educated ministers; one of the first things they did was establish Harvard College in 1636. The social emphasis of these people was on family and community, and their way of life in a new environment seemed to be unusually healthy. Their numbers reached 100,000 by 1700, although only about 25,000 had immigrated. Total religious conformity proved to be

impossible to maintain, and dissident factions moved away, particularly to Rhode Island.

As in the Chesapeake Bay region, Indian leaders opposed the continued expansion of the colonists into Indian farming and hunting areas. There were two major wars: the Pequot war of 1637 and the suppression of the resistance led by Metacomet, the Wampanoag leader known as "King Philip," in 1676, concurrent with Bacon's Rebellion in Virginia. But not all Indian relations were hostile. Indian trading was an important commercial activity in the colony. Some efforts at Indian conversion were successful, beginning with the establishment of four "Praying Towns" for a combined population of about 1000 Indians. Land was granted for these communities, which eventually numbered 15.

In 17th-century life along the Middle Atlantic coast, Dutch people also played an important role. Their base was New Netherlands, a colony established in 1623 on the lower Hudson River with a capital at New Amsterdam (later New York City). The Dutch were the leading traders of the world at this time, with a commercial network extending to South America, Africa, India, the East Indies, and Formosa. From their base on Manhattan Island, Dutch trading posts spread to Connecticut, and down to the Delaware River Indian communities in Pennsylvania and New Jersey, as well as up the Hudson River.. Fort Orange (later Albany) was the interior headquarters for developing trade in furs with the Mohawk and other Indian nations.

The Dutch also made large grants of land in the Hudson River valley to "patroons," creating a kind of local gentry. One of the largest holdings, Rensselaerswyck, covered 700,000 acres of land near present-day Albany, New York. They transported about 10,000 colonists to New Netherlands, including not only Dutch but Protestant populations from other European countries: French Huguenots, Walloons from present-day Belgium, English, Finns, and Swedes. There were also Portuguese and Portuguese Jews from Brazil, and Africans. In 1638, the Swedes established a trading fort on the Delaware River at the present-day site of Wilmington. The Dutch colony lasted only 50 years, transferring to England in 1675 following 10 years of warfare between England and Holland, and henceforth became New York. The Dutch heritage and diverse population of New York City remained, however. Descendants of old Dutch families carry names well known in modern America, such as Roosevelt and Vanderbilt.

In settling North America, people paid a great deal of attention to religion and religious beliefs. Opposition to official state religions was a strong motivation for the Pilgrims and Puritans in settling New England. Far more radical were the ideas of the Quaker people who came to Pennsylvania when the colony was established by William Penn in 1681. The Quaker belief that each person has an "inner light" to guide their behavior placed individuals outside the authority of others. True to Quaker beliefs in pacifism and religious tolerance, William Penn invited people of all sects to a new society where persecution for one's beliefs did not exist. In England and in Massachusetts, Quaker beliefs were considered so dangerous and fanatical that outspoken leaders were hanged.

Penn alone among colonial leaders included Indian people in his ideas for a social system. He immediately established peaceful relations with Delaware leaders and stated that his goal was to live in friendship. He promised not to assign any land without first purchasing it from the Delaware. He also promised to provide adequate trade goods and prohibited the sale of alcohol. Impressed by this unusually hopeful attitude, Shawnee and other refugees from inter-tribal warfare moved into Pennsylvania. Unfortunately, Penn left the colony in 1701, and his successors were not as altruistic. Quaker farmers found good agricultural land in Pennsylvania and prospered almost immediately. By 1700, Philadelphia was the largest city on the Atlantic seaboard. The addition of Scots-Irish, German, and Swiss settlers brought the population of Pennsylvania up to about 20,000 but the newcomers were eager for more land and did not adhere to Penn's strict policies for dealing with Indian people.

Nevertheless, the treatment of Indian people in the early years of the Pennsylvania colony stood in stark contrast to the situation in Carolina, established in 1669. Governors of Carolina promoted, and sometimes led, raids on Indian communities to capture those who were young and strong, and sell them as slaves to planters in the West Indies. The Carolina slave raids destroyed the Spanish missions of the Georgia-Florida region, striking as far south as the Everglades by 1711. About 10,000 Indians were enslaved in the Southeast, and Indian slavery preceded and overlapped the introduction of large numbers of Africans at the outset of the 18th century.

The leading people of South Carolina were the plantation owners, many of whom came from Barbados. The development of rice and cotton in the tidewater region, using enslaved Africans as a principal labor source, created a flourishing economy. With the growth in plantation production, the African population increased to the point where it became three times that of the white population. In the vicinity of Charleston, Africans comprised close to 90 percent of the population. The tidewater region of South Carolina centered on Charleston differed from all other English colonial regions in the numerical dominance of African people.

The population make-up in the backcountry provides another social portrait. The Scots and Germans who moved into the southern Appalachians became independent farmers and cattle raisers, impinging on the hunting grounds of Cherokees. One of the important business enterprises of Charleston merchants was trade with the Indians to get deerskins for export to Europe. Charleston traders penetrated the interior southland, and even crossed the Mississippi River before 1700.

From the beginning of settlement, the wars carried on by the different European monarchs cast a shadow over the relationships between the different peoples in North America. The Carolina colonies were carved out of territory originally claimed by Spain. People were brought to Georgia, boldly established in 1733, to serve as a protec-

Right: a map of the St Anthony Falls in the Mississippi River, which was surveyed by Captain Carver on November 17, 1766. Errors were often made as surveyors, paid piece rates by their government employers, worked for speed rather than accuracy

tion for South Carolina. Georgia started out as a philanthropic venture to provide new opportunities for Englishmen imprisoned for debt, and at the same time to have them available for military service if necessary. Other settlers, whose ocean voyages were not similarly subsidized, also came to Georgia, creating a backcountry population similar to that of South Carolina. The intermittent periods of English–Spanish warfare kept the people living on both sides of the St Mary's River, Georgia–Florida border, in a state of antipathy. Military expeditions, chiefly by sea, between St Augustine and Charleston or Savannah took place up to 1819 whenever war erupted in Europe or Latin America.

From the abbreviated account of arriving Europeans and Africans up to this point, it is clear that settlements and isolated communities of different kinds came into existence all along the Atlantic seaboard during the 17th century. Some were transplanted and some were new communities. In considering this process, it is important to keep in mind the continuing presence of Indian people, who formed a majority population for the early decades of settlement, but were gradually forced back from the coastline or confined to reserved land whittled away by aggressive white neighbors. For Indians, the arrival of Europeans with their technologically advanced possessions, notably guns, hatchets, and cloth, introduced new "tribes" into local and inter-regional affairs. Indian people too had different kinds of communities, some towndwelling, and others intinerant. The more highly organized tribal people were also more involved in complex inter-tribal diplomacy. As in Europe, Indian people over the centuries had developed traditional allies and enemies. To plan raids or revenge expeditions, councils were held regularly, usually in the spring. These councils received representatives from other tribes, held ceremonies commemorating leaders who had died, determined the time and direction of warfare for the season, and arranged inter-tribal feasts and sports competitions. European participation in Indian alliances and hostilities preceded Indian participation in North American battles brought on by wars between European monarchs.

French settlement began in the St Lawrence River valley of Canada, with the establishment of Québec 300 miles due north of Boston in 1608, and Montreal 200 miles north of Albany in 1642. Before Charleston and Philadelphia were founded, French traders had made their way 800 miles west through the upper Great Lakes, and by 1700 a second French settlement area had been established on the Gulf of Mexico prior to the founding of New Orleans in 1718. The small French population—about 15,000 in 1700, was spread thinly over a vast interior. The principal settlers in the lower St Lawrence River heartland of French Canada were the "habitants" who

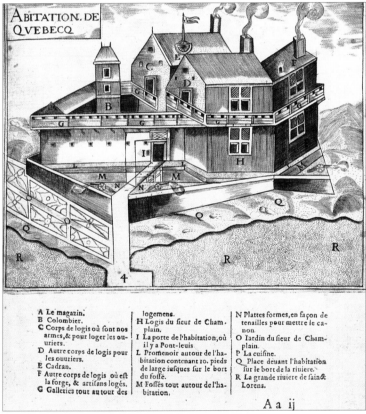

Top: French explorer Samuel Champlain in a bloody encounter with Iroquois warriors on the border between Canada and New York State in 1609. Two Indian chiefs, who had never before been confronted with firearms, were shot dead

Bottom: Champlain's residence on the banks of the St Lawrence River in Quebec

occupied small "ribbon farms"—narrow strips of land along the St Lawrence river that extended away from the river banks for a considerable distance. The parish chapel was the central focus for each district. The French government wanted to create a stable agricultural population bringing in substantial harvests of wheat and other foods which they preferred to Indian corn. Ribbon farms with river frontage were also surveyed for "habitants" along the Detroit River, in French villages on the Mississippi

River in the Illinois country, and in the New Orleans district, as well as around other French forts. Southern Louisiana had a population of small farmers and cattle ranchers, but the people with power were the plantation owners who raised cotton, rice, and indigo with workforces of enslaved Africans.

In Canada, the important people (aside from the governor's staff, military officers, and missionaries) were the merchant traders, for the fur trade was the principal economic enterprise of the colony. The forts established to protect the trade, and the subsidiary posts, scattered small clusters of French at strategic points along trade routes throughout Canada and Louisiana. Since only a limited number of licenses were issued, 600–800 unlicensed traders, called "coureurs de bois," annually flaunted the laws and carried trade goods to Indian country. They took Indian wives "according to the custom of the country," and raised families in the Indian communities where they traded.

French policy in Canada encouraged intermarriage between French men and Indian women, with the goal of forming "one nation," but expected marriages to be performed by Catholic priests and the ensuing families to be French rather than Indian. From prior experience with the dye wood trade in Brazil, the Frenc h government had observed the importance of making family alliances with Indian communities in order to facilitate trade. In North America, the second generation of "coureurs de bois" were Métis ("mixed"), who formed a separate population group which is recognized in Canada today. Indian leaders did not object to the marriage alliances of their daughters with French traders, even when they knew that the trader had a French wife back in Montreal, for they themselves believed in polygamy. Even the French

governors had an Indian as well as a French wife.

The French also came to understand the Indian view of trade as a reciprocal gift exchange, which was one aspect of the Indian regard for balance in all relationships. More difficult for the French to understand initially was the Indian handling of a major infraction of social behavior, such as murder. In the Indian communities of Canada, such an act called for the entire community to heal the damage. Relatives gathered to offer gifts to compensate the family that had suffered a loss, or find a person to replace the victim and take over similar labor and responsibilities. To kill the murderer would be to create further damage to the social order.

All in all, many French and very few English settled in Indian communities. French family names found on Indian reservations in North America also appear in Montreal and Québec city telephone directories. The experience of the French in North America illustrates the adjustments made by people of different customs, beliefs, and value systems in order to live in the same area. By 1750, Europeans from many countries had settled in North American colonies governed by England, France, and Spain. The population numbers and distribution varied. The Spanish population in what is now the U. S. was approximately 10,000, with about 4000 in New Mexico and close to 3000 in Texas and in Florida. The French colonies had about 55,000 people, including 50,000 in Canada, 2000 in the Illinois country, and 3000 in Louisiana. Far greater was the population of the English colonies, comprising 250,000 Europeans and 240,000 Africans, including about 10,000 who had gained their freedom. The Indian population of North America in 1750 is estimated at 500,000 in present-day Canada and 1,500,000 in the area of the U. S. and the Mexican border regions.

TIMELINE
AD 1515–1763

NORTH AMERICA	THE CARIBBEAN, CENTRAL & S. AMERICA	EUROPE, AFRICA, & ASIA
	c.1515 Inca empire at its greatest extent	1517 Martin Luther posts 95 theses at Wittenberg, triggering Reformation
	1519–21 Spanish conquer Aztec empire in Mexico	
1524 Giovanni Verrazano explores coast of North America	1524 12 Franciscan friars arrive in New Spain	
	1525 Inca Huayna Capac dies, possibly of a European disease. Civil war between his successors Huascar and Atahualpa	1529 Ottoman Turks besiege Vienna
	1530s Portuguese begin to colonize Brazil	1531 King Henry VIII becomes head of Church of England
	1533 Spanish conquer Peru	1533 Pope Clement VII excommunicates Henry VIII
1534 Jacques Cartier establishes short-lived French colony at Québec	1534 Spanish found Quito, Ecuador	1534 Henry VIII of England breaks with Rome
	1535 Spanish found Lima, Peru	
	1537 Spanish found Asunción, Paraguay	
	1538 Spanish found Bogotá, Colombia	
1539–42 Spaniards Coronado and de Soto lead expeditions to Great Plains and Florida	1541 Spanish found Santiago, Chile	1541 Promulgation of order making Protestantism the state religion in Ireland
	1545 Spanish discover silver at Zacatecas, Mexico and Potosí, Bolivia	
	1546 Spanish complete conquest of Maya	
	1548 Spanish found La Paz, Bolivia	
1550s French fur traders penetrate Gulf of St Lawrence. Plains Indians begin to use horses		1562–92 Wars of Religion in France
1562 150 French Protestants found colony on St Johns River, Florida		
1565 Spanish massacre French colonists in Florida and found St Augustine, first permanent European settlement in future U.S.		1566 Dutch rebel against Spanish rule in the Netherlands
		1569 Spanish take possession of Philippines
	1572 Last Inca stronghold at Vilcabamba falls to Spanish	1572 St Bartholomew's Eve massacre of French Protestants in Paris
		1580 King Philip II of Spain succeeds to throne of Portugal, uniting the two countries
1585 Short-lived English colony at Roanoke Island	1586 Francis Drake sacks Cartagena, Colombia	1587 Russian expansion into Siberia begins. Queen Elizabeth I grants Sir Walter Raleigh 40,000 acres in Ireland, where he plants tobacco
	1588 Jesuit missionaries gather Guaraní Indians of Paraguay into mission towns and build a trade empire from the sale of their produce	1588 Spanish attempt to invade England fails
1598 Juan de Oñate leads settlers from Mexico to upper Rio Grande		1598 Edict of Nantes gives religious freedom to Protestants in France
1599 First French dwelling in Canada at Tadoussac		
1607 English found Jamestown, Virginia		
1608 French found Québec		
1609 Spanish found Santa Fé, New Mexico		1609 Dutch gain independence from Spain. "Articles of Plantation" open 5000 acres in Ireland to settlers from England and Scotland
		1618 Outbreak of Thirty Years War between Catholic and Protestant states in Europe
1619 20 Africans brought to Jamestown, Virginia		1619 Dutch colonization of East Indies begin
1620 Pilgrim Fathers arrive at Plymouth		
1625 Dutch found New Amsterdam		
	1627 English settle in Barbados	
1630 English Puritans settle in Massachusetts. 20,000 English migrate to New England by 1640	1630 Dutch invade northeast Brazil	
1635 English found colony of Connecticut	1632 Pirate "Brethren of the Coast" established on Ile de la Tortue off Haiti	
1636 English found colony of Rhode Island		

NORTH AMERICA	THE CARIBBEAN, CENTRAL & S. AMERICA	EUROPE, AFRICA, & ASIA
1638 Pequot War in New England. Swedish settlement founded on Delaware River		1640 Portugal independent of Spain once again
		1641 Insurrection against English rule in Ireland
1642 French found Montréal		1642–49 Civil War in England and Scotland
		1648 Peace of Westphalia ends Thirty Years War. Ukrainian rebel Chmielnicki massacres Jews in Poland
		1649 Oliver Cromwell, protector in England and Scotland (to 1658), massacres civilians at Drogheda and Wexford in Ireland. Russians reach Pacific
1654 23 Jews settle in New Amsterdam	1654 Expelled from Brazil, Dutch colonize Guyana	1653 "Act of Satisfaction" proclaims rebellion in Ireland is ended. Order for transportation of 8000 Irish to the Caribbean
	1655 English capture Jamaica from Spanish	1660 Monarchy restored in Britain
1663 Charles II grants Carolinas to eight proprietors. Québec recognized as French colony		
1664 English seize Dutch colonies: Fort Orange renamed Albany, New Amsterdam New York		
1670 Hudson's Bay Company granted charter	1670 Spanish recognize English claim to Jamaica	
1680 Pueblo Indians expel Spanish from New Mexico		
1682 William Penn founds Pennsylvania		1683 Ottoman Turks besiege Vienna
1684 La Salle claims Mississippi Valley for France		1685 Revocation of Edict of Nantes in France prompts Protestant emigration
1685 La Salle founds short-lived settlement on Matagorda Bay		1688 William of Orange deposes James II of England
1689–93 Spanish reconquer New Mexico		1689–97 King William's War, between France and Grand Alliance (Britain, Austria, the Netherlands)
	1696 Gold discovered at Minas, Brazil	1690 William of Orange defeats James II's Catholic forces at the Battle of the Boyne
1698 Spanish build fort at Pensacola		
1700 Father Kino founds Arizona missions		1700 Rise of Asanti on Gold Coast
		1701–14 Queen Anne's War (War of Spanish Succession) between Britain and France
1706 Spanish found Albuquerque		1703 Tsar Peter II founds new capital St Petersburg as part of drive to "westernize" Russia
1711–13 War between settlers and Tuscarora in N. Carolina. Tuscarora move north to become sixth nation of Iroquois League		
1714 Treaty of Utrecht: France cedes Acadia, Newfoundland, and Hudson's Bay to Britain		
1715 Yamassee War in the Carolinas	1717 Viceroyalty of New Granada created	1715 First Jacobite Rebellion in Scotland
1718 French found New Orleans		
1728 Bering begins Russian exploration of Alaska		
1733 Colony of Georgia founded		
1735 French destroy Natchez Grande Village		
1739–48 King George's War: French and Indians raid Saratoga, Albany, and Maine. British capture Fort Louisbourg	1741 British fail to capture Cartagena, Colombia	1739 Prussian annexation of Silesia triggers King George's War (War of Jenkins' Ear); Britain and France again on opposing sides
1751 Pimas rebel against Spanish in Arizona	1745 French scientific expedition to Ecuador introduces enlightenment ideas to S. America	1745 Second Jacobite rebellion in Scotland
1754 British capture Fort Duquesne (Pittsburgh) from French, opening French and Indian War		1756–63 North American conflict spills over to Europe in Seven Years War between Britain and France
1759 Québec falls to British		
1763 Treaty of Paris ends French rule in N. America		1760 George III succeeds to British throne. British win control of eastern India

THEIR NUMBER BECOME THINNED
THE FIRST CENTURY OF CONTACT, 1515–1615

The first European settlements in North America were no more than footholds, but their effect was catastrophic. The newcomers carried diseases, and Native Americans, who had no immunity to them, died in their millions.

The first regular contacts probably occurred in Newfoundland early in the 16th century. Portuguese fishermen were paying duties on their Newfoundland catches by 1506, and the following year a vessel from Rouen in Normandy brought seven native captives to France. By 1515 Bretons were selling salt cod-fish at Rouen, and by 1525, the Portuguese had set up a fish processing station onshore. The Beothuk of Newfoundland were one of the first Native American people to be hit by European diseases; by the mid-18th century, they had almost completely died out.

During the first half of the 16th century, the Spanish launched a series of ambitious expeditions, involving armies of hundreds of men, to North America. In 1526, 500 settlers, soldiers and enslaved Africans established a settlement, San Miguel de Gualdape, at the mouth of the Savannah River. Many of the settlers, including their leader Ayllón, died of illness or starvation, or in clashes with Indians; 150 survivors were evacuated after a few months. Two years later, Pánfilo de Narváez landed in south Florida with an army of 400. By the time they reached Appalachee Bay, half the soldiers were dead. The survivors built rafts and tried to sail along the coast to Mexico. Shipwrecked near Galveston Bay, they transmitted to the natives of the Texas coast a pathogen—possibly typhus or typhoid —that killed half of them. Just four survivors made it back to Spanish territory eight years later. Crossing northern Chihuahua in 1535, one of them, Cabeza de Vaca, reported a sudden illness with a relatively low mortality rate among the Indians.

That same year, a French expedition led by Jacques Cartier visited the Laurentian Iroquois and set up a short lived settlement, Ste-Croix, near the later site of Quebec. The French transmitted an unknown pathogen to Laurentian Iroquois who, by 1600, had disappeared as a people. Those who survived presumably amalgamated with the Mohawks.

The 1540s saw two major Spanish expeditions into the North American interior. Francisco Vásquez de Coronado's army visited the Pueblo country and traveled onto the plains as far as present-day Kansas, leaving little besides 12 burned pueblos, a soon-abandoned mission, and a variety of diseases. Hernando de Soto's expedition was even more disastrous. Obsessed with finding gold, he led an army of 600 through the swamps of the southeast, forcing local people to act as guides, kidnapping and torturing those who refused. "They made neither settlement nor conquest," wrote the Spanish historian Oviedo, "but caused desolation of the land and loss of liberty of the people."

By the end of the century, the Spaniards had established just two settlements in North America: St Augustine (1565) in Florida, and San Juan (1598) in New Mexico (> *pages 44–5*). Their English rivals fared no better. Walter Raleigh tried to establish a colony on Roanoke Island in 1585. The first group of settlers was evacuated after a year; the replacements, who arrived in 1587, had disappeared by 1590. The survivors may have become assimilated into the Indian tribes of area. Even this tentative settlement was enough to spread disease, however: Englishmen reported Roanoke Island natives dying by scores in 1585.

The European presence also altered the political structures of Native America. In some areas such as the St Lawrence, depopulation created a political vacuum into which new groupings of peoples moved. Sometimes Europeans intervened directly in Indian affairs: in 1609 the French explorer and trader Samuel Champlain used European firepower to assist his Huron, Algonquin and Montagnais allies in a war against the Iroquois. Perhaps the most striking instance, however, was that of the Powhatan state that grew up on the shores of Chesapeake Bay in the early 17th century. As a young man, Powhatan had been kidnapped by the Spanish, who took him to New Spain. There, the viceroy personally sponsored him and had him formally educated. The young man returned with Jesuit missionaries to Chesapeake Bay in 1570, and immediately escaped and rejoined his native people. He organized the destruction of the mission the following year. He was probably influential in welding together the previously autonomous villages into the Powhatan paramount chiefdom.

2: The Powhatan paramount chiefdom, c.1570–1620

approximate extent of Powhatan's territory ■ chief's house
○ English settlement

SUSQUEHANNOCK
Pennsylvania
Quadroque
Sepowig · Sasquesahannock
Atquanachuke ■
New Jersey
Tockwough ■
Ozinie ■
West Virginia
Maryland
Delaware Bay
Washington D.C.
Wighcocomoco ■
MANAHOAC
Hassnioga · Pawtuxent ■
Shackakonia ■ · Patawomke ■ · Acquintanacksuak ■
Mahaskahod ■ · Sekowocomoco ■
Cuttawomen ■ · Pissaseck ■ · Wighcocomoco ■
Nandranghtacund ■
Toppa-hannock ■
Virginia
Uttamussack ■
Kupkipcock ■ · Wighcocomoco ■
Chickahominy ■
Powhatan ■ · Menapacant ■ · Accohannock ■
Arrohatoc ■ · Waenoc ■ · Werowocomio ■
Appamattuc ■ · Accomac ■
Paspahegh ■ · Archer's Hope ○
Quiyoughcohannock ■ · Warraskoyack ■
Jamestown (1607) · Nansemond ■
ATLANTIC OCEAN
MONACAN
MANGOAK
Chawanoac ■
Raleigh's "Lost Colony" (1585–90)
North Carolina
Albemarle Sound
Roanoke Island
0   50 miles

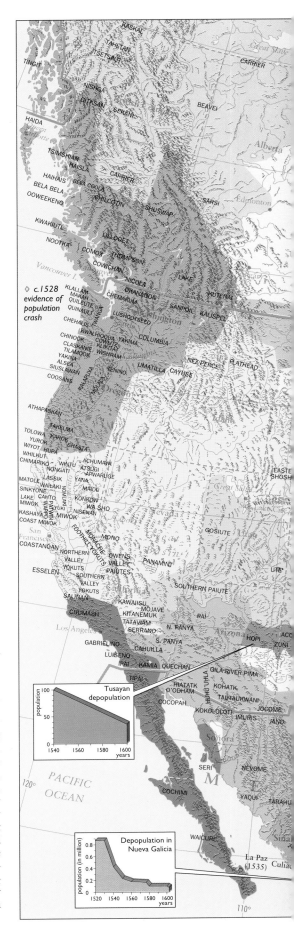

◇ c.1528 evidence of population crash

Tusayan depopulation
population
100
50
0
1540 1560 1580 1600 years

Depopulation in Nueva Galicia
population (in million)
0.8
0.6
0.4
0.2
0
1520 1540 1560 1580 1600 years

PACIFIC OCEAN

La Paz (1535)

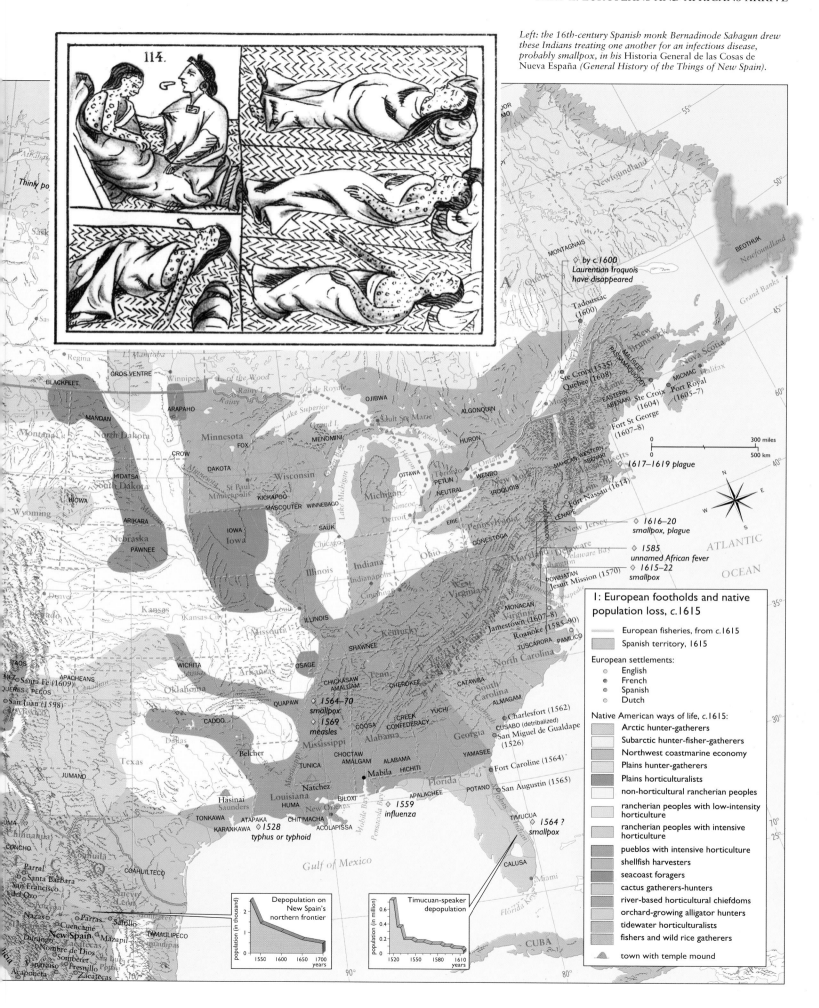

Left: the 16th-century Spanish monk Bernadinode Sahagun drew these Indians treating one another for an infectious disease, probably smallpox, in his Historia General de las Cosas de Nueva España (General History of the Things of New Spain).

1: European footholds and native population loss, c.1615

— European fisheries, from c.1615
▨ Spanish territory, 1615

European settlements:
○ English
● French
◍ Spanish
◌ Dutch

Native American ways of life, c.1615:
Arctic hunter-gatherers
Subarctic hunter-fisher-gatherers
Northwest coastmarine economy
Plains hunter-gatherers
Plains horticulturalists
non-horticultural rancherian peoples
rancherian peoples with low-intensity horticulture
rancherian peoples with intensive horticulture
pueblos with intensive horticulture
shellfish harvesters
seacoast foragers
cactus gatherers-hunters
river-based horticultural chiefdoms
orchard-growing alligator hunters
tidewater horticulturalists
fishers and wild rice gatherers
▲ town with temple mound

Depopulation on New Spain's northern frontier
Timucuan-speaker depopulation

THE RIM OF CHRISTENDOM
SPANISH COLONIZATION OF NORTH AMERICA, 1492—1680

Spain colonized the populous regions of Mesoamerica decades before any other European power could contest its claim to all of North America.

The year 1492, when Columbus first landed in Hispaniola, saw the completion of the Spanish conquest of the Iberian peninsula from the Muslims. The Reconquist had provided new lands on which military adventurers could form large estates, and an outlet for Christian zeal. Within a generation, the Americas came to provide a new arena for these impulses, which influenced the nature of Spanish colonization. Unlike the English colonists of the northeast, who consisted largely of communities in search of religious freedom and land to farm, the Spanish were mostly adventurers in search of wealth and power, or celibate priests. They were relatively few in number, and had no intention of working the land themselves. They needed the Indians as a labour force so that, despite the effects of disease and atrocities, the native people were never displaced as completely as they were from areas colonized by North Europeans. And, as the Spanish did not at first bring women with them, a substantial mestizo population came into being.

The Aztec empire fell to Hernán Cortés in 1521, and its capital, Tenochtitlán, became Mexico City, the administrative center and springboard for the colonization of New Spain. Rumours of great empires to the north encouraged other conquistadors. Though they found no "New Mexicos" to conquer, they did find

Below: the church of San Miguel at Santa Fé—founded in 1610, destroyed in the Pueblo uprising and rebuilt after the Spanish reconquest in the 1690s—is the oldest Christian church in the U.S.

rich silver ores at Zacatecas. From 1545, prospectors and miners pushed the frontier of colonial New Spain northward, seeking more mineral wealth.

In the wake of the conquistadors came Roman Catholic missionaries to convert the Indians on what became known as "The Rim of Christendom." Some missionaries tried to protect the Indians from the worst brutalities of the conquistadors, but their relations were inevitably colonial. They extracted labor from the Indians to raise crops and livestock, and to process raw materials into products which could be sold to finance their missions. They were protected by military garrisons. On the Atlantic coast, the frontier post, or *presidio*, was a European-style fortification manned by a relatively large garrison. Inland, small military garrisons of less than 100 men profoundly influenced the Indian inhabitants. Spanish

ranchers were granted estates—known as *estancias* and *haciendas*—to raise cattle on semi-arid lands to provide hides and tallow for the mines.

The galleons carrying silver to Spain had to pass through the Straits of Florida. Spain had claimed Florida in 1513, but had made no permanent settlement. In 1562, 150 French Huguenots settled at Fort Caroline on the St Johns River. The Spanish were alarmed, and sent a fleet under Pedro Menéndez de Avilés. He massacred the French, renamed their settlement San Mateo, and built a fort, San Pedro, to dominate the river mouth. A further string of forts guarded the Atlantic coast, while Franciscans established missions to the Indians to the north. The only successful colony, however, was the capital San Augustín; by the 18th century its population had reached 3–4,000. The first permanent European settlement in the future U.S.,

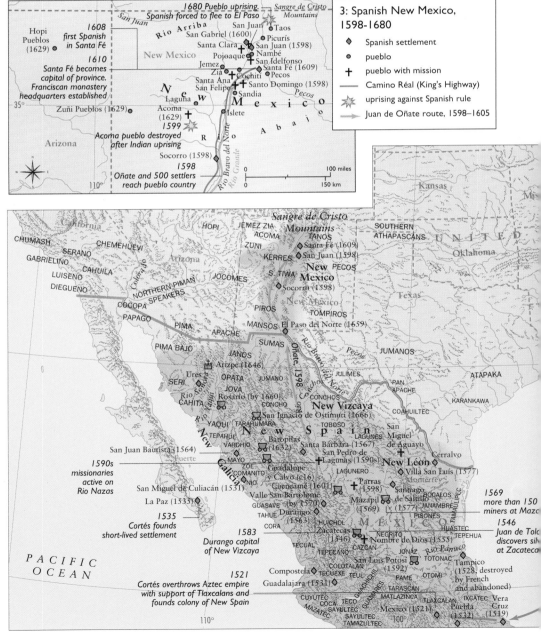

3: Spanish New Mexico, 1598-1680

- ◆ Spanish settlement
- ○ pueblo
- ✚ pueblo with mission
- ── Camino Réal (King's Highway)
- ✸ uprising against Spanish rule
- → Juan de Oñate route, 1598–1605

it is now St Augustine, a city with over 400 years of continuous occupation.

In 1598 Juan de Oñate led a group of 500 settlers, mostly recruited from Mexico City and Zacatecas, and including many women and children, to the pueblo country of the upper Rio Grande. The Indians of Acoma Pueblo did not take kindly to the incursion, and in 1599 an uprising was brutally suppressed. The new Spanish province, of which Oñate became the first governor, was a thin salient along the Rio Grande. The southern area, Rio Abajo (down-river), was low-lying and dry, with a long growing season; to the north, Rio Arriba (upriver), was high, wetter, and wooded. Oñate's successor, Pedro de Peralta, made Santa Fé the capital in 1610; the main plaza, with its governor's palace and church, still exists today. Spanish settlements sprang up between the pueblos, and by the late 17th century there were about 2500 people of Spanish descent in New Mexico.

Franciscan missionaries set out to convert the Pueblo Indians. Poor sanitary conditions in the missions meant that many Indians succumbed to disease, so the missionaries recruited immigrants from near and far. Besides fundamentally altering Indian lifeways and attempting to suppress their religion, the Spanish changed the landscape, overgrazing the range and over-cutting scarce trees. In 1680 these tensions caused an uprising among the Pueblo Indians. Led by a Tewa medicine man, Popé, an army of 500 Indians drove the Spanish out of Santa Fé. Some 600 Spaniards were killed, and the remainder fled to El Paso. Popé and his followers attempted to erase all traces of Spanish religion and culture, but after his death the movement faltered and by 1693 the Spanish had reestablished their hold on New Mexico.

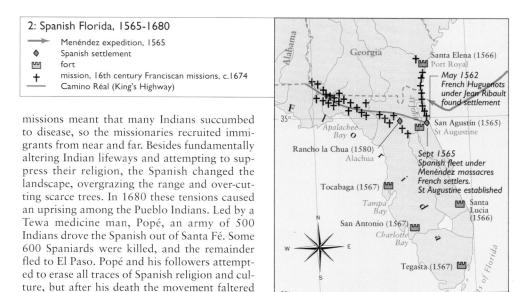

2: Spanish Florida, 1565-1680

→ Menéndez expedition, 1565
◆ Spanish settlement
♜ fort
+ mission, 16th century Franciscan missions, c.1674
— Camino Réal (King's Highway)

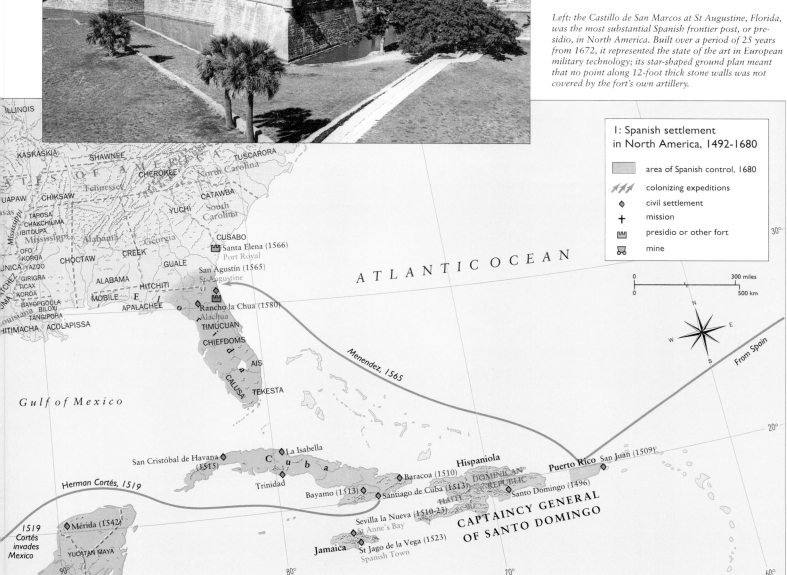

Left: the Castillo de San Marcos at St Augustine, Florida, was the most substantial Spanish frontier post, or presidio, in North America. Built over a period of 25 years from 1672, it represented the state of the art in European military technology; its star-shaped ground plan meant that no point along 12-foot thick stone walls was not covered by the fort's own artillery.

1: Spanish settlement in North America, 1492-1680

▨ area of Spanish control, 1680
⇗ colonizing expeditions
◆ civil settlement
+ mission
♜ presidio or other fort
🛒 mine

PILGRIMS AND PLANTERS
ENGLISH SETTLERS AND INDIANS ON THE ATLANTIC COAST, *c.* 1660

In the course of the 17th century, English settlers consolidated their hold on the eastern seaboard of North America, ousting the Dutch and pushing the Indians inland.

By 1670, the non-native population of what would become the 13 British colonies consisted of about 100,000 Europeans and 4000 Africans. They were concentrated in four areas: New England and eastern Long Island; Manhattan, eastern New Jersey, the Hudson River, and western Long Island; the lower Delaware River and northern Chesapeake Bay region; and Maryland, Virginia, and the north shore of Albemarle Sound in Carolina.

The population of New England in the 1660s was about 50,000. Most immigrants came from East Anglia, London and the surrounding areas, and the southwest of England. From the first settlements in eastern Massachusetts, the population spread out in sub-regional clusters: around Massachusetts Bay and Plymouth, in the Connecticut River valley, around New Haven (including eastern Long Island), near Narragansett Bay in Rhode Island, and in the Portsmouth area of New Hampshire. Smaller scattered groups settled on the coast of Maine, Cape Cod, and two large nearby islands, Martha's Vineyard and Nantucket. In all these areas, villages multiplied as dissidents broke away from older communities and younger sons sought larger or independent land allotments.

When the English seized New Netherland from the Dutch in 1664, the European population in that colony was about 9000, about half of whom had arrived after 1657 from the Netherlands and other north European countries. New Netherland's population was about 40 percent Dutch, 19 percent German, 15 percent English, 7 percent Scandinavian, 7 percent African, 5 percent French, and 5 percent Flemish and Walloon. Settlement concentrated around Manhattan, which had a population of around 1800. Western Long Island contained about 2000 settlers in five "Dutch" towns and five "English" towns, and 500–600 people lived in East Jersey. The predominantly Dutch areas were in the Hudson Valley around Albany-Schnectady (around 750 people) and at Kingston (around 325 people). The settlement pattern varied. The city of New Amsterdam was surrounded by small farms (boweries) and villages; the Hudson valley contained one palisaded town (Beverwyck) surrounded by farms and tiny villages, and three mid-valley village-like settlements surrounded by farms.

By 1670, the Delaware valley contained Dutch, Finns, Swedes, French Huguenots, Danes, Frisians, Holsteiners, and English, who lived on both banks of the Delaware River. The population of about 1000, including 60–70 Africans, was the smallest of the four main regions, and was very much in flux. The first immigrants settled on the west bank of the Delaware River, where the population still concentrated in the 1660s. Some of the Swedes and Finns moved downriver and built farms in the upper Chesapeake Bay. Settlement patterns varied with nationality. The Swedes and Finns preferred scattered farms, while the Dutch tried to impose a village pattern on the Delaware landscape.

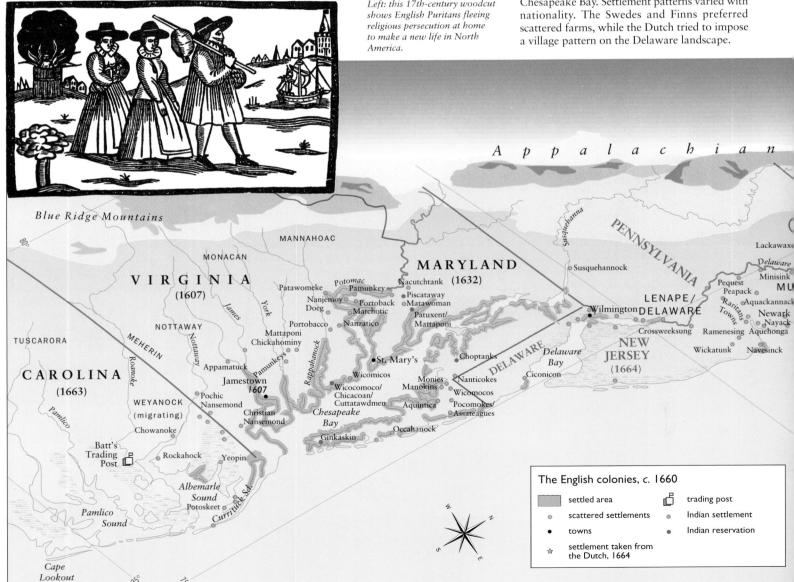

Left: this 17th-century woodcut shows English Puritans fleeing religious persecution at home to make a new life in North America.

Blue Ridge Mountains

Appalachian

MANNAHOAC

MONACAN

VIRGINIA (1607)

MARYLAND (1632)

PENNSYLVANIA

Susquehannock

Lackawaxe

Delaware

Pequest · Minisink
Peapack

LENAPE/
Wilmington DELAWARE

Patawomeke · Potomac · Pamunkey · Nacutchtank
Nanjemoy · Portoback · Piscataway
Doeg · Matchotic · Matawoman
Portobacco · Nanzatico · Patuxent/Mattaponi

Aquackannack
Raritans
Towns · Newark
Crossweeksung · Ramenesing · Aquehonga Nayack

NOTTAWAY

Mattaponi
Chickahominy

TUSCARORA

Appamatuck

St. Mary's

Choptanks

NEW
JERSEY
(1664)

Wickatunk · Navesinck

DELAWARE
Delaware
Bay

MEHERIN

Wicomicos
Monies · Nanticokes
Manokins
Wicomocos
Aquintica · Pocomokes/
Assateagues

Ciconicon

CAROLINA (1663)

Jamestown
1607
Pochic
Nansemond

WEYANOCK
(migrating)

Christian
Nansemond

Wicocomoco/
Chicacoan/
Cuttatawdmen

Chesapeake
Bay

Occahanock

Chowanoke

Ginkaskin

Batt's
Trading
Post

Rockahock · Yeopin

Albemarle
Sound
Potoskeet

Pamlico
Sound

Cape
Lookout

The English colonies, *c.* 1660

- settled area
- scattered settlements
- towns
- ⚷ trading post
- Indian settlement
- Indian reservation
- ☆ settlement taken from the Dutch, 1664

About as many people lived in the Chesapeake district, including the northern Albemarle Sound area, as lived in New England. Virginia contained 30,000–35,000 settlers, Maryland about 10,000–11,000, and between 1000 and 4000 lived in the Albemarle region. The Chesapeake area had a high immigration rate, but also a high mortality rate; as a result, most of the inhabitants in the 1660s were recent immigrants, in contrast to New England where the majority were born in the colony. Most of the immigrants were, or had been, English indentured servants. Free immigrants were also mainly from England. A few free and indentured Irish and Scots came as well. Original settlement in Virginia had concentrated around the James River, with migrations to the eastern shore of Virginia as early as the 1620s. After 1630, most migrants went north to the York, Rappahannock, and Potomac rivers, and inland towards the falls of those rivers.

In Maryland, during the first decade of settlement, the English stayed close to their original location at St Mary's, near the entrance to the Potomac River. In 1649–50, Puritans from the James River migrated to the Severn River on the northwest shore of the bay. During the 1650s and 60s, people pushed westward up the Potomac and Patuxent rivers and across the bay to the eastern shore of the Delaware peninsula. Virginians who lived on the southern end of the Eastern Shore moved up into present-day Maryland. From the mid 1660s, small groups of people in Virginia started moving south into the Albemarle and Currituck Sound areas in what would become the Carolina Proprietary, an area first known as Virginia's "Southern Plantation." Throughout the Chesapeake area, colonists lived on isolated farms and plantations, with few concentrated settlements.

At this period, Indian people still remained in their homelands throughout most of the Atlantic coastal region, though they were steadily hemmed in and dislodged by increasing numbers of settlers. The English were close to success in the Chesapeake Bay region, where they had already destroyed the power of Powhatan and other chiefdoms. Less than 3000 Indians remained in the coastal plain of Virginia. All the good agricultural lands along the main bays and rivers were being taken over by new settlers, who either bought land from the Indians or drove them away. On the mainland, Indian communities had been forced to retreat upriver into the back country. With the fall in population, groups had combined. Some, like the Ginkaskins, had been reassigned land which they tried to preserve from encroaching settlers. On the Eastern Shore,

Right: Pocahontas, the daughter of Powhatan, who ruled a powerful state in the Chesapeake Bay region. Shown here in European dress, she married an English settler, John Rolfe, and traveled to England, where she died of smallpox in 1616, and is buried at Greenwich.

Indians were moving inland in the 1660s; the Choptanks were assigned a reservation in 1669.

In New England, Indian people were still numerically superior, but they were affected by religious dissension and intercolonial rivalry. By 1670, seven "praying towns" existed as a result of missionary effort; seven more were established after 1671. To the north, settlement had not yet encroached on the Abenaki, who were more in the orbit of French activity along the St Lawrence River. Many Indian settlements were occupied temporarily by groups who moved seasonally from agricultural areas to fishing or hunting grounds. King Philip's War (1675–76), organized by the Wampanoag leader from Rhode Island, marked the final attempt of New England Indians to resist English control of their land. At the same time the hostilities of Bacon's Rebellion (1675–77) in Virginia brought about the final subjugation of the Indian people in the Chesapeake Bay area.

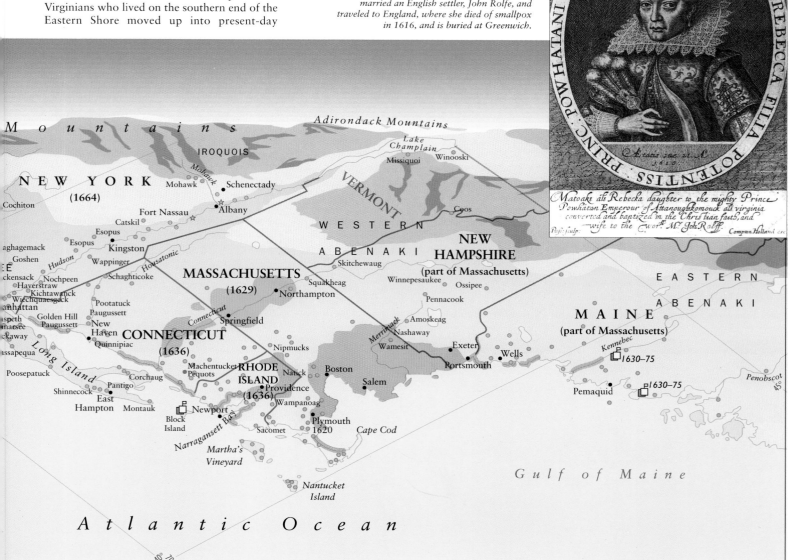

FROM THE ST LAWRENCE TO THE MISSISSIPPI

THE FRENCH IN NORTH AMERICA, 1608–1763

From their initial foothold on the St Lawrence, the French expanded through the Great Lakes and down the Mississippi, leaving a thin scattering of settlers over a vast arc of North American territory.

Above: Quebec was first established as a base on the St Lawrence River by the French explorer Samuel de Champlain in 1608. By the time of this engraving, from Popple's American Atlas of 1730, it was a substantial city with a population of almost 5000.

The French colonial population in North America first settled at Quebec in the early 17th century. Although the French king envisaged a series of peasant agricultural settlements similar to those in France, what developed in the Great Lakes and Mississippi valley was rather a series of Franco-Indian communities engaged principally in trade. French explorers arrived at Green Bay, Wisconsin in 1634, and went down the Mississippi by 1673 to reach the Gulf of Mexico in 1682. The French colony in Louisiana was not firmly established until a fort was set up on Mobile Bay in 1702.

French settlers, principally from the Ile de France and Normandy, concentrated in the lower St Lawrence River around Trois Rivières, Quebec, and Montreal. Here they laid out the land in the characteristic long-lot pattern; each *habitant* had a parcel of land stretching back into the bush from a narrow river frontage. Satellite images show that the land is still marked by this pattern, not only on the Mississippi and St Lawrence rivers, but also at Detroit and at Vincennes on the Wabash River in Indiana. A different system was used in Louisiana, where attempts were made at plantation development after New Orleans was founded in 1718. The Illinois country had the most distinctive system, for here were not only slaves but also a system of communal management reminiscent of late-medieval France where villages made joint decisions about where to plant and when to open common fields for grazing. In the rich bottom lands, the French raised corn and other food crops to supply the poorly-fed residents of the lower Mississippi, where soldiers were sent to live with Indian families when commissary supplies were short. Close by were villages of Illinois Indians who raised crops but also hunted buffalo and raided tribes across the Mississippi to bring back slaves.

New France had a small population of immigrants, at first principally single young men, but families had many children. The population of Canada was only about 15,000 in 1700 and 50,000 at the peak of the French colonial era in 1750. There were about 2500 inhabitants in the Illinois country at this time, but in Louisiana only about 2000 French and German colonists along with 5000 Africans, trying to make a success of cotton and indigo production (> *pages 52–3*). Their Indian neighbors numbered between 200,000 and 300,000. In 1729, the Louisiana colony suffered a serious setback as a consequence of the uprising of the Natchez Indians, who killed about 10 percent of the French settlers. Two years later, the military retaliation destroyed this last surviving Mississippi valley chiefdom, and most of the Natchez sought refuge with the Chickasaws.

Centered in Montreal, the significant economic activity in New France was the fur trade, the process of collecting from Indian hunters the prized skins and hides of the beaver, as well as those of deer, otter, marten, fox, and muskrat. In return, Indians received hatchets, knives, kettles, metal cups, fish hooks, cloth, beads, needles, mirrors, and soon guns and liquor. Although the French government tried to control trade through licensing, illegal traders known as *coureurs de bois* (runners of the woods) established connections with Indian families throughout the country of the Great Lakes and Mississippi valley. They ventured northwest into present-day Manitoba and Saskatchewan, southwest to Spanish Santa Fe, and even to meet the British governor in Charleston, South Carolina. Indian leaders learned to speak French, and *coureurs de bois* usually learned Indian languages. By the 1730s, probably 800 or more were active, operating in groups of 12 to 20 and essentially living among the Indians. Family names listed in Quebec telephone books—Amiotte, Duchesneau, Pelletier, and Beaubien—are also found on the Indian reserves of North America.

After the French government temporarily withdrew most of the western forts at the beginning of the 18th century, a new program of fort building in the *pays d'en haut* (Upper Country) began with the establishment of Fort Michillimackinac at present-day Mackinack City, Michigan in 1715. These forts became centers for Indian trading, and families of dual French and Indian heritage grew up around them. As rivalry with the British over the expansion of the fur trade in the Ohio country intensified, the French built a line of forts from present Toronto across Lake Erie into what is now part of Pennsylvania. During the French and Indian war, which began in 1754, the French forts fell to the British (> *pages 66–7*).

Left: the building of the French post at New Biloxi, Louisiana, in December 1720. This engraving, from a drawing by Jean-Baptiste le Buteaux, shows buildings going up and boats being constructed. In the foreground, a typical Mississippi flatboat lies near its moorings. The site, just across Biloxi Bay from Fort Maurepas (Old Biloxi), was abandoned within two years, and the settlement transferred to New Orleans.

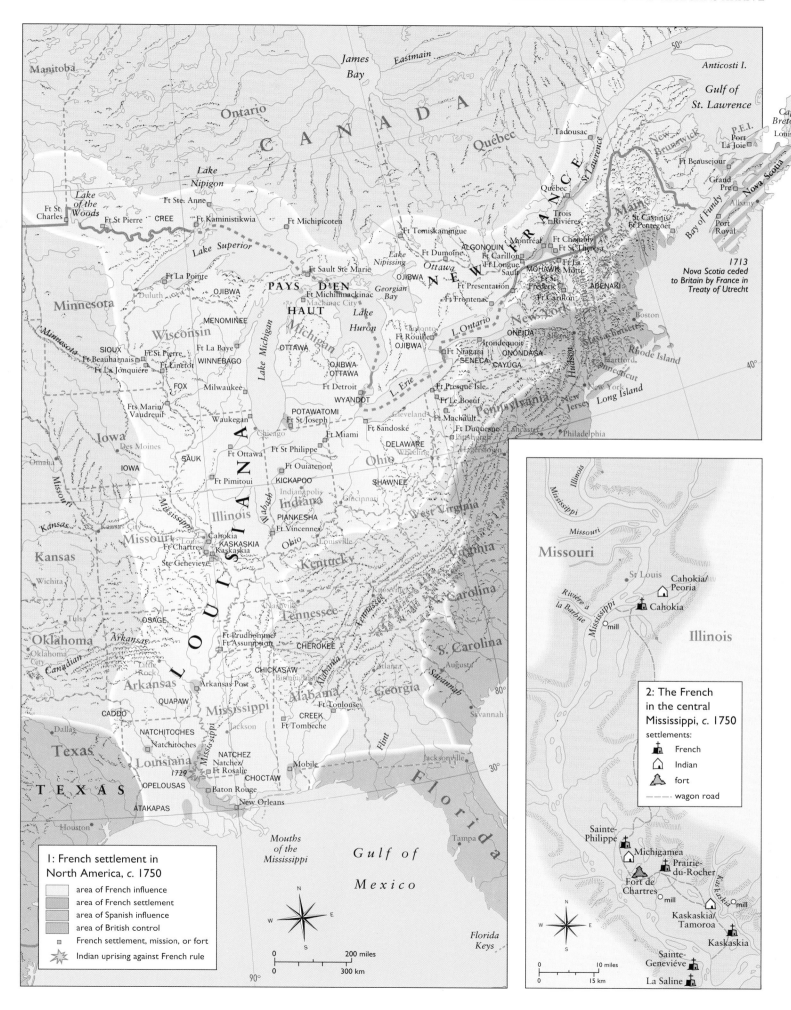

1: French settlement in North America, c. 1750

area of French influence
area of French settlement
area of Spanish influence
area of British control
▫ French settlement, mission, or fort
✳ Indian uprising against French rule

2: The French in the central Mississippi, c. 1750

settlements:
⛪ French
⌂ Indian
⛰ fort
--- wagon road

1713
Nova Scotia ceded to Britain by France in Treaty of Utrecht

THE BOUGHT AND SOLD PEOPLE
THE FORCED MIGRATION OF AFRICANS, 1650–1800

While most migrants to North America came of their own free will, millions of Africans were forcibly transported from their homelands and into slavery.

The 20 Africans who arrived at the Jamestown colony in 1619, along with the small number brought to Boston in 1639, were the first of 10,000 who came to the American colonies in the 17th century. Institutionalized slavery did not begin immediately. The first Africans were imported to fill the need for laborers when colonists found that they could not force Indians to work in their fields. The Africans were indentured servants, and they worked on

the tobacco plantations alongside white laborers. In 1675, there were only 4000 Africans scattered across Maryland and Virginia; in 1708, there were just 4000 in Carolina. But as the number of Africans in North America grew, the plantation owners began to fear their potential power and implemented regulations which made slaves of them.

In Africa, the slave trade was linked to warfare among rival kingdoms. The successful army brought back slaves as booty, and they were often sold by one ruler to another as well as to European traders. Slavery in Africa, however, was neither hereditary nor racial, as it became in the Americas. Moreover, European slavers

forced many African states to participate in the trade by paying for slaves with guns. Rulers who refused to do business risked being conquered by better-armed neighbors.

The captive Africans came from many ethnic groups in widely separated regions of Africa, though all spoke languages of the Niger–Congo family. All Africans were farmers; some were fishers and herders. All had knowledge of iron and textiles; all had elaborate religious and cultural traditions. Africans were skilled in raising tobacco, the principal plantation crop of the Chesapeake Bay region, as well as rice and indigo, the basis for the tidewater economy in Carolina and Georgia.

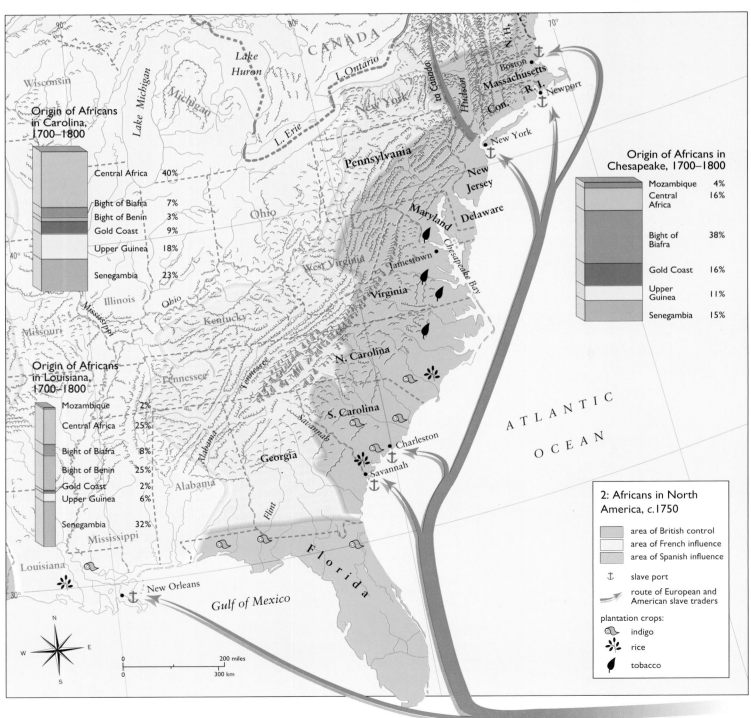

Origin of Africans in Carolina, 1700–1800

Central Africa	40%
Bight of Biafra	7%
Bight of Benin	3%
Gold Coast	9%
Upper Guinea	18%
Senegambia	23%

Origin of Africans in Chesapeake, 1700–1800

Mozambique	4%
Central Africa	16%
Bight of Biafra	38%
Gold Coast	16%
Upper Guinea	11%
Senegambia	15%

Origin of Africans in Louisiana, 1700–1800

Mozambique	2%
Central Africa	25%
Bight of Biafra	8%
Bight of Benin	25%
Gold Coast	2%
Upper Guinea	6%
Senegambia	32%

2: Africans in North America, c.1750

- area of British control
- area of French influence
- area of Spanish influence
- ⚓ slave port
- → route of European and American slave traders

plantation crops:
- 🌿 indigo
- 🌿 rice
- 🍃 tobacco

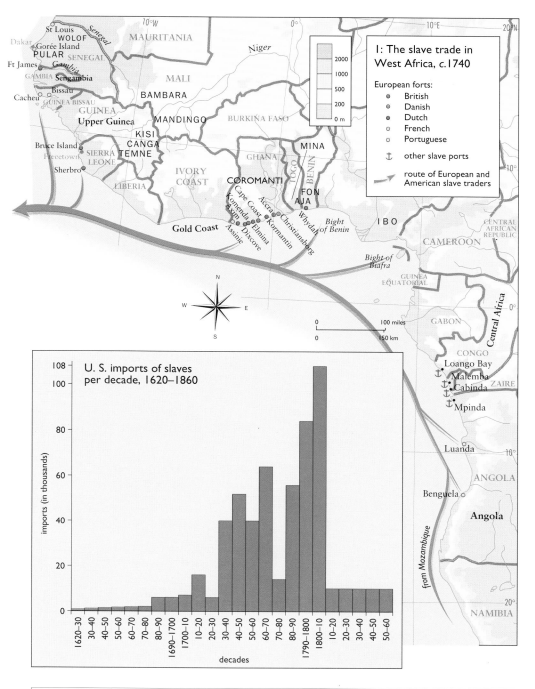

I: The slave trade in West Africa, c.1740

European forts:
- British
- Danish
- Dutch
- French
- Portuguese

⚓ other slave ports

↗ route of European and American slave traders

U. S. imports of slaves per decade, 1620–1860

imports (in thousands)

decades

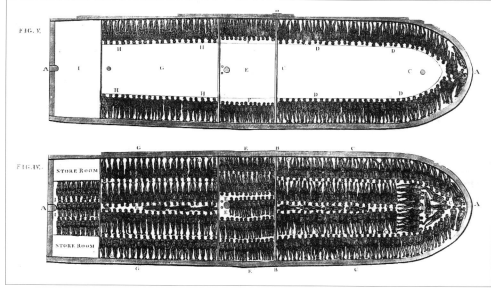

Native rice had been domesticated in Africa about 1500 BC. African women used yarn dyed with indigo and other colors to weave cloth with distinctive symbolic patterns. Their garden plots also produced corn, peas and melons. Skilled artisans worked in gold, silver and copper, and made hatchets, knives and horseshoes from iron.

During the 18th century, the total number of Africans in the Atlantic seaboard colonies rose to 350,000, although this was only a small portion of the six million African slaves brought to North and South America during that period. Some found homes in the northern colonies; in 1700 an estimated 40 percent of households in New York City had African slaves. The largest numbers, however, went to the Chesapeake Bay region and to South Carolina; about 150,000 each. In addition, about 30,000 Africans landed in Louisiana under French and Spanish rule. Others went to Florida, to Canada, and to northern colonies from Pennsylvania to Massachusetts. By 1725 there were 45,000 Africans in the Chesapeake area, and by 1760 their numbers had reached 185,000. In Carolina, the number of Africans had reached 90,000 by 1775. Slave imports rose to a peak in mid-18th century (somewhat later in Louisiana), then leveled off, until they were abolished in 1808. With U. S. independence, several northern states abolished slavery, following the lead of Vermont in 1777. Upper Canada (now Ontario) abolished the slave trade in 1793.

The overall sex ratio among arriving slaves, about two males per female, varied by ethnic group. Some ethnic groups, such as Mandingo and Ibo, were close to the African coast: slaves from these groups included about 50 percent women. Other groups, such as Bambara and Hausa, lived as much as 800 miles inland: slaves from these groups were almost all male. In Louisiana, half the women came from ethnic groups providing only 15 percent of the men. For slaves born of African mothers in Louisiana, almost half of them came from a few ethnic groups: Wolof and Mandingo (Senegambia), Kisi (Upper Guinea), Aja and Fon (Bight of Benin), and Ibo (Bight of Biafra).

Their large numbers enabled the Africans of the plantation south to retain something of their homeland heritage. In South Carolina, over 40 percent of slaves came from the rice-growing regions of Upper Guinea and Senegambia. Another 40 percent came from Angola. The largest group going to the Chesapeake area was from the Bight of Biafra, dominated by the yam-growing Ibo people. In Louisiana the largest group, from Senegambia, included the Pular or Fulbe, who grew rice and kept cattle. The large group from the Bight of Benin brought the religion of *vodun* (voodoo); Central Africans brought decorative arts patterns.

Left: this 18th-century engraving of a slave ship vividly illustrates the appalling conditions on board. Many Africans died of disease on the journey; others committed suicide by jumping into the sea. If conditions improved slightly in the later 18th century, it was a result not of humanitarian considerations but of a desire to preserve a financially valuable cargo.

SETTLING THE INTERIOR
SOUTHERN AND WESTERN EXPANSION, *c.* 1760

By the mid-18th century, there were more than one and a half million settlers in Britain's American colonies. Their diverse origins and independent mindset foreshadowed the character of the U.S.

The year 1760 was a landmark in North American history, setting the scene for the American Revolution 15 years later. In England, George III succeeded his grandfather as king, and in America British forces captured Montreal, completing their conquest of New France. Three years later, in the Treaty of Paris that settled the Seven Years War, France and Spain formally ceded to Britain all their colonies east of the Mississippi River. Britain's colonial frontier had lost an important external restraint, and its colonists were poised to expand across the Appalachians. Anxious to avoid further hostilities with the Indians, the British government issued a proclamation in 1763 banning settlement west of the Appalachians, but the settlers paid little heed.

Approximately 1,600,000 persons were settled in the British colonies in 1760, more than 14 times the estimated population in the 1660s. About 80 percent were Europeans, some 20 percent Africans. (By contrast, the number of colonists in the former French territories was under 80,000, while only about 3000 people of European descent lived in Spanish Florida.) Colonial settlement filled nearly every mile of coast from Maine to Georgia. Over the preceding century, several new colonies had been founded: Pennsylvania (1681) and Delaware (1704) in the mid-Atlantic region; Carolina (1663, divided into North and South Carolina in 1691) and Georgia (1732) in the south. The cities of Charleston, founded in 1670, and Savannah (1733) grew into the focal points for colonial development south of Virginia.

The main cause of the population explosion was natural increase, but there was also substantial immigration from Europe. A few thousand French Huguenots emigrated to America (chiefly to New York, Massachusetts, and South Carolina) after the formal revocation of religious freedom in France in 1685. Nearly a quarter of a million immigrants arrived in the British colonies from Scotland and Ireland. Most of those who came directly from Scotland were Covenanters escaping the established Anglican church or Jacobites who supported the restoration of the Catholic King James II or his son. By far the largest number were Scots-Irish Presbyterians who had been living in the north of Ireland and emigrated to escape a bad economy and the demands of the Anglican church for religious conformity. A substantial number of Germans from the region around the upper Rhine and Main rivers (the modern states of Bavaria and Rhineland-Palatinate) emigrated in the 18th century to escape crop failures and the carnage of the War of the Spanish Succession by taking advantage of a liberalization of British and colonial immigration laws.

The Germans initially moved into New York along the Hudson River; eventually they filtered down the Susquehanna River and into south central Pennsylvania. Some of the Scots-Irish settled in Maryland on the eastern shore of Chesapeake Bay, but over the decades most made their way to the western reaches of Pennsylvania and Maryland and then down the Shenandoah valley to the frontier areas of Virginia, the Carolinas, and Georgia. Africans —most of them slaves but a small number of them free—could be found throughout the colonies, but the great majority of them were concentrated in the south (> *pages 54–5*).

The English constituted well over half the total population in the 13 colonies, and more

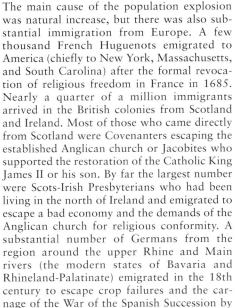

arrived each year. Nevertheless, the total growth from natural increase was greater than that from immigration. Even Africans, terrible though their living conditions were, developed a rate of natural increase that added more to their numbers than did the slave trade. After 1700 the overall rate of population growth was around 3 percent, one of the highest in history; one effect of this was that the average age of the population was under 17 years.

The attitudes, experience, culture, and goals of the settlers were as important as their numbers. The German and Scots-Irish immigrants, for example, were independent-minded people who desired economic success and acted on their dissatisfaction with the established church and government in their homelands. The presence of many settlers with this anti-authoritarian cast of mind may well have helped to build support for the cause of independence in the American Revolution.

Left: after the failure of the 1745 Jacobite uprising, the speaking of Gaelic was banned in Scotland, and many highland villages were depopulated by deportation and eviction. Later many tenants left for America as the land was cleared in favor of sheep farming; some landlords even paid their fare in order to get them off the land. The evictions, and the emigrations, continued into the 19th century, when this scene was painted by Thomas Faed.

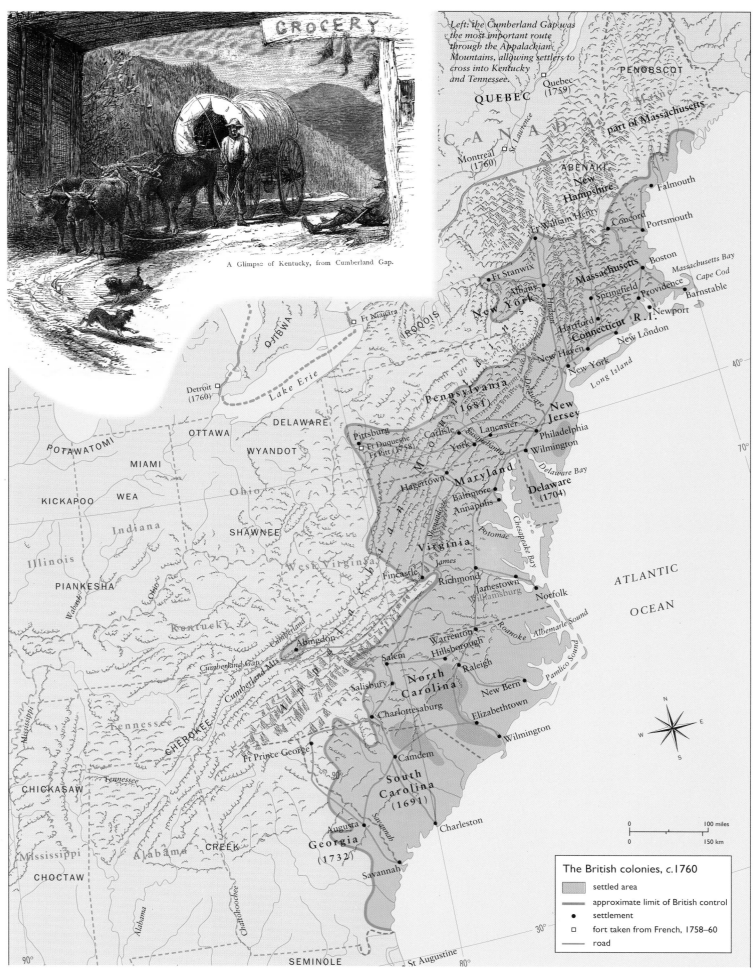

GROCERY

A Glimpse of Kentucky, from Cumberland Gap.

Left: the Cumberland Gap was the most important route through the Appalachian Mountains, allowing settlers to cross into Kentucky and Tennessee.

PENOBSCOT

QUEBEC

Quebec (1759)

CANADA

part of Massachusetts

Montreal (1760)

St. Lawrence

ABENAKI

New Hampshire

Falmouth

Fr William Henry

Concord

Portsmouth

Ft Stanwix

Massachusetts

Boston

Albany

Massachusetts Bay

Cape Cod

Ft Niagara

Springfield

Providence

Barnstable

New York

Hartford

Connecticut

R.I.

Newport

OJIBWA

IROQUOIS

Hudson

New Haven

New London

Long Island

New York

40°

Lake Erie

Pennsylvania (1681)

New Jersey

70°

Detroit (1760)

DELAWARE

Pittsburg

Carlisle

Lancaster

Philadelphia

OTTAWA

WYANDOT

Ft Duquesne

Ft Pitt (1758)

York

Susquehanna

Wilmington

Delaware

POTAWATOMI

MIAMI

Hagertown

Maryland

Baltimore

Delaware Bay

Delaware (1704)

WEA

Ohio

Annapolis

KICKAPOO

Potomac

Chesapeake Bay

Indiana

SHAWNEE

Shenandoah

Virginia

James

Illinois

West Virginia

Fincastle

Richmond

Jamestown

ATLANTIC

PIANKESHA

Ohio

Williamsburg

Norfolk

OCEAN

Wabash

Kentucky

Roanoke

Albemarle Sound

Cumberland

Abingdon

Warrenton

Tennessee

Cumberland Gap

Cumberland Mts

Salem

Hillsborough

Raleigh

Pamlico Sound

CHEROKEE

Salisbury

North Carolina

New Bern

Charlottesaburg

Mississippi

Tennessee

Ft Prince George

Elizabethtown

Camdem

Wilmington

CHICKASAW

South Carolina (1691)

N

Alabama

CREEK

Augusta

Savannah

Charleston

0   100 miles
0   150 km

Mississippi

Georgia (1732)

Savannah

CHOCTAW

Chattahoochee

Alabama

The British colonies, c.1760

settled area

approximate limit of British control

● settlement

□ fort taken from French, 1758–60

road

SEMINOLE

St Augustine

30°

90°   80°

CHAINED TO THE COLONIES
AFRICANS AND INDIANS IN LOUISIANA, 1768–1800

In Spanish Louisiana, Africans came to outnumber European settlers. They worked alongside Indians on the plantations, and formed independent, mixed communities in the swamps and bayous.

Less than 6000 Africans were brought to colonial Louisiana during the French regime, almost all during the decade beginning in 1721. On plantations they worked alongside enslaved Indians and some ran away together, often joining with Indians to oppose French rule. In 1746, the total population of Louisiana was given as 4730 Africans and 3200 white people. Under Spanish rule beginning in 1768, the population increased—particularly after the trade in African slaves was opened up in the 1780s.

Spanish Louisiana grew from a 1766 population of about 11,000 (5000 slaves, 700 free people of color, and 5000 Europeans), to an 1800 population of 44,000 (24,000 slaves, 3000 free people of color, and 17,000 Europeans). The growth came mostly from European immigration and the importation of African slaves. As in the French era, Senegambia (the region between Senegal and Gambia rivers) sent the largest number of enslaved Africans to Louisiana, followed by the Bight of Benin and Central Africa. Women came in the largest numbers from the coastal African groups—the Mandingo, Wolof, Kisi, Canga, Aja, and Fon (> *pages 50–1*). During this period the free population of color also increased, as a result of manumission and by natural growth.

The capital, New Orleans, had a population of 5000 in 1800. The majority consisted of slaves, among whom women predominated. The population of the area immediately around New Orleans was more than twice that of the city itself, and consisted largely of slave men. The rest of Louisiana's population was concentrated along the Mississippi, its tributaries and bayous. Everyone participated in an economy focused on the production of rice, cattle, indigo, tobacco, and timber, especially cypress. Sizable groups of Africans speaking similar languages were gathered on plantations, in communities of free people, and in the "maroon" or runaway bands, perpetual sources of insurrection who controlled the area downriver of New Orleans, with centers at Balize and Barataria.

Louisiana's Africans included a number from Islamic regions of Africa, where they had gone to schools, and learned to read and write Arabic. Stories brought from Africa, folk tales, and proverbs have all made their way into American literature. Africans also brought knowledge of herbal medicine, and an ability to make charms and use poisons to kill their enemies. Religion permeated their lives, and included music, dancing, and song. Prayer preceded playing the harp, an instrument that promoted harmony and balance in the world. The use of large gourds as resonators, the small harps, bells, and various drums, led to the development of modern musical instruments including the marimba, banjo (a Bantu African word) and percussion instruments such as the congas.

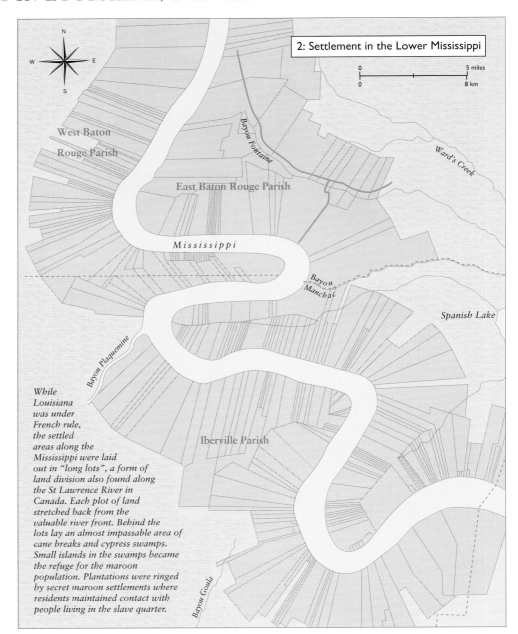

2: Settlement in the Lower Mississippi

While Louisiana was under French rule, the settled areas along the Mississippi were laid out in "long lots", a form of land division also found along the St Lawrence River in Canada. Each plot of land stretched back from the valuable river front. Behind the lots lay an almost impassable area of cane breaks and cypress swamps. Small islands in the swamps became the refuge for the maroon population. Plantations were ringed by secret maroon settlements where residents maintained contact with people living in the slave quarter.

Left: slaves who escaped would often live among the Indians. This 1735 drawing by Alexandre de Batz shows an African among a group of Indians of different tribes, in a cypress clearing. Many mixed communities such as this existed in Louisiana backwaters behind the plantations.

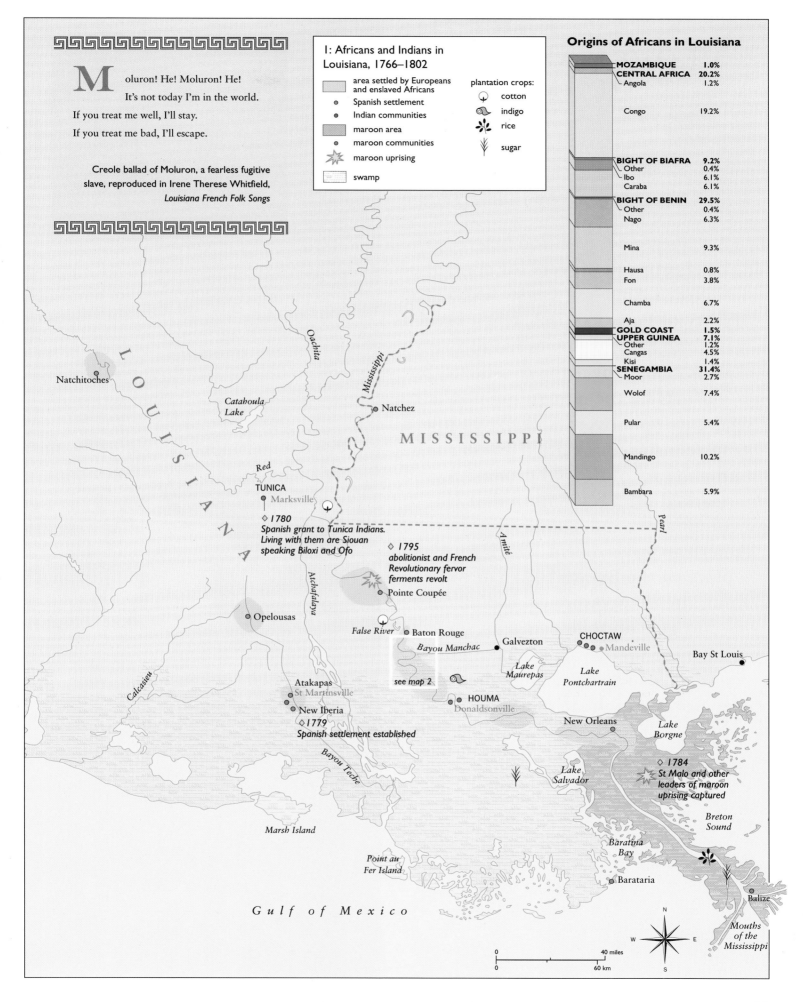

Moluron! He! Moluron! He!

　It's not today I'm in the world.

If you treat me well, I'll stay.

If you treat me bad, I'll escape.

Creole ballad of Moluron, a fearless fugitive
slave, reproduced in Irene Therese Whitfield,
Louisiana French Folk Songs

1: Africans and Indians in Louisiana, 1766–1802

　　area settled by Europeans and enslaved Africans
　●　Spanish settlement
　●　Indian communities
　　maroon area
　⚘　maroon communities
　✸　maroon uprising
　　swamp

plantation crops:
　🌿 cotton
　🐚 indigo
　❀ rice
　🌾 sugar

Origins of Africans in Louisiana

MOZAMBIQUE	**1.0%**
CENTRAL AFRICA	**20.2%**
Angola	1.2%
Congo	19.2%
BIGHT OF BIAFRA	**9.2%**
Other	0.4%
Ibo	6.1%
Caraba	6.1%
BIGHT OF BENIN	**29.5%**
Other	0.4%
Nago	6.3%
Mina	9.3%
Hausa	0.8%
Fon	3.8%
Chamba	6.7%
Aja	2.2%
GOLD COAST	**1.5%**
UPPER GUINEA	**7.1%**
Other	1.2%
Cangas	4.5%
Kisi	1.4%
SENEGAMBIA	**31.4%**
Moor	2.7%
Wolof	7.4%
Pular	5.4%
Mandingo	10.2%
Bambara	5.9%

Ouachita

Mississippi

Natchitoches

Catahoula Lake

● Natchez

MISSISSIPPI

Red

TUNICA
　Marksville

◇ *1780*
*Spanish grant to Tunica Indians.
Living with them are Siouan
speaking Biloxi and Ofo*

Atchafalaya

◇ *1795*
*abolitionist and French
Revolutionary fervor
ferments revolt*

● Pointe Coupée

Amité

Pearl

● Opelousas

False River ● Baton Rouge

Bayou Manchac ● Galvezton

CHOCTAW
　Mandeville

● Bay St Louis

Lake Maurepas

Lake Pontchartrain

see map 2

Atakapas
● St Martinsville

● HOUMA
Donaldsonville

● New Iberia

◇ *1779*
Spanish settlement established

New Orleans

Lake Borgne

◇ *1784*
*St Malo and other
leaders of maroon
uprising captured*

Calcasieu

Bayou Teche

Lake Salvador

Breton Sound

Baratina Bay

Marsh Island

Point au
Fer Island

● Barataria

● Balize

Gulf of Mexico

N

W　E

S

0		40 miles
0		60 km

*Mouths
of the
Mississippi*

LOUISIANA

PART III: PEOPLE AS PAWNS OF IMPERIAL POWERS

Introduction
by John H. Long

Fierce competition between the European powers for control of North America was stalled by the Treaty of Paris in 1763, when French and Spanish losses led to British dominance over the continent. But efforts by the new ruling power to secure its hold over its newly-acquired empire inspired rebellion amongst the inhabitants of the old provinces, and sparked off a revolution that was to culminate in independence. The new American government which took the place of the British began at once to put intense pressure on Indian tribes to give up their territory, and the opening up of vast tracts of land to settlement was to change the face of the North American continent within just a few decades.

Right: a dramatic scene from the siege of Yorktown in October 1781, painted by Louis Charles Auguste Couder (1790–1873). Although the Revolutionary War between Great Britain and its American colonies was to continue for two more years, General Lord Cornwallis's surrender to Washington on October 19, 1781, was a decisive factor in the final outcome, and succeeded in bringing the war to a virtual close

Looking back to February 10, 1763, when representatives of Britain, France, and Spain signed the Treaty of Paris that ended the French and Indian War (the Seven Years War in Europe), there is irony in the fact that Britain's victory was so lopsided. From France, Great Britain gained all of Canada and Louisiana east of the Mississippi River, plus islands in the Caribbean, and from Spain it took Florida, a territory stretching from just east of New Orleans to the Atlantic and around the Gulf of Mexico to the islands at the southern tip of the peninsula. In addition, by the secret Treaty of Fontainebleau (November 3, 1762), France compensated Spain for its loss of Florida by ceding to Spain its claim to what remained of Louisiana, the western drainage basin of the Mississippi River.

For over a century and a half these European powers had competed for control of North America, but the losses of France and Spain seemed to guarantee that for the indefinite future colonial affairs east of the Mississippi River, at least, would be managed for the benefit of Great Britain alone and the colonists would speak only English. Yet less than 20 years later the political situation had changed radically, thanks in great part to the results of the Seven Years War, and the future of North American settlement was set on an entirely different path. Great

Britain's efforts to centralize and manage its new empire led to rebellion and revolution by the colonists in its old provinces and to their eventual independence. By the second decade of the 19th century, the direction of the new path was clear: the central band of the continent would be occupied and exploited by the remarkably diverse people of a vigorous, new nation whose growth, both in territory and in population, would be unusually large and rapid.

When the Treaty of Paris was concluded, the total number of non-Indians in the British colonies, free and slave together, exceeded 1,500,000. By comparison, the numbers for the Spanish and French colonies seem anemic: Florida had around 3000; Louisiana, including settlements near the mouth of the Mississippi, could count only about 10,000 in the 1760s, half of whom were African slaves, and in Canada along the St Lawrence River and in the Maritimes (not counting British Nova Scotia) there were only about 80,000 more. The war itself, as well as the treaty settlement, produced some modest population movement. In the 1750s, as war became imminent, the British commander in Nova Scotia forcibly deported thousands of Acadians because he deemed them an internal threat. (When asked to take loyalty oaths, these long-resident, French-speaking

Left: the facade of Westover Plantation House, Virginia, built around 1730 by William Byrd. The plantation system relied on a slave population which had risen to almost 700,000 by 1790. The state of Virginia, which defined black slaves as "real estate [which] shall descend unto heirs and widows," was home to the largest number of slave laborers

farmers declared their loyalty to the British throne but would not pledge to bear arms against its enemies, which seemed to imply a residual loyalty to France.) Reacting to the change in imperial jurisdiction following the war, some French and Spanish colonists tried to evade their new rulers—most Spanish in Florida left within a year of the treaty, while some of the French settlers who had been living on the east bank of the Mississippi River created St Louis on the west bank as a refuge from British rule—but the total number involved was not great.

that when it was over the British tried to brake the westward thrust of its own colonists, just as the French had done. Britain was trying to cope with its greatly enlarged American empire by instituting some of the central controls it had neglected to establish in the preceding 150 years. The government in London did not want to stop expansion completely; it merely wanted to control it. To that end, a royal proclamation was issued in October 1763 that created new provincial governments for the conquered colonies (in North America they

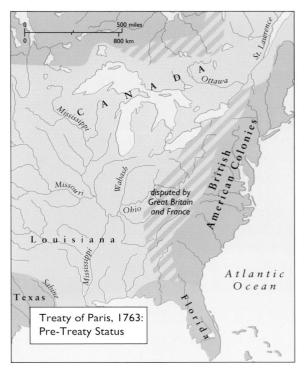

Treaty of Paris, 1763: Pre-Treaty Status

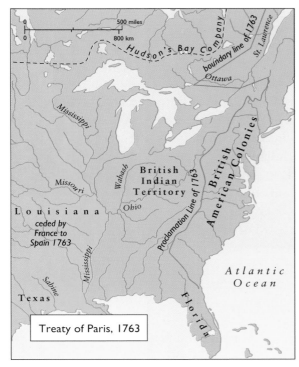

Treaty of Paris, 1763

One cause of the French and Indian War was France's desire to contain the westward pressure of settlement from the 13 British colonies. A significant difference between the French and Spanish colonies and those of the British was in the sizes of their populations. Britain's North American provinces had developed with little centralized control from London, often serving as havens for those who did not fit well into the home country's society and economy, and in nearly every case growing into diverse, self-sufficient communities; settlers worked the land, extracted natural resources, provided a market for British goods, and grew in number. The French and Spanish had concentrated more on the extraction of American resources (e.g. fur trapping, Indian trade) and therefore had much less incentive than the British to build a large, self-sustaining colonial population. In the 1750s the French had tried to block British expansion into the trans-Appalachian interior by establishing a chain of posts in the eastern Mississippi basin and then taking military control of the Ohio valley. The British counterattack made the conflict a full-fledged war.

One irony at the end of the French and Indian War was

were Québec in Canada and East Florida and West Florida as separate colonies in the former Spanish province), and that declared restrictions on the colonial penetration of the interior. Chief among those restrictions was a prohibition against settling west of the Appalachian divide and a requirement that Indian traders be licensed. In effect, the proclamation created a territory for the Indians between the Mississippi River and the ridge of the Appalachian mountain chain. The new rules were meant to protect the colonists and Indians from each other. The prohibition on western settlement was to be temporary until the government set up a mechanism to regulate expansion, but it stayed in effect until nullified by the outbreak of the American Revolution. While most British colonists (who had little interest in moving west) simply resented the restriction, others chose to ignore it and created new settlements on the Clinch, Holston, and on other rivers that flow into the Mississippi from parts of modern Tennessee, Kentucky, and Pennsylvania.

The British authorities did not rest on the Proclamation of 1763. They began almost immediately to arrange "treaties" (meetings meant to produce a document of agreement between the participating groups) with the many Indian tribes for the purpose of acquiring title to land for future expansion of colonial settlement. All together, these treaties created what became known as the Indian Boundary Line, a line between Indian and European settlement that was recognized by both sides and could be surveyed and marked on the ground. In 1768 the Treaty at Fort Stanwix, New York, resulted in the British securing Indian deeds to all land south of the Ohio River from Pittsburgh south to the mouth of the Tennessee River (an area far larger than the British home government wanted), in addition to a large area between Pittsburgh and Fort Stanwix. When news of the Fort Stanwix line became public, land-hungry colonists started to move into the region south of the Ohio. By 1771 British negotiators and surveyors in the south had succeeded in gaining the agreement of many southern Indian tribes to a line that paralleled the Proclamation Line from Florida north to the boundary between North Carolina and Virginia near the head of the Kanawha River, ran generally westward from there to the head of the Kentucky River, and thence downstream to the Ohio. When the War of the American Revolution ended with the Treaty of Paris in 1783, the Indian Boundary Line served de facto as a starting point for U.S. efforts to acquire more land from the Indians. Many Americans who wanted to try a move westward saw the line as having opened much of Kentucky.

On the other side of the continent, Russia was starting to plant small outposts along the Pacific Coast, principally in Alaska but also extending as far south as northern California. Also, the British developed an interest in the region around Vancouver Island after James Cook's visit in 1778. Spain responded by planting outposts at San Diego (1769), Monterey (1770), and eventually at San Francisco (1776). Franciscan missions were established at these posts and at others founded later in the 1770s and 1780s to complete a chain along the coast north of Baja California. Spanish outposts in what is now Texas and southern Louisiana saw little new activity. The expansion of settlement in California was limited to the coastal mission posts and involved only a small number of non-Indian settlers.

The American Revolution's effect on settlement was not limited to opening the trans-Appalachian west to white settlement. A much larger and more immediate effect on the settlement of North America was the departure of thousands of Loyalists from the U. S. Perhaps as many as 500,000 men and women and their children tried to remain loyal to King George III and the British cause—some even forming militia units to fight the American rebels—and in the end 30,000 to 40,000 of them left the U. S. as refugees, most of them never to return. The largest contingent went to Canada, others to the West Indies, and still others to England. The British government set up programs to help the Loyalists reestablish themselves. These included land grants, food,

Treaty of Paris, 1783

Jay Treaty, 1794
Treaty of
San Lorenzo, 1795

Right: the mission belltower in San Diego, California, where Franciscan missionaries arrived in 1769, introducing draft animals and European farming techniques to the Indian inhabitants of the Monterey and San Diego areas

equipment, and the like, but the measures were never adequate to eliminate the hardship completely or to compensate for the loss of an established home. A significant proportion of those who left went involuntarily as the slaves of loyal masters. On the other hand, the British made it their policy to offer slaves their freedom, if they would escape to British lines; many of these African-American Loyalists became disillusioned at receiving less assistance than was accorded their white counterparts, and a group of nearly 1,200 eventually departed their new settlements in Nova Scotia to help found the fledgling colony of Sierra Leone in Africa. The ranks of Loyalists also included Indians who had thrown in their lot with the British. Descendants of the Loyalists still form a distinctive and important part of the population in the Bahamas and Canada.

Most American leaders, as well as the average citizens, believed in the desirability of growth in the population of the U. S. and in an enlargement of the settled area. In their eyes, expansion would support democracy and economic wellbeing and imbue the national character

Right: the battle of Bunker Hill in Charlestown, where a 3000-strong American force successfully confronted 2300 redcoats in an attempt to loosen the British grip on Boston. Although the Americans were eventually forced to beat a hasty retreat after running out of ammunition, their morale was boosted by the confrontation

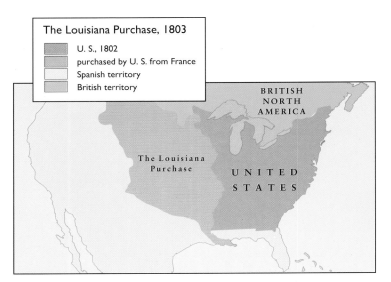

The Louisiana Purchase, 1803

- U. S., 1802
- purchased by U. S. from France
- Spanish territory
- British territory

BRITISH NORTH AMERICA

The Louisiana Purchase

UNITED STATES

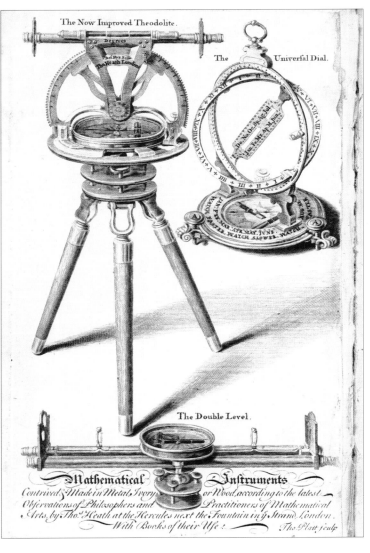

The Now Improved Theodolite.

Degrees

The Universal Dial.

The Double Level.

Mathematical Instruments Contrived & Made in Metal, Ivory or Wood, according to the latest Observations of Philosophers and Practitioners of Mathematical Arts, by Thos. Heath at the Hercules next the Fountain in ye Strand, London. With Books of their Use.

with long life by giving as many families as possible the opportunity to realize the ideal of becoming independent farmers. In one sense, they looked forward to making certain that each American would have a fair share of the national pie by continually enlarging the pie. The Constitution of 1787 created a governmental structure that anticipated growth in many ways, not least of which was the provision for adding new states, rather than the creation of satellite colonies. To leaders like James Madison and Thomas Jefferson, growth and expansion were more than desirable, they were necessary. Little wonder that when Napoleon offered to sell Louisiana (the western Mississippi basin) in 1803, President Jefferson hardly hesitated. At a single stroke he made the potential for national growth practically limitless and set a precedent for future territorial expansion.

The American government started providing for the orderly expansion of non-Indian settlement well before the war was over. States that had any claim to land west of the Appalachian Mountains by virtue of their colonial charters were persuaded to cede those claims to create a

Left: a selection of instruments employed by land surveyors as they extended the frontier, plotting a daily average of 27,000 acres of land for the nation to grow into

public domain of land owned and administered by the national government. (Connecticut retained a small area in northeastern Ohio, the Western Reserve, that it finally turned over to the federal government in 1800.) Then the national government passed the Land Ordinance of 1785, which established the principles and procedures by which surveyors would demarcate the public land into townships six miles on a side, each township further divided into sections one mile square. The national domain and the rectangular survey system were meant to provide for the orderly spread of settlement under a system of centralized control at least as comprehensive and detailed as the British had imagined before the Revolution, and it worked. Over the next century, that system facilitated the settlement of the territory outside the original 13 states and Texas.

Providing for the orderly description and management of the land and its sale would not be sufficient by itself. There had to be some way in which settlers could reach their new lands. This problem in transportation could be solved only in the most rudimentary way for as long as roads and natural water courses were all that were available. Until better transportation became available, the speed with which settlement expanded westward was unavoidably slow.

There was also the problem of land being available for settlement. Most western territory was already occupied by indigenous Indians whose prior settlement gave them a legal and moral claim that the American government

recognized. It became the responsibility of the national government, which had taken the place of the British government in this regard, to deal with the Indian tribes. This government quickly adopted the policy of buying Indian land to make it available for settlement from the East. Fighting was supposed to be a last recourse; when war with Indians did occur, as it did in the region north of the Ohio River in the late 1780s and early 1790s (in what was actually a continuation of the War of the American Revolution), federal forces were brought to bear, and in the end, supported by a greater population and greater resources, they won, as they would win in the future. The Greenville Treaty of 1795 was imposed on the losing Indian confederation and opened up over half the state of Ohio to white settlement faster than the land could be surveyed.

By the eve of the War of 1812, approximately 50 years after the British had driven France and Spain out of the eastern half of North America, Spain was back in control of Florida, and Britain's colonies were confined to the region north of the Great Lakes, the St Lawrence River, and the St Croix River. The new U. S. found itself with jurisdiction over the East Coast and the entire Mississippi drainage basin. The British provinces were more numerous because they held many more people than had lived there under the French in 1763, and the American states and territories were growing at a remarkable rate. The Indians were under constant pressure to give up more land and then move west. The stage was set for even more dramatic changes in the next few decades.

Above: the powerful warrior Tecumseh, chief of the Shawnee, united Indians of the Northwest Territory against frontier settlers. He is seen here sporting the tunic and medal of his British supporters

TIMELINE
AD 1763–1815

NORTH AMERICA

THE CARIBBEAN, CENTRAL & S. AMERICA

EUROPE, AFRICA, & ASIA

NORTH AMERICA	THE CARIBBEAN, CENTRAL & S. AMERICA	EUROPE, AFRICA, & ASIA
1763 Treaty of Paris ends French rule in N. America; Acadians deported from Canada to Louisiana; Spain cedes Florida to Britain. British proclamation tries to reserve land west of Appalachians for Indians, but settlers soon encroach beyond this line. Ottawas, led by Pontiac, rebel against British	1763 Rio de Janeiro replaces São Salvador de Bahia as capital of Brazil	1763 Treaty of Paris concludes Seven Years War. Peasant agitation in Ulster
		1763–9 Senegambia in West Africa made a British Crown Colony
1764 St Louis established by French expelled from Illinois		
1766 British Stamp Act imposes duties on American colonies	1766 British take possession of Falkland Islands	
	1767 Spanish expel Jesuits from New Spain	
1768 Treaty of Fort Stanwix: Iroquois cede Ohio Country to English colonists; Ohio River declared boundary between Indians and white settlers. Andrew Turnbull's Minorcan colony established at New Smyrna in Florida		1768 Catholicism becomes state religion in Poland
1769 British settlers move into Kentucky. Spanish Franciscans set up Californian missions		c. 1770–80 Approximately 15,000 slaves exported from Africa to N. America
		1771 Benjamin Franklin visits Ireland
1773 Boston Tea Party—American colonists protest at British duty on tea		1772 First Partition of Poland as Russia, Austria, and Prussia annex its territory
1774 Québec Act sets up permanent government for Canada, makes French the official second language and allows religious tolerance for Catholics. Lord Dunmore's War between settlers and Shawnees in Virginia		
1775 American Revolution begins with Battle of Lexington. Spanish found presidio at Tucson, Arizona		1775 4000 British troops withdrawn from Ireland to fight American revolutionaries
1776 U.S. Declaration of Independence. Spanish found San Francisco	1776 Spanish colonial reforms. Argentina separated from Viceroyalty of Peru to become new Viceroyalty of the Río de la Plata, with its capital at Buenos Aires	
	1780 Tupac Amaru II, a mestizo claiming descent from the Incas, leads uprising against Spanish in Peru	1778 France allies with U.S. against Britain
		1780–94 War between Britain and the Netherlands
1781 British commander Lord Cornwallis surrenders at Yorktown, ending War of the American Revolution	1781 Communero revolt against Spanish rule in Socorro, Colombia	c. 1780–90 Approximately 55,000 slaves exported from Africa to N. America
1782 Ohio settlers massacre christianized Delaware Indians		
1783 Second Treaty of Paris: Britain recognizes American independence; Florida returns to Spanish rule; French Louisiana ceded to Spain, except for New Orleans. 30,000 pro-British colonists leave U.S. for Canada and the Caribbean	1783 Spain issues decree encouraging immigration to Trinidad	1783 Russia annexes the Crimea
1784 First permanent Russian settlement in America, on Kodiak Island. Province of New Brunswick created from Nova Scotia	1786 Spanish King Carlos III appoints 12 intendants to rule New Spain, replacing *acaldes*, *mayores*, and *corregidores*	
1787 U. S. Congress passes Northwest Ordinance, accelerating westward expansion		1787–94 War between Russia and Turkey
	1788 Brazilian uprising against Portuguese rule	1788 British found first penal colony in Australia
1789 George Washington first U. S. president		1789 French Revolution
1790 First Federal Census gives U.S. population of 3,900,000. There are 73,000 white settlers in Kentucky and 3000 in Ohio		c. 1790–1800 Approximately 85,000 slaves exported from Africa to N. America
1791 Québec divided into two provinces, Upper and Lower Canada. Vermont becomes a State of the Union.	1791 Slave uprising led by Toussaint L'Ouverture in French colony of Haiti	1791 Second Partition of Poland between Prussia and Russian empire

NORTH AMERICA

1792 Kentucky becomes a state. Pennsylvania buys Erie Triangle. 1196 African-American loyalists sail from Nova Scotia to found Sierra Leone in West Africa

1793 Eli Whitney invents cotton gin

1795 Treaty of Greenville: 12 Indian nations agree to boundary between Indians and settlers in the Northwest Territory (U.S. Public Land)

1796 Tennessee becomes a State of the Union

1797 John Adams becomes U.S. president

1798 Spain cedes Mississippi Territory to U.S.

1799 Russian American Fur Company chartered

1800 Spain cedes Louisiana to France

1801 Thomas Jefferson becomes U. S. president

1802 Tlingit uprising against Russians on Sitka Island, Alaska

1803 U.S. purchases Louisiana from France. Ohio becomes a State of the Union.

1804 Lewis and Clark set out from St Louis to explore territory acquired from Spain

1806 U.S. Congress authorizes construction of Cumberland Road, aiding flow of settlers to West. Aaron Burr conspires unsuccessfully to annexe Spanish territory in Southwest

1808 Astor's American Fur Company receives charter

1809 Treaty of Fort Wayne gives settlers 2.5 million acres of Indian land in Ohio and Indiana. St Louis Missouri Fur Company receives charter

1809–11 Shawnee chief Tecumseh unites tribes of old Northwest, South, and Mississippi against U.S.

1812 Louisiana becomes a State of the Union. Russians establish post at Fort Ross, California

1812–15 War of 1812 between Britain and U.S. Tecumseh, a brigadier general on the British side, is killed at Battle of Moravian Town (1813)

1813–14 Creek War; Andrew Jackson deprives Creeks of their land

1814 Treaty of Ghent ends War of 1812 in December, but news does not reach North America until February 1815

1815 Treaties of Portages des Sioux open Indian lands below Lake Michigan to white settlement

THE CARIBBEAN, CENTRAL & S. AMERICA

1797 British take Trinidad from Spain. Smallpox epidemic among Indians in Mexico

1801 Toussaint l'Ouverture captured by Leclerc and imprisoned in France, where he dies

1802 Haitian revolution rekindles after French try to reintroduce slavery

1804 Haiti gains independence from France with Jean Jacques Dessalines as emperor

1806 Unauthorized British expedition takes Buenos Aires, but is captured by the citizens. Salvador Miranda attempts to free Venezuela from Spanish rule. Dessalines assassinated; Haiti divided between Pétion in north and Christophe in south

1807 Portuguese royal family flee to Brazil to escape French invasion. Rio de Janeiro becomes the seat of Portuguese government. Simón Bolívar returns to South America from Europe

1810 Hidalgo's uprising in Mexico; wars of independence begin throughout Spanish America

1811 Rebel state of New Granada (Venezuela, Colombia, and Ecuador) formed in opposition to Spanish rule

1813 Mexico declares independence from Spain.

EUROPE, AFRICA, & ASIA

1792 France at war with Austria and Prussia. Second Partition of Poland

1793 Louis XIV guillotined in France; Britain and France at war

1794 Kosciuszko's rising against Russians in Poland

1795 Third Partition of Poland—Russia, Austria, and Prussia annex all remaining Polish territory. British conquer Cape of Good Hope

1798 Wolfe Tone's rebellion against British rule in Ireland

1799 Napoleon proclaimed First Consul in France. Crop failure and famine in Ireland

1800 Act of Union between Britain and Ireland

c. 1800–10 Approximately 108,000 slaves exported from Africa to N. America

1803 Robert Emmet's uprising against British rule in Ireland

1804 Napoleon crowned emperor of France

1807 Napoleon invades Portugal. Slave trade abolished in British Empire

1808 Napoleon invades Spain and replaces King Ferdinand VII with his own brother, Joseph Bonaparte

1810 Napoleon annexes Holland

1812 Napoleon invades Russia

1813 Napoleon defeated at Leipzig

1814 Napoleon abdicates and is exiled to Elba; Congress of Vienna restores Bourbon monarchy in France and Spain, inaugurating conservative rule throughout Europe which leads many to migrate

1815 Napoleon escapes from exile but is defeated at Waterloo and imprisoned on St Helena by British

DEPORTEES AND DISSENTERS
THE ODYSSEY OF THE ACADIANS, 1755–78

French-speaking refugees from British Canada migrated to Louisiana, where they form a distinctive element of the community to this day.

The French and Indian War (1755–63) disrupted no group more severely than the Acadians. Catholic in religion and French in language, these people were descended from French colonists who had settled in Acadia (present Nova Scotia and eastern New Brunswick) early in the 1600s. In the autumn of 1755, the Acadians numbered about 13,000 and the British commander in Nova Scotia feared they would be an internal threat in the developing war with France. They refused to swear full allegiance to the British crown, so he ordered troops to deport them by force. Many tried to escape into the forest or to French-held territory, but whenever the British captured a new French area they removed the Acadians who had sought refuge there.

Above: this typical Cajun house near Rayne, Louisiana, was photographed in the 1930s. The large gabled roof and built-in porch are characteristic of old Acadian houses throughout North America.

north to Chaleur Bay the majority of the population is descended from Acadians who successfully resisted exile, and they have preserved the memory of their ancestors' ordeal through commemorative events and museums such as the Village Historique Acadien, a recreated settlement constructed in Caraquet.

In the U. S. there are Acadians in northern Maine, descended from a group of returned exiles who settled on the upper Saint John River, and in southern Louisiana, where "Cajun" has evolved as an informal version of "Acadian." Over the years Cajuns expanded west of the Mississippi with the result that today neither New Orleans nor Baton Rouge lies within the region that the state officially designated Acadiana in 1971. The number of people in that area who can claim descent from the Acadian exiles has grown from less than 3000 in 1785 to more than 750,000 today.

Left: one of the best-known aspects of Cajun culture is its distinctive music, in which accordions and violins play a prominent part. Here, a modern Cajun band entertains dancers at the Rendez Vous Des Cajuns at the Unis Liberty Theatre in Eunice, Louisiana.

The war ended with the transfer of Spanish Florida to Britain, when some 3000 Spaniards and several hundred Indians were evacuated to Havana in 1764. Apparently the Acadians still posed a threat a decade later, for the British deported a final contingent from St Pierre and Miquelon Islands in 1778 when France declared its support for the American Revolution. Many Acadians made their way back to the Maritime region after the war, but few were able to recover their former homes. Many went to Sainte Domingue (now Haiti) before moving on to Louisiana. Nearly a thousand returned from France to St Pierre and Miquelon, and in 1785 another 1600 sailed to Louisiana.

The Acadians not only survived their persecution but have left a powerful cultural legacy that enriches both the U. S. and Canada. In Canada they are the dominant non-British ethnic group in New Brunswick, Prince Edward Island, and Nova Scotia. Along the coast from Moncton

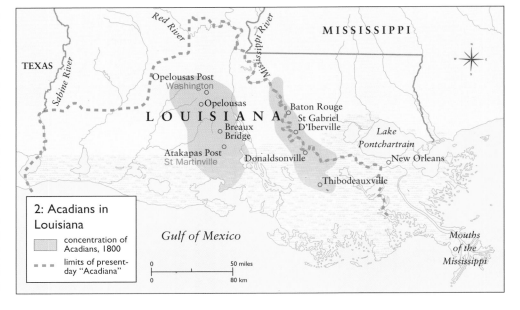

2: Acadians in Louisiana

concentration of Acadians, 1800

limits of present-day "Acadiana"

0   50 miles
0   80 km

3: Acadians in New Brunswick

concentration of Acadians, 1800

0 — 30 miles
0 — 50 km

1: Forced exile of French speakers, 1755–78

concentration of Acadians:
- 1755
- 1800
- → route of Acadians

political control, 1763:
- British
- French
- Spanish

Newfoundland
1758, 3500 to France
1765, 67, 78, 2000 to France
1760, 300 to France
1762, 1500
2000
1755
700
250
500
1000
1100
1756, 1100 to England
500
Charleston 500
400
1785, 1600 from France

Spanish to 1763
British 1763–84
Spanish 1784–1819

THE MEDITERRANEAN COMES TO FLORIDA
MINORCAN, ITALIAN AND GREEK SETTLERS, 1767–90

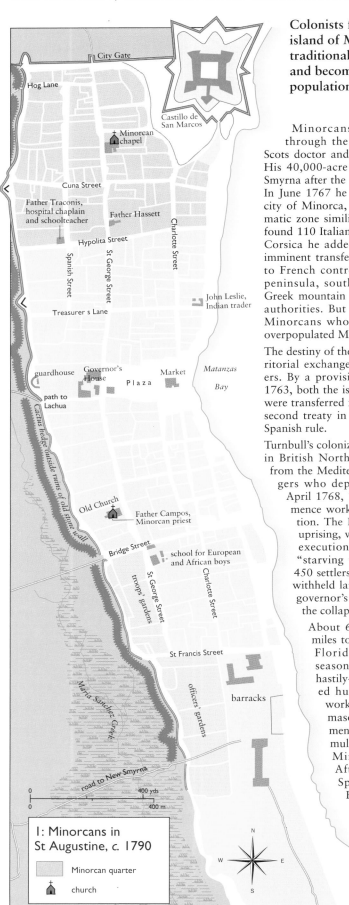

Colonists from the Mediterranean island of Minorca brought their traditional lifeways to Florida and become the backbone of the population of St Augustine.

Minorcans came to British Florida through the commercial ambitions of a Scots doctor and merchant, Andrew Turnbull. His 40,000-acre plantation was named New Smyrna after the birthplace of his Turkish wife. In June 1767 he sailed from Mahon, the port city of Minorca, to recruit settlers from a climatic zone similiar to Florida. At Livorno he found 110 Italians, unemployed single men. At Corsica he added 55 Greeks who feared the imminent transfer of the island from Genoese to French control. From the Peloponnesian peninsula, southwest of Athens, came 200 Greek mountain tribesmen fleeing the Turkish authorities. But the majority were the 1000 Minorcans who abandoned their poor and overpopulated Mediterranean island.

The destiny of the Minorcans was linked to territorial exchanges among the European powers. By a provision of the Treaty of Paris of 1763, both the islands of Minorca and Florida were transferred from Spanish to British rule; a second treaty in 1783 returned them both to Spanish rule.

Turnbull's colonizing expedition was the largest in British North America, and the only one from the Mediterranean. Of the 1403 passengers who departed aboard eight ships in April 1768, 1255 reached Florida to commence work on Turnbull's indigo plantation. The Italians and Greeks staged an uprising, which was suppressed with the execution of two leaders. During the "starving time" of the first two years, 450 settlers died. Forced labor, droughts, withheld land allotments, and the British governor's antipathy to Turnbull led to the collapse of the colony in 1777.

About 600 survivors walked the 75 miles to St Augustine, capital of East Florida. Through the first rainy season, they endured hardships in hastily-constructed palmetto-thatched huts. Gradually they took up work as farmers, carpenters, stonemasons, shopkeepers, and fishermen, using their skills at catching mullet, a species common to both Minorca and coastal Florida. After Florida was returned to Spanish rule and most of the British departed, the combined Minorcans, Greeks, and Italians became the largest section of the civilian population of St Augustine.

Their devoted priest, a Father Pedro Campos, who had traveled

Above: a Minorcan woman in traditional costume. Minorcans have continued to live in St Augustine, keeping alive their folk traditions and honoring their patron saints.

with them from Minorca, continued to preach in Catalan. The northern section of the town was identified as the Minorcan Quarter, though more prosperous merchants and shipowners moved to homes near the central plaza or the wharfs.

The Minorcans formed a cohesive group within a diverse community of about 1700 living in and around the town. About two thirds were of European origin, and the remaining third of African heritage. The small Spanish population was limited to the governor, Vincente Manuel de Zéspedes, his household, several officials, and five families from the Canary Islands .

The permanent Cuban battalion included "Floridanos"—Spanish Americans born in St Augustine who had lived in Cuba during the 20 years the British ruled Florida. The Irish parish priest, Father Thomas Hassett, had been trained in Spain. John Leslie, a Scot, managed the local Indian trade. Seminoles and Creeks came to barter venison and deerskins, and hold councils with the governor.

Map labels

City Gate
Hog Lane
Castillo de San Marcos
Minorcan chapel
Cuna Street
Father Traconis, hospital chaplain and schoolteacher
Father Hassett
Hypolita Street
Charlotte Street
Spanish Street
St George Street
John Leslie, Indian trader
Treasurer's Lane
guardhouse
Governor's House
Plaza
Market
Matanzas Bay
path to Lachua
Cactus hedge outside ruins of old stone wall
Old Church
Father Campos, Minorcan priest
Bridge Street
school for European and African boys
St George Street troops' gardens
Charlotte Street
St Francis Street
Maria Sanchez Creek
officers' gardens
barracks
road to New Smyrna

0   400 yds
0   400 m

1: Minorcans in St Augustine, c. 1790

▢ Minorcan quarter
⛪ church

N / S / E / W

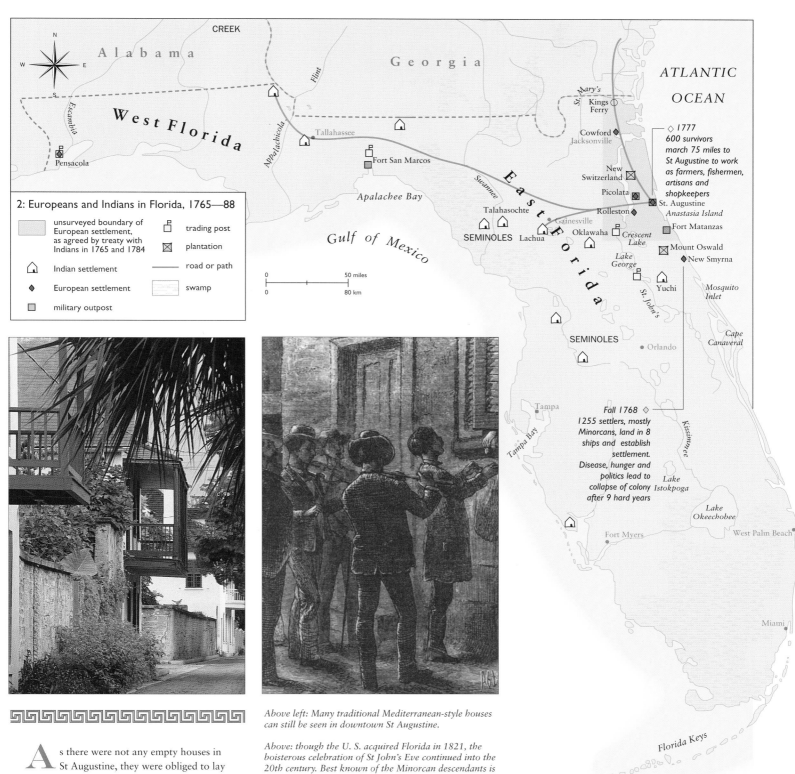

2: Europeans and Indians in Florida, 1765—88

- ▨ unsurveyed boundary of European settlement, as agreed by treaty with Indians in 1765 and 1784
- ⌂ Indian settlement
- ◆ European settlement
- ▪ military outpost
- ⌂ trading post
- ⊠ plantation
- — road or path
- ▱ swamp

◇ *1777*
600 survivors march 75 miles to St Augustine to work as farmers, fishermen, artisans and shopkeepers

Fall 1768 ◇
1255 settlers, mostly Minorcans, land in 8 ships and establish settlement. Disease, hunger and politics lead to collapse of colony after 9 hard years

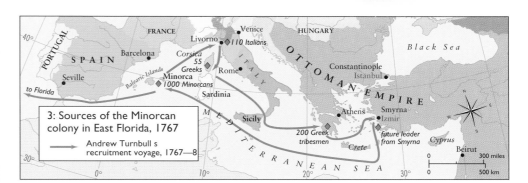

Above left: Many traditional Mediterranean-style houses can still be seen in downtown St Augustine.

Above: though the U. S. acquired Florida in 1821, the boisterous celebration of St John's Eve continued into the 20th century. Best known of the Minorcan descendants is the American poet Stephen Vincent Benét (1898–1943), whose great-great-grandfather came from Minorca.

A s there were not any empty houses in St Augustine, they were obliged to lay under Trees, and at the sides of old Walls in the rains of August and September, which diseased and dropsied them in such a manner as must end in Death, a few of the young and robust excepted... Their want is now so great, that above a hundred of the women and Children went to the Governor's House some days ago and demanded sustenance in the most clamourous Manner.

Dr Andrew Turnbull to Lord Germain,
8 December, 1777

3: Sources of the Minorcan colony in East Florida, 1767

→ Andrew Turnbull s recruitment voyage, 1767—8

110 Italians
Corsica 55 Greeks
Minorca 1000 Minorcans
to Florida
200 Greek tribesmen
future leader from Smyrna

AMERICAN LOYALISTS
EXILES FROM THE AMERICAN REVOLUTION, 1776–92

The American Revolution dislocated a greater number of people in North America than any other event on the continent up to that time.

During the American War of Independence (1776–83), a significant number of Americans —probably 500,000 of the 2,500,000 non-Indians in the 13 colonies—preferred to remain within the British Empire. Most of these people stayed at home during the war, but approximately 15 to 20 percent of them were permanently uprooted or dispersed. Many of these exiles, known as the American Loyalists, had to move two or three times before reaching new permanent residences.

Among loyal colonists, support for the British ranged from not cooperating with revolutionary measures to taking up arms in one of the Loyalist military units that served alongside the British army. Indians and African-Americans, former freemen and ex-slaves alike, also formed military forces. Britain tried to compensate the exiles who suffered for their loyalty, especially those who fought to preserve the empire. That aid usually consisted of land grants in Canada, the Bahamas, and the West Indies, plus supplies to help them start new lives; many were granted pensions. In addition, the British government helped all American Loyalists to make formal claims for compensation for the farms, buildings and other property they had had to leave behind, and which the states had confiscated.

The Loyalists were a diverse group. Most were British colonists who openly opposed the revolution and who left the United States when the British military evacuated the area; some depart-

Above: General Burgoyne surrenders his British army at the New York town of Saratoga on 17 October, 1777.

ed voluntarily while others were forced out. Thousands of those counted as Loyalists were African-American slaves who were forced to move when their masters fled with the British army. The British tried to damage the revolutionary cause by enticing slaves to escape to freedom and to a better life than they had known or could expect in the United States. In fact the support provided for black exiles was much less than that given to whites, and some were sold back into slavery. Hundreds of Indians, especially tribes in the New York region, chose the British side.

There were Loyalists in every state, and the moment hostilities erupted some of them began to leave for safer locales. First were about a thousand New England Loyalists who left Boston for Halifax in Nova Scotia when the British army departed in 1776. A large number moved out of West Florida and north to Canada after the Spanish captured Pensacola and Mobile. The largest group had gathered in New York City (the British Army's head-

quarters) over a number of years; about 30,000 left en masse for Canada in 1783 when the formal peace was settled. Thousands had fled from Charleston and Savannah to St Augustine and its environs in East Florida when the British forces pulled out of Georgia and South Carolina in 1782 and 1783, and had to move again when it became known that the peace settlement (the Treaty of Paris of 1783) restored Florida to Spanish rule after 20 years in British hands. Several thousands of Loyalists who initially arrived in Nova Scotia soon moved on to the Upper St Lawrence Valley in Quebec. Approximately 9000 eventually settled in England, traveling as families or in small contingents, not as a large, single group. The last major group to move all together consisted of 1196 African-American Loyalists. In 1792 they left their inadequate lands outside Shelburne, Nova Scotia, where the British government had settled them, and sailed to Africa to help establish Sierra Leone.

The absolute size of the Loyalist migration was significant. Immigration to Canada more than doubled the population there, and in 1784 led to the creation of the province of New Brunswick from Nova Scotia. In 1791 Quebec was divided into two provinces of Upper and Lower Canada, again for the purpose of providing administration and services for the thousands of Loyalists who had moved into the Upper St Lawrence Valley. The Loyalist migrations temporarily quadrupled the population of the Floridas, and permanently doubled that of the Bahamas. Throughout the United States many Loyalists who had left their homes during the war returned after the peace rather than face permanent exile. In the South, for example, it has been estimated that from 1783 almost as many Loyalists returned to Georgia and South Carolina from East Florida as moved to the Bahamas.

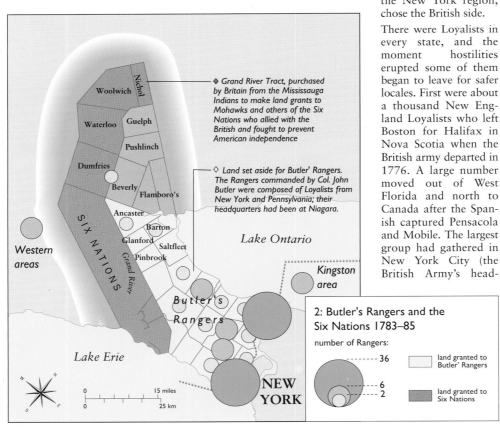

◆ Grand River Tract, purchased by Britain from the Mississauga Indians to make land grants to Mohawks and others of the Six Nations who allied with the British and fought to prevent American independence

◇ Land set aside for Butler' Rangers. The Rangers commanded by Col. John Butler were composed of Loyalists from New York and Pennsylvania; their headquarters had been at Niagara.

2: Butler's Rangers and the Six Nations 1783–85

number of Rangers:

- 36
- 6
- 2

land granted to Butler' Rangers

land granted to Six Nations

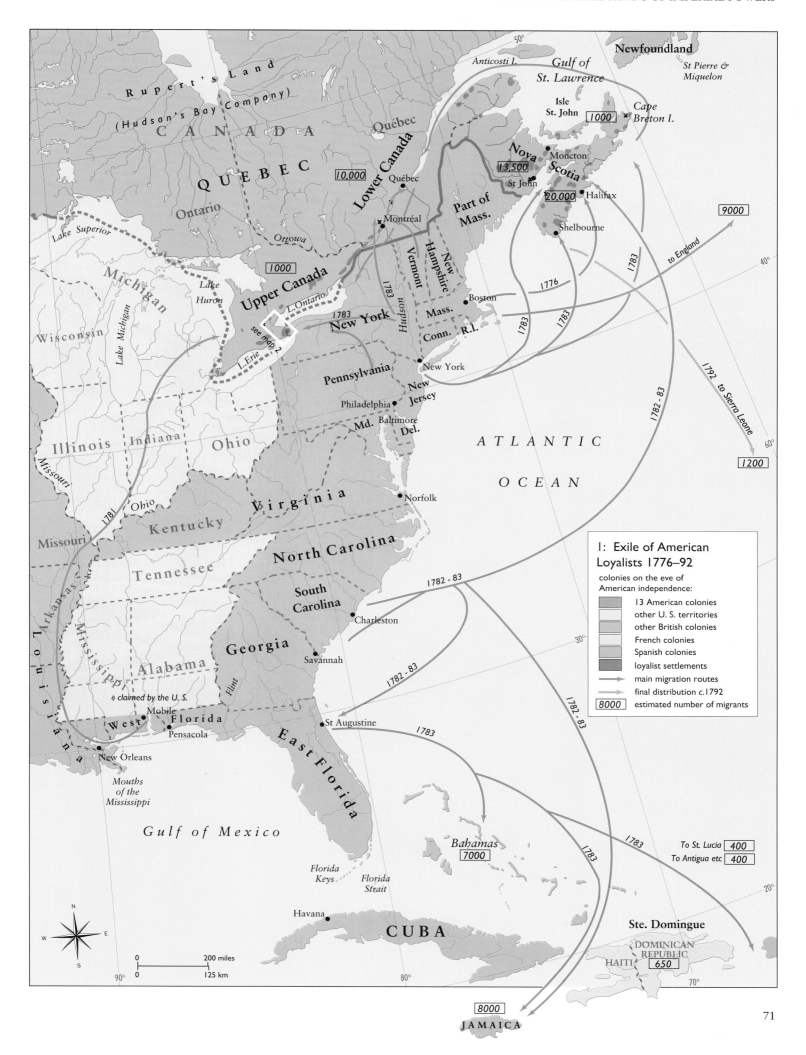

Newfoundland

St Pierre & Miquelon

Anticosti I.   Gulf of
St. Lawrence

Isle
St. John   1000   Cape
Breton I.

Rupert's Land

(Hudson's Bay Company)

C A N A D A   Québec

Nova   Moncton
Scotia

Q U E B E C   13,500

Ontario   10,000   Lower Canada

Québec   20,000   Halifax

St John

Part of
Mass.   Shelbourne

Lake Superior   Montréal   9000

Ottawa   New
Hampshire

Michigan   New
Vermont   1783   to England

Lake
Huron   1000   1776   40°

Wisconsin   Upper Canada   L.Ontario   1783   Mass.   Boston   1783

see map 2   New York   1783

L.Erie   Conn.   R.I.   1792   to Sierra Leone

Lake Michigan   New York

Pennsylvania   New
Jersey   A T L A N T I C   60°

Illinois   Indiana   Ohio   Philadelphia   Md. Baltimore
Del.   O C E A N   1200

Missouri   Ohio   Virginia   Norfolk

1781   Ohio

Kentucky

Missouri   Tennessee   North Carolina   1: Exile of American
Loyalists 1776–92

Arkansas   South
Carolina   1782 - 83   colonies on the eve of
American independence:

Georgia   Charleston   13 American colonies

Alabama   other U. S. territories

Mississippi   Savannah   1782 - 83   other British colonies

Louisiana   Flint   French colonies

claimed by the U.S.   Spanish colonies

Mobile   loyalist settlements
West   Florida   St Augustine   1783
Pensacola   East Florida   1783   main migration routes
New Orleans   final distribution c.1792

Mouths
of the
Mississippi   8000   estimated number of migrants

Gulf of Mexico   1782 - 83

Bahamas   1783   To St. Lucia   400
7000   To Antigua etc   400

Florida
Keys   Florida
Strait

N   20°

W   E   Havana   Ste. Domingue

S   C U B A

0   200 miles   DOMINICAN
REPUBLIC
0   125 km   HAITI   650

90°   80°   70°

8000

JAMAICA

71

THE WILDERNESS ROAD
EURO-AMERICAN SETTLEMENT BEYOND THE APPALACHIANS, 1790–1810

Following the American Revolution, the non-Indian population of the U. S. grew rapidly. Over wilderness trails and down the Ohio River by flatboat, settlers flooded into the Indian hunting grounds.

In the 20 years between the first Federal Census in 1790 and the third in 1810, the total number of people nearly doubled from 3,900,000 (including 757,000 non-white Americans) to 7,224,000 (including 1,378,000 non-whites), an average growth rate of more than 35 percent per decade. Only about 150,000 of these new people were immigrants; the rest were the product of natural increase.

Canada's population grew more slowly than that of the U. S. By 1810 the estimated total for all Canada, including New Brunswick and Nova Scotia, was approximately 460,000. Only about 75,000 people were living west of Montreal, strung along the lower courses of the rivers and the north shores of Lakes Erie and Ontario. As in the U. S., most population growth in this period resulted from natural increase, with only a small contribution by immigration.

Beyond the Appalachians, the American population advanced in a series of major waves. Whether pushed by overcrowding, undesirable social conditions or diminished opportunities in the East, or drawn by the prospect of cheap land and greater freedom, Americans could not have flooded the new western areas as they did without overcoming the obstacles of poor transportation and prior Indian settlement. The territory south of the Ohio River in Kentucky and northern Tennessee had long been used by the various Indian tribes not for habitation but as a common hunting ground, and some of it had been ceded to Britain in treaties before the Revolution.

The first wave flowed into Kentucky. At the outset of the American Revolution in 1775, there were only about 400 settlers there; by 1790 there were 73,000. The second wave concentrated on Ohio. In 1790 there were only about 3000 white people in Ohio, challenging the agreed boundary between Indian and white settlement. This had been established on the Ohio River by a treaty between the British and the Indians at Fort Stanwix in 1768, which was recognized by the new American government in 1778. In defense of this agreement, Indians resisted white settlement north of the Ohio River, but were defeated at the Battle of Fallen Timbers in 1794. This led to the signing of the Greenville Treaty in 1795, in which the 12 tribes agreed to give up two thirds of Ohio. New settlers rushed in, and within 15 years some 230,000 of them were living in the state of Ohio. Other treaties followed, pushing the tribes further west and north.

The newly-opened regions were crisscrossed with trails, but to settle an area people must be able to carry bulky and heavy objects and large quantities of material, and boats and wagons were the only means available at the time. The Ohio River was the principal route, but roads were necessary to cross the mountains to the waterways that fed the Ohio and ultimately the Mississippi. From the 1790s, land speculators, states, and even the Federal Government promoted wagon roads to the west. The most famous of these was the Wilderness Road running though Cumberland Gap into central Kentucky and, after 1810, to the Ohio River.

Nearly all were rough cuts through the forest, quagmires when wet and dusty when dry, but they sufficed. With the removal of the Indian settlements, these roads and rivers carried a flood of settlers that flowed steadily for years.

The result in the U. S. was the creation of new states: Kentucky in 1792, Tennessee in 1796 and Ohio in 1803, just as New Brunswick and Upper and Lower Canada had been created in response to population growth. The purchase of Louisiana (which then comprised the whole western half of the Mississippi drainage basin) from France in 1803 encouraged the westward flow of people to continue.

Below: "Mad Anthony" Wayne and his officers confer with members of the Twelve Tribes. Wayne defeated the Indians at Fallen Timbers in 1794, paving the way for the Treaty of Greenville the following year, which opened much of Ohio to settlers. This picture was painted by a member of Wayne's staff.

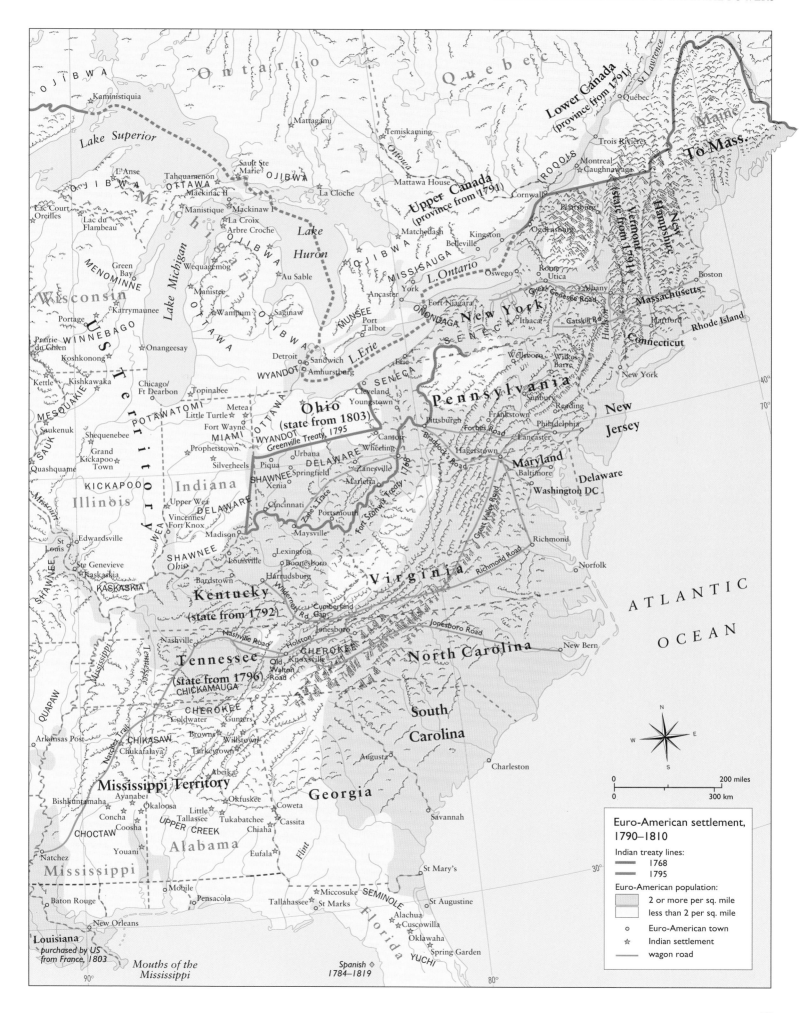

OJIBWA

Ontario

Kaministiquia

Lake Superior

Mattagami

Temiskaming

Quebec

Lower Canada
(province from 1791)

Québec

St. Lawrence

IROQUOIS

Trois Rivières

Maine
(state from 1791)

To Mass.

OJIBWA

L'Anse

OJIBWA

Tahquamenon

OTTAWA

Sault Ste Marie OJIBWA

Mattawa House

Montreal
Caughnawaga

New Hampshire

Lac Court Oreilles

Lac du Flambeau

Manistique

Mackinac I.

Mackinaw I.

La Croix

Arbre Croche

OJIBWA

Lake Huron

La Cloche

Upper Canada
(province from 1791)

Matchedash

Belleville

Kingston

MISSISAUGA

Cornwall

Plattsburg

Ogdensburg

Vermont
(state from 1791)

Boston

Green Bay

MENOMINNE

Wequagemog

Saginaw

OTTAWA

OJIBWA

Au Sable

MUNSEE

Port Talbot

York

Ancaster

Fort Niagara

L. Ontario

Oswego

Rome
Utica

Great Genesee Road

Albany

Massachusetts

Hartford

Connecticut

Rhode Island

Wisconsin

U S

Manistee

WINNEBAGO

Wampum

OTTAWA

New York

SENECA

Wellsboro

Wilkes Barre

Hudson

Catskill Rd.

Ithaca

New York

40°

Portage

Prairie du Chien

Koshkonong

Onangeesay

WYANDOT

Detroit

Sandwich

Amhurstburg

L. Erie

Erie

SENECA

Pennsylvania

Sunbury

Reading

70°

Kettle

Kishkawaka

Chicago/
Ft Dearbon

Topinabee

Cleveland

Youngstown

Pittsburgh

Forbes Road

Frankstown

Philadelphia

Lancaster

New
Jersey

MESQUAKIE

SAUK

Saukenuk

POTAWATOMI

Metea

Little Turtle

Fort Wayne

Ohio
(state from 1803)

WYANDOT

Greenville Treaty, 1795

Canton

Wheeling

Braddock's Road

Hagerstown

Maryland

Baltimore

Delaware

Quashquame

Grand Kickapoo Town

Shequenebee

Silverheels

MIAMI

Prophetstown

Piqua

Urbana

Springfield

Xenia

DELAWARE

Zanesville

Marietta

Fort Stanwix Treaty

Washington DC

KICKAPOO

Indiana

SHAWNEE

Cincinnati

DELAWARE

Zane's Trace

Portsmouth

Richmond

Illinois

Upper Wea

WEA

Vincennes/
Fort Knox

Madison

Maysville

Wilderness Rd.

Virginia

Great Valley Road

Richmond Road

Norfolk

St Louis

SHAWNEE

Ohio

Louisville

Lexington

Boonesboro

Ste Genevieve

SHAWNEE

Kaskaskia

Edwardsville

KASKASKIA

Bardstown

Harrudsburg

Kentucky
(state from 1792)

Cumberland Rd. Gap

Jonesboro

Jonesboro Road

ATLANTIC

OCEAN

Missouri

Nashville Road

Holston

Nashville

Tennessee
(state from 1796)

Old Walton Road

CHEROKEE

Knoxville

North Carolina

New Bern

QUAPAW

CHICKAMAUGA

CHEROKEE

Coldwater

Gunters

Browns

South
Carolina

Arkansas Post

Natchez Trail

CHIKASAW

Chukafalaya

Willstown

Turkeytown

Augusta

Charleston

Abeika

Okfuskee

Coweta

Mississippi Territory

Bishkuntamaha

Ayanabe

Okaloosa

Little

Tallassee

Tukabatchee

Chiaha

Cassita

Georgia

Savannah

Concha

Coosha

CHOCTAW

UPPER CREEK

Youani

Alabama

Eufala

Flint

Natchez

Mississippi

St Mary's

30°

Mobile

Baton Rouge

Pensacola

Miccosuke

Tallahassee

St Marks

SEMINOLE

St Augustine

Alachua

Cuscowilla

New Orleans

Louisiana
purchased by US
from France, 1803

Mouths of the
Mississippi

Spanish
1784–1819

Oklawaha

YUCHI

Spring Garden

Florida

80°

90°

N
W E
S

0   200 miles
0   300 km

Euro-American settlement,
1790–1810

Indian treaty lines:
——— 1768
——— 1795

Euro-American population:
▨ 2 or more per sq. mile
☐ less than 2 per sq. mile
○ Euro-American town
★ Indian settlement
——— wagon road

73

ONTO THE PLAINS

INDIAN MIGRATION ONTO THE GREAT PLAINS, 1515–1800

Spanish colonists unintentionally revolutionized the lives of many Indian peoples who acquired horses from New Mexico by barter or theft and migrated onto the Great Plains, which had been almost uninhabited for millennia.

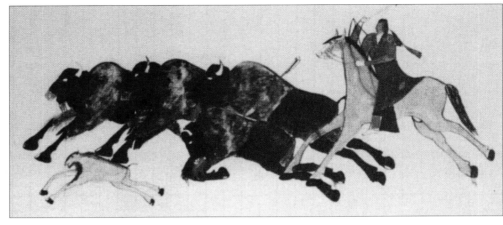

Plains Apaches, migrating south from the interior of Canada, first appeared in the Texan Panhandle area as early as 1515. In the course of the 17th century, they expanded across the southern Plains, splitting into the Lipan, Jicarilla, Mescalero, and other western Apaches. Further north, the Lakota (Sioux) were also moving onto the Plains. The Yankton Lakota moved west from the area of Red Lake, Minnesota into North Dakota, while the Teton Lakota moved from the head of the Minnesota River to the region west of the Missouri, following the Cheyenne who preceded them. Both nations hold the Black Hills as sacred. The Ojibwa and Cree moved out onto the Canadian plains from the Great Lakes, the Cree after suffering population loss in an epidemic in 1700.

These migrations, and the adoption of the horse, gave rise to the distinctive lifestyle of the Plains Indians. There they made bison—augmented by elk, antelope, and deer—the basis of their subsistence. The Plains hunters were linked to the world market system: Plains women tailored skin clothing, and tanned buffalo robes to trade for muskets acquired from the French, powder, lead, pigments, beads, jewelry, agricultural products, and liquor.

Fighting one another for hunting territories as well as horses, Plains tribes developed the best light cavalry contingents on the continent. During the 18th century, the Comanche and Wichita, armed with French trade guns, defeated the Plains Apaches and forced them to retreat southwards to the Spanish borderlands. These areas had previously been inhabited by Coahuiltecan-speaking Indians, Navajos, and Jumano traders, but the spread of European diseases around the Spanish missions had drastically reduced the population. The Spanish had been driven out of New Mexico from 1680 to 1693 by the Pueblo uprising, and saw in the newcomers an opportunity to consolidate their position. Missionary work, previously directed at the Pueblo Indians, now concentrated on the Apaches and detribalized Indians known to the Spanish as *Genízaros*. Many of these were the mestizo offspring of Indian women who married Spaniards, or were kidnapped as children and brought up as Hispanic Christians.

Above: the acquisition of horses allowed the Plains Indians to pursue herds of buffalo over considerable distances. This painting of a buffalo hunt, by the Gros Ventre artist George Bear, was made in 1884, just as white hunters equipped with repeating rifles were driving the great herds, and the Plains lifeway that depended upon them, to extinction.

Together with a natural increase in population, they allowed the New Mexican colonists to found new forts, missions, and towns, notably Albuquerque in 1706.

The Apaches crossed the upper tributaries of the Rio Brazos under attack from the Wichita, and reached the Red River. Lipan Apaches raided Spanish San Antonio and negotiated temporary accommodation with the Spanish. The colonists tried to establish a mission among the Lipan Apaches on the San Sabá tributary of the Colorado River in 1757, but it was destroyed the following year by a confederacy of Indians led by the Hasinai, who did not want their Apache enemies to acquire weapons from the Spanish. Franciscans also established two unofficial missions to the Lipans on the upper Nueces River from 1762 to 1771. The region was not free from raiders from further afield; the Osage, based in southwestern Missouri, mounted raids as far west as Santa Fé and as far south as the Caddoan villages of Louisiana. By the 1790s, however, the Spanish frontier was largely peaceful. The Lipans reached the Gulf of Mexico coast around 1796, and also negotiated with Spanish officials at the military post at El Paso. During the 19th century, Lipan Apaches ranged in western Texas and along the lower Pecos valley into northern Coahuila.

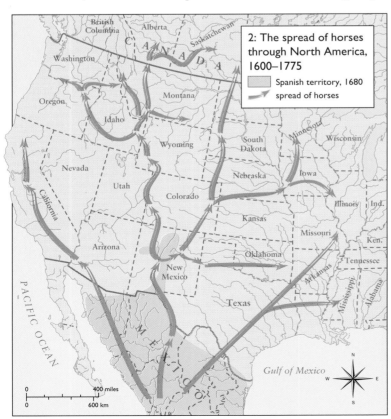

2: The spread of horses through North America, 1600–1775

Spanish territory, 1680

spread of horses

Below: the Hopi Pueblo of Walpi was built on this commanding position at the top of First Mesa after the Pueblo uprising of 1680. Although the Spanish regained control of the Rio Grande and Acoma pueblos, the Hopi of Arizona remained independent until the 19th century.

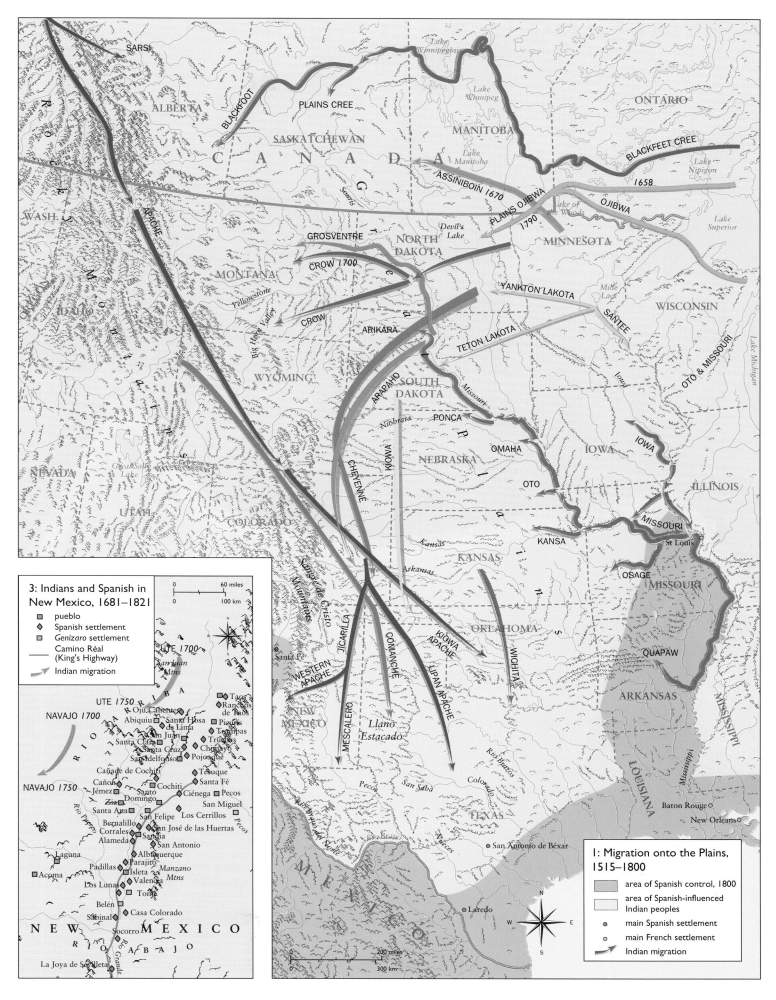

3: Indians and Spanish in New Mexico, 1681–1821

- ☐ pueblo
- ◆ Spanish settlement
- ☐ *Genízaro* settlement
- —— Camino Réal (King's Highway)
- ➤ Indian migration

0 — 60 miles
0 — 100 km

UTE 1700
UTE 1750
NAVAJO 1700
NAVAJO 1750

San Juan Mtns

Taos
Ranchos de Taos
R. Oju. Caliente
Abiquiu
Santa Rosa de Lima
Picurís
San Juan
Trampas
Santa Clara
Trujillos
Santa Cruz
Chimayó
San Ildefonso
Pojoaque
Cañada de Cochiti
Tesuque
Cañon
Santa Fé
Jémez
Cochiti
Santo
Ciénega
Pecos
Domingo
Zia
San Miguel
Santa Ana
San Felipe
Los Cerrillos
Bernalillo
San José de las Huertas
Corrales
Sandia
Alameda
San Antonio
Laguna
Albuquerque
Acoma
Padillas
Parajito
Isleta
Manzano Mtns
Los Lunas
Valencia
Tomé
Belén
Casa Colorado
Sabinal
Socorro
La Joya de Sevilleta

RIO ARRIBA
RIO ABAJO
Rio Puerco
Rio Grande

NEW MEXICO

1: Migration onto the Plains, 1515–1800

- ▨ area of Spanish control, 1800
- ☐ area of Spanish-influenced Indian peoples
- ● main Spanish settlement
- ○ main French settlement
- ➤ Indian migration

SARSI
BLACKFOOT
PLAINS CREE
ALBERTA
SASKATCHEWAN
MANITOBA
ONTARIO
Lake Winnipegosis
Lake Winnipeg
Lake Manitoba
BLACKFEET CREE
Lake Nipigon
ASSINIBOIN 1670
PLAINS OJIBWA
1790
1658
OJIBWA
Lake of the Woods
Lake Superior
C A N A D A
WASH.
APACHE
GROSVENTRE
Devil's Lake
NORTH DAKOTA
MINNESOTA
Mille Lacs
WISCONSIN
Lake Michigan
CROW 1700
MONTANA
Yellowstone
CROW
Big Horn Valley
ARIKARA
YANKTON LAKOTA
SANTEE
IDAHO
OREGON
TETON LAKOTA
OTO & MISSOURI
WYOMING
ARAPAHO
SOUTH DAKOTA
Niobrara
PONCA
Missouri
Iowa
NEVADA
Great Salt Lake
KIOWA
CHEYENNE
NEBRASKA
OMAHA
IOWA
IOWA
UTAH
OTO
COLORADO
ILLINOIS
Sangre de Cristo Mountains
Kansas
KANSA
MISSOURI
St Louis
Arkansas
KANSAS
OSAGE
MISSOURI
JICARILLA
KIOWA APACHE
OKLAHOMA
WESTERN APACHE
Santa Fé
COMANCHE
WICHITA
QUAPAW
NEW MEXICO
MESCALERO
LIPAN APACHE
Llano Estacado
ARKANSAS
Rio Braços
Pecos
San Sabá
Colorado
Mississippi
LOUISIANA
Rio Grande del Norte
TEXAS
Nueces
San Antonio de Béxar
Baton Rouge
New Orleans
MEXICO
Laredo

0 — 200 miles
0 — 300 km

IMPERIAL SPAIN: THE FINAL THRUST

SPANISH "DEFENSIVE COLONIZATION" OF NORTH AMERICA 1680–1821

Alarmed by the arrival of French settlers in the Gulf of Mexico, Spain's 18th-century Bourbon kings ordered a "defensive expansion" of New Spain into Texas and California.

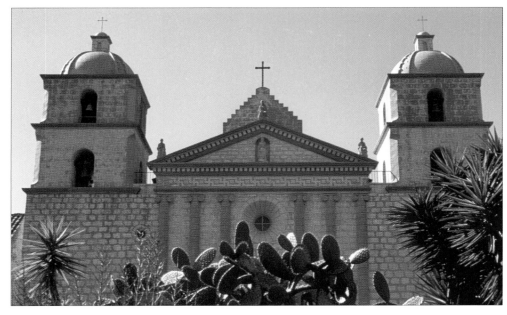

Above: the mission church at Santa Barbara was founded by Franciscan monks in 1782. The Californian missions were the focus of agricultural communities of friars and Indians, but the region attracted few Spanish colonists.

In 1685 the French explorer La Salle established a fort at Matagorda Bay on the Gulf coast of Texas. Spain's Council of the Indies decided that "prompt action" was needed to deal with this "thorn in the heart of America." Most of the French soon perished from hunger and disease, or at the hands of the Karankawa Indians. A few survivors found refuge with the Hasinai Indians who lived east of the Trinity River. The possibility that France might drive a wedge between New Spain and Spanish Florida remained, and from 1699, Spanish subjects contested the lower Mississippi and the Gulf coast with French—and later Canadian—colonists. Father Damián Massenet established two Spanish missions in Texas by 1690, and in the following year Texas became a province under the governorship of Domingo de Téran. In West Florida in 1698, the Spanish built a fort at Pensacola to block French expansion eastward. The Texan missions were soon abandoned, but when the French established a fort at Natchitoches in 1714, Spanish expansion into Texas began again, leading to the creation of San Antonio and a small fort at Los Adaes. By the end of Spanish rule in 1821, about 4000

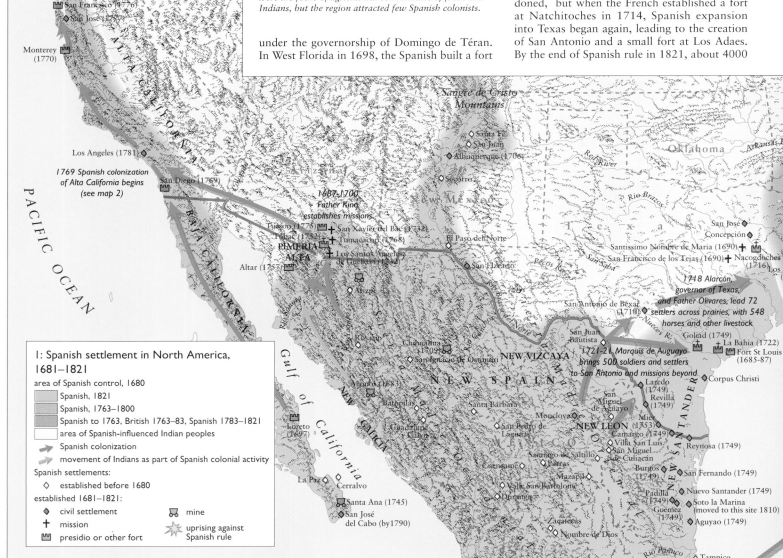

1: Spanish settlement in North America, 1681–1821

area of Spanish control, 1680

- Spanish, 1821
- Spanish, 1763–1800
- Spanish to 1763, British 1763–83, Spanish 1783–1821
- area of Spanish-influenced Indian peoples

→ Spanish colonization

→ movement of Indians as part of Spanish colonial activity

Spanish settlements:

◇ established before 1680

established 1681–1821:

- ◆ civil settlement
- ✝ mission
- 🏰 presidio or other fort
- ⛏ mine
- ✦ uprising against Spanish rule

Spaniards lived in Texas, mostly at San Antonio, Goliad, and Nacogdoches.

Behind the line of the Spanish advance, the province of New Santander was strengthened as towns and missions were settled by Spaniards, mestizos, and Indians who had been relocated, sometimes forcibly. Franco-Spanish rivalry along the Gulf coast came to an end in 1763, when the first treaty of Paris transferred French Louisiana to Spain. This Spanish gain was offset by the transfer of Florida to Great Britain.

Missionaries were also active among the Pima Indians of northern Sonora and southern Arizona, an area known to the Spanish as Pimería Alta. Notable among them was the Jesuit Father Eusebio Kino. After his death in 1711, missionary activity declined in the face of Apache raids, and in 1751 the Pimas rose up against Spanish rule. Tabac, Arizona owed its existence to this event; it was founded as a presidio in 1752 to pacify the troubled region.

The rocky desert peninsula of Baja California was—and still is—only sparsely settled, though by 1730 there were 29 soldiers, 41 sailors, six cowherds and muleteers along with 99 other settlers, at Loreto. Santa Ana, above La Paz, was a short-lived boom town: in 1767, half the colonists on the peninsula congregated around its silver mine; by 1809 it was deserted.

In 1769, however, the peninsula provided the springboard for the colonization of the much more promising region of Alta California to the north. This was to be the last of Spain's "defen-sive expansions" in North America; this time, the perceived threat was from Russian fur traders advancing south from Alaska. The colonization was carried out by land and sea simultaneously, the fleet leaving from La Paz and the land party, under Gaspar de Portola, from Loreto. In the course of their grueling 11-week journey they established settlements at San Diego and at Monterey, the capital of the new province. In 1775–76, a party of 240 settlers, soldiers, and muleteers led by Juan B. Anza and accompanied by Father Pedro Font made the trek north from Sonora to the Golden Gate; the settlement they founded there was San Francisco. A chain of Franciscan missions was founded along the coast in the following decades, and provided the backbone of the new colony. Many missions were agricultural, growing fruit and cereals, and rearing livestock; the labor force was largely Indian. There were Hispanic settlers, however; by 1821, they probably numbered around 4000–5000.

By the time the last of these Californian missions was established at Sonora in 1823, Spain's American empire had crumbled. In 1800, with Spain itself threatened by Napoleon's armies, it had been forced to return Louisiana to the French, who sold it to the U. S. three years later. The prestige and authority of Spain were irretrievably weakened, and in the second decade of the 19th century Hispanic Americans from Mexico to Chile opted for independence. Despite attempts to put down these insurrections, the Spanish proved as unsuccessful as the British in holding on to their American colonies.

2: Spanish missions in Alta California, 1769–1823

Spanish colonizing expeditions:
- Portola, 1769
- Portola's support fleet
- Anza, 1775-76

Spanish settlements:
- ○ civil town
- ✝ mission
- 🏰 fort
- ◆ Russian settlement
- ⬭ Russian-Aleut otter hunting fields
- ✦ uprising against Spanish rule

1812 Fort Ross established with 95 Russians and 80 Aleuts

1809 Russians establish temporary post, bringing Aleut hunters in search of furs

1806 Russian ships arrive to trade for food for Alaskan countries

1811 Aleut hunters gather 1200 furs from San Francisco Bay

Ross (1812)
Bodega Bay
Kostromitinov Farm — Tschernisch Farm
Port Rumiontsov
Point Reyes
Drake's Bay
Khlebnikov Farm
Farallon Station
Golden Gate
Yerba Buena
San Rafael Arcángel (1817)
San Francisco Solano (1823)
San Francisco de Asis (1823)
Santa Clara de Asis (1777)
San José de Guadalupe (1797)
San José (1777)
Santa Cruz (1791)
Mar 1776 Anza reaches San Francisco Bay; founds mission and presidio
Monterey Bay
Monterey (1770)
San Juan Bautista (1791)
San Carlos Borromeo de Carmelo (1791)
Oct 1769 Portola reaches Monterey
Nuestra Señora de la Soledad (1791)
San Antonio de Padua (1771)
San Miguel Arcángel (1797)
San Luis Obispo de Tolosa (1772)
La Purisima Concepción (1787)
Buellton
Santa Barbara (1782)
Santa Inés (1804)
San Buenaventura (1782)
San Fernando Rey de España (1797)
Santa Monica Bay
Los Angeles (1781)
San Gabriel Arcángel (1771)
Gulf of Santa Catalina
San Juan Capistrano (1776)
San Luis Rey de Francia (1797)
Jan 1776 Anza helps put down Indian uprising
July 1769 Portola and settlers reach San Diego
San Diego
San Diego de Alcalá (1769)
Oct 1775 Anza, with 240 settlers, soldiers and muleteers
from La Paz
from Loreto
from Sonora

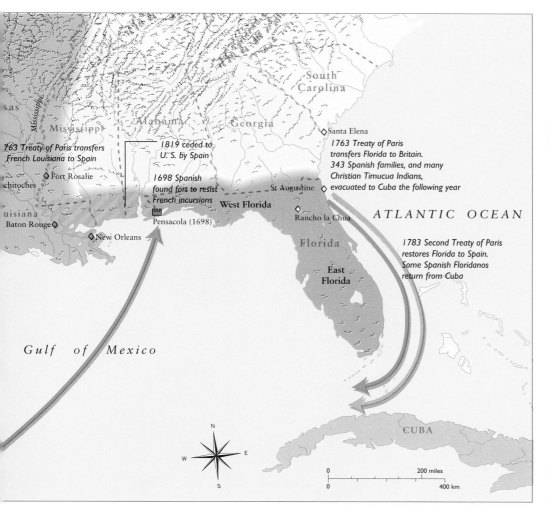

South Carolina
Alabama
Georgia
Mississippi
Santa Elena

1763 Treaty of Paris transfers French Louisiana to Spain

1819 ceded to U. S. by Spain

1698 Spanish found fort to resist French incursions

1763 Treaty of Paris transfers Florida to Britain. 343 Spanish families, and many Christian Timucua Indians, evacuated to Cuba the following year

Fort Rosalie
Natchitoches
Louisiana
Baton Rouge
New Orleans
Pensacola (1698)
West Florida
St Augustine
Rancho la Chua
Florida
East Florida

ATLANTIC OCEAN

1783 Second Treaty of Paris restores Florida to Spain. Some Spanish Floridanos return from Cuba

Gulf of Mexico

CUBA

PART IV: IMMIGRATION AND EXPANSION

Introduction
by John Long

Between 1815 and 1860, the population of North America increased enormously. Its geographical distribution changed as settlers moved steadily westwards, and its composition shifted as new arrivals from Ireland and Germany began to outweigh the Anglo-Saxons and African-Americans who had arrived in the previous century. The underlying conditions of settlement—matters of land title and national jurisdiction, freedom and slavery, technological innovation and economic inducements, cultural values and religious beliefs—were hotly contested and underwent widespread and rapid change.

Right: an 1861 lithograph shows Staten Island and the Narrows seen from Fort Hamilton. Fort Richmond can be seen on the extreme left, while Fort Lafayette is prominent in the harbor between the trees

Over the course of the first half of the 19th century, the population of British North America grew markedly. An extremely high birth rate and low death rate combined to produce a steep increase in French-speaking people with virtually no assistance from immigration. Natural increase was important elsewhere, but immigration played a large role also. It has been estimated that in the Maritime provinces, for example, the burst of population growth from less than 200,000 around 1825 to more than half a million in 1851 was due in large part to heavy immigration from Scotland and Ireland. Many immigrants settled in the cities, a development that gave Montreal an English-speaking majority by 1867.

During the 1850s, after the Oregon agreement with the U. S., growth was steady, yet slow, in all provinces save British Columbia. In 1861 the population was distributed roughly as follows: the province of Canada (the St Lawrence River and northern Great Lakes drainage basins) was home to nearly 2 million people, almost equally divided between Canada West and Canada East; Nova Scotia had over 250,000 and New Brunswick was over 200,000; Prince Edward Island was much smaller, with only a little over 60,000, while the count in British Columbia was about 50,000.

Even though Canadian and American settlement paralleled each other to a certain extent, the population neither increased nor pushed westward as fast in British North America as it did in the U. S.: in 1851, 73 percent of the total non-Indian population was settled in Canada, while 25 percent was settled in the Maritimes, and only 2 percent was in the West. From the end of the War of 1812 to the eve of the Civil War in the U. S., the Indian population declined whilst the non-Indian population increased at the phenomenal rate of almost 35 percent per decade, raising the density in well established areas in the East, filling nearly all the land east of the Mississippi River, spreading westward across that river almost to the 100th meridian, and leapfrogging the western plains and mountains to the states of California, Oregon, Utah, and New Mexico.

Most of the increase in total population arose from natural increase, thanks mostly to a birth rate which had started a gradual decline in the 1800s but was nonetheless quite high; the proportion of foreign born in the total population never exceeded 15 percent during this period. The proportion of African-Americans declined from over 21 percent in 1820 to just under 17 percent in 1860 as the total population of about 9.6 million in 1820 rose to about 31.5 million in 1860.

Immigrants were drawn to the U. S. in the decades before the Civil War chiefly by economic opportunity, the prospect of jobs in construction and manufacturing or the acquisition of virgin land in the West or even the Gold Rush in California. There were events that pushed people to emigrate—the failure of the potato crop in 1845 and five subsequent years of famine in Ireland, and economic hard times and the unsuccessful revolutions in Europe in 1830 and 1848—but they would not have headed for America if there was nothing there for them. Many who immigrated, especially the Irish escaping the famine, were extremely poor. Unable to pay for better passage than steerage, they were carried as return cargo in the holds of ships that had hauled lumber, cotton, or some other bulk product to Europe from America. When they arrived, they were virtually penniless.

The northeastern port cities of New York and Boston

Above: a basic meal is distributed in the steerage of a ship bound for the U. S. Poorer immigrants, who could only afford to make the crossing at the cheapest rate, had to endure cramped conditions and great hardships during the long and arduous journey.

both saw the proportion of foreign born in their populations pass above 50 percent well before the Civil War. Eventually, unskilled jobs on large construction projects like canals and railroads helped many immigrants leave the city. Others, who had good connections to earlier immigrants and who had some capital, were able to move immediately beyond the eastern cities into the trans-Appalachian agricultural areas; some immigrant communities grew so well that they impressed their character on their city, as the Germans did on Milwaukee. Most immigrants avoided the South, where they could not compete with the system of slavery.

The expansion of the U. S.

Early in the 1800s, much of North America that eventually became the U. S. was claimed, and sometimes was actually controlled, by one or another European county. Throughout the first half of the 19th century many

Americans continued to think of Great Britain as an implacable enemy, despite ties of language, commerce, and kinship. A recurring concern of American foreign policy was preventing European states from threatening American sovereignty, security, and prosperity. Of particular importance was the possibility that Great Britain or France would gain influence or outright possession of neighboring Spanish colonies. Ultimately, this goal found its best known expression in 1823 in the Monroe Doctrine, when President James Monroe declared that North and South America "are henceforth not to be considered as subject for future colonization by any European powers…" Gaining jurisdiction over additional territory and securing European acceptance and recognition would help achieve the desired security and remove external obstacles to American development.

After the Louisiana Purchase, the U. S. next acquired Florida. When, in 1810, a group in the far western end of the Florida panhandle, almost next door to New Orleans, rebelled against the Spanish and asked for annexation to the U. S., President James Madison welcomed them. Another piece of western Florida around Mobile was acquired in 1813. In 1818, U. S. General Andrew Jackson and his troops invaded East Florida. Jackson acted without official authorization, claiming he was trying to stop Seminole Indian raids on American settlements and trying to close a haven for escaped slaves. This military occupation put such pressure on Spain that in 1819 it agreed to the Transcontinental or Adams–Onis Treaty: in return for special trading status in Florida ports and U. S. assumption of Spanish debts to Americans, Spain ceded Florida to the U. S., settled the southwestern limit of the Louisiana Purchase along the Sabine, Red, and Arkansas rivers to the Rocky Mountains, capped Spain's territorial claims with the parallel of 42 degrees north latitude from the Rockies westward to the Pacific Ocean, and ceded Spain's relatively weak claim to the Oregon Country.

Both Great Britain and the U. S. had strong interests in the Oregon Country, a huge, imprecisely-defined region lying west of the Rocky Mountains and extending from Alaska to the northern limit of California. Many in the U. S. advocated trying to take all of Oregon north to the latitude of 54 degrees, 40 minutes. In 1818 Britain and the U. S. agreed that the boundary between the U.S. and British North America would run along the 49th parallel from the Lake of the Woods to the Rockies, thereby putting the northern fringe of the Louisiana Purchase into British hands and giving the upper drainage basin of the Red River of the north to the U.S. That same convention also said Oregon was to be administered jointly by the two countries for a period of ten years, an arrange-

ment that in 1827 was extended indefinitely. The Oregon question was settled for good in 1846 when the U. S. and Britain agreed to extend the boundary along the 49th parallel from the Rocky Mountains to the Pacific Ocean, except for Vancouver Island, which was to be all British. The U. S. president James K. Polk was criticized for not pressing the American claim to a more northern boundary, but to the south Polk was facing a war with Mexico, and he wanted to be rid of this nagging controversy. Small but long-standing disputes over details of the boundary with Maine and Lake Superior were settled in 1842. These northern boundary settlements opened the way for the westward expansion of settlement in both America and Canada.

Except for a relatively minor disagreement with the U. S. over the interpretation of the line around the islands at the southern tip of Vancouver Island, the Oregon agreement left Great Britain with unchallenged authority in what today is Canada. (An agreement with Russia had settled the Alaska boundary in 1825.) The land area of Canada (then called British North America) is 3,849,000 square miles, making it the largest nation in the western hemisphere. By 1860 the British had organized the area into a number of separate provinces: Vancouver Island, British Columbia, Canada (the St Lawrence and northern Great Lakes drainage basins), New Brunswick, Prince Edward Island, Nova Scotia, and Newfoundland (including the Labrador coast); in addition, in the northern and central area the Indian territory which was not in Rupert's Land (under the Hudson's Bay Company) nor in British Columbia was designated the Northwestern Territory and was placed under direct British rule. This

Below: "Terry's Texas Rangers," painted by Carl von Iwonski in 1845. The previous year, 15 Texas Rangers had launched an attack on 300 Comanche Indians, killing over half of them and severely intimidating the rest with their Colt six-shooters.

relatively stable territorial situation could only favor the expansion of settlement.

The war between Mexico and the U. S. erupted in 1846 following the American annexation of Texas, then an independent republic. Anglo-American settlers, recruited in the early 1820s after Mexico won its independence from Spain, formed the core of Texans who fought for their independence in 1836, and many of them desired annexation to the U. S. Annexation per se might not have ignited war with Mexico because Mexico had accepted the independence of Texas, but the U. S. accepted the Texans' version of their boundary with Mexico. Mexico steadfastly insisted that the boundary was the Nueces River, not the Rio Grande as claimed by Texas, and the difference was so great that war was all but inevitable.

Above: General Zachary Taylor defeats the Mexicans at Palo Alto in May 1846, when what had begun the previous month as a skirmish on the banks of the Rio Grande developed into a full-scale war which would last until the Treaty of Guadalupe Hidalgo in 1848. Mexico then renounced its claim to Texas and to present-day New Mexico and Upper California, and the U. S. gained vast tracts of land.

The Treaty of Guadalupe-Hidalgo ended the war in 1848; its provisions included establishment of the Texas line along the Rio Grande and also American payment of $15 million and other considerations for the enormous area lying between Texas and the Pacific shore and between the 42nd parallel and approximately the southern limit of California. With the Gadsden Purchase in 1853 (buying land for a southern transcontinental railroad route), the final boundaries of the U. S. (the area now known as the contiguous 48 states) were set.

American territorial expansion between 1810 and 1860 nearly doubled the area of the country. The absolute figures are noteworthy: the area of the original 13 states was about 889,000 square miles, the Louisiana Purchase of 1803 added 827,000 square miles, and the total net gain of territory from 1810 through 1853 was just over 1,300,000 square miles. By way of comparison, the land area of modern France is about 220,000 square miles,

modern Mexico is around 762,000 square miles, and the United Kingdom of Great Britain and Northern Ireland is around 94,000 square miles.

Some Euro-Americans did not wait for the Federal government to settle the issues of international jurisdiction before heading west in search of good sites for new settlement. Reports from missionaries to the Indians in the Pacific Northwest arrived in the East full of glowing praise for the rich farmland in the Willamette valley and helped spread what became known as "Oregon Fever." Adventurous families gathered their possessions and, starting in 1842, headed west from Independence, Missouri, in trains of wagons. The reports that drew settlers across the mountains were not so exaggerated that any significant number of pioneers complained that the hardships of the 2000-mile trip were too steep a price. Over the next few decades, until the 1870s when railroad trains replaced the wagon trains, the Oregon Trail was traveled by tens of thousands of migrants seeking new lives and good fortune in the Pacific Northwest.

Oregon's new farmers were squatters who had to provide their own order, and they wanted the benefits of regular governmental institutions and services. They petitioned Congress to organize a territorial government for Oregon, but Washington initially showed little interest Finally, in August 1848, after growing conflict between the new Oregonians and native Indians resulted in the deaths of over a dozen whites, the federal government delayed no longer and created Oregon Territory.

Utopia in the desert

The other large group that moved west beyond the limits of the Louisiana Purchase before the U. S. had secured sole jurisdiction of the region was the Mormons. Joseph Smith published *The Book of Mormon* in 1830 and shortly thereafter founded the Church of Christ, renamed in 1834 the Church of Jesus Christ of Latter-Day Saints. The Mormons did not own slaves, experimented with communal property ownership, and ignored many traditional standards of conduct; they usually were not popular with their mainstream neighbors and suffered considerable persecution. Their proselytizing was successful, however, and by 1840 there were almost 17,000 members. The Mormons' mission included converting Indians and establishing their city of Zion at some divinely appointed place. Smith and his growing band of followers moved from New York to Ohio, where they lived for a period in Kirtland, a community where the entire population had been converted by Mormon missionaries. Shortly afterward they moved on to Independence, Missouri, but in Missouri the Mormons were unable to

Mormon. The boundaries of Deseret took in the drainage basin of the Great Basin and extended to the Pacific coast approximately from Los Angeles to San Diego; a good overland road (which they improved) ran from the coast to Salt Lake City and the Mormons anticipated relatively heavy traffic by the immigrant converts whom their missionaries were winning in Europe.

Brigham Young and his followers did not pursue independent nationhood and, instead, after the Mexican War petitioned Washington for statehood in the American Union. The statehood campaign did not succeed, but in 1850 Utah Territory was established (eliminating the need for Deseret) and Young was named governor, an office he held until 1857.

For effect on population migration and settlement patterns, the California Gold Rush dwarfs the Mormon and Oregon movements. News of the 1848 gold strike spread fast, and from all over the world, tens of thousands of Forty-Niners broke away from their normal activities and headed for the gold fields on the west side of the Sierra Nevada Mountains. Many came overland, following the Oregon and Mormon trails to the Rockies and then, after crossing the continental divide at South Pass, turning southwestward along the California Trail to the Central Valley. Others traveled on ships, some sailing from Europe and the East Coast all the way around South America, while others went to Panama and then crossed the isthmus to catch another ship on the Pacific Ocean side. One measure of the impact of gold fever is the accompanying burst in U.S. immigration: 226,000 in 1848, 297,000 in 1849, 370,000 in 1850, and rising to 428,000 in 1854 before declining.

find toleration, let alone acceptance, and were driven away with great loss of property. The next move took them to Nauvoo, Illinois. Despite creating a near city-state in Nauvoo, Smith could neither avoid controversy nor escape the regular system of state and federal authority. Joseph Smith and his brother were arrested by Illinois officials and, while they were incarcerated at Carthage, Illinois, a mob stormed the jail and killed both men. Missionaries in other parts of the U. S., in Canada, and in Europe were increasingly successful in swelling the ranks of their brethren, but after Joseph Smith's murder, it was clear that the Mormons had to move again.

Of the many men who tried to take Smith's role, Brigham Young became Smith's successor. Under his leadership, during the summer of 1846 the Mormon population of Nauvoo, about 12,000, abandoned the place and headed westward across Iowa. From winter quarters at about the site of Omaha, Nebraska, Young set out the next summer with a small band and founded the Mormons' new home by the Great Salt Lake. The remaining Mormons joined the new settlement over the course of the next few years as the entire community worked at making the Great Basin a comfortable and fruitful home. By 1850 the church had 51,839 members on its rolls, more than 40 percent of them to be found in England, Canada, and other countries. Realizing they were beyond the official jurisdiction of the U. S. government and having little interest in again living under the authority of others who did not share their beliefs and values, the Mormons set about deliberately establishing their own theocratic state whose name, Deseret, they took from *The Book of*

Transport and technology

The remarkable spread of settlement in North America, especially the U. S., was helped greatly by changes in technology. In the field of transportation, the development of steamboats for river traffic was of high importance. They carried large loads at speeds many times greater than what had been possible with keel boats and barges, and they could power their way upstream against river currents. The opening of the Erie Canal, connecting Lake Erie and the Hudson River, was a revolutionary improvement over the roads and natural waterways that had been the means by which people traveled west and shipped agricultural produce and other materials to and from markets. One scholar has estimated that the Erie Canal cut travel time by almost 70 percent and cut costs by 90 percent from what they had been before the canal opened. The impact on what today is the Midwest was almost instantaneous, especially at the west end of Lake

Erie around Detroit where the population seemed to explode. New York City, which was perfectly situated at the mouth of the Hudson, became the nation's shipping center and, as a sort of natural corollary, the principal destination of immigrants who wanted to make their way westward. New Englanders suddenly found westward travel relatively easy and cheap, and many moved into the states of the Old Northwest—Ohio, Indiana, Illinois—which in turn yielded a northern, anti-slavery dominance of the region.

Canal fever spread rapidly throughout the country, but struck most heavily in Pennsylvania and Ohio. It became possible to move people and goods from Buffalo or Albany to Philadelphia or Pittsburgh or Baltimore by boat. Ohio created several canals that linked Lake Erie with the Ohio River and, along the way, opened much of the interior of that state to direct canal connections. Crossing the Appalachians was difficult, however, and the trip from Philadelphia to Pittsburgh entailed a short trip over the mountains on a railroad. Except for the Erie, most canal projects were not financial successes. The Canal Era did not last long because the railroad followed close behind. The first two railroads in the U. S., short lines at a mine and a quarry, started operation in 1826, only a year after the Erie Canal opened. By 1840 the total trackage in America was nearly 3000 miles, almost twice the miles of track that could be found in all of Europe. By 1860 railroads in America were still concentrated east of the Mississippi River, where more than 30,000 miles of track had been laid.

The beginnings of the industrial factory system—particularly textile mills in Massachusetts—increased jobs and signalled a future direction of the economy. Of equal importance were some technological breakthroughs in agriculture. Starting in 1837 John Deere's self-polishing plow transformed plowing the rich but sticky prairie soil into a manageable task. In 1832 Cyrus McCormick demonstrated his reaper, which greatly facilitated the harvest, but it did not actually go into production until the 1840s. Together, the new plow and the reaper made farming on a commercial scale in the near west an attractive prospect and practically guaranteed that the land would draw and sustain a heavy influx of new settlers.

The most significant technological development of all during this period was probably the cotton gin, invented in 1793 by Eli Whitney. Being able to separate the cotton fibers from the seeds and husks quickly and efficiently made cotton a potentially important commercial crop. The timing was almost perfect, for the gin's appearance coincided with the rise of the cotton cloth industry in England. The impulse to expand the cultivation of cotton to its maximum had widespread consequences: it con-

Above: "Wooding Up" on the Mississippi in 1863. Steamboats had been proved commercially viable as early as 1807, and by 1830 dominated the Arkansas, Mississippi, Missouri, Ohio, and Red rivers, playing an essential part in the opening up of the West. Their reign was destined to be brief, however, as railroads came to challenge their ascendancy

tributed to the displacement and removal of the Cherokees, Choctaws, and other southern Indians who occupied land that was just right for cotton; it injected new life into the southern slave system; and it produced a major shift in where southerners, especially African-American slaves, lived and worked, from Virginia and the other southeastern states to a deep southern band from East Texas to the Georgia coast. In the 1830s, when the Indians were removed from the area, Alabama and Mississippi experienced phenomenal growth: Alabama's population increased 90 percent from 309,527 in 1830 to 590,756 in 1840, while Mississippi grew 175 percent from 136,621 to 375,651; during the same decade Virginia experienced a 1.8 percent loss of population. Eventually, cotton became the country's most important commercial crop, for both export and domestic processing, and slaves became the most valuable type of property in the South.

The conflict over slavery

In 1832 the Virginia legislature responded to Nat Turner's bloody rebellion in part by conducting a long debate on the effects of slavery, which was followed by votes on a number of emancipation and anti-slavery proposals, including one to provide for the gradual abolition of slavery in the state, all of which were defeated. For many, these debates signify a turning point in the South's attitude. It was not long before southerners developed positive arguments in defense of slavery, and the slave states enacted tighter slave codes, set new restrictions on free African-Americans, and erected new legal barriers to emancipation and manumission.

In addition to their arguments against the institution,

opponents of slavery tried a variety of measures to free slaves. Many northern states passed personal liberty laws meant to obstruct and thwart the national fugitive slave law, but none were very successful. By 1860 the American Colonization Society, founded in 1817 in Richmond, Virginia, to emancipate slaves and "return" them to Africa, had managed to send about 12,000 to Sierra Leone and Liberia (founded by the society in 1822), but it suffered a sharp decline in support in the early 1830s. Probably the most effective was the Underground Railroad, whose participants helped as many as 50,000 slaves escape to Canada between 1830 and 1860. Nearly all of the "conductors" on the Underground Railroad were free blacks. Despite these successes, the numbers seem tiny compared to the size of the enslaved population: according to the U. S. Census, in 1860 American slaveholders "owned" approximately 4 million black men, women, and children.

As the years passed, slavery infected nearly every issue touching the organization of new states and territories and the expansion of settlement. For example, many of the Anglo-Americans who colonized Texas in the 1820s brought slaves with them, contrary to Mexican law, and the possibility that British agents might persuade Mexico to enforce its ban on slavery had prompted many early demands for American annexation of Texas. The creation of territorial governments and the admission of new states in the 1840s and 1850s became more and more difficult and complicated as it became impossible to avoid the issue of restricting slavery or letting it grow and spread into new regions.

The rise of nativism

The 1830s also saw the rise of nativism. This was aimed especially at Roman Catholics, and has been attributed to negative reaction to Catholic missionaries from Europe and to the steady flow of immigrants from places such as Ireland. In the 1850s the Know-Nothing party, which was chiefly an anti-Catholic and anti-immigrant political party, temporarily attained national standing. The common complaint of the native-born, white Protestants who were the usual members of nativist groups was that Catholics could not sustain the American republican form of democratic government because it required an electorate of virtuous, educated, and independent citizens, while Catholics were superstitious, ignorant, and controlled by their priests. Nativist opposition to continued heavy immigration was not very effective until the late 19th century.

Settlers and Indians

As non-Indians, both immigrant and native-born, continued to push westward, the inevitable conflicts with the various tribes of Indians grew in frequency and intensity. The U. S. officially recognized Indian tribes as autonomous entities with a right to the soil by original occupancy, but the government also tried to buy as much land from the Indians as it could and to move them out of the way of the unstoppable flood of settlers from the East. The government adopted a policy of removal, aiming to buy the lands of eastern Indians and then to relocate them to areas west of the Mississippi where they would be out of the way and could be protected from unscrupulous whites. The "Trail of Tears," as the forced removal of the Cherokees in 1838 is known because of the harsh conditions and treatment inflicted on the Indians, became a symbol of white injustice towards the Indian. The Federal Government's position and policy, bad as they may have been, were mild compared to what some civilian groups of non-Indians attempted. More and more whites came to see Indians as wild savages who did not, and would not, make full and efficient use of the land (i.e., farm it in the white man's fashion), and they also came to reject the idea of any Indian rights to the land.

In Texas, a number of local whites tried to exterminate or drive away all the Indians in the state. In one instance, Robert S. Neighbors, the federal Indian agent, feared the worst after a series of white attacks on reservation Indians and led a group of Indians north out of one of the federal reservations in Texas into the Indian territory that would become Oklahoma. Not long afterward, Neighbors was gunned down by a white man angered by the agent's assistance to the Indians. In Oregon, the native Indians hardly welcomed the pioneers from the Oregon Trail, and there were bloody clashes between whites and Indians over who would occupy the rich soil of the Willamette valley. In California, as in Texas, there was a concerted effort to kill all resident Indians. The overall, unsurprising result was a steep decline in Indian population and the displacement of tribes both in the East and, in reaction to the influx of emigrant Indians from the East, in the West. Through 1860 the development of new technologies in agriculture, manufacturing, and transportation, and the stabilization of international boundaries set the stage for future developments in the settlement of the continent. Increasing controversy and conflict over the nature of immigration, the future of slavery, and Indian-white relations promised that those future developments would not be easy or peaceful.

TIMELINE
1815–60

NORTH AMERICA	THE CARIBBEAN, CENTRAL & S. AMERICA	EUROPE, AFRICA, & ASIA

1816 Selkirk incident in Red River valley, Canada, where settlers and Métis clash over farmland. Indiana becomes State of the Union

1815 Brazil elevated to equal status with Portugal. Spanish troops under Pablo Morillo land in Colombia and attempt to suppress independence movement with campaign of terror

1816 Famine in Germany and Ireland

1817 Mississippi becomes a State of the Union. James Monroe becomes U.S. president

1817–18 First Seminole War: Andrew Jackson invades Spanish Florida

1818 Illinois becomes a State of the Union

1818 Simón Bolívar returns to South America from exile in the Caribbean

1818 Peasants' Revolt in Norway

1819–24 Kickapoo resist removal from Illinois Country

1819 U.S. purchases Florida from Spain

1819 Simón Bolívar defeats Spanish at Boyacú, Colombia

1820–22 Liberal uprising in Spain

1820 Maine becomes a State of the Union. Missouri Compromise maintains balance between free and slave states

1820 British King George III dies

1821 Alabama and Missouri become States of the Union

1821 Mexico becomes independent under Agustín de Iturbide. San Martín takes Lima, Peru. By 1826 all Spanish colonies on the American mainland win independence

1821 Greek War of Independence from Turkey begins

1822 Plans for slave uprising in Charleston discovered; 35 African-Americans hanged and strict system of slave control imposed in South

1822 Pedro I, son of Portuguese King, becomes emperor of an independent Brazil. Quito, Ecuador, liberated from Spain at Battle of Pichincha. Haitians under General Boyer occupy Santo Domingo

1822 State of Liberia established in West Africa as a national home for freed slaves from America. Red Star Line begins regular monthly sailings from Liverpool to New York

1823 Monroe Doctrine declares America and Europe to be separate political spheres and proclaims non-intervention

1823 Iturbide flees Mexico after proclaiming himself emperor

1823 French army restores Bourbon monarchy in Spain

1824 Battle of Ayacucho: decisive victory of South American republicans over Spanish colonial forces. Iturbide returns to Mexico, but is shot; Estados Unidos Mexicanos organized

1825 Opening of Erie Canal
John Quincy Adams becomes U.S. president

1825 Decembrist uprising provokes autocratic clampdown in Russia

1827 Publication of *Freedom's Journal*, the first black newspaper to be published in the U.S. Winnebago uprising in Wisconsin

1827 Turks defeated at Battle of Navarino

1829 Andrew Jackson becomes U.S. president

1829 Venezuela breaks away from Republic of Gran Colombia

1830 U.S. Congress passes Indian Removal Act

1830 Ecuador breaks away from Republic of Gran Colombia. Mexican colonization law bans further immigration into Texas

1830 July Revolution in France replaces Bourbon king with constitutional monarchy. Polish uprising against Russian rule crushed. Greece and Serbia achieve autonomy from Turkish empire. Belgium becomes independent of the Netherlands

1830–40 French conquer Algiers

1831 Santa Ana begins first of six terms as president of Mexico. Slave revolt in Jamaica

1832 Duchy of Warsaw incorporated into Russia

1832 Black Hawk's War. Removal of southeastern tribes (the "Trail of Tears")

1835–37 Toledo War (Ohio and Michigan Boundary War) breaks out among settlers

1835–42 Second Seminole War

1835 Population growth in Republic of Texas

1836 Arkansas becomes a State of the Union. Texas gains independence from Mexico

1837 Michigan becomes a State of the Union. Martin Van Buren becomes U.S. president

1837 Queen Victoria succeeds to British throne

NORTH AMERICA

THE CARIBBEAN, CENTRAL & S. AMERICA

EUROPE, AFRICA, & ASIA

1838 First regular transatlantic steamship service

1838–39 Cherokees relocated (Trail of Tears)

1841 John Tyler becomes U.S. president

1843 Russian Orthodox church establishes mission school for Alaska Inuit

1845 U.S. annexation of Texas leads to war with Mexico. Florida and Texas become States of the Union. James Knox Polk becomes U.S. president

1846 U.S. forces capture Los Angeles from Mexico. Iowa becomes a State of the Union. Britain cedes Oregon Country to U.S.

1847 Mormon settlers found Salt Lake City

1847–54 1.6 million Irish migrate to U.S. Some 6000 die of typhus and dysentery at the quarantine station on Grosse Isle, Canada

1848 U.S. conquers Mexican territory to Rio Grande. Nova Scotia is the first colony of British North America to achieve "responsible government." Gold discovered in California. Wisconsin becomes a State of the Union

1849 California Gold Rush. Courthouse rebellion of Métis in Canada's Red River valley. Zachary Taylor becomes U.S. president

1850 California becomes a State of the Union. Mariposa War between miners and California Indians. Clay Compromise restricts spread of slavery in new states. Millard Fillmore becomes U.S. president

1853 Gadsden Purchase of land in southern Arizona from Mexico completes U.S. mainland territorial acquisitions. Franklin Pierce becomes U.S. president

1854 Opening of Great Northern Railway in Canada. Kansas–Nebraska Act liquidates northern part of Indian territory and creates state of Kansas and territory of Nebraska

1855 Ottawa becomes Canada's capital by royal decree

1855–58 Third Seminole War in Florida

1857 Supreme Court rules Missouri Compromise unconstitutional in Dredd Scott case. James Buchanan becomes U.S. president

1858 Minnesota becomes a State of the Union. Colorado Gold Rush

1859 Oregon becomes a State of the Union

1860 British government transfers control of Indian affairs to Canada

1838 Slaves freed in British Caribbean islands

1843 Haitian leader Boyer ousted in coup

1844 Dominicans drive out Haitian forces and reestablish republic

1845 Mexican president Santa Ana declares war on U.S. over annexation of Texas

1847 Mexican army under Santa Ana defeated by U.S. at Buena Vista; U.S. forces occupy Mexico City

1850 Importation of slaves abolished in Brazil

1855 Santa Ana retires as president of Mexico for the last time and goes into exile

1857–60 Liberal constitution in Mexico sparks Civil War

1858 Benito Juarez elected president of Mexico

1839 British parliament rejects first Chartist petition

1840–42 Opium War between Britain and China

1842 British parliament rejects second Chartist petition

1845 Marx and Engels write *Communist Manifesto*

1845–8 Potato blight leads to severe famine in Ireland.

1846 Corn Laws repealed in Britain

1848 Year of revolutions throughout Europe. French monarchy overthrown; Second Republic proclaimed with Louis Napoleon (nephew of Napoleon Bonaparte) as president

1849 Proclamation of republic in Tuscany and Rome marks beginning of Italian unification movement

1851 Military uprising in Portugal

1852 Louis Napoleon proclaimed Emperor Napoleon III in France. Chinese workers recruited to work on sugar plantations in Hawaii

1853 Japan opened to Western trade

1853–56 Crimean War

1857 Indian Mutiny; British East India Company dissolved; India put under rule of British viceroy. French begin conquest of Indochina (Vietnam). Britain and France at war in China

THE CALL OF THE WEST

NORTH AMERICA, c. 1830

North America's non-Indian population was on the threshold of another spurt of expansion in 1830, aided by road and canal building, and the beginning of steam navigation.

From 1810 to 1830 the U. S. population of European descent swelled from 7,224,000 to 12,901,000. During the same period, the population of British North America doubled, although the total number of inhabitants was still less than a million. Only 213,000 of them lived in Upper Canada west of Montreal, with an isolated population of about 600 in the Red River district around present-day Winnipeg. The Euro-American population west of the Appalachians continued to expand. To accommodate the settlers, more land was acquired from Indian tribes through land sale treaties. Indians were also removed from briefly-held reservations north of the Ohio River, and driven from large areas in the south (> *pages 90–1*).

Water transport was still the key to reaching new homes in new lands. The construction of a canal around the falls of the Ohio River between 1825 and 1830 boosted both the river traffic and the local population to make Cincinnati the eighth largest city in the U.S. in 1830. The opening of the Erie Canal, connecting Hudson River at Albany with Lake Erie,

An emigrant who is rich may settle near a large town, find society, libraries, and a great many comforts. If he does not object to holding slaves, Kentucky offers him great advantages. But if he is not rich, or is ambitious, the Illinois and Missouri territories, and… Alabama country, will hold out advantages that will pay him for all sacrifices.

Elias Pym Fordham,
Letter from Illinois, 1818

spurred people on to the western country, shifting the main flow of settlers north from the old Ohio River route. A canal system for Ohio was constructed to connect with Lake Erie, as a continuation of the new transportation artery. Between 1825 and 1842, 1000 miles of canals were built in Ohio, mostly by Irish immigrant laborers. These canals connected ports in Upper Canada as well as the U. S. with the Ohio–Mississippi River route to New Orleans.

Adventurous people from New York and New England used the Erie Canal and Lake Erie vessels to reach Detroit, the launching point for overland travel toward newly opened land

around Chicago. Close to 84,000 people flocked into southern Michigan between 1831 and 1834. The year 1826 marked the peak for sales of government land, bought from Indians at two cents an acre and sold to settlers and developers for $1.25 an acre. The road west from Detroit, begun in 1827, at first used by stagecoaches twice a week, was soon traveled four times a day. The road struck the shore of Lake Michigan near the present-day Indiana-Michigan stateline, and followed the lakes' beach to Chicago.

The three large blocks of land still held by southern Indians in 1830 were soon acquired, and these rich agricultural lands became available for the expansion of plantation agriculture (> *pages 92–3*). But at this time, few North Americans envisioned a dense population beyond the Mississippi valley. Canada's area of settlement was still confined to a narrow band, and government efforts to purchase blocks of land adjoining Lakes Huron and Superior were not undertaken until 1855. A scattered population of fur traders, European, and *métis*, continued to share the land in Indian country. But the fur trade was on the decline as a result of heavy harvesting of animal skins in previous decades.

2: The Ohio canal system, 1825—42

— canal built, 1825—42
---- canal proposed but not built
▨ land granted by Federal Government for canal building

Below: settlers travel along the Ohio River in a flatboat with their possessions and merchandise. During the 1830s, the construction of a canal network in Ohio and the development of the paddle steamer gradually superseded this method of transport.

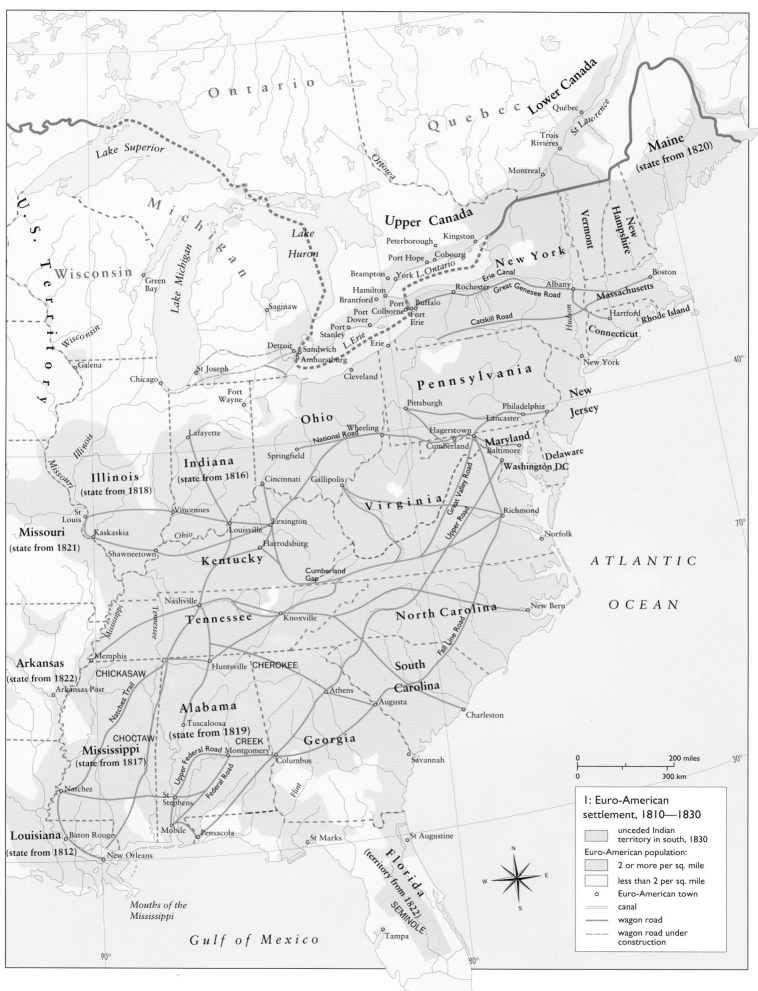

Ontario

Quebec

Lower Canada

Québec

St Lawrence

Trois Riviéres

Maine
(state from 1820)

Montreal

Lake Superior

U.S. Territory

Lake Michigan

Michigan

Lake Huron

Upper Canada

Vermont

New Hampshire

Wisconsin

Green Bay

Saginaw

Peterborough   Kingston

Port Hope   Cobourg

New York

Boston

Massachusetts

Wisconsin

St Joseph

Chicago

Detroit

Sandwich
Amhurstburg

Galena

Fort Wayne

Lafayette

Springfield

Indiana
(state from 1816)

Cincinnati

Gallipolis

Ohio

Brampton   York L.Ontario

Hamilton

Brantford

Port Colborne
Dover

Port Stanley

Cleveland

Erie

L. Erie

Wheeling

Rochester   Erie Canal

Great Genesee Road

Catskill Road

Albany

Hudson

Hartford

Connecticut

Rhode Island

New York

Pennsylvania

Pittsburgh

Philadelphia

Lancaster

New Jersey

National Road

Hagerstown
Cumberland

Maryland

Baltimore

Delaware

Washington DC

Buffalo
Fort Erie

Illinois
(state from 1818)

St Louis

Kaskaskia

Missouri
(state from 1821)

Shawneetown

Missouri

Illinois

Vincennes

Ohio

Louisville

Harrodsburg

Lexington

Kentucky

Cumberland Gap

Great Valley Road

Upper Road

Virginia

Richmond

Norfolk

70°

ATLANTIC

OCEAN

Nashville

Tennessee

Knoxville

North Carolina

New Bern

40°

Arkansas
(state from 1822)

Memphis

CHICKASAW

Huntsville   CHEROKEE

Natchez Trail

Arkansas Post

Alabama
(state from 1819)

Tuscaloosa

CHOCTAW

Mississippi
(state from 1817)

CREEK

Upper Federal Road   Montgomery

St Stephens

Natchez

Federal Road

Louisiana
(state from 1812)

Baton Rouge

Mobile

New Orleans

Pensacola

Flint

Georgia

Columbus

Fall Line Road

South Carolina

Athens

Augusta

Savannah

Charleston

St Marks

St Augustine

Florida
(territory from 1822)

SEMINOLE

Tampa

Mouths of the Mississippi

Gulf of Mexico

90°   80°   30°

200 miles

0

0   300 km

I: Euro-American
settlement, 1810—1830

unceded Indian
territory in south, 1830

Euro-American population:

2 or more per sq. mile

less than 2 per sq. mile

○ Euro-American town

canal

wagon road

wagon road under
construction

N
W   E
S

TRAILS OF TEARS AND DEATH
INDIAN RELOCATION, 1829–40

The removal of 60,000 southern Indians to lands west of the Mississippi in the 1830s is a tragic story of uprooted peoples. At the same time, some 10,000 living around the southern Great Lakes were also moved west.

The idea of moving Indians beyond the Mississippi where, it was then presumed, American people would never want to settle, had been in the minds of Federal administrators since the early 19th century. The U. S. government erected a line of forts from Fort Snelling in Minnesota (1819) to Fort Jesup (1842) in western Louisiana to prevent white encroachment on Indian lands and subdue inter-tribal hostilities. During removal the garrisons also took charge of distributing provisions and helping Indian immigrants settle in their newly assigned territory. Western Indians clearly resented the intrusion of eastern tribes into their country.

Measures to transfer Indians across the Mississippi became far more aggressive after 1830 when the Indian Removal Bill was narrowly passed to appease the inexorable demands, particularly of Southerners, to acquire Indian land. Through questionable "treaties," the five major tribes in the southern U. S. "sold" about 100 million acres of their tribal estates for $68 million and 32 million acres in present Oklahoma, to which they were required to move according to a schedule using a variety of routes. The first to leave were contingents of Choctaws. Collected in holding camps, they marched to Memphis in the fall of 1831 for the river crossing. By the spring of 1834, they were able to assemble a total of about 13 or 14 thousand of their people in the Red River district. About 7000 were left behind in Mississippi, the wealthy through political influence and the impoverished largely because they were in debt. Emigrating Creeks from Alabama and Georgia suffered heavy losses when a steamship sank, but successfully transferred 14,500 to the Canadian River country.

The Chickasaws, who had a significant plantation-owning elite, enrolled 4000 for removal.

They were congregated in holding camps and marched to Memphis beginning in October 1837. Their better financed expeditions managed to cross the Mississippi with less suffering. With them they had their slaves and 4 or 5 thousand horses. Altogether, the five "civilized" tribes owned about 8000 enslaved African-American at the time of removal.

Although they had established a constitutional government, applied for admission as a state, and secured the legal support of a favorable Supreme Court decision, 16,000 Cherokees were nevertheless rounded by in surprise raids and marched west at bayonet point in 1838, burying about a quarter of their population along the trail. About a thousand escaped removal by fleeing to the mountains of North Carolina, where they eventually acquired their own reservation. Surviving stories include heart-breaking account of walking barefoot and without blankets during cold and stormy weather, and deaths from disease and hunger.

Close to 3000 Seminoles, the smallest of the five southern tribes being removed, eventually went to Oklahoma. Several hundred more held out in the Florida Everglades, despite U.S. Army expenditure of $20 million to dislodge them during seven years of campaigns.

The removal experience of northern Indians was less severe. The westward emigration of Indians from the southern Great Lakes region had been under way since the 1780s. In cooperation with Spanish authorities at St Louis, Delaware, Shawnee, and Cherokee veterans of frontier warfare on the Ohio River led the movement into Upper Louisiana. By later American treaties, in 1818 and 1819, Delaware and Kickapoo from Indiana and Illinois agreed to relocate further west around modern Kansas City, Kansas. In the early 1830s, a few hundred each of Seneca, Shawnee, and Ottawa vacated their reservations in northwestern Ohio. These were all just small segments of tribes with principal locations in other places. In an exception to the general pattern of removal, the Seneca were assigned to a portion of the country which had been designated for the Cherokee but not yet occupied by them.

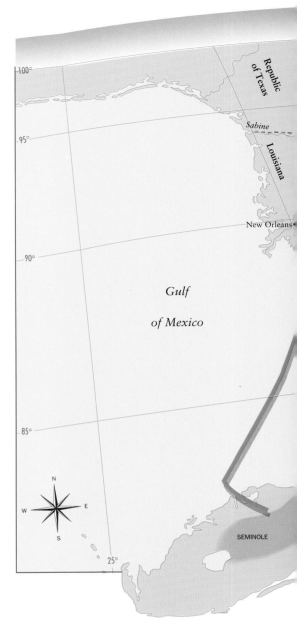

The painter George Winter lived among the Potawatomis from 1837 to 1839, when part of the tribe was removed to the west. He made portraits of many individuals, whose personalities are vividly recalled in his diaries, and recorded scenes of daily life. Here, the women cook, chop wood and fetch water while the men hunt, sleep and seek recreation. The Potawatomi, who had long been in contact with French traders, were a prosperous tribe; their brightly colored clothes were made of high quality European fabrics.

The Potawatomi, numbering about 9000 and spread around the base of Lake Michigan and into the Indiana-Michigan border zone, resisted migration. About 2000 from northwestern Indiana were the only bands forcibly removed. Probably half of the removed Potawatomi were soon back in Wisconsin and Michigan; another 2000 fled to Canada. The rest initially moved to land set aside in western Iowa. The Miami delayed departure from their Wabash River homeland in Indiana; they had signed a treaty in 1838 that enabled some to remain. Last to give up their reservations in "The Old Northwest" were the Wyandots of Ohio and southeastern Michigan who nevertheless signed a treaty in 1842 and carried out their own removal the following year. Finding no acceptable land unoccupied in Kansas, they purchased from the Delaware a tract at the confluence of the Missouri and Kansas rivers.

The initial removals of the northern tribes were only temporary bases. Because of increasing traffic up the Missouri River and across the plains, Federal authorities transferred Indian people out of the corridor, shifting them several times during the next decades toward a concentration in present Oklahoma. Despite the removal program, thousands of Indians remained in the region east of the Mississippi.

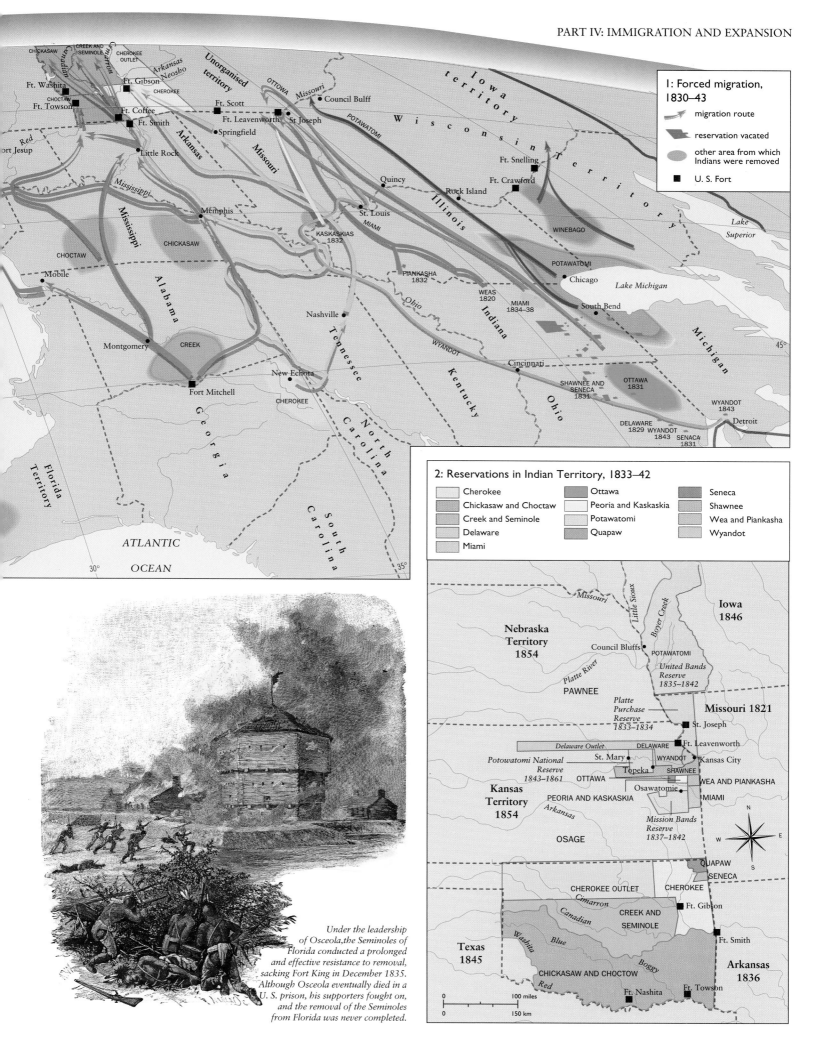

1: Forced migration, 1830–43

→ migration route

▰ reservation vacated

⬤ other area from which Indians were removed

■ U. S. Fort

2: Reservations in Indian Territory, 1833–42

- Cherokee
- Chickasaw and Choctaw
- Creek and Seminole
- Delaware
- Miami
- Ottawa
- Peoria and Kaskaskia
- Potawatomi
- Quapaw
- Seneca
- Shawnee
- Wea and Piankasha
- Wyandot

Under the leadership of Osceola, the Seminoles of Florida conducted a prolonged and effective resistance to removal, sacking Fort King in December 1835. Although Osceola eventually died in a U. S. prison, his supporters fought on, and the removal of the Seminoles from Florida was never completed.

THE COTTON KINGDOM EXPANDS
THE MOVEMENT OF AFRICAN-AMERICANS IN THE SOUTH, 1830–60

Technological innovation and the demand for cotton gave a massive boost to the plantation economy of the South, and saw the growing population of African-Americans expand to the west.

Above: the cotton gin, invented by Eli Whitney in 1793, made it possible to separate cotton fibers from other parts of the plant many times faster than was possible by hand. The machine gave slavery a new lease of life; once cotton could be processed in industrial quantities, it had to be produced in industrial quantities too.

Ironic as it may seem, the acceleration of the Industrial Revolution in Britain was a powerful force driving both the removal of Indians from land east of the Mississippi River and the expansion of slavery in the southern U. S. The key was the world's insatiable demand for cotton cloth, which England's textile mills strived to fill throughout the first half of the 19th century. American farmers in the South began to produce cotton for export to England soon after the invention of the cotton gin at the end of the 18th century. Except for a few years around the economic panics of 1819 and 1837, the market for cotton grew steadily right through the American Civil War. In 1802 the U. S. exported $6 million in tobacco, long the country's leading commercial crop, and only $5 million in cotton. By 1830 cotton exports were worth $30 million while tobacco remained at $6 million; by 1860 the figures were $192 million and $16 million respectively. As early as the 1840s, the U. S. was producing three quarters of the world's cotton.

This explosion of production would have been impossible without expanding the area under cultivation. Cotton growing started in the upcountry of South Carolina and Georgia, then spread south and west. Pressure was put on the federal government to open Indian land to the profitable crop. The Chickasaws, Choctaws, Cherokees and Creeks were removed from northern Mississippi, Alabama, and Georgia in the 1830s (>pages 90–1), and little time was lost before their territories were being worked for cotton. The annexation of Texas as a slave state in 1845 appeared to provide a natural extension of the productive land beyond the Mississippi.

More than suitable land and technology was required to create the phenomenon known as King Cotton. That other ingredient was the slave labor force that was exploited to clear and cultivate the enormous Cotton Kingdom that eventually stretched across the South from South Carolina to east Texas. Cotton could be grown on small farms—unlike rice and sugar, the other labor-intensive crops cultivated by slave labor—but large-scale production had important advantages. Cotton needs attention most of the year, and many tasks such as weeding and picking could be performed by specialized gangs of men and women. On a large plantation, the older and less fit slaves could tend livestock, work on food crops, or care for chil-

dren. Industrial-style agriculture was also practiced in the rice plantations of South Carolina and in the rice and sugar delta of Louisiana, but by 1860 these crops enjoyed neither the demand nor the vast acreage of suitable land that propelled cotton to the forefront of the economy.

Although relatively few Africans were brought to North America after Congress made illegal the international slave trade in 1808, the total number of people in bondage grew from a little over 2 million in 1830 to nearly 4 million in 1860, the natural result of more births than deaths within the African-American population. The Cotton Kingdom absorbed that phenomenal population growth, and thrived on it. Slave labor made a high level of prosperity attainable from a single cash crop, cotton. Slaves made up the majority of the population in the most successful cotton-growing areas, and became the principal form of wealth in the South: the average slaveholder was ten times richer than the average non-slaveholder.

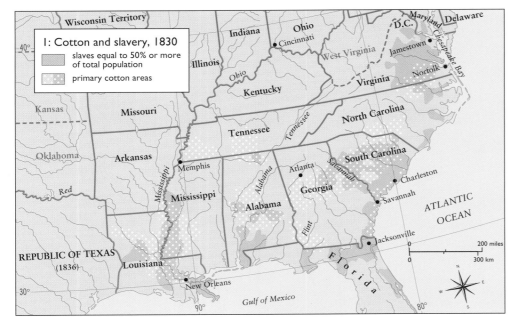

1: Cotton and slavery, 1830

- slaves equal to 50% or more of total population
- primary cotton areas

I t was the cotton interest that gave a new desire to promote slavery, to spread it, and to use its labor.

Daniel Webster, 1850

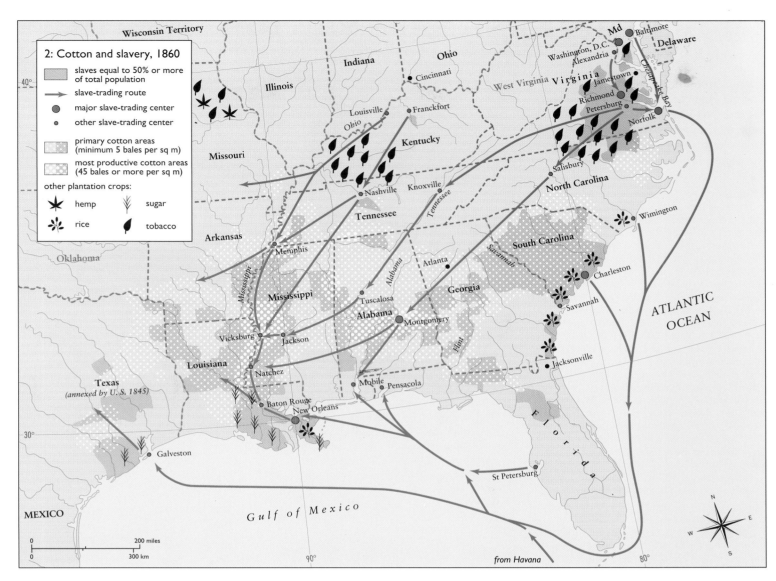

2: Cotton and slavery, 1860

slaves equal to 50% or more of total population

→ slave-trading route

● major slave-trading center

• other slave-trading center

primary cotton areas (minimum 5 bales per sq m)

most productive cotton areas (45 bales or more per sq m)

other plantation crops:

✴ hemp   ⚜ sugar

✳ rice   🍃 tobacco

Right: a cotton-growing plantation on the Mississippi. As the demand for cotton increased, plantation farming became organized on "production line" principles, with specialized labor gangs allotted to specific tasks.

FROM FAMINE AND PERSECUTION
MIGRANTS FROM WESTERN AND NORTHERN EUROPE, 1815–60

Famine and political repression in Europe after the end of the Napoleonic Wars in 1815 began a new period of mass migration that culminated in the great exodus from Ireland that followed the potato blight of the late 1840s.

Many people emigrated to North America from areas where high birth rates had caused overpopulation. In southwest Germany, where agriculture had been devastated by the fighting and where the division of land between heirs had fragmented holdings, a severe famine developed in the winter of 1816–7. In Ireland, an agricultural slump, aggravated by a poor harvest in 1816, led 20,000 people to emigrate in 1818. Political persecution also drove people to leave, as reactionary régimes were reestablished across Europe in the wake of Napoleon's defeat. Agrarian unrest in Ireland was met by increasingly repressive legislation. Irish migration to North America was encouraged by a liberalization in attitudes to Catholics, and by cheap transatlantic fares: £3.10s from Liverpool in 1831. Between 1831 and 1841, almost 200,000 people left Ireland for Canada; many of these went on to the U. S., while a further 20,000 traveled there directly. By 1843, Jesuit missionaries in Montreal were relying on recently arrived Irish Catholics to guard their missions from the Indians, who had burned a mission on Walpole Island near Detroit.

The late 1840s brought a new wave of migration. The revolutions that occurred all over Europe in 1848 led to a political crackdown that forced many people into exile. Among those fleeing Europe in 1848–9 were German, Czech, and

T he passengers were sealed below... Three blinking lanterns... gave enough light to make out the ghostly forms of the hundreds of passengers in various states of trying to bed down in bunks or on the floor. The rolling and creaking of the ship in the storm was frightening. The stench from refuse and excreta was nauseating. I wondered how the people could possibly survive six or eight weeks when it was this bad after about two days.

Gerald Keegan, *Famine Diary*, 1847

Above: in Ireland, evictions continued throughout the famine years. This 1848 engraving from the Illustrated London News *shows a landlord evicting a tenant and his family while their cottage is destroyed. British soldiers stand by to quell any protest. An estimated 30,000 families were evicted during the famine years of 1845–8.*

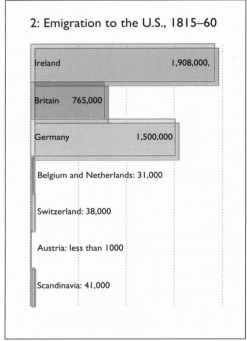

2: Emigration to the U.S., 1815–60

Ireland	1,908,000,
Britain	765,000
Germany	1,500,000
Belgium and Netherlands: 31,000	
Switzerland: 38,000	
Austria: less than 1000	
Scandinavia: 41,000	

1: Causes of emigration 1815–60

- low population growth
- high population growth
- famine
- revolution
- Chartist movement
- migration routes

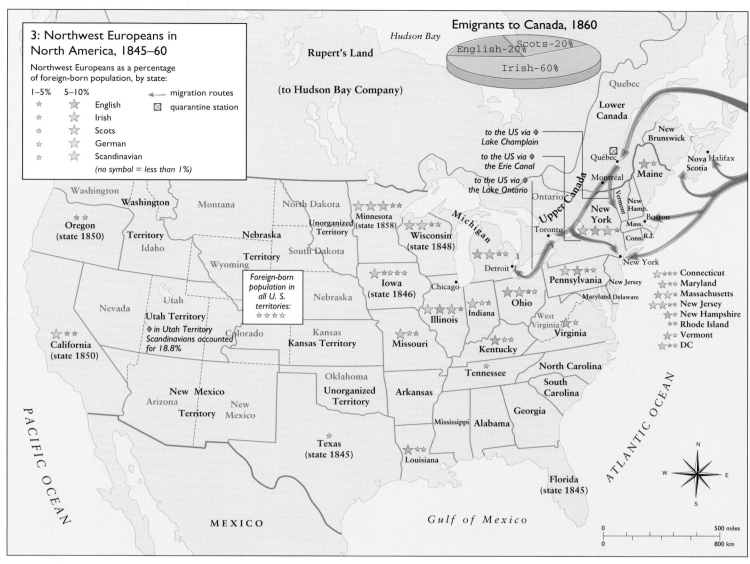

3: Northwest Europeans in North America, 1845–60

Northwest Europeans as a percentage of foreign-born population, by state:

1–5%	5–10%		
☆	★	English	← migration routes
☆	★	Irish	⊠ quarantine station
☆	★	Scots	
☆	★	German	
☆	★	Scandinavian	
		(no symbol = less than 1%)	

Emigrants to Canada, 1860

English–20% Scots–20%
Irish–60%

Hudson Bay

Rupert's Land

(to Hudson Bay Company)

Quebec

Lower Canada

to the US via ◇
Lake Champlain

to the US via ◇
the Erie Canal

to the US via ◇
the Lake Ontario

New Brunswick

⊠ Québec

Nova Scotia Halifax

Montreal

★★ Maine

Ontario

Upper Canada

Washington

Washington

Montana

North Dakota

★★★★★

Minnesota (state 1858)

Michigan

Toronto

New Hamp.

Vermont

New York

Boston

★★ Oregon (state 1850)

Territory

Idaho

Nebraska

Unorganized Territory

★★★★

★★★★ Wisconsin (state 1848)

★★ New York

Mass.

Territory

Wyoming

South Dakota

Detroit

★★★ Pennsylvania

Conn. R.I.

Foreign-born population in all U. S. territories:
★★★★

Nevada

Utah

★★★★ Iowa (state 1846)

Chicago

★★★ Indiana

Ohio

New Jersey

New York

Utah Territory

◇ *in Utah Territory Scandinavians accounted for 18.8%*

Colorado

Nebraska

Illinois

West Virginia

★★ Virginia

Maryland Delaware

★★★ California (state 1850)

Kansas

★★ Missouri

★★ Kentucky

☆★★★	Connecticut
★★★	Maryland
★★★	Massachusetts
★★★	New Jersey
★★	New Hampshire
★★	Rhode Island
★★	Vermont
★★★	DC

New Mexico

Arizona Territory

New Mexico

Kansas Territory

Oklahoma Unorganized Territory

Arkansas

☆ Tennessee

North Carolina

South Carolina

Georgia

Mississippi Alabama

★ Texas (state 1845)

★★★ Louisiana

MEXICO

Florida (state 1845)

Gulf of Mexico

PACIFIC OCEAN

ATLANTIC OCEAN

N W E S

0	500 miles
0	800 km

Hungarian democrats and Chartist labor reformers from Britain. In Ireland, a fungus that destroyed the potato crops led to the terrible famine of 1845–8. The sheer number of emigrants—more than 85,000 in 1847 alone—meant that outdated, unseaworthy ships were pressed into service. One such "coffin ship" sank shortly after leaving Westport in County Mayo, drowning all its passengers in sight of their relatives on the quayside. The ships which made it across the Atlantic were unsanitary, and typhus and dysentery became epidemic. Most berthed in Canada. The quarantine station at Grosse Isle near Quebec, described by the Montreal Immigrant Society Bulletin in 1848 as "the great charnel house of victimized humanity," is today the site of a memorial to the 6000 Irish men, women, and children who died in its filthy sheds.

Migration from England and Scotland continued, fostered by family ties between earlier generations of migrants and their relatives in Britain. The major immigration lasted to 1860, peaking at 60,000 a year in the early 1850s. The new arrivals tended to cluster in the cities; English speakers became a majority in Montreal in this period, and Quebec City acquired a significant English minority. Germans also benefited from the information passed on by earlier migrants. In those parts of Europe with no tradition of migration, people were slow to follow: Scandinavians, Dutch,

Belgians, and Swiss came only in small numbers. There was little migration from France, despite the existence of French-speaking areas in North America, although a few hundred Acadians returned to Lower Canada and New Brunswick in this period. The French Canadian population was doubling every 30 years; by the 1840s French Canadians were migrating to the U. S.

The migration of this period involved entire families, although often the fathers or both parents went abroad to earn enough money for their families to join them later. Migrants never came from the poorest sections of society, since they had to be prosperous enough to pay their fare, raise enough capital to buy land, and survive their first year without a harvest. Farming remained a struggle for families who had settled in agricultural regions in Texas, the trans-Appalachian West and the Midwest by the late 1830s. Craftsmen and skilled workers were in demand in the rapidly-expanding cities. Some cities developed ties with towns and villages in Europe which ensured them a supply of workers skilled in specific crafts: house painters from London, carpet weavers from Glasgow, Cornish stonecutters, and German furniture-makers and brewers. Farm workers seeking unskilled labor in similar areas were less successful.

Below: although the revolutionary upheavals of 1848 prompted many people to emigrate from Germany, daily oppression by petty officialdom was probably a stronger motive, as this 1849 cartoon points out. "My dear people," the official asks, "Is there no way to keep you here?" "Sure, sir," the old peasant replies. "If you would leave, we would stay."

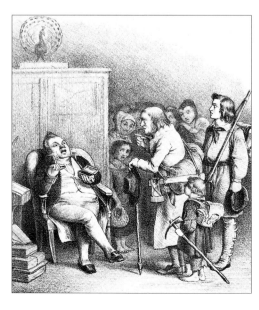

THE AMERICANIZATION OF TEXAS
EURO-AMERICANS ADVANCE INTO MEXICAN TERRITORY, 1821–60

Anglo-American settlers in Texas broke away from Mexico in 1836 to form their own republic. After the state joined the U. S. nine years later, its non-Indian population exploded.

Shortly after gaining independence from Spain in 1821, Mexico launched a program to encourage immigration into Texas. The government planned large land grants to contractors, known as *empresarios*, who agreed to bring in a certain number of families to colonize their assigned areas. These grants were much in demand, and soon covered over half the modern state. Many *empresarios* brought in immigrants, some from as far away as Ireland.

In 1830, however, the Mexican government, dissatisfied with the results of the program, closed Texas to Anglo-American colonization. Few of the contracts had been fulfilled, and those immigrants who did come often failed to observe the Mexican prohibition of slavery. Even successful *empresarios* such as Stephen Austin and Green DeWitt had not introduced large numbers of immigrants: in 1826, after five years of existence, Austin's colony had a population of only 1800, including 443 slaves. Rather than a loyal population that would strengthen Mexican rule in Texas, the program had helped to fill the territory with Americans who wished to join the U. S. The Texas revolution succeeded in 1836 after

a brief war that is famous in the U. S. chiefly for the massacres at the Alamo in San Antonio and at Goliad, and the spectacular Mexican defeat at San Jacinto. Despite unstable conditions, the expanses of empty land continued to draw immigrants. The new Texas Republic (1836–45) embarked on a scheme to promote immigration. This extended even to Europe, where the Society for the Protection of German Immigrants in Texas recruited thousands of Germans, many of whom settled in the Texas hill country north and west of the traditional frontier along the old road between San Antonio and Nacogdoches. The 1834 white and black population of Texas, including slaves, has been estimated at 24,700; in 1836 there were 30,000 Anglo-Americans, 5000 African-Americans (mostly slaves), 3470 Mexicans and 14,200 Indians. For 1845 an estimate based on voting rights in the Texas presidential election puts the total number of non-Indians at 125,000.

During its decade of existence, the Texas Republic was constantly preoccupied with the regional Indian population, engaging in councils and treaties as well as frequent hostilities. Sam Houston, the first president of the republic, had lived among the Cherokee in Oklahoma, and knew how to negotiate with Indian people, but he was generally unable to convince other leaders that Indian problems could be mediated.

The Caddo living in East Texas (the region east

of the Trinity River) and the adjoining Red River country of Louisiana had long been the most influential tribe between the Mississippi and the Rio Grande. In the 1830s they were surrounded by immigrant Indian allies, including bands of Shawnee, Delaware, Cherokee, Potawatomi, Kickapoo, and Coushatta, who had been around for 15 years and more. More recent arrivals—Choctaw, Biloxi, Cherokee, Seminole, Apalache, Alabama, Creeks, and others—had come in reaction to the U. S. removal program of the 1830s (> *pages 126–7*). Around Nacogdoches in the 1830s. there were representatives of 20 tribes, with some rival factions, all as eager for assurances of land and hunting grounds as the non-Indian settlers. After Houston lost his influence, anti-Indian sentiments favored warfare to get rid of all Indians, who were suspected of treasonous contacts with Mexican agents. Most feared by the settlers and most reluctant to attend any councils were the Comanches, whose territory included the western hill country. At the invitation of Mexico, bands of Cherokee, Seminole, Kickapoo, Creek, and Caddo took refuge near Nacimiento. The Kickapoo remained there; the others went to Oklahoma or hid in the hills.

The U. S. finally annexed Texas in 1845, triggering war with Mexico. The U. S. victory in 1848 not only confirmed the separation of Texas from Mexico, but also extended U. S. territory to include the northern half of Mexico, roughly the area south of Oregon and west of Texas. American representatives appeared eager to establish peaceful relations with Texas tribes. In 1854, two reservations were established on the upper Brazos River, one for the Comanches that was never really occupied, and a second for associated Caddoan-speaking bands along with long-time allied Shawnee and Delaware. Learning that a vigilante band planned to destroy the reservation Indians, their agent Robert S. Neighbors led them on an emergency trek across the Red River into Oklahoma in August 1859. He was murdered on his return.

As a part of the U .S., Texas achieved a stability that increased its attractiveness to immigrants. In 1821 the estimated population had been around 7–800; in 1860 the U. S. Census Bureau counted 604,125. Immigration accounted for most of that growth. By 1850, the area settled by two or more people per square mile barely crossed the Trinity River, with just two outcrops extending to Austin and San Antonio. A decade later the same general area had a population density of between six and 18 people per square mile. Most new settlers came from the southern U. S. They moved first into East Texas, then spread south and west. The population nearly tripled from 212,592 in 1850 to over 600,000 in 1860, but the 14,000 Indians present in 1834 were no longer in evidence.

I: Empresario grants in Texas, 1821–30
- Mexican territory
- U. S. territory
- – – – *empresario* grants

Right: the Alamo in San Antonio. First built as a Franciscan mission in 1745, it became the symbol of the Texan struggle for independence from Mexico after its 183 defenders died in their attempt to hold off Santa Ana's Mexican army in February and March of 1835.

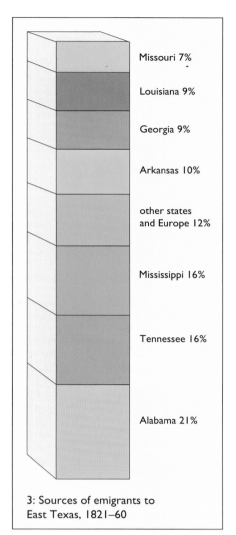

3: Sources of emigrants to
East Texas, 1821–60

Missouri 7%

Louisiana 9%

Georgia 9%

Arkansas 10%

other states
and Europe 12%

Mississippi 16%

Tennessee 16%

Alabama 21%

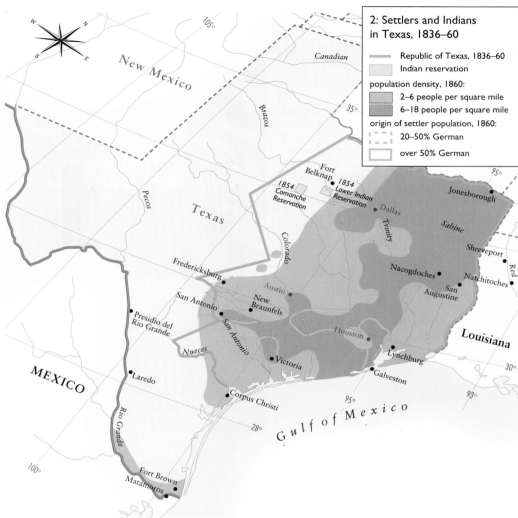

2: Settlers and Indians
in Texas, 1836–60

Republic of Texas, 1836–60

Indian reservation

population density, 1860:

2–6 people per square mile

6–18 people per square mile

origin of settler population, 1860:

20–50% German

over 50% German

GOD AND GOLD

MORMON UTAH AND THE CALIFORNIA GOLD RUSH, 1847–51

Settlers were drawn to the West for a wide range of motives. Some were driven by religious idealism, others by the lure of gold, while some were simply searching for land to farm.

The Oregon Trail, a route from the lower Missouri River to the Willamette valley near the mouth of the Columbia River, had been known for many years before the first, small wagon train of settlers from the East completed the 2000-mile journey in 1842. The success of that intrepid group inspired others, and the next year a thousand more made the trek; within two years the annual number of men, women and children exceeded 3000, and it remained high until the transcontinental railroads were built and rendered the trail obsolete in the 1870s. Federal Census takers counted over 13,000 non-Indians in Oregon in 1850 and over 52,000 in 1860, nearly all of whom had arrived by the Oregon Trail.

In 1846, shortly after traffic on the Oregon Trail reached its high annual average, members of the Church of Jesus Christ of the Latter-day Saints—the Mormons—fled their settlement in Nauvoo, Illinois, after the murder of their founder Joseph Smith. Brigham Young, their new leader, determined to remove the church and its adherents to a new home in the Great Basin between the Rocky Mountains and the Sierra Nevada. These exiles, numbering 15,000 or 16,000, made their winter quarters near the site of present-day Omaha, Nebraska. The next summer, Young and less than 150 pioneers established a new settlement near the Great Salt Lake. Others followed that same year, and the remainder migrated from Omaha at a rate of about 3000 per year. Converts to Mormonism arrived from Europe, principally England, at about the same rate. The Federal Census of Utah recorded over 11,000 non-Indians there in 1850 and more than 40,000 in 1860.

The Mormons, like the farmers in the Willamette valley, had occupied their land as squatters when jurisdiction was still an international controversy. In 1849 they organized their own government, chose borders that gave them a huge territory between the Rockies and the Sierras, and called it the state of Deseret. They petitioned Washington to admit Deseret to the Union as a state, but instead Congress created Utah Territory, covering most of modern Nevada and Utah, and parts of Colorado and Wyoming, which effectively ended Deseret. Under the authority of Deseret, the Mormons had extended their settlements south and west from Salt Lake City, especially into San Bernardino, Las Vegas, St George and other places that lay along the corridor to the ports of southern California where they expected to receive new converts from Europe, but by the early 1850s they had pulled back closer to the Great Salt Lake.

The impressive migrations along the Oregon and Mormon Trails were surpassed by the tidal wave of people who flooded into California after the news spread that gold had been found in a stream that flows into the Sacramento River. The gold field along the west side of the Sierra Nevada mountains proved to be extensive, and remained productive for years. The immediate impact of the Gold Rush on the peopling of the continent was to increase California's population from 14,000 in 1848 to 100,000 by the end of 1849. Part of the 1850 Federal Census for California is lost, but estimates place the total population for 1852 above 250,000, and in 1860 the Federal Census reported 380,000.

Overall population growth was paralleled by a rapid decline in the native Indians. In California, the voluntary militia and bands of ranchers and miners tried to eliminate the Indians, supported by community fundraising and bounties paid for scalps. During the 25-year period from 1845 to 1970, California's Indian population declined by 80 percent from 150,000 to only 30,000. More fatalities were caused by disease (72,000) than by outright killing (48,000).

The "Forty Niners" who flocked to California not only arrived faster and in greater numbers than those who went to Oregon and Utah, but they were nearly all men rather than families. Only about half actually engaged in gold mining; the rest hoped to make their fortunes supplying the miners. Although most came from the eastern third of North America, a remarkable number arrived directly from Europe, Australia, Chile and other South American countries, as well as from China. California's Gold Rush was only the first of many strikes that drew men to the mountainous West. In 1859, just west of Denver, a second gold rush began, and in 1860 both gold and silver were discovered east of Lake Tahoe in an area around Virginia City, the famous Comstock Lode (> *pages 128–9*).

Left: the 1849 Gold Rush brought the first Chinese immigrant laborers to California, where they undertook the heavier tasks on behalf of the mine owners. These first Chinese, who named the place "The Golden Mountain," were joined in the 1850s by others who came as craftsmen and shopkeepers and, later on, to work on the railroads. As in Australia, where they were also employed in gold mines at this period, they found themselves the focus of considerable race hatred and discrimination.

Below right: Mormon migration to the Great Salt Lake continued after the original settlement. In July 1856 about 600 men, women and children set out on foot across the Great Plains from Florence, Nebraska. As this contemporary woodcut shows, they pulled their household goods behind them in handcarts. Since this means of conveyance was unusual at the time, their journey soon became known as the "Handcart Migration".

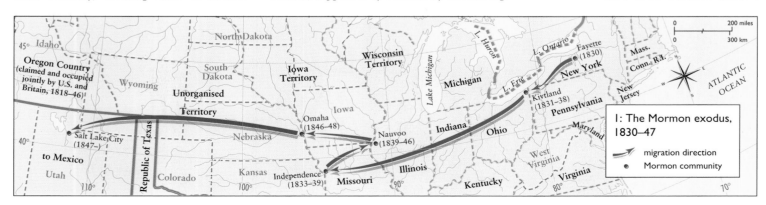

I: The Mormon exodus, 1830–47

migration direction

Mormon community

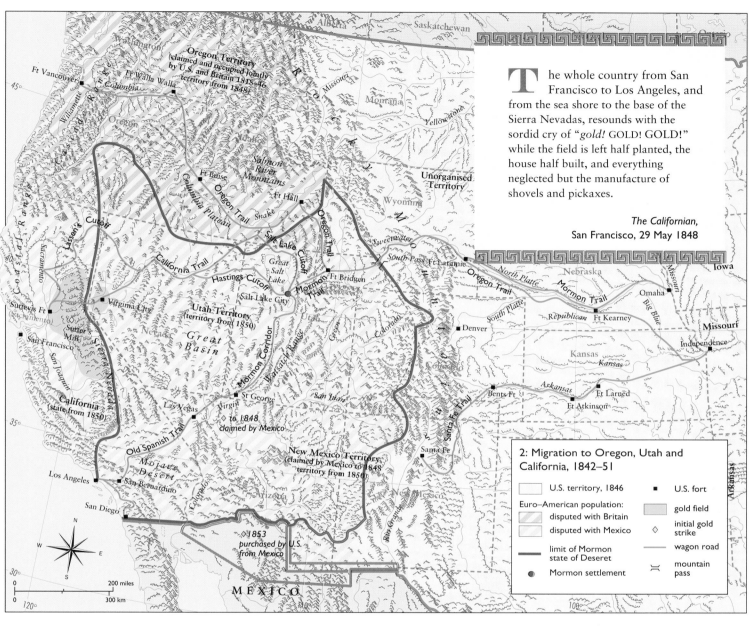

The whole country from San Francisco to Los Angeles, and from the sea shore to the base of the Sierra Nevadas, resounds with the sordid cry of "*gold!* GOLD! GOLD!" while the field is left half planted, the house half built, and everything neglected but the manufacture of shovels and pickaxes.

The Californian,
San Francisco, 29 May 1848

2: Migration to Oregon, Utah and California, 1842–51

☐ U.S. territory, 1846	■ U.S. fort
Euro–American population:	
▨ disputed with Britain	▨ gold field
▨ disputed with Mexico	◇ initial gold strike
—— limit of Mormon state of Deseret	—— wagon road
● Mormon settlement	⊃⊂ mountain pass

THE EVE OF CONFLICT

NORTH AMERICA, 1860

By 1860, settlers had pushed across the Mississippi while the cities of the east were swelled by new arrivals from Europe. Few could have known that the decade ahead held conflict and changes that would affect nearly everyone.

The American Civil War that broke out the following year may be the best known of these events, but other developments took place which were also to have profound effects: the Canadian Confederation of 1867, followed by the Métis rebellion in the Red River district in 1870; the Indian wars in the western U. S.; and the ending of the Russian presence on the continent through its 1867 sale of Alaska to the U. S. (> *pages 130–31*).

The non-native population of Canada in 1861 was little under 3,250,000, a total that reflected both natural increase (about 641,000) and immigration (152,000) over the preceding decade. The distribution of that population had spread slowly; the greatest expansion and increase in density were along the St Lawrence River and in the Maritime provinces, with the scattered beginnings of settlement in the interior. On the west coast, settlement spread out from the southern tip of Vancouver Island, where the population totaled about 50,000 far fewer than the 80,000 on Prince Edward Island in the east.

The population of the U. S. in 1860 topped 31 million, of which more than 2.5 million had emigrated from other countries since 1850. As in Canada, the American population was predomi-

nantly rural, with less than 20 percent living in settlements of 2500 or more. In Canada and in the northeastern and central U. S., most people were engaged in agriculture and were producing surpluses for sale; relatively small numbers worked as tradesmen or were involved in mining, lumbering, and fishing. The older farms in the East tended to concentrate on providing perishable foods for the cities. Farmers in the more recently cleared and cultivated lands produced increasing quantities of corn, wheat, and other grains, beef, pork, and wool, and other products for the European market. This commercialization of agriculture was made possible in part by the invention of the steel plow, the mechanical

Above: Hunted Slaves, *an oil painting by Richard Ansdell. Painted in 1862 just after the outbreak of the Civil War, this heroic image of escaped slaves fending off hunting dogs sent after them was powerful propaganda for the abolitionist cause.*

reaper, and other improvements in agricultural technology, as well as by the transportation systems of rivers, canals, roads, and railroads that had facilitated the opening and settlement of the new farming regions. Population distribution in the U. S. exhibited the results of the steady push westward, with early islands of white settlement reflecting the California Gold Rush and the Mormon establishment around the Great Salt Lake (> *pages 98–9*), and the successes of those who braved the Oregon Trail to the Willamette Valley and the Santa Fe Trail to the Rio Grande (> *pages 96–7*). The frontier had pressed inexorably across the Mississippi, but had just reached the practicable limit of traditional agriculture marked by the 100th meridian.

According to the Federal Census of 1860, there were 488,070 free African-Americans in the U. S. They could be found in nearly every county, the most notable exceptions being along the Mississippi River in Mississippi and Arkansas. Along the East Coast, especially in cities, their ranks were sometimes increased by the bureaucratic practice of classifying native Indians as "Negro" in official records. African-Americans achieved freedom through escape, emancipation, or (especially in the early years of slavery) by buying themselves from their owners. A few became rich, but most remained poor. Wherever they lived, free African-Americans had to carry papers proving they were not slaves, and in the South they were non-citizens whose movements, employment, and political and legal status were severely limited. In the whole country they could vote in only four of the New England states and some places, like Missouri, banned their entry across state lines. They constituted nearly the entire corps of "conductors" on the Underground Railroad, and struggled long to achieve the abolition of slavery nationwide.

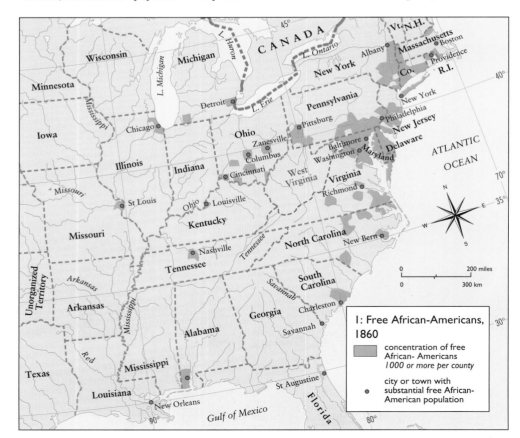

1: Free African-Americans, 1860

concentration of free African-Americans 1000 or more per county

● city or town with substantial free African-American population

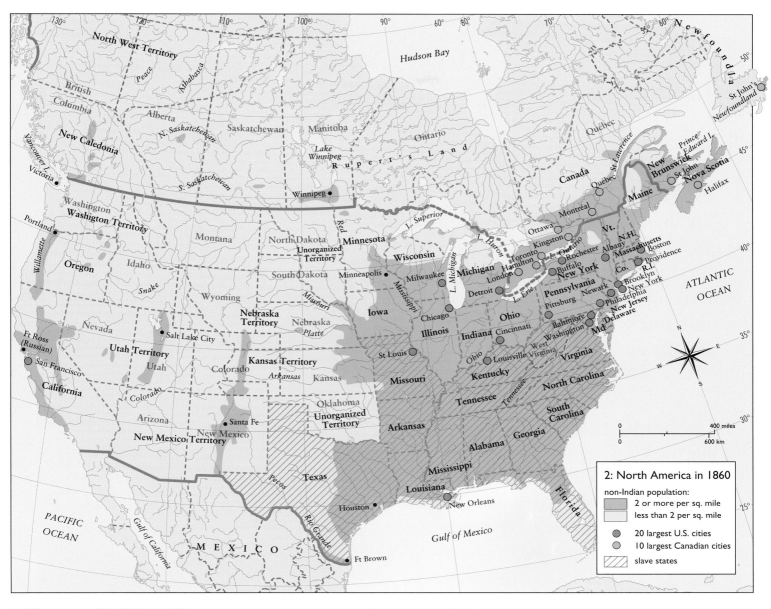

2: North America in 1860

non-Indian population:

- 2 or more per sq. mile
- less than 2 per sq. mile

- 20 largest U.S. cities
- 10 largest Canadian cities
- slave states

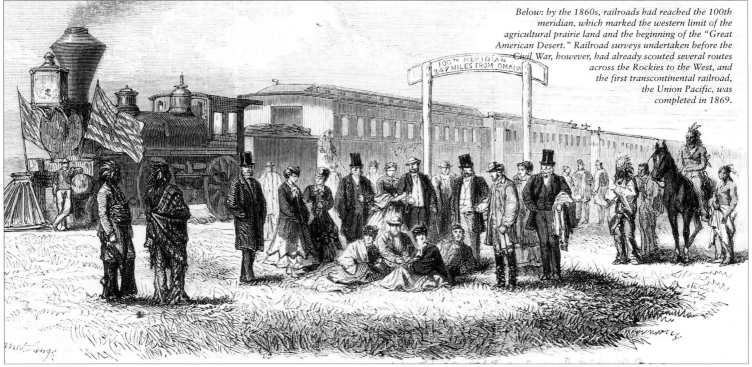

Below: by the 1860s, railroads had reached the 100th meridian, which marked the western limit of the agricultural prairie land and the beginning of the "Great American Desert." Railroad surveys undertaken before the Civil War, however, had already scouted several routes across the Rockies to the West, and the first transcontinental railroad, the Union Pacific, was completed in 1869.

PART V: MASS MIGRATION

Introduction
by Dirk Hoerder

Canadian Confederation and the end of the Civil War in the U. S. heralded a period of mass migration to North America which was only halted by the intoduction of restrictive policies in the 1920s and by the dark years of the Depression. Four major migration systems were in operation, encompassing both voluntary and involuntary movement, both exploiters and the exploited. For those who saw North America as a "land of opportunity" there were often bitter disappointments in store, but networks of mutual support and encouragement sprang up to help newcomers adjust to the difficulties and perplexities of American life.

Right: New arrivals in the crowded waiting room at Castle Garden, the main immigration station for New York before Ellis Island was built in 1892.

The main era of European immigration to North America encompassed the years following the Civil War in the U. S. (1861–1864) and the period of expansion in Canada following Confederation in 1867. Canada's main periods of immigration were the 1880s and the years from 1900 to 1930, when the international economic depression began. The era came to a close after World War I, when restrictive legislation was passed in both nations in the 1920s.

The boatloads of mainly European people who arrived in North America during the period of "mass migration" were not an isolated stream. They were but one element in the Atlantic migration system, one of four major systems of population transfer covering the entire globe. The Atlantic migration system reached from Central and Eastern Europe to the western edge of the North American continent and into South America.

A second system of emigration from Europe was the Russo-Siberian migration system, which carried a population wave eastward toward Manchuria and China. The dividing line between the two streams of exodus from Europe was in Russia, on a line from Lake Peipus, near Leningrad, along the Dneiper River to Odessa and the Black Sea. Settlement had already taken place in the plains of South Russia during the 18th century and the first half of the 19th century. This eastward European expansion, which continued into the Caucasus Mountains and across the Aral Sea, involved in the region of 10 million people.

A third system, the Asian contract labor migration system (often called the "coolie system"), came into being in the 19th century in response to worldwide labor demands which arose when the widespread enslavement of African people ended. Shiploads of Asians were taken to the Americas, primarily to work on railroads built in western America as well as Peru and Chile. Until restrictions curtailed the population flow across the Pacific, both the Asian and the Atlantic migration system contributed to immigration into North America.

International investment and imperial economic expansion contributed to the development of a comparatively small-scale network which is known as the colonial migration system. European countries such as England, Germany, France, and Italy created new enterprises overseas. Merchants, colonial administrators, soldiers, and some settlers moved along the routes to flourishing plantation economies and to small industrial centers. International markets for tropical produce such as cocoa, bananas, coffee, rice, rubber, oils, and sugar grew, necessitating large-scale production. The need for clerical workers and administrative personnel, and sometimes for

Below: sharecroppers in the Deep South, painted by William Aiken Walker. When cotton crops were devastated by an infestation of boll-weevils during the Depression, many African-Americans migrated north to industrial cities such as Chicago and Pittsburgh.

additional labor, led to colonial immigration.

Of the four major migration systems, it was the Atlantic system that increased the population of North America the most. Transatlantic emigration from Europe to Argentina, Uruguay, Chile, and Brazil was in progress when North America received the first big waves of European newcomers. The peak era of migration took place in the later years (1880–1910) of a century (1815–1915) in which 48 million people crossed the Atlantic Ocean to settle in the Americas. Why did they go? One way to explain this phenomenon is to describe what was happening in Europe to cause millions of people to depart, and what drew them to a region still called "The New World."

Immigrants were "pushed" and "pulled," often at the same time. Among the factors tending to "push" people out of Europe were overpopulation and land shortage. At a time when most families lived off the land, the growing population of Europe was faced with increasingly scarce land resources. Internal colonization had led young people to move into infertile hill country or wet marshes, terracing and draining lands previously considered unfit for cultivation. The home production of cloth and clothing provided landless children with income, but

Above: The Wagons, *painted by Charles M. Russell (1865–1926). The massive influx of Europeans to the West via the new railroad networks closed off much of the land to its original Indian inhabitants, who were often forced to relocate to small settlements as colonialists took over their territories*

often at starvation level. Once textile production was concentrated in large, centrally located factories and had ceased to be a home industry, workers were obliged to leave their farms in order to to seek work. In the long run, however, manufacturing jobs were too scarce to take care of all young people without land, and intercontinental migration was the result. Other probable factors behind emigration were the famine caused by the potato blight in Ireland, labor unrest, revolutions and warfare, and, in the later 19th century, religious persecution and the anti-Jewish pogroms.

The "pull" to America for many early immigrants was the availability of land in regions opened up as a consequence of treaties negotiated with Indian tribes. By the mid-19th century, however, immigrants were more varied in terms of occupation and training. Only about 30 percent of the newcomers were farmers, with similar percentages of skilled and unskilled laborers, and 10 percent working in professional and other jobs. By 1900, the percentage of farmers had fallen below 5 percent, that of skilled workers had fallen to about 20 percent, while unskilled workers accounted for more than 70 percent of the immigration.

In the late 19th century, jobs for industrial laborers were a main factor in decisions to come to North America. Many newly arrived workers had already made the shift in Europe from rural labor to the shops and factories opened during industrialization. They had already made at least one transition to a new community, and had sometimes led a more or less transient existence on the continent. Cities such as Vienna, Berlin, Paris, and London included people from many countries in their working-class populations. In Eastern and Southeastern Europe, a mixture of ethnic groups interacted. Popular languages were supplemented by administrative languages used in the locality, and sometimes by other languages used in markets and workplaces.

America offered a chance to settle more permanently. By the late 19th century, new immigrants usually had relatives or friends who had arrived earlier, resulting in a chain of migrants from one particular region of Europe to a new American center where family or former neighbors lived. The decision to leave Europe was often discussed in village communites, and the mythologizing of North America may have been involved, firing the imagination of prospective immigrants. America became the "land of opportunity" where, regardless of background or inheritance, an independent newcomer could become a "self-made man." This was often a necessity: when an elder son, inheriting the family's land, had to pay off his brothers and sisters, he often had to migrate to earn the money. He would usually become one of many temporary immigrants who came to North America to make money and took their savings back to their homeland.

Many enthusiastic new immigrants were unaware of the dangers of being settled on swampy lands, unfit for agriculture or habitation, or in tenement areas where life was as hard as it had been back home. But they formed support associations, usually according to local or provincial origin. Every European nation contained various peoples (Great Britain, for instance, included Irish, Scottish, and Welsh), and provinces were used for self-identity. Immigrants defined themselves as Bavarian, Prussian, or Swabian after regions united under the German Empire in 1871. Basques came from both France and Spain. From Italy came peoples as diverse as Lombardos and Sicilians. Only in America did they become German, Italian, or French.

Most European immigrants settled in familiar and established communities. Once "pioneer migrants" were established in a new location, they sent information back to their villages or cities, inducing others to join them.

This resulted in the phenomenon of chain or sequential migration. At the turn of the century, 94 percent of migrants arriving in the U. S. joined family or friends. Migration was also facilitated by prepaid tickets sent back home by those who arrived earlier.

Immigrants' concepts of distance and geographic space did not reflect actual measureable distances. The "mental maps" of incoming Europeans conflated places of work, places where relatives lived, and places where overseas communities could be found. A Polish man talking about his cousins might mention in the same breath one working in the mines of the Ruhr district and another in

Below: "The Mott Street Barracks" in New York City from Jacob Riis' How the Other Half Lives. Conditions in the prison-like tenements of American cities were harsh, and life for those who lived there was often as gruelling as it had been "back home."

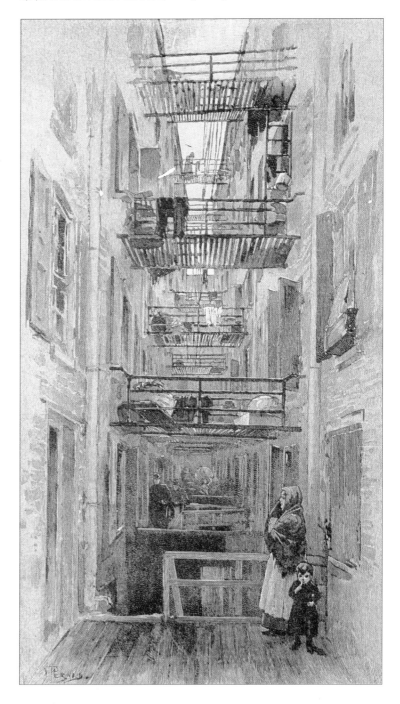

Pennsylvania; an Irish woman's friends included one in Liverpool and another in Montreal. The waystations in the mind of a Russian traveling to Pennsylvania might consist of the Russian border, the crossing, and Ellis Island. The three points represented the danger spots, where passport problems, shipping disasters, or refusal of entry were to be feared.

Time and distance seemed incidental. A Finn in Timmins, Ontario, located about half way between northern Lake Huron and James Bay, wrote his family in Helsinki, asking them to join him. His directions were simple: get on the train in Halifax, Nova Scotia, where the boat landed, and get off in Timmins. He did not mention the fact that the trip took three days and that it would be wise to carry food. His family arrived very hungry. Distance or a remote location was often of no import: a Sardinian working on the Panama Canal, or in Mulberry Street

returning to Europe was concentrated in a few major ports as steamships increased in size. In the first half of the 19th century, British, Dutch, and Scandinavian ports handled the bulk of the traffic. Since railroad connections on the continent were few, prospective immigrants came down the Rhine to Dutch and Belgian ports. When Hamburg and Bremen were connected by tracks to the hinterland, much of East Central and Eastern European migration came through the two German ports. Southeastern European migration passed through Black Sea or Greek ports, the Adriatic ports of Fiume and Trieste, and through Genoa and Naples.

The system of agents selling ship tickets, legally or illegally, spread deep into the Czarist and Austro-Hungarian empires. Tickets could be bought from the village of origin to the port of destination. Commercial promotions by steamship and railroad companies stimulated and facili-

Left: A photograph taken at the turn of the century shows an Italian immigrant family anxiously awaiting the determination of their fate at Ellis Island immigrant station in New York.

Above: A bustling scene in New Orleans harbor in 1884. New Orleans was founded by the French in 1718 as a commercial gateway to the Mississippi. In 1811, it gave its name to the SS New Orleans, the first Mississippi steamboat.

(New York City), or in a small town outside New York would always live in a community of Sardinians.

A major factor behind "mass migration" was improvements in both land and sea transport. The development of large passenger and cargo steamships increased the volume of traffic far beyond the capacity of sailing vessels. At the same time, transcontinental railroads enabled new immigrants to reach the hinterland, although many chose to remain in port cities. The process of leaving and

tated immigration from Europe. Directories, maps, and advertisements for land were included in the special guides published to encourage immigration. Railroad companies had all received grants of land adjacent to their transcontinental lines, and the sale of land tracts to immigrants and to westward-moving Americans and Canadians was an important source of revenue.

The two principal ports in North America for arriving immigrants were Québec and New York City. The Grand

Isle at Québec acquired an unfortunate reputation as a "deadly island" when seriously ill and dying passengers arrived from Ireland. Although Ellis Island in New York has been described as a place of hope, it was also known as an "isle of tears," although only for the 2 percent or less excluded after arrival. The first screening which occurred was actually of those arriving at the borders of the German Reich on their way to the major ports. Steamship agents rejected about 5 percent of passengers before departure from Europe to protect their companies from the expense of shipping back excluded persons.

"Selective immigration" began in Canada in 1896, when the government called for settlers to populate the western prairies. Large agricultural families were sought, as there was an underlying wariness of single men, who might be shiftless or of radical political orientation. There was a great fear of foreign anarchists and labor agitators. Immigrants from the British Isles and North Europe were preferred, but these countries could not provide sufficient settlers. The next choice was East European peasants, seen as inferior but nevertheless of good quality. These "men in sheepskin coats" were to be accompanied by their "stout wives" and plenty of children to provide a labor force in the agricultural communities of the future. This search for immigrant families contrasted with the common pattern of working-class, single men, who had made up 90 percent of arrivals in Canada. These men could not initially support wives and families, but brought them over later. Women from their home communities often came on prepaid tickets as "mail order brides," selected with the help of family and friends.

In the late 19th century, a change in the direction of immigration streams took place in both Canada and the U. S., from a preponderance of North European arrivals to an increasing number of people from Southern and Eastern Europe. German migration reached its final peak in the 1880s and slowed to a low level in 1893, and migration from North Europe and the British Isles

Above left: a gang of railroad workers lay track for the Union Pacific Railroad in the 1860s. From 30,500 miles of track by 1860 (already the same as the rest of the world combined), the transcontinental railroad network grew to a staggering 93,000 miles by the 1870s
Above: thousands of wood-burning locomotives distributed millions of tons of freight across the rail network

Below: an advertising map of 1870 for the Central and Union Pacific Railroads. Keen to secure California within the Union, Abraham Lincoln had ordered the Union Pacific Railroad in 1862. It was to link with the Central Pacific between Omaha, Nebraska, and Sacramento, California

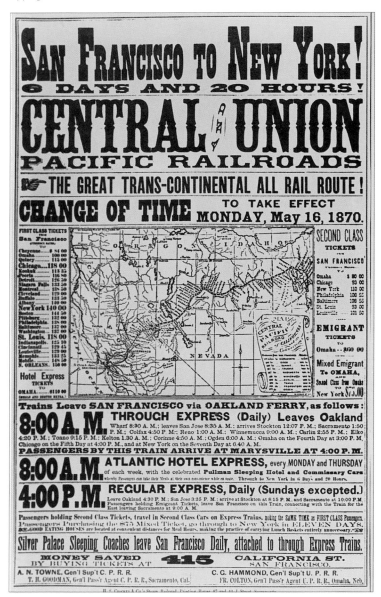

continued at a reduced rate. The "new immigrants" from Eastern and Southern Europe were viewed with suspicion by an American population that considered Slavs, Magyars, Sicilians, and Jews as alien people whose habits and beliefs prevented them from being assimilated and living "the American way."

In the U. S., antipathy toward Chinese laborers, combined with other labor concerns, led to the first comprehensive federal immigration law, which was passed by Congress in 1882. The Treasury Department had the authority to enforce the act, but individual states had the responsibility of inspecting immigrants and ensuring that incapacitated persons, convicts, and "idiots" were sent back. Deportation could be carried out by the federal government. In 1891, the post of superintendent of immigration was established, and building of a new reception center on Ellis Island began. Antipathy toward all foreigners increased when President William McKinley was assassinated by an anarchist in 1901.

In addition to more stringent examinations, a literacy requirement was added in 1917 for all newcomers over the age of 16. The peak of restrictive legislation came in 1921 and 1924. The latter law reduced immigration by setting the annual quota for each country at 2 percent of the number of people born in that nation who were resident in the U. S. at the time of the 1890 census. The choice of the 1890 census was, like the Canadian policy, highly discriminatory, as it effectively reduced immigration from Southern and Eastern Europe. For Italians, Greeks, and Slavs, the quotas represented about 3 percent of their pre-war annual immigration. There were "non-quota" admissions for artists, actors, ministers, and professors, and a few other special categories.

In the long story of the settling of North America, a major interval occured when the restrictive policies of the 1920s brought to an end the era of "mass migration." But it is important not to overlook the fact that internal population movements were progressing at the time. The new railroads that opened up the west for settlement by Europeans and North Americans also closed off much of the western country to the original Indian inhabitants. As the non-Indian population grew, Indians were resettled and confined to smaller reserved areas. The railroad system also brought in immigrants from south of the Mexican border, and carried African-Americans northward on their "Great Migration."

Left: The registration hall at Ellis Island, photographed in 1910. One immigrant described his experience there as "the nearest earthly likeness to the Final Day of Judgment, when we have to prove our fitness to enter Heaven."

TIMELINE
1860–1920

NORTH AMERICA	THE CARIBBEAN, CENTRAL & S. AMERICA	EUROPE, AFRICA, & ASIA
1860 Paiute War in Nevada	1860 Liberal leader Benito Juarez wins control of Mexico City	1860–70 Unification of Italy
1861 Kansas becomes a State of the Union	1861 Juarez suspends Mexico's foreign debt. García Moreno establishes theocratic rule in Ecuador. Spanish reoccupy Dominican Republic	1861 Liberation of serfs in Russia
1861–65 American Civil War		
1861–63 Apache uprisings in Southwest		
1862 Homestead Act passed by U.S. Congress, opening Indian land in Kansas and Nebraska to settlers	1862 French invade Mexico	1862 Bismarck, the architect of German unification, becomes prime minister of Prussia
1862–64 Sioux uprising in Minnesota and North Dakota		
1863–66 Navajo War in Arizona and New Mexico		
1864 Nevada becomes a State of the Union 300 Indians massacred at Sand Creek	1864 French make Archduke Maximilian of Austria emperor of Mexico	
1865 Abraham Lincoln assassinated. Andrew Johnson becomes president. 13th Amendment abolishes slavery in U.S.	1865 Paul Bogle leads uprising in Jamaica. Spanish ousted from Dominica	
1866 U.S. Congress passes Railroad Act, allowing railroad companies to appropriate Indian lands		1866 Austria defeated by Prussian–Italian alliance; Italians take Venice. International Red Cross founded
1867 British North America becomes Dominion of Canada, with own parliament. U.S. buys Alaska from Russia. Nebraska becomes a state	1867 Maximilian captured and shot in Mexico; Juarez re-elected president. War of the Triple Alliance: Paraguay v. Brazil, Uruguay, and Argentina	
1868 14th Amendment denies Indians the right to vote in the U. S.	1868 Uprising against Spanish rule in Cuba	1868 France establishes protectorate in Indochina
1869 Ulysses S. Grant becomes U.S. president. Riel rebellion of Métis in Manitoba suppressed. 15th Amendment gives vote to freed slaves in U.S. Prince Rupert's Land, Manitoba (1870) and British Columbia (1871) joins Canada		1869 Suez Canal completed
		1871 Franco–Prussian War. Napoleon III abdicates. Paris Commune. German States unified under Prussia to form German Reich
1872 Modoc War in Oregon and California		
1874 Gold discovered in S. Dakota		
1874–75 Red River War in southern plains: Comanches, Kiowas, and Cheyennes are led by Quanah Parker	1875 Ecuadorean president García Moreno assassinated and replaced by liberal regime	
1876 Colorado becomes a State of the Union	1876 Porfirio Diaz becomes dictator in Mexico with U.S. support	1876–78 Russo–Turkish War establishes independent Bulgaria
1876–77 Sioux, Cheyennes, and Arapahoes fight to defend their lands in Black Hills, S. Dakota		
1877 Desert Land Act passed by U.S. Congress. Chief Joseph's War (Nez Perce). Blackfeet cede land to Canadian government		1877 Britain annexes Transvaal
1877–80 Apache resistance in Southwest		
1878 Bannock War in Idaho	1880 Spain sends 250,000 troops to suppress renewed Cuban uprising	
1881 U.S. President Garfield assassinated	1881 Chile defeats Peru in war to win control of nitrate reserves in Atacama Desert	1881 Assassination attempt on British Queen Victoria. Russian Tsar Alexander II assassinated. Pogroms against Jews in Russian empire. French establish protectorate in Tunisia
1881–85 392,802 Canadians migrate to U.S.		
1882 U.S. bans Chinese immigration. New provinces of Alberta, Saskatchewan, and Assiniboia in Canada		1882 "May Laws" impose discriminatory restrictions on Russian Jews
1885 Métis rebellion of Louis Riel defeated in Saskatchewan. Canadian Pacific Railroad completed		
1886 Mohawk Indians trained in high-steel construction to build bridge across St Lawrence River		
1887 General Allotment Act parcels out reservation land among individual Indians		1887 Britain annexes East Africa

NORTH AMERICA

1888 Benjamin Harrison wins U.S. presidential election with minority of popular vote

1889 Oklahoma land rush: 2 million acres of reservation land are given to white settlers. Montana, N. & S. Dakota, and Washington become states

1890 Low point of Indian population in U.S. (less than 250,000). Ghost Dance movement gains influence. U.S. troops massacre 350 Sioux at Wounded Knee. Idaho and Wyoming become states

1896 New Canadian policy encourages immigrants. 100,000 people swarm into the Yukon during the Klondike goldrush. These were the richest gold deposits ever found. Utah becomes a state

1898 Spanish–American War. Curtis Act abolishes Indian tribal governments

1901 Population of Canada reaches 5.37 million. President McKinley assassinated; Theodore Roosevelt becomes U.S. president. Creek Indian uprising in Oklahoma Territory

1903 Boundary between Alaska and British Columbia settled by arbitration

1905 Provinces of Alberta and Saskatchewan established by Autonomy Bill

1908 National Association for the Advancement of Colored Peoples founded in U.S. by W. E. B. du Bois

1909 William Howard Taft becomes U.S. president

1912 New Mexico and Arizona become states

1913 Woodrow Wilson becomes U.S. president

1916 Pancho Villa raids U.S. territory, sacking Columbus, New Mexico, and killing 18 Americans

1917 U.S. Immigration Act excludes Asian laborers. U.S. enters World War I. African-American migration to northern cities begins

1919 Volstead Act prohibits liquor in the U.S.

1920 19th Amendment gives women the vote in U.S.

THE CARIBBEAN, CENTRAL & S. AMERICA

1888 Abolition of slavery completed in Brazil

1889 Brazil becomes a republic

1895 Cuban uprising against Spain breaks out again

1897 Spain gives Cuba autonomy but not full independence; fighting continues

1898 U.S. intervenes in Cuban war

1899 Spain cedes Cuba and Puerto Rico to U.S. Liberal revolt in Colombia sparks "War of a Thousand Days," which leaves 100,000 dead

1903 U.S. encourages Panama to secede from Colombia and leases Canal Zone from new government

1911 Mexican dictator Porfirio Diaz is overthrown: Mexican Revolution begins

1912 Eloy Alfaro, former liberal president of Ecuador, lynched in Quito, ushering in period of instability and military rule

1914 First Venezuelan oil well drilled

1915 U.S. invades Haiti

1916 U.S. invades Dominican Republic. War between U.S. and Mexico

1917 Queretaro Congress drafts new anti-clerical constitution in Mexico. Wartime demand for nitrates, used in explosives, earns Chile $30 million

1919 Assassination of Emiliano Zapata in Mexico

EUROPE, AFRICA, & ASIA

1891 Russian Jews expelled from St Petersburg and Moscow. Trans-Siberian Railway built. Jewish Colonization Association set up to promote Jewish emigration from Russia and Poland

1894 Sino-Japanese War. Dreyfus case in France

1897 First Zionist Congress held in Basle, Switzerland

1898 U.S. annexes Guam, Puerto Rico, Philippines, and Hawaii

1899 Boer War

1900 Boxer rebellion in China

1901 British Queen Victoria dies

1903 Publication of forged *Protocols of the Elders of Zion* fuels antisemitism. Pogroms against Jews in Russia

1904 Britain and France sign Entente Cordiale

1904–5 Russo-Japanese War. Strikes and demonstrations throughout Russia

1907 France and Russia sign Entente Cordiale

1911 Russia's reforming Prime Minister, Stolypin, assassinated

1912–13 First and Second Balkan Wars

1913 Gandhi leads Great March of Indians in South Africa

1914 Aug: outbreak of World War I

1915 Massacre of Armenians in Turkey

1916 Easter Rising in Dublin against British rule: 64 nationalists, 132 British soldiers and policemen killed

1917 March: Tsar Nicholas II of Russia abdicates; Provisional Government established.
Balfour Declaration: British foreign secretary pledges support for national home for Jews in Palestine.
Nov: Bolsheviks take power in Russia. British capture Jerusalem from Turks

1918 March: Russia withdraws from war.
April: U.S. troops in action in France.
Nov: Armistice ends World War I

1919 Treaty of Versailles imposes peace terms on defeated powers. Poland, Czechoslovakia, Yugoslavia, and the Baltic States become independent nations. World War I has left millions homeless

THE WORLD ON THE MOVE
A CENTURY OF WORLD MIGRATION, 1815-1915

The 35 million European immigrants who arrived in North America from 1815 to 1915 were part of a world in flux; at a time when some 1,551 million people lived on the planet, about 81 million of them were on the move.

Throughout the world, railroad building, canal construction, river regulation, and harbor improvements mobilized men for unskilled physical labor. Textile industries and urban households needed women workers. Manufacturing plants and steam-powered factories demanded the concentration of large labor forces. Many came from nearby rural areas; others were brought across oceans. The major migration streams flowed from Europe to North and South America (35 and 8 million respectively); Europe to the rest of the world (5 million including transfers to colonial areas); from Russia to Siberia (6 million directly, plus 4 million moving southeast beyond the Caspian Sea); internal migration within Asia and India (14.5 million, with an additional million to North and South America, mainly as contract laborers). Another 7 million Europeans returned to their homelands from North and South America during this time. As yet there was no migration from the colonial areas into Europe or North America, except for short-term contract labor.

Railroads made land travel over the Eurasian and North American continents easier and faster. Four transcontinental lines were completed in the U. S. between 1869 and 1883, three in Canada between 1885 and 1915, and one in Russia in 1904. Cutting across continents, the Suez Canal, built by 20,000 conscripted *fellaheen* (itinerant Egyptian laborers), was completed in 1869; by 1914 the Panama Canal, built by immigrant workers, replaced the railroad which had spanned the isthmus since 1855. These interoceanic canals reduced travel time by 25 to 50 percent on their respective routes. The change from sail to steam, accomplished on the major routes in the 1870s, cut travel time in half.

By 1900 the European powers and the U. S. had divided the world's tropical zones among themselves for economic development. From South America to Southeast Asia, plantation systems produced cash crops for the international trade: foodstuffs, stimulants such as tea and coffee, and "industrial crops". The most famous of these was cotton, which was turned into cloth in the factories of the northern hemisphere, while palm oil from West Africa lubricated the machinery of the industrializing world. It was not only the goods that traveled; these plantation economies set local and regional migration systems in motion throughout the southern hemisphere, causing large numbers of people to move—voluntarily or otherwise—great distances. At the end of the 19th century Europe and North America, with their 507 million inhabitants, controlled the movements of nearly 1044 million people who lived in the other continents.

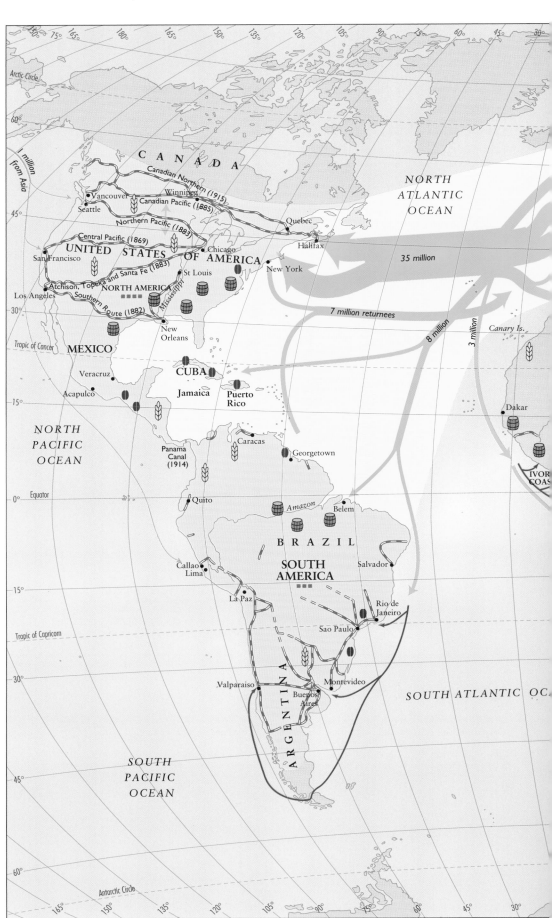

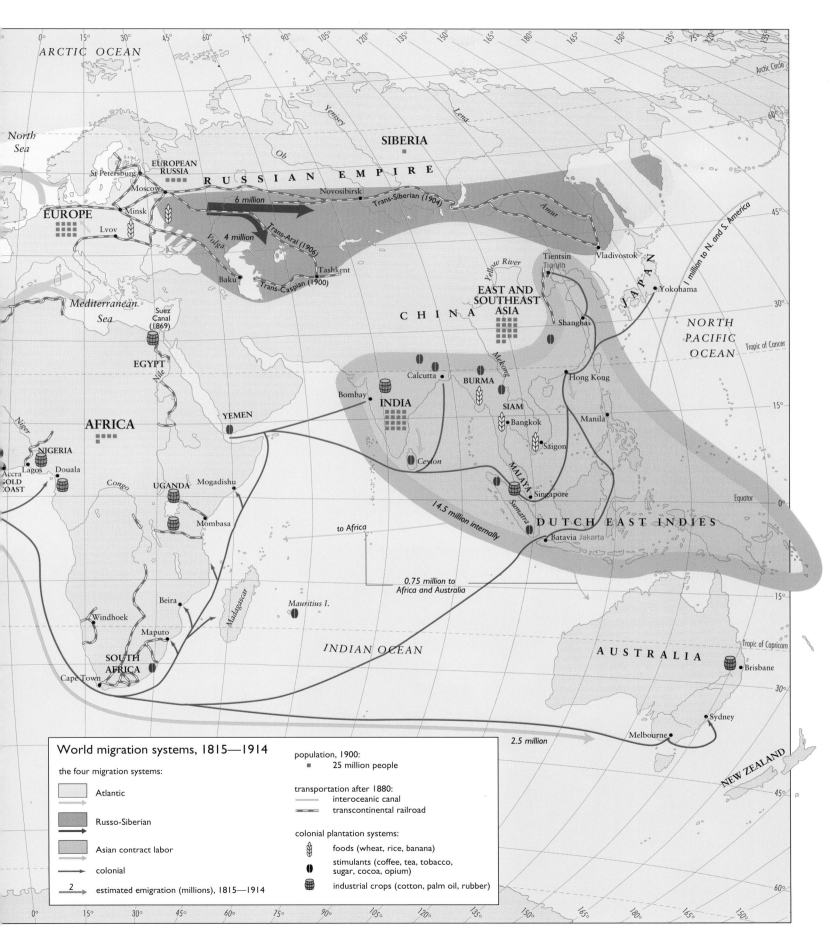

ARCTIC OCEAN

Arctic Circle

North
Sea

SIBERIA

EUROPEAN
RUSSIA

St Petersburg

Moscow

RUSSIAN EMPIRE

Novosibirsk

Trans-Siberian (1904)

Amur

6 million

EUROPE

Minsk

Vladivostok

Lvov

4 million

Volga

Trans-Aral (1906)

Tashkent

Baku

Trans-Caspian (1900)

Yellow River

Tientsin
Tianjin

JAPAN

1 million to N. and S. America

Yokohama

Mediterranean
Sea

Suez
Canal
(1869)

EAST AND
SOUTHEAST
ASIA

CHINA

Shanghai

NORTH
PACIFIC
OCEAN

Tropic of Cancer

EGYPT

Nile

Calcutta

BURMA

Hong Kong

Bombay

INDIA

Mekong

Manila

AFRICA

YEMEN

SIAM

Bangkok

Niger

NIGERIA

Ceylon

Saigon

Accra
GOLD
COAST

Lagos

Douala

Congo

UGANDA

Mogadishu

MALAYA

Singapore

Equator

Mombasa

14.5 million internally

DUTCH EAST INDIES

to Africa

Batavia Jakarta

Beira

Madagascar

Mauritius I.

0.75 million to
Africa and Australia

Windhoek

Maputo

INDIAN OCEAN

AUSTRALIA

Tropic of Capricorn

Brisbane

SOUTH
AFRICA

Cape Town

Sydney

Melbourne

2.5 million

NEW ZEALAND

World migration systems, 1815—1914

the four migration systems:

population, 1900:
■ 25 million people

Atlantic

transportation after 1880:
interoceanic canal
transcontinental railroad

Russo-Siberian

colonial plantation systems:

Asian contract labor

foods (wheat, rice, banana)

colonial

stimulants (coffee, tea, tobacco,
sugar, cocoa, opium)

2   estimated emigration (millions), 1815—1914

industrial crops (cotton, palm oil, rubber)

PEOPLE IN TRANSIT
EUROPEAN EMIGRATION ROUTES, 1860–1914

As steamships took to the seas and rail networks extended across the continent, migrants flooded out of Europe to North America.

Many emigrants to North America came from the agricultural heartlands of Central Europe, far from any sea, and in the earlier part of the 19th century they faced a long, hard journey even before they reached their port of embarkation. They traveled on foot or by cart to river ports. In Western Europe, most migrants then sailed down the Rhine to Dutch and Belgian ports; in the east, the main artery was the Danube, which carried migrants to the Black Sea ports of Constanta and Varna, from where they had a long sea journey before they reached the Atlantic.

The beginnings of the railroads in the 1830s eased the journey across Europe somewhat, and in the 1870s steamships began to replace sailing ships on trans-Atlantic routes. By the end of the century an efficient railroad network carried migrants from the agricultural regions inland to the major northern ports of Bremen, Bremerhaven, Hamburg, and Liverpool, or to the southern port of Naples. Migrants also sailed from Scandinavia to the English port of Hull, crossed the island by train and began their trans-Atlantic voyage at Liverpool. The passenger ships departing from these ports at the turn of the century could each carry more than a thousand emigrants. Many villages in East Central, Eastern, or Southern Europe suffered a massive decline in population as a result of this mass migration.

The U. S. introduced regulations in 1882 prohibiting entry to those it regarded as undesir-able on the grounds of health, morals, and political affiliation; Canada followed suit in 1896. In 1892 a major cholera epidemic in Hamburg was blamed on Russians and Jews passing through the city on their way to North America, giving rise to animosity against migrants in general. As a result, millions were subjected to health inspections and fumigation at border control stations, and many complained of ill-treatment at the hands of discourteous officials. Although the exclusion rate at Ellis Island amounted to no more than one or two percent, about five percent of migrants were screened out by shipping companies prior to departure to avoid the expense of shipping them back. Others were turned back at the border stations of the German Reich.

On the whole, however, travel from a remote village in European Russia or the Ukraine to North America had become a relatively easy affair. Those considering emigration could benefit from the experience of relatives who had already migrated, and who wrote home encouraging their families and friends to follow them. Once the decision had been made, an agent of the North German shipping companies, usually a local teacher or cleric, was contacted. The agent would then sign a contract, advise the head office at Bremen or Hamburg, and receive a departure date and voucher for the ticket—the famous "Schiffskarte"—which he would hand to the emigrant. The latter would arrive at the port just before departure, but if there were a

Below: entry procedures at New York's Ellis Island were quick but harsh for those rejected. Despite its low turn-back rate, it became known as the "island of tears." Hundreds were always waiting to be processed, so that there were many witnesses to the rare but unexplained exclusions: would their own family be torn apart too?

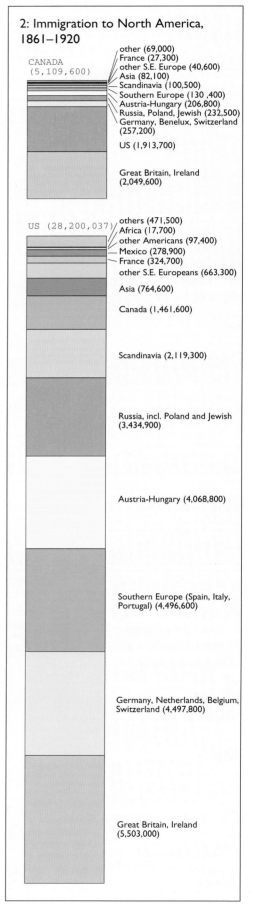

2: Immigration to North America, 1861–1920

CANADA (5,109,600)

other (69,000)
France (27,300)
other S.E. Europe (40,600)
Asia (82,100)
Scandinavia (100,500)
Southern Europe (130,400)
Austria-Hungary (206,800)
Russia, Poland, Jewish (232,500)
Germany, Benelux, Switzerland (257,200)
US (1,913,700)

Great Britain, Ireland (2,049,600)

US (28,200,037)

others (471,500)
Africa (17,700)
other Americans (97,400)
Mexico (278,900)
France (324,700)
other S.E. Europeans (663,300)

Asia (764,600)

Canada (1,461,600)

Scandinavia (2,119,300)

Russia, incl. Poland and Jewish (3,434,900)

Austria-Hungary (4,068,800)

Southern Europe (Spain, Italy, Portugal) (4,496,600)

Germany, Netherlands, Belgium, Switzerland (4,497,800)

Great Britain, Ireland (5,503,000)

delay of more than three days the Bremen shipping companies had to pay for board and lodging. The companies realized that treating the emigrants well—up to a point—was the best way of attracting more business. At Bremerhaven, the city authorities had railtracks built right up to the embarkation point so that travelers could step directly from the train onto the ship. On the other side of the Atlantic, ports such as New York, Halifax, Quebec City, and Montreal were connected by rail with the rest of the continent. By 1900 there were few areas which were not accessible by train.

Right: the port of Bremerhaven in 1904. On the right is the German steamship Crown Prince William, *on the left the departure station of the Norddeutscher Lloyd shipping line. Bremerhaven, built in the early 19th century at the mouth of the River Weser to replace Bremen, which was affected by silting, was the most up-to-date port in Europe, and emigrants could step directly from the train onto their ship.*

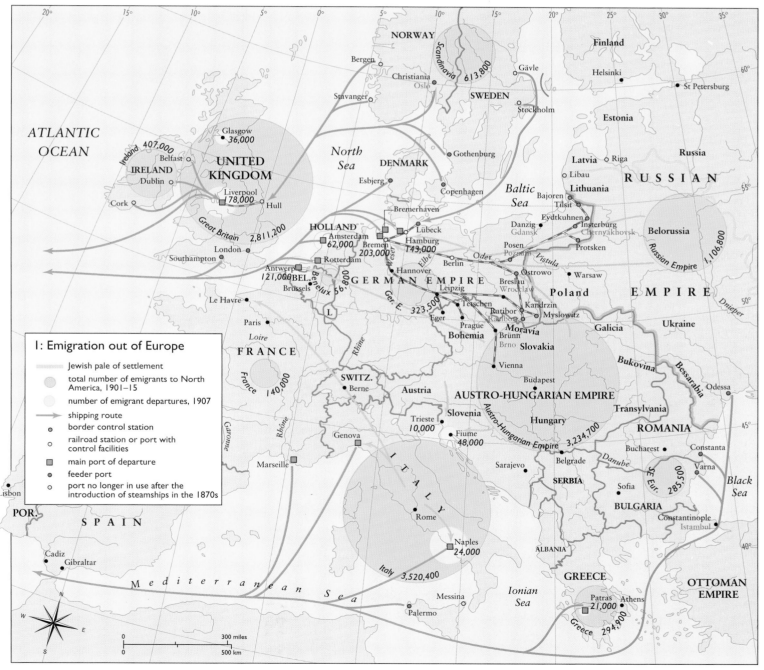

1: Emigration out of Europe

- Jewish pale of settlement
- total number of emigrants to North America, 1901–15
- number of emigrant departures, 1907
- shipping route
- border control station
- railroad station or port with control facilities
- main port of departure
- feeder port
- port no longer in use after the introduction of steamships in the 1870s

115

MID EUROPE TO MID WEST
IMMIGRATION FROM WEST CENTRAL EUROPE, 1860–1920

German-speaking peoples formed the largest group of immigrants after English-speakers. Their impact on North American culture and society was profound, especially in the Midwest.

In the mid-19th century, German speakers were spread across a vast area of central Europe. Germany was of a patchwork of small states, whose dialect and culture differed widely despite their common mother tongue. In 1871 they were unified to form the German Reich. Among its many minorities, the Reich included Danes, Alsatians, Poles and Sorbs (a small Slavic group from the area around Cottbus). To the south and east lay the Austro-Hungarian empire; dominated by German-speaking Austrians, it too included many ethnic minorities, most of them Slavs. German speakers also lived in Switzerland, the Balkans and southeast Russia.

Germany and Austria, like the U. S. and Canada, industrialized later than their European neighbors, and industrialized rapidly. This imposed great stresses on their social fabric. Central Europe had a long tradition of migration—North German farm workers had been moving to Dutch areas for two centuries—and this trend increased throughout the 19th century. Seasonal work at harvest time accustomed people to cash wages, and this often led them to migrate to the cities, either at home or abroad. Some areas experienced a dramatic rise in population, while many rural areas became severely depopulated. At the turn of the century, over half the urban population in Germany had not been born in the cities. Germany became the second largest labor-importing country after the U. S., and 95 percent of Austro-Hungarian migration consisted of internal movement of workers to large cities.

Increasing numbers of farm workers from the northeast were drawn to the wages to be had in North American cities. More than 4 million left for North America between 1860 and 1920, with emigration peaking between 1864 and 1873 and again between 1880 and 1893. The later wave of migration included 230,000 Swiss, several hundred thousand Austrians and Balkan Germans, and members of German-speaking religious groups—including Mennonites, Amish and Hutterites—from Russia, where the government had abolished their privileges in 1872.

These German-speakers combined with around 150,000 other migrants from Belgium, the Netherlands and Luxembourg.

The German immigrants settled mainly in the cities of Ontario and the northeastern U. S., as well as in the Midwest and Alberta. German-speaking communities could also be found in Louisiana and Texas. Most German-speaking immigrants in the U. S. came from the Reich. In Canada, on the other hand, 80 percent of immigrants came from other German-speaking areas. In addition to this, further migration within North America also brought the "Dutch" settlers of Pennsylvania to Ontario and the Canadian prairies.

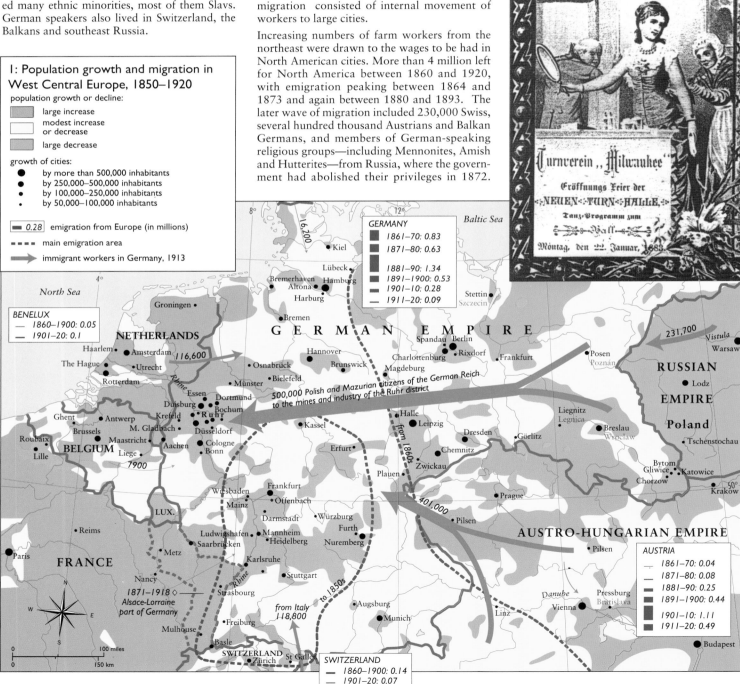

1: Population growth and migration in West Central Europe, 1850–1920

population growth or decline:

- large increase
- modest increase or decrease
- large decrease

growth of cities:

- ● by more than 500,000 inhabitants
- ● by 250,000–500,000 inhabitants
- ● by 100,000–250,000 inhabitants
- • by 50,000–100,000 inhabitants

▭ *0.28* emigration from Europe (in millions)

- - - - main emigration area

➜ immigrant workers in Germany, 1913

BENELUX
— 1860–1900: 0.05
— 1901–20: 0.1

GERMANY
1861–70: 0.83
1871–80: 0.63
1881–90: 1.34
1891–1900: 0.53
1901–10: 0.28
1911–20: 0.09

AUSTRIA
1861–70: 0.04
1871–80: 0.08
1881–90: 0.25
1891–1900: 0.44
1901–10: 1.11
1911–20: 0.49

SWITZERLAND
1860–1900: 0.14
1901–20: 0.07

500,000 Polish and Mazurian citizens of the German Reich to the mines and industry of the Ruhr district

231,700

116,600

16,200

7900

401,000

from 1860s

to 1850s

from Italy 118,800

1871–1918 ◇ Alsace-Lorraine part of Germany

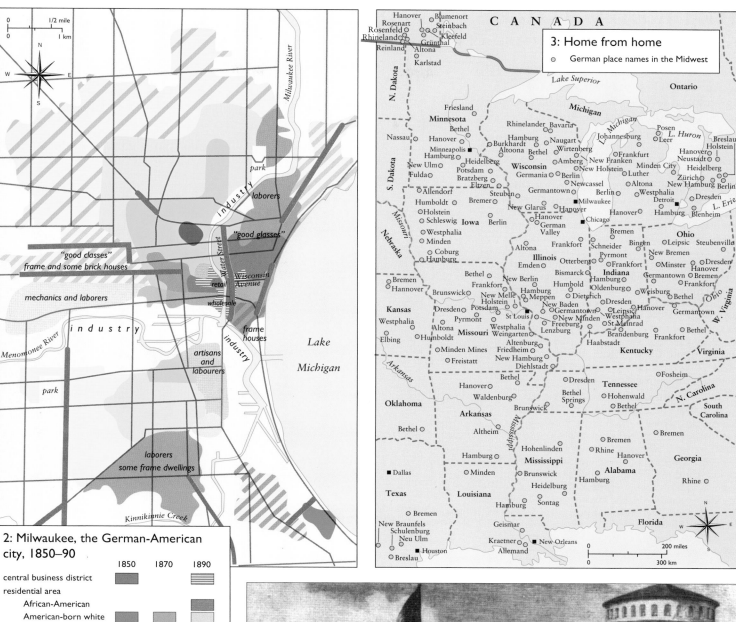

3: Home from home

○ German place names in the Midwest

2: Milwaukee, the German-American city, 1850–90

	1850	1870	1890
central business district			
residential area			
African-American			
American-born white			
German			
Irish			
Italian			
Polish			
Russian-Jewish			
Scandinavian			
Dutch and Bohemian			
other			

Above left: a program for a ball held at the Turnverein in Milwaukee, where Sunday concerts prompted one satisfied German customer to conclude that it was "not proper to miss it...because it costs only fifteen cents on a season ticket, and the music fits in with the slumbrous Sabbath feeling that follows a dinner of Knoedel and Sauerbraten. Also, the setting is meant for relaxation," he continued. "There are tables and chairs...and when we come in the hall is already misty with cigar smoke... waiters [come] laden with steins [and] waitresses bring trays of coffee and cakes..."

Right: Castle Garden was the main entry station for immigrants at New York until Ellis Island was built. The poster, in German, is recruiting new arrivals from Germany into the U. S. Army in 1861.

BETWEEN FOREST AND PRAIRIE
SCANDINAVIAN IMMIGRATION, 1865-1914

Railroad and shipping companies recruited families from the depressed agricultural regions of Scandinavia to populate the prairies of the Midwest and southern Canada.

Scandinavians had come to the Midwest before the Civil War in relatively small numbers. But after 1865, tens of thousands deserted the fjords and river valleys of southern Norway and the forests of central and southern Sweden. Few people felt the need to emigrate from rich agricultural districts such as coastal Norway, the interior plains of Sweden, and much of Denmark. By the late 1860s, agents for land, railroad and shipping companies were actively recruiting emigrants, while those already in America sent thousands of prepaid tickets to waiting friends and relatives. The shipping trade was dominated by the North German lines and the six firms that made up the Liverpool Circle, but by the 1880s more than 20 companies were competing for the emigrant traffic from Scandinavia.

Once in America, most immigrants were ferried to their destination by rail. Most early immigrants settled in rural areas. Pre-Civil War settlements often served as staging areas for the new arrivals, who then moved on to found daughter settlements. Large agricultural settlements clustered along a broad arc stretching from northern Illinois to the Red River valley on the Minnesota-North Dakota border along the westward advancing frontier. This transition zone between forest and prairie provided an attractive environment for many settlers, who sought rich prairie soils near both wood and water. They had to adapt rapidly. Many Scandinavians had experience of forest work back home, so they were able to spend their first few winters working as loggers until they had raised enough money to buy a farm. Wheat, seldom grown in Scandinavia, was the great frontier crop.

In the rural areas Scandinavian immigrants formed closely-knit, insular communities. Swedes and Norwegians rarely mixed with one another, let alone with non-Scandinavian settlers, although Norwegians often lived alongside Danes. Many settlements consisted of people from the same province, district and sometimes even from the same extended family. In the cities, however, interaction was more intense, particularly when the groups had to combine to support their first organizations and newspapers. Large Scandinavian communities developed in Worcester, Massachussetts, Chicago, Seattle and Tacoma, Washington, and in other cities.

After 1880, the pattern changed. Scandinavian immigration soared to its highest recorded levels—80,000 in 1882—but instead of families looking for land to farm, the new emigrants were young adults in search of employment: farm hands, maidservants, artisans and laborers. They gravitated to the cities, especially in the Middle West. Most of them were Swedes, since fewer Danes and Norwegians came from

1: Scandinavians in North America, 1865—1915

Areas settled by Scandinavians, 1890:

moderate (10—25% of population)

substantial (over 25% of population)

○ city with major Scandinavian population, 1890

original migration

second-generation migration, 1911

railroad

towns or had skills suitable for the expanding urban labor markets.

Nearly a million Scandinavian-born people were living in North America by 1890. The vast majority had settled in the Upper Middle West, although other concentrations were scattered from Pennsylvania to Puget Sound. Although Quebec was a major port of arrival, most of the Scandinavians settled in the U. S. until 1890.

After 1890, once much of the land in the Midwest had been taken, large numbers of Scandinavians and second generation Scandinavian–Americans migrated to a scattering of settlements in North Dakota or on the newly-opened lands of the Canadian prairie provinces of Manitoba, Saskatchewan and Alberta. When joined by new immigrants coming directly from Scandinavia, they eventually made up a sizable Scandinavian presence in Western Canada.

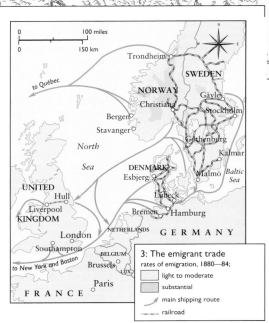

3: The emigrant trade
rates of emigration, 1880—84:

light to moderate

substantial

main shipping route

railroad

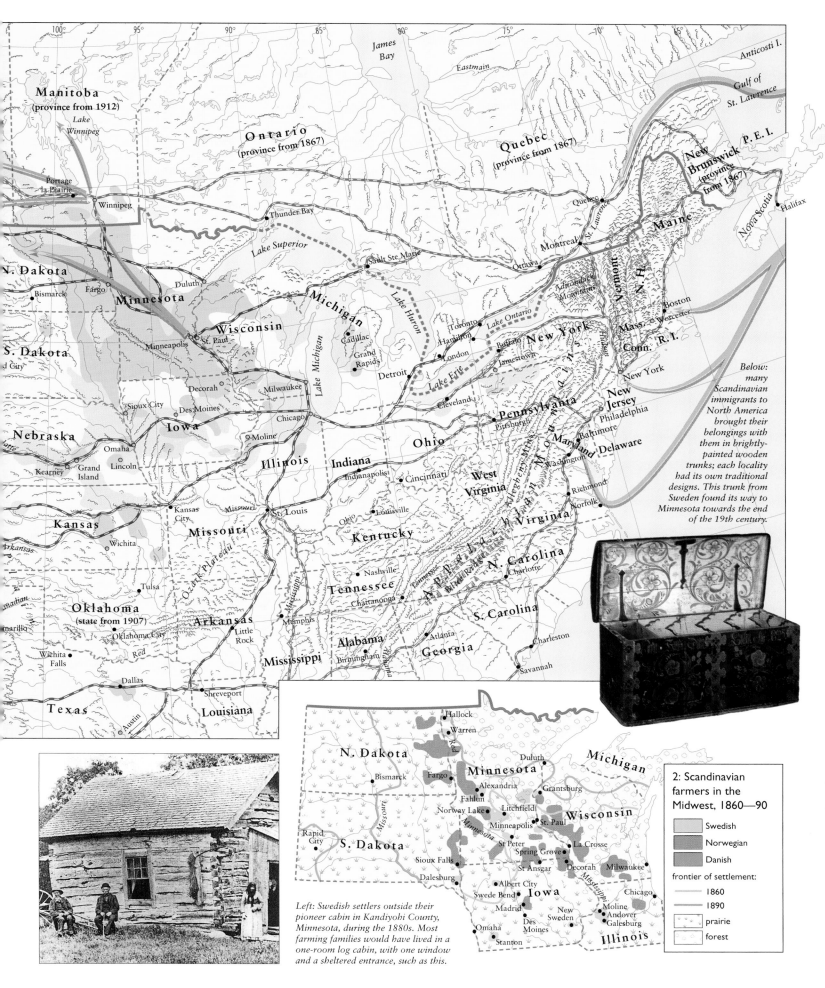

Below: many Scandinavian immigrants to North America brought their belongings with them in brightly-painted wooden trunks; each locality had its own traditional designs. This trunk from Sweden found its way to Minnesota towards the end of the 19th century.

2: Scandinavian farmers in the Midwest, 1860—90

Swedish
Norwegian
Danish

frontier of settlement:
1860
1890
prairie
forest

Left: Swedish settlers outside their pioneer cabin in Kandiyohi County, Minnesota, during the 1880s. Most farming families would have lived in a one-room log cabin, with one window and a sheltered entrance, such as this.

119

FROM FEAR TO FREEDOM
EAST CENTRAL AND EASTERN EUROPEAN MIGRATION, 1882–1920

In some respects, the living patterns of East European migrants remained similar after they arrived in America. In cities such as Cleveland (below) they continued to hold markets very much like this one at Kolomyi in Galicia (left). But in many ways people's lives were vastly changed as they moved from small agricultural plots or shtetls —the Jewish villages of Poland—into underground mine work or the belching steel factories.

The pogroms and poverty of Eastern Europe in the late 19th century brought a new wave of migrants to the industrial cities of North America.

East Central and East European immigrants had come to North America in very small numbers before the Civil War, but after the mid-1890s migration from the west of the Russian Empire and the eastern part of the Austro-Hungarian monarchy increased. With the beginning of anti-Jewish pogroms in Russia in 1882, whole families of Russian Jews began a flight that brought 2 million men, women and children to North America, almost one third of the total East European Jewish population. Other Central and Eastern Europeans were generally single men with little money—$12–20 in the early 1900s—who brought women relatives later. Women came if jobs were available for them; often they worked as boardinghouse keepers, caring for up to two dozen men.

Eastern Europe's troubled history of migrations and wars had created regions of mixed ethnic settlement and small islands of people in the midst of larger communities. These patterns were repeated in North America. Even illiterate migrants often had a grasp of more than one language; at home, they might speak their neighbor's language, and also had to know the imperial administrative language, Russian or German. As a result, migrant groups were able to communicate with each other after they arrived in America.

Some newcomers, including Jewish migrants, settled as farmers. In 1896 Canada began recruiting East European settlers for the plains region of Saskatchewan and Alberta. But most migrants went to the cities as unskilled laborers. Small groups settled in southern New Jersey and New England, but in the east, the majority went to Philadelphia and the coalmining areas of Scranton and Wilkes Barre, Pennsylvania. Most migrants went on to Buffalo, Cleveland, Detroit, Chicago and the Canadian cities. Prejudice against East and South Europeans in the U. S. led to exclusionary moves in 1917 and in the 1920s, and so the major period of immigration lasted only from the 1890s to 1914; in Canada it continued into the 1920s.

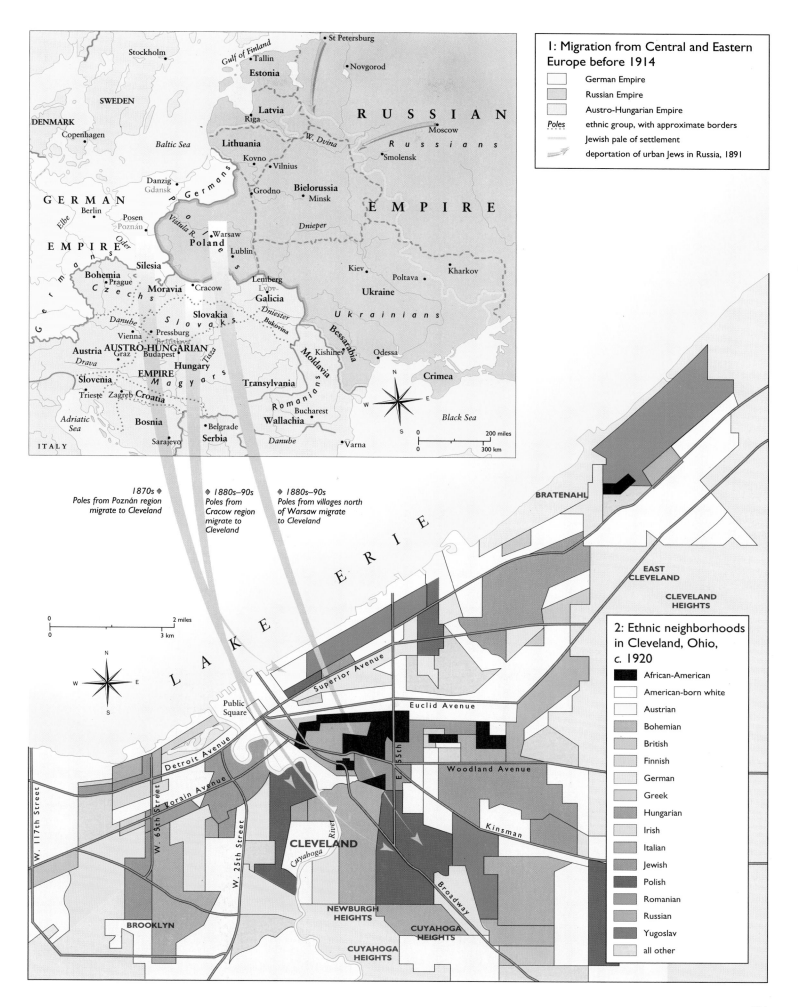

1: Migration from Central and Eastern Europe before 1914

- German Empire
- Russian Empire
- Austro-Hungarian Empire
- *Poles* ethnic group, with approximate borders
- Jewish pale of settlement
- deportation of urban Jews in Russia, 1891

Stockholm

SWEDEN

DENMARK
Copenhagen

Gulf of Finland
Tallin
Estonia

St Petersburg
Novgorod

RUSSIAN

Baltic Sea

Latvia
Riga

Lithuania
Kovno
Vilnius

Moscow

Russians

W. Dvina

Smolensk

EMPIRE

Danzig
Gdansk

Germans

Grodno

Bielorussia
Minsk

GERMAN
Berlin

Posen
Poznán

Elbe
Oder
Poles

Vistula R.
Warsaw
Poland

Dnieper

EMPIRE

Lublin

Kiev
Poltava
Kharkov

Silesia

Bohemia
Prague
Moravia
Czechs

Cracow

Lemberg
Lvov
Galicia

Ukraine

Germans

Danube

Slovakia
Slovaks

Dniester
Bukovina

Ukrainians

Vienna
Pressburg
Bratislava

AUSTRO-HUNGARIAN

Bessarabia

Kishinev

Odessa

Austria
Graz
Budapest

Drava
Hungary
Magyars

Moldavia

Crimea

Slovenia

EMPIRE
Tisza
Transylvania

Trieste
Zagreb
Croatia

Romanians

Black Sea

Adriatic Sea

Bosnia
Belgrade

Romania

Bucharest
Wallachia

Sarajevo
Serbia

Danube

Varna

ITALY

0   200 miles
0   300 km

1870s
Poles from Poznán region migrate to Cleveland

1880s–90s
Poles from Cracow region migrate to Cleveland

1880s–90s
Poles from villages north of Warsaw migrate to Cleveland

LAKE ERIE

BRATENAHL

EAST CLEVELAND

CLEVELAND HEIGHTS

0   2 miles
0   3 km

Superior Avenue

Public Square

Euclid Avenue

Detroit Avenue

Lorain Avenue

E. 55th

Woodland Avenue

W. 117th Street

W. 65th Street

W. 25th Street

Cuyahoga River

CLEVELAND

Kinsman

Broadway

NEWBURGH HEIGHTS

BROOKLYN

CUYAHOGA HEIGHTS

CUYAHOGA HEIGHTS

2: Ethnic neighborhoods in Cleveland, Ohio, c. 1920

- African-American
- American-born white
- Austrian
- Bohemian
- British
- Finnish
- German
- Greek
- Hungarian
- Irish
- Italian
- Jewish
- Polish
- Romanian
- Russian
- Yugoslav
- all other

"GO MAKE AMERICA"

MIGRATION FROM THE MEDITERRANEAN, 1870–1920

The unification of Italy began a wave of immigration from southern Europe, and Greek, Spanish, Portuguese, and Italian enclaves began to spring up throughout the U.S. and Canada.

Emigration from Italy began earlier than from other southern European countries, and by 1880 there were an estimated 56,000 Italians in the U. S. This was mainly due to strife arising from the unification of the small principalities and territories into a single Kingdom of Italy in 1861. The arrival of 2 million Italian immigrants in the United States between 1900 and 1910 was the most dramatic mass migration from the Mediterranean, but they were followed by lesser numbers of migrants from other South European countries: Greece, Spain, and Portugal. These Mediterranean immigrants were generally single men, and around half of them returned to Europe within a few years. Some even made the round trip several times.

The stream of departures began in northern Italy, then shifted to the central and southern regions. Early north Italian immigrants tended to settle in New Orleans and San Francisco, although there were also smaller enclaves in Canadian cities such as Montreal, Toronto, Vancouver, and Winnipeg. The majority of Italian immigrants, however, eventually came from the impoverished rural south of Italy. They rapidly replaced the Irish as day-laborers in the burgeoning milltowns of the northeastern U. S. Only 60,000 Italians migrated directly to Canada during the same period, but they made up about half the work force in the railroad camps of the Canadian

Above: despite initial hardships, many Italian immigrants succeeded in establishing themselves as shopkeepers and artisans. This thriving Italian grocery was photographed in New York's Lower East Side in the 1890s.

prairies and the American West. There was a sharp fall in immigration with the outbreak of World War I in 1914, and by the time the U. S. passed restrictive legislation in 1920, the number of Italian-born residents had decreased by 50 percent within ten years.

In the 1890s significant numbers of Greek immigrants began to join the work force in the industrial towns of the northeastern and north-central U. S. They came both from Greece itself, a young nation-state which had declared its independence from the Ottoman Empire in 1821, and from areas of Turkey which were still under Ottoman rule, where their civil rights were severely curtailed. By 1910, Greek immigration to the U. S. had increased tenfold.

Most Portuguese immigrants came from the Azores, a group of islands a thousand miles west of Lisbon, although some also came from the mainland and from the Madeira Islands 500 miles to the southwest. They settled mainly in Connecticut, Rhode Island, and Massachusetts,

Left: an Italian home under a dump, from Jacob Riis's book The Children of the Poor. *The dumps—wooden bridges from which garbage was dumped into river barges—provided the poor with both shelter and a source of material they could use or sell.*

where some worked in the fishing industry. Spanish immigrants arriving before 1900 settled in the former Spanish colonies of Louisiana, California, and Florida. After 1900 a further Spanish contingent arrived, containing a higher proportion of literate and skilled workers. They formed sizable enclaves in the industrial northeast of the U. S., including New York, New Jersey, Pennsylvania, Connecticut, and Michigan.

By 1920 there were a total of one and a half million immigrants from Spain, Portugal, Italy, Greece, and parts of Turkey living in North America; of these, more than a million were Italian. For them, the U. S. was a land of opportunity. The popular Italian expression for emigration—whether to some remote railway construction camp in the middle of the Canadian prairies or to the burgeoning milltowns of the northeastern U. S.—was to "fare l'America": "go make America."

T he townsmen of some Italian villages, when there is sufficient number of them within reach, club together to celebrate its patron saint, and hire a band and set up a gorgeous altar in a convenient back yard. The fire escapes overlooking it are draped with flags and transformed into reserved-seat galleries with the taste these people display under the most adverse circumstances.

Jacob Riis, *The Children of the Poor*, 1892

2: South European homelands of migrants to America, c. 1919

→ shipping routes

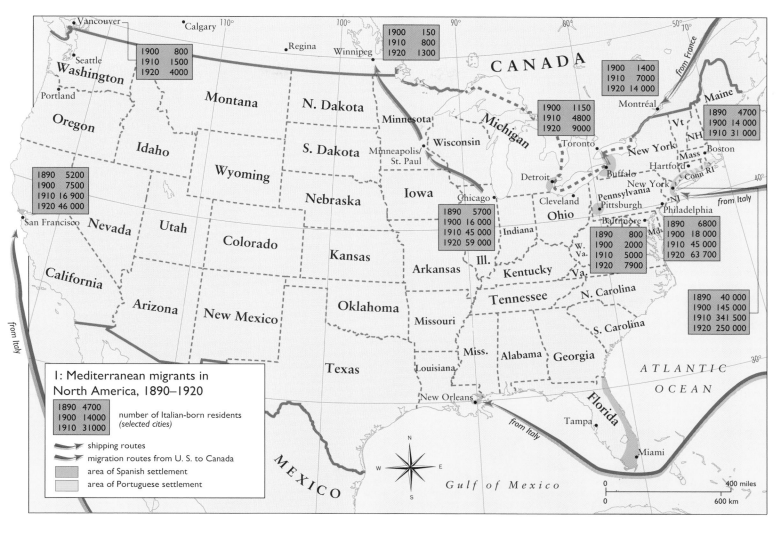

1: Mediterranean migrants in North America, 1890–1920

1890	4700
1900	14000
1910	31000

number of Italian-born residents *(selected cities)*

shipping routes

migration routes from U. S. to Canada

area of Spanish settlement

area of Portuguese settlement

Left: many Italian immigrants in New York lived in overcrowded and insanitary rear tenements such as this one on Roosevelt Street. This engraving, again based on a photograph by Jacob Riis, comes from his book How the Other Half Lives. Riis was a Danish photographer who campaigned to improve the conditions of immigrant families in New York.

3: South European immigrants to the U. S., 1900–20

- Italy
- Greece
- Portugal
- Spain

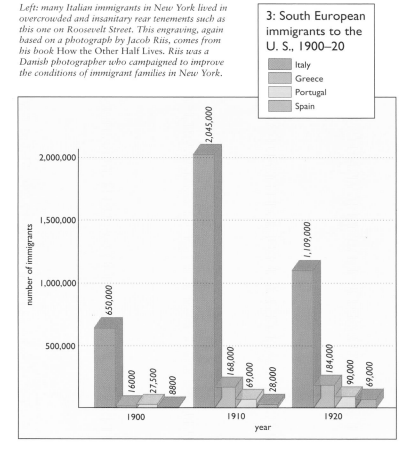

123

PRAIRIES AND PLAINS
MIDWESTERN AND WESTERN CULTURAL PATTERNS, 1865–1920

Germans and Scandinavians, East Europeans and African-Americans pushed westward to people the prairies and plains of the "Great American Desert" and Canada's "Last Best West."

In the U. S., settlement west of the Mississippi increased rapidly after the end of the Civil War in 1865. In 1862 the U. S. Congress had passed the Homestead Act, giving settlers a claim to a quarter section—160 acres—if they lived on the land for five years. While "sturdy settlers" moved west, cattle herders drove stock north onto the plains from Texas (> *pages 128–9*). West of the 100th degree, low rainfalls seemed to prohibit settlement in what for long had been called the "Great American Desert." But new plant breeds and irrigation made the area tillable, and the Desert Land Act of 1877 regulated the sale of lands in whole sections at low cost. Even then, the area remained far more sparsely settled than more hospitable lands to the east.

The frontier was never one continuous westward advance of settlers. They were preceded first by fur traders, then in some areas by loggers, in others by miners. Areas which were only partially fertile were passed over; in other places an advance guard of settlers would forge ahead of the main stream. Parallel to settlement, Irish and Italian railroad laborers advanced from the east, while Chinese track crews came from the west, working on the transcontinental railroads which were completed between 1868 and 1885. The railroad companies then sold adjoining parcels of land to settlers.

The predominant groups were Germans and Scandinavians, who settled in a broad belt across the northwest of the U. S. and the southern Canadian prairies; African-Americans moving from the southeast through Texas; and Mexican-Americans along the Mexican border. Many smaller groups added to the cultural mix of the West. Chinese landed on the west coast of Canada and spread eastward across the prairies, opening restaurants in many small towns. From Russia and Austria-Hungary, the old empires that ruled Central and Eastern Europe's patchwork of peoples, came a variety of religious and ethnic minorities. Many of the newcomers settled alongside compatriots from the same region or even the same village, preserving their old

cultural patterns in the Canadian, and U. S. West. Ukrainians from the Austrian provinces of Galicia and Bukovynia concentrated in Southern Manitoba. German-speaking Mennonites from Russia also settled there and in North Dakota, while members of a Russian religious sect called the Doukhobors—the name means "spirit wrestlers"—went to the Canadian prairies.

The settlement of the Canadian west began later, and continued longer, than that of the U. S. prairies and plains. The Dominion of Canada—today's Canadian state—was established in 1867. Three years later, in 1870, it incorporated Rupert's Land, a vast tract of the northwest which had previously belonged to the Hudson's Bay Company, and created the Province of Manitoba in the same year. But large numbers of people did not move to the Western Prairies until the 1880s and 1890s. The soil and climate of much of this land was only marginally suitable for agriculture, so settlement was mostly confined to a more fertile belt of aspen-poplars in the south, continuing into the Peace River valley in Alberta and British Columbia in the 1920s.

Not everyone moved from east to west. While Ontarians moved onto the prairies and

Left: Swedish pioneers in the late 19th century. From the American Midwest, many Scandinavians moved up the Red River valley to settle the Canadian prairies.

2: Ethnic distribution in the Canadian prairies, 1904–11

▨	populated area (more than 2 people per square mile), 1911
▫	aspen poplar belt

ethnic origin (by township):

- First Nation Reserves
- Métis
- American (including Canadians returned from U. S.)
- Canadian (British)
- Canadian (French)
- English, Scots, and Welsh
- Austrian Empire (including Ukrainians)
- German and Mennonite
- Scandinavian
- railroad
- railroad land grant

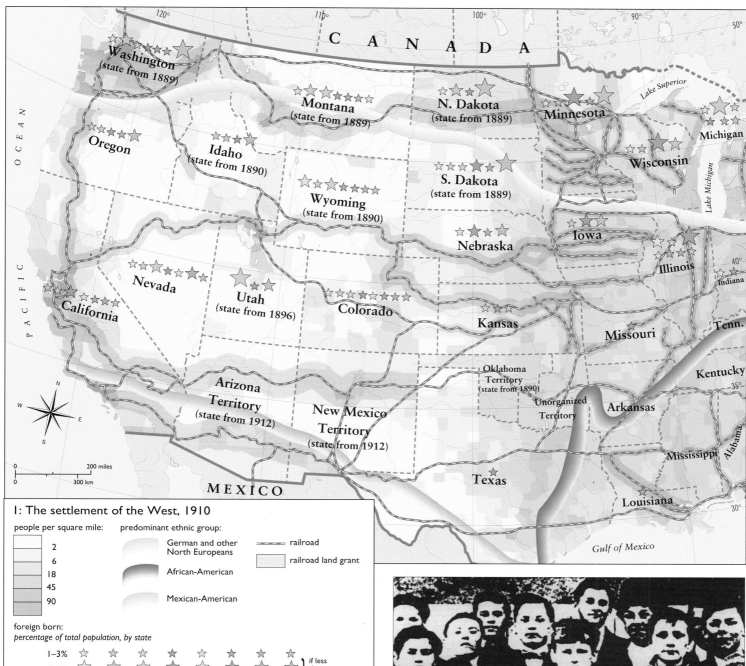

1: The settlement of the West, 1910

people per square mile:

2
6
18
45
90

predominant ethnic group:

German and other North Europeans

African-American

Mexican-American

railroad

railroad land grant

foreign born:
percentage of total population, by state

1–3%
3–5%
more than 5%

if less than 1%- no symbol

Austrian Empire
Canadian
English, Scots and Welsh
German
Irish
Italian
Russian Empire
Scandinavian

American farmers often made several moves westward, millions of native-born and new Canadians moved south into the U. S. plains, and millions of Americans, including Mormons from Utah and Idaho, went north across the 49th parallel to settle in Canada. The population of the U. S. prairies and plains grew from 600,000 in 1860 to 9.2 million in 1920, and that of Canada's "Last Best West" from 100,000 in 1881 to 2 million in 1921. But there was a limit to the numbers that these regions could absorb. The surplus sons and daughters of farming families formed a steady eastward stream that filled the cities, and from 1891 on, Canada's urban population grew faster than that of its rural areas.

Right: a group of Ukrainian schoolboys and their teacher pose for a class photograph in Teulon, Manitoba, 1911. Many Ukrainians settled in southern Manitoba, where they maintained their traditional lifeways and allegiances, even building houses in the distinct styles of their native provinces.

RESERVATIONS AND RESISTANCE

INDIANS AND MÉTIS, 1850–96

As settlers pushed on beyond the 100th parallel, all the Indians in the western U. S. fought to defend their homelands and avoid confinement on reservations.

From the 1850s to the 1890s, the U. S. Army engaged in over 1000 battles to subdue Indian resistance, taking on one group at a time in campaigns involving up to 4000 or 5000 soldiers. Where settlements were being formed, organized militia and volunteers joined in the hostilities. In the Northwest Pacific coast region, where the boundary between the U. S. and British Columbia was settled in 1846, numerous Indian groups had been forced through treaties to accept reservations in the 1850s. But there were always holdouts.

Violence intensified over a broad range of territory in the 1860s. In the East, the battles of the Civil War involved about 4000 Indian soldiers in the Union Army and close to 10,000 on the Confederate side. At the war's end, the Federal government took the western part of Indian Territory from the five slave-holding tribes as punishment for their support of the Confederacy. Part of the land became reservations for western tribes, but a portion became Oklahoma Territory in 1890, and attracted a land rush. On the western plains, settlers and miners streamed into Indian hunting grounds. The army command ordered Indian people to stay away from the "Holy Road," reserved for non-Indians headed west. The long wagon-trains drove away the buffalo herds, depleting water resources and grazing lands. In retaliation, Indian raiders burned wagons, seized stage coaches and attacked railroad crews and travelers. The army adopted a strategy of deliberate starvation; by 1885, the buffalo herds had all been destroyed. Officers also seized Indian ponies to immobilize the bands, and exploited tribal hostilities by using scouts and warriors from one tribe against their traditional enemies.

A number of events mark the course of a brave and tragic era of frontier warfare. The Minnesota Sioux uprising in 1862 was a reaction to crowding by settlers, and to hunger caused by the government's long overdue payment of annuities for land sales and the refusal of a local trader to extend credit. Although only a part of the Sioux were responsible for the initial attacks on traders and settlers, retaliatory warfare spread throughout Minnesota and Dakota Territory in the ensuing years. The "hostiles" fled to Canada while the "friendlies" who gathered obediently in prison camps bore most of the punishment. On 26 December 1863, 39 Sioux—including some who were innocent—were hanged; 247 were imprisoned in Iowa; and 1300 exiled to a Missouri River reservation at Crow Creek in 1866. At Sand Creek in southeastern Colorado in 1864, militiamen killed a hundred sleeping Cheyenne women and children, part of a group trying to return to their home country. When 8000 Navajos surrendered the same year, many were forced 300 miles east to Bosque Redondo, a camp guarded by Fort Sumner. They did not return from this Long Walk until 1868. There were many deaths from starvation along the way, and among the thousands who avoided capture by going into hiding.

The Modoc War (1872–73) on the northern Californian border ended in the exile of the Modocs to a reservation in Indian Territory. The resounding Sioux and Cheyenne victory at Little Big Horn in Montana in June 1876 was followed by military suppression. A second, more dramatic campaign in 1877 pitted the Army against Chief Joseph and a band of Nez Perces who had refused to leave their fertile valley and move to Idaho. After a 1700-mile chase, the Army cornered the talented leader just 40 miles below the border of Canada, where Sitting Bull of the Sioux had taken refuge the previous year. Geronimo, last of a line of Apaches unreconciled to accepting reservation life, outwitted the army until 1886, when he was captured in Mexico and imprisoned at St Augustine, Florida, before being sent to Oklahoma. Ultimately he became a legendary hero who rode in President Theodore Roosevelt's inaugural parade in 1905.

Canada's far less populous western provinces experienced only two serious military confrontations, the Riel uprisings of 1868–70 and 1885. The first was provoked by plans to end the Hudson's Bay Company government of Ruperts Land and establish a province of Manitoba within the Canadian Confederation. The Red River Métis—part French Catholic, part Indian—had small reason to expect that their land and civil rights would be respected under Anglo–Protestant rule. Led by Louis Riel, they attempted to resist settlement. When the military finally gained control, Riel fled to Ojibwa protection at Red Lake, Minnesota, before making his way west to Montana where he became a schoolteacher and a U. S. citizen.

The Métis went west, establishing a sizable community along the South Branch of the Saskatchewan River near related Cree and Salteaux bands. By 1884, the buffalo had disappeared and the Indians were starving; the completion of the Canadian Pacific Railroad had opened the area to settlers; and government land prices were high. The Métis recalled Riel, who set up a provisional government at Batoche in 1885. Troops arrived within a week and gained control after several military engagements. The Cree leader Big Bear tried unsuccessfully to organize pan-Indian support, but finally surrendered at Fort Carleton. Louis Riel and eight Indians were hanged, while two whites were acquitted. Some refugees, Indian and Métis, fled over the border to Montana.

In both Canada and the U. S., administrators of Indian affairs pursued the same goals: to transform Indians into Christian farmers who cut their hair and lived like their neighbors of European ancestry. Both governments employed the same methods: they tried to enforce a pass system to keep Indians on reservations, and to eliminate native languages and traditions such as the sun dance and potlatch. Resistance continued, but decades were to pass before renewed vitality became apparent among the First Nations of North America.

Below: U. S. troops force-march Cheyenne prisoners, most of them women and children, through the snow after General Custer's attack on Black Kettle's village on the Washita in November 1868.

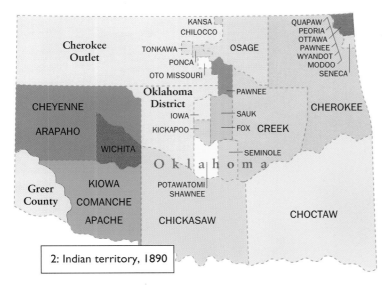

2: Indian territory, 1890

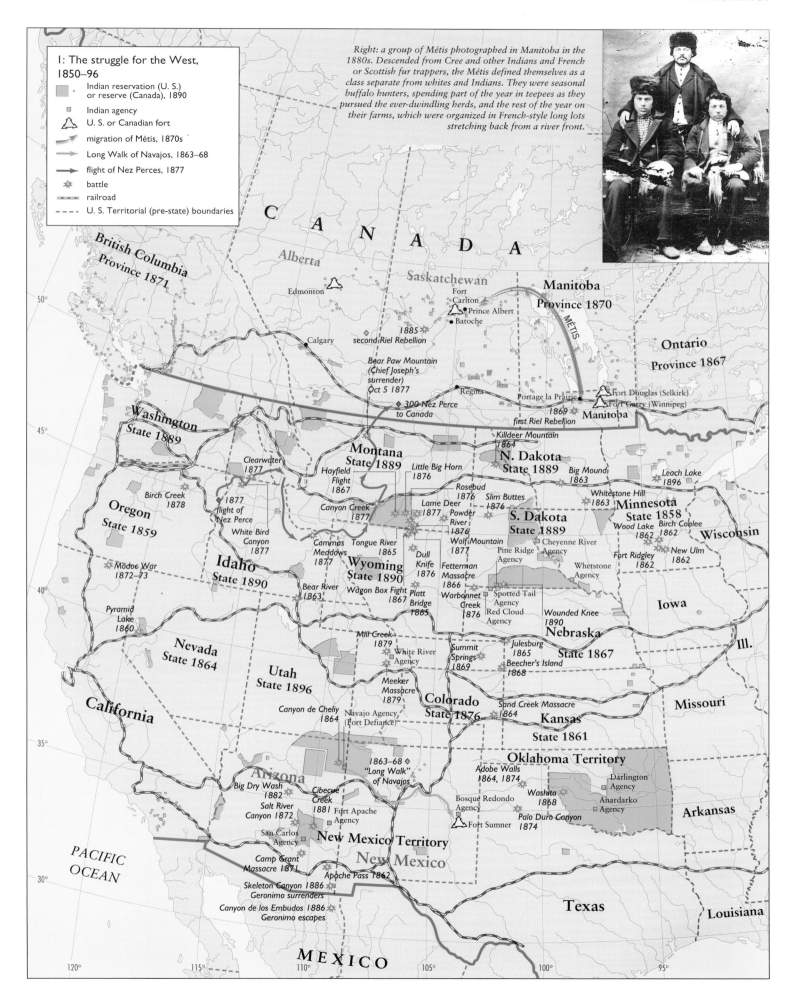

1: The struggle for the West, 1850–96

- Indian reservation (U.S.) or reserve (Canada), 1890
- Indian agency
- U.S. or Canadian fort
- migration of Métis, 1870s
- Long Walk of Navajos, 1863–68
- flight of Nez Perces, 1877
- battle
- railroad
- U.S. Territorial (pre-state) boundaries

Right: a group of Métis photographed in Manitoba in the 1880s. Descended from Cree and other Indians and French or Scottish fur trappers, the Métis defined themselves as a class separate from whites and Indians. They were seasonal buffalo hunters, spending part of the year in teepees as they pursued the ever-dwindling herds, and the rest of the year on their farms, which were organized in French-style long lots stretching back from a river front.

CANADA

British Columbia Province 1871

Alberta

Saskatchewan

Manitoba Province 1870

Edmonton

Fort Carlton

Prince Albert

Batoche

Ontario Province 1867

Calgary

1885 second Riel Rebellion

Bear Paw Mountain (Chief Joseph's surrender) Oct 5 1877

Regina

Portage la Prairie

Fort Douglas (Selkirk)

Fort Garry (Winnipeg)

1869 first Riel Rebellion

Manitoba

MÉTIS

300 Nez Perce to Canada

Washington State 1889

Clearwater 1877

Hayfield Flight 1867

Montana State 1889

Little Big Horn 1876

Killdeer Mountain 1864

N. Dakota State 1889

Big Mound 1863

Leach Lake 1896

Birch Creek 1878

Canyon Creek 1877

Rosebud 1876

Slim Buttes 1876

Whitestone Hill 1863

Minnesota State 1858

Oregon State 1859

1877 flight of Nez Perce

White Bird Canyon 1877

Lame Deer 1877

Powder River 1876

S. Dakota State 1889

Wood Lake 1862

Birch Coolee 1862

Wisconsin

Cammas Meadows 1877

Tongue River 1865

Wolf Mountain 1877

Cheyenne River Agency

Fort Ridgley 1862

New Ulm 1862

Idaho State 1890

Wyoming State 1890

Dull Knife 1876

Pine Ridge Agency

Whetstone Agency

Modoc War 1872–73

Bear River 1863

Wagon Box Fight 1867

Platt Bridge 1865

Fetterman Massacre 1866

Warbonnet Creek 1876

Spotted Tail Agency

Red Cloud Agency

Wounded Knee 1890

Iowa

Pyramid Lake 1860

Mill Creek 1879

White River Agency

Summit Springs 1869

Julesburg 1865

Beecher's Island 1868

Nebraska State 1867

Ill.

Nevada State 1864

Utah State 1896

Meeker Massacre 1879

Colorado State 1876

Sand Creek Massacre 1864

Kansas State 1861

Missouri

California

Canyon de Chelly 1864

Navajo Agency (Fort Defiance)

1863–68 "Long Walk" of Navajos

Oklahoma Territory

Arizona

Big Dry Wash 1882

Cibecue Creek 1881

Fort Apache Agency

Adobe Walls 1864, 1874

Darlington Agency

Salt River Canyon 1872

Bosque Redondo Agency

Washita 1868

Anardarko Agency

Arkansas

San Carlos Agency

New Mexico Territory

New Mexico

Fort Sumner

Palo Duro Canyon 1874

Camp Grant Massacre 1871

PACIFIC OCEAN

Skeleton Canyon 1886 Geronimo surrenders

Apache Pass 1862

Canyon de los Embudos 1886 Geronimo escapes

Texas

Louisiana

MEXICO

THE PEOPLE OF THE FAR WEST
MIGRATION TO CALIFORNIA AND THE FAR WEST, 1870-1920

In the 50 years from 1870 to 1920, immigrants came to the West from many directions, developing a multi-layered population of ranchers, miners, truck farmers, and laborers.

The dominant group of American and western Canadian newcomers came to include North Italian, German, and Irish immigrants from across the Atlantic. The Italians started vineyards and wineries, laying the basis for a major industry. The Chinese and Japanese represented the significant recent immigration from a new direction, across the Pacific Ocean. California's older population was composed of unobtrusive surviving Indians and the descendants of landowning Spanish colonists, along with later arriving Mexicans who continued to move north across the international border established in 1848 and 1853. By 1920, Mexicans made up more than 10 percent of the population of Arizona and California, but less than 5 percent of New Mexico and Colorado.

The big period for Chinese immigration, from 1854 to 1883, brought in more than 288,000 shopkeepers, craftsmen, and laborers, principally from the southeastern coastal provinces of Fukien and Kwangtung, and the region of Canton and the delta of the Pearl River. Chinese worked in mines, and on the railroads, and established tiny communities in towns along the railroad lines. Japanese immigration, from rural areas of all the islands, was highest between 1890 and 1908 when over 150,000 came to California, clustering in the central valley. Truck gardening became their special niche. Other gardeners came from the Philippine Islands, acquired by the U. S. in 1898 at the end of the Spanish-American War. Resentment against the Asian workers brought about legislation to exclude the Chinese in 1882, and curtail Japanese immigration in 1907, but exceptions to this legislation permitted men to bring in wives and families.

By the 1890s, the Indians had been assigned reservation "islands" in the vast country. Other "island" populations existed at sites of mineral discoveries, where communities rapidly changed from boom towns to ghost towns. A few rich veins like the Comstock Lode created longer-lasting cities. In order to stabilize society when immigration was high and mineral discoveries created transient populations, women in all western states except New Mexico received equal voting rights between 1890 and 1912.

Ranchers and farmers of the sparsely occupied interior Far West raised horses, cattle, sheep, hay crops, and some grain. From Colorado and New Mexico westward to California, land rights were contested in former Mexican territory, and most Mexican-owned properties were appropriated by Americans. The ranches hired "cowboys" of Euro-American, Mexican, African, and Indian heritage.

Right: ranchers of the West acquired many horses by breaking in wild mustangs, and displayed this skill at championships. Fanny Sperry Steele became Lady Bucking Horse Champion of the World at the first Calgary Stampede in 1912.
Below: North America's first "Chinatown" grew up in San Francisco, where this photograph of a butcher was taken by Arnold Genthe around 1900.

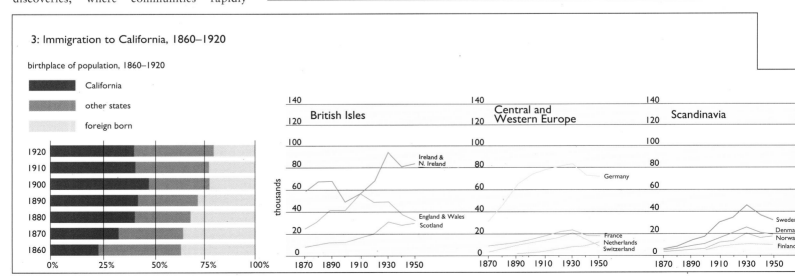

3: Immigration to California, 1860–1920

birthplace of population, 1860–1920

- California
- other states
- foreign born

British Isles

Central and Western Europe

Scandinavia

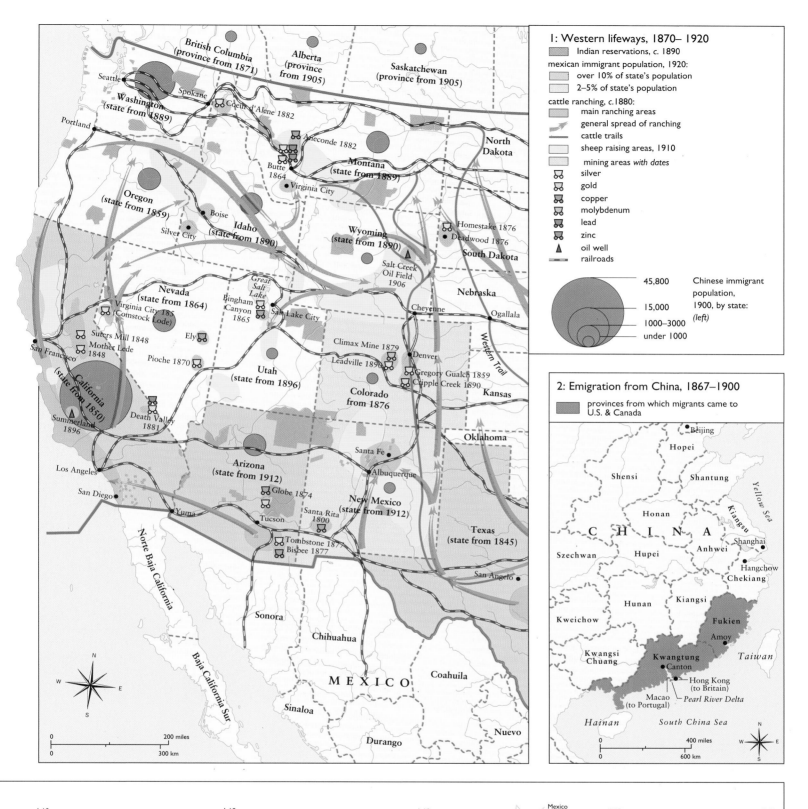

1: Western lifeways, 1870– 1920

Indian reservations, c. 1890

mexican immigrant population, 1920:
- over 10% of state's population
- 2–5% of state's population

cattle ranching, c.1880:
- main ranching areas
- general spread of ranching
- cattle trails
- sheep raising areas, 1910
- mining areas *with dates*
  - silver
  - gold
  - copper
  - molybdenum
  - lead
  - zinc
- oil well
- railroads

45,800 — Chinese immigrant population, 1900, by state: *(left)*
15,000
1000–3000
under 1000

British Columbia (province from 1871)
Alberta (province from 1905)
Saskatchewan (province from 1905)

Seattle
Spokane
Coeur d'Alene 1882
Washington (state from 1889)
Portland
Anaconde 1882
Butte 1864
Montana (state from 1889)
North Dakota
Virginia City
Oregon (state from 1859)
Boise
Idaho (state from 1890)
Silver City
Wyoming (state from 1890)
Homestake 1876
Deadwood 1876
South Dakota
Salt Creek Oil Field 1906
Great Salt Lake
Nevada (state from 1864)
Bingham Canyon 1865
Salt Lake City
Nebraska
Virginia City 185 (Comstock Lode)
Cheyenne
Ogallala
Suters Mill 1848
Mother Lode 1848
Ely
Pioche 1870
Climax Mine 1879
Leadville 1890
Denver
Gregory Gualch 1859
Cripple Creek 1890
Western Trail
San Francisco
Utah (state from 1896)
Colorado from 1876
Kansas
California (state from 1850)
Summerland 1896
Death Valley 1881
Los Angeles
Arizona (state from 1912)
Santa Fe
Albuquerque
Oklahoma
San Diego
Yuma
Globe 1874
Tucson
Santa Rita 1800
New Mexico (state from 1912)
Tombstone 1877
Bisbee 1877
Texas (state from 1845)
San Angelo
Norte Baja California
Sonora
Chihuahua
MEXICO
Coahuila
Baja California Sur
Sinaloa
Durango
Nuevo

N W E S

0 — 200 miles
0 — 300 km

2: Emigration from China, 1867–1900

provinces from which migrants came to U.S. & Canada

Beijing
Hopei
Shensi
Shantung
Honan
Yellow Sea
Kiangsu
CHINA
Szechwan
Hupei
Anhwei
Shanghai
Hangchow
Chekiang
Hunan
Kiangsi
Kweichow
Fukien
Amoy
Kwangsi Chuang
Kwangtung
Canton
Taiwan
Hong Kong (to Britain)
Macao (to Portugal)
Pearl River Delta
Hainan
South China Sea

0 — 400 miles
0 — 600 km

N W E S

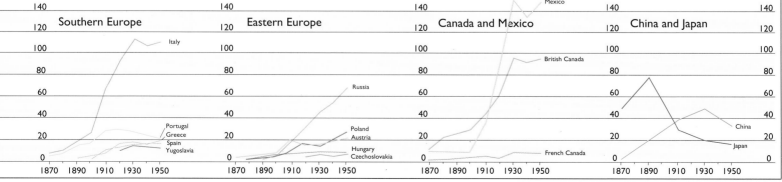

Southern Europe
140
120
100 — Italy
80
60
40
20 — Portugal / Greece / Spain / Yugoslavia
0
1870 1890 1910 1930 1950

Eastern Europe
140
120
100
80
60 — Russia
40
20 — Poland / Austria / Hungary / Czechoslovakia
0
1870 1890 1910 1930 1950

Canada and Mexico
140 — Mexico
120
100
80 — British Canada
60
40
20 — French Canada
0
1870 1890 1910 1930 1950

China and Japan
140
120
100
80
60
40 — China
20 — Japan
0
1870 1890 1910 1930 1950

THE PACIFIC NORTHWEST
MIGRATION TO ALASKA AND BRITISH COLUMBIA, 1783–1900

In the last region of North America to be settled by people of European origin, Russian fur traders were followed by sawmill and cannery workers, and thousands of migrants in search of gold.

Russian *promyshlenniki* (fur hunters) moved along the Aleutians from Siberia during the 18th century in pursuit of sea otters. Their first permanent base was set up by Grigory Shelikov in 1783 at Three Saints Harbor on Kodiak Island. His deputy, Alexander Baranov, moved it to St Paul's Harbor in 1792; today it is the city of Kodiak, the oldest non-native settlement in Alaska. After Shelikov's death his Russian American Company, now led by Baranov, obtained a charter from the Tsar in 1799 granting it a monopoly of the Russian American fur trade. The Russians were always few, and depended on the Aleut for the success of their enterprise, reducing them to near-slavery as hunters and domestic servants. To the south, the Tlingit put up fierce resistance, sacking the Russian post on Sitka Island in 1802.

Russian and Aleut hunters continued down the coast as far as northern California. By the 1820s, a second generation of *promyshlenniki* was largely composed of creoles of mixed Russian-Aleut parentage. The disruption and disease arising from Russian activity devastated the Aleut population: out of the estimated 30,000 living in the north when the Russians reached the Aleutians, only 3000 remained when Alaska was sold to the U. S. in 1867.

To the south, in what is now British Columbia, the coastal peoples lived semi-sedentary lives. Fishing provided a plentiful food supply, while the coastal rainforests furnished timber for sub-stantial plank-built houses. Nineteen distinct languages were spoken by the communities of the region. In the first half of the 19th century they developed trade relations with merchants from both British Canada (and occasionally Montreal) and Europe. Agents of companies such as Astor's Pacific Fur explored much of the area, while the Northwest Company surveyed parts of the Peace, Fraser, and Columbia rivers, which later became Hudson's Bay Company territory. In 1811 the first sawmills and tanneries began to appear along the coast.

The Pacific Northwest saw its greatest influx of migrants as a result of the gold rushes of the second half of the 19th century. Because the gold discovered was free or placer gold, which can be panned by amateurs (unlike hardrock gold, which requires expensive equipment to mine), large numbers of people traveled to the region in the hope of making their fortunes; the Fraser River gold rush of 1857–9 brought about 30,000 in one year. Between 1860 and 1866,

Above: the Russian settlement at New Archangel in 1826. This lithograph by F.H. von Kittlitz, a Russian veteran of the Napoleonic wars, shows "the most important and crowded area of the city." An Aleut watches from a rock which, "according to convention... belongs to the natives" as the Russians make their way to church.

further discoveries were made at Williams Creek, in the Barkerville area, at Kootenay, and at Cariboo. The last great gold rush took place in Alaska at the end of the century, following reports of strikes along a tributary of the Klondike River. The population of Dawson City grew to 25,000. British Columbia became a colony in 1858 to regulate the influx of gold-rush migrants, but the boost was temporary; after the end of the Cariboo rush, the population of British Columbia dropped from over 16,000 to 5000 before stabilizing at 9000–10,000. Industry and communications had a more lasting impact. The first fish canneries were opened in 1878, and their production quadrupled over the next 35 years. The Canadian Pacific Railway reached Vancouver in 1886, with shipping lines across the Pacific to China and Australasia opening the way for an Asian immigrant population. By the 1880s, towns such as Victoria and New Westminster had a large, mixed population, with the indigenous Indians living alongside Euro-Canadians and Chinese immigrants who worked on the railroads and in the canneries. Here too, contact spread infectious diseases and brought about a catastrophic reduction of the indigenous population. By 1885 they were a minority; by 1901 they constituted less than one eighth of the total population of British Columbia.

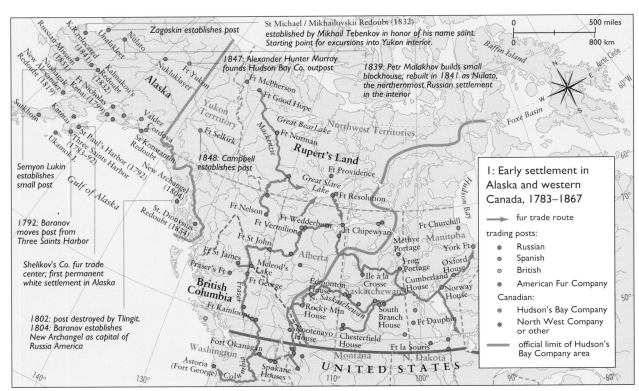

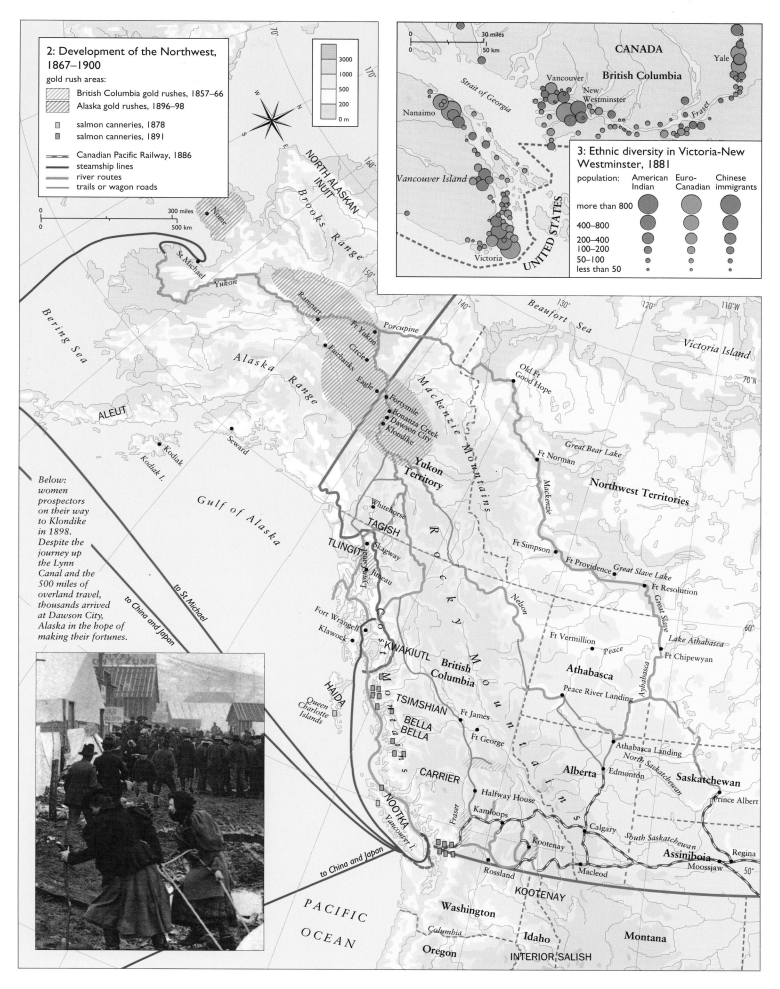

2: Development of the Northwest, 1867–1900

gold rush areas:

- ▨ British Columbia gold rushes, 1857–66
- ▨ Alaska gold rushes, 1896–98

- ▫ salmon canneries, 1878
- ▪ salmon canneries, 1891

⎯ Canadian Pacific Railway, 1886
⎯ steamship lines
⎯ river routes
⎯ trails or wagon roads

3000
1000
500
200
0 m

0   300 miles
0   500 km

3: Ethnic diversity in Victoria-New Westminster, 1881

population:	American Indian	Euro-Canadian	Chinese immigrants
more than 800			
400–800			
200–400			
100–200			
50–100			
less than 50			

Below: women prospectors on their way to Klondike in 1898. Despite the journey up the Lynn Canal and the 500 miles of overland travel, thousands arrived at Dawson City, Alaska in the hope of making their fortunes.

CANADA
British Columbia
Yale
Vancouver
New Westminster
Nanaimo
Fraser
Strait of Georgia
Vancouver Island
Victoria
UNITED STATES

NORTH ALASKAN INUIT
Brooks Range
Nome
St. Michael
Yukon
Bering Sea
ALEUT
Kodiak
Kodiak I.
Seward
Gulf of Alaska
Alaska Range
Rampart
Ft. Yukon
Porcupine
Circle
Fairbanks
Eagle
Fortymile
Bonanza Creek
Dawson City
Klondike
Yukon Territory
Whitehorse
TAGISH
Skagway
TLINGIT
Juneau
Lynn Canal
Fort Wrangell
Klawock
KWAKIUTL
HAIDA
Queen Charlotte Islands
TSIMSHIAN
BELLA BELLA
CARRIER
NOOTKA
Vancouver I.
Fraser
Kamloops
Halfway House
Kootenay
Rossland
KOOTENAY
to St. Michael
to China and Japan
to China and Japan
PACIFIC OCEAN

Mackenzie Mountains
Old Ft Good Hope
Great Bear Lake
Ft Norman
Mackenzie
Beaufort Sea
Victoria Island
Northwest Territories
Ft Simpson
Ft Providence
Great Slave Lake
Ft Resolution
Great Slave
Lake Athabasca
Ft Chipewyan
Ft Vermillion
Peace
Athabasca
Peace River Landing
Ft James
Ft George
British Columbia
Rocky Mountains
Coast Mountains
Nelson
Athabasca Landing
North Saskatchewan
Alberta
Edmonton
Saskatchewan
Prince Albert
Calgary
South Saskatchewan
Macleod
Assiniboia
Regina
Moossjaw
Washington
Columbia
Oregon
Idaho
Montana
INTERIOR SALISH

70°N
60°
50°

PEOPLING AMERICA'S INDUSTRY

THE MOVE TO THE CITIES, 1860-1920

The rapid growth of industry and its demand for labor promoted the development of North America's great cities and their diverse, multicultural mosaic of immigrant neighborhoods.

The half century between 1865 and 1917 was, in the U. S., a period of rapid industrialization and urbanization. More and more newcomers went to the urban centers. The earlier migrants—English, Scots, Germans, and Scandinavians—were mostly employed as skilled laborers. With the increase in mass production and the shift away from craft work, later arrivals, including many Irish, Germans from east of the River Elbe, Eastern Europeans, and Italians had to make do with semi-skilled or unskilled work. In the Chicago stockyards, for example, skilled butchers were replaced in the 1890s by a "disassembly line" of men performing one particular task. In the Detroit auto factories some 20 years later, the introduction of assembly lines deskilled the work in a similar manner.

Women worked in many jobs, including skilled ones, particularly in the textile industry. Immigrant women often entered the new society through domestic work. Housed and fed by their employers, they became economically independent of their families and were initiated into North American ways of housekeeping and the English language. They often found that the live-in arrangements restricted their individual freedom, however, and third generation German and Scandinavian women tended to leave domestic jobs to more recent arrivals. There were several major shifts in production patterns in this period. The textile industry expanded from the New England states into the new southern industrial belt. Slaughtering and

meat-packing grew in a belt from Columbus, Ohio, to Omaha, Nebraska. The Great Lakes were circled from Rochester, New York, to southern Wisconsin by an arc of automobile and automobile parts factories. Steel production shifted from Pennsylvania to the Gary–Chicago area. Oil drilling, once started in Pennsylvania, extended from southeastern Kansas to the Texas Gulf Coast. In Canada large-scale industrial development did not get under way until the 1890s, and was largely concentrated in Ontario

Above: industrious workers assemble oscillating shuttles at the Singer Manufacturing Company at Elizabethport, New Jersey, in the 1880s. The company catalog lauded the factory grounds as "pastoral and quiet, conducive to the good morals and excellent discipline.... among the thousands of men and women employed here."

and the Montreal area. Some industry was also located in the maritime provinces: the paper mills at Saint John processed New Brunswick timber, while the coal, iron, and steel industries of Pictou County and Cape Breton Island accounted for 20 percent of Nova Scotia's industrial workforce.

Each of these developments was accompanied by human moves. The areas of urbanization and industrialization were the main settlement areas for East and South European immigrants. People migrated within North America too, from agricultural areas to the cities. African-Americans were mobilized first for southern textile factories, then for production centers in the North. In the cities, migrant communities formed a mosaic of ethnic groups, whose quarters usually extended no more than a few streets. Groups intermingled along the borders and sometimes succeeded each other over time in the same area. In a few cities one group—such as Germans in Milwaukee (> *pages 116–7*)—predominated; in others, a single group—the Polish communities in Cleveland (> *pages 120–1*), for example—were interspersed with migrants from other areas. The city with the greatest diversity in this period, however, was Chicago (> *pages 134–5*).

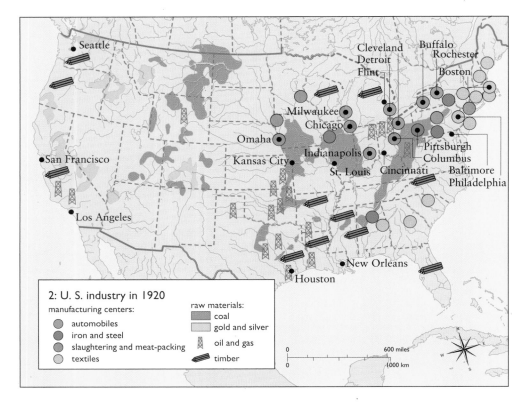

2: U. S. industry in 1920

manufacturing centers:
- automobiles
- iron and steel
- slaughtering and meat-packing
- textiles

raw materials:
- coal
- gold and silver
- oil and gas
- timber

0   600 miles
0   1000 km

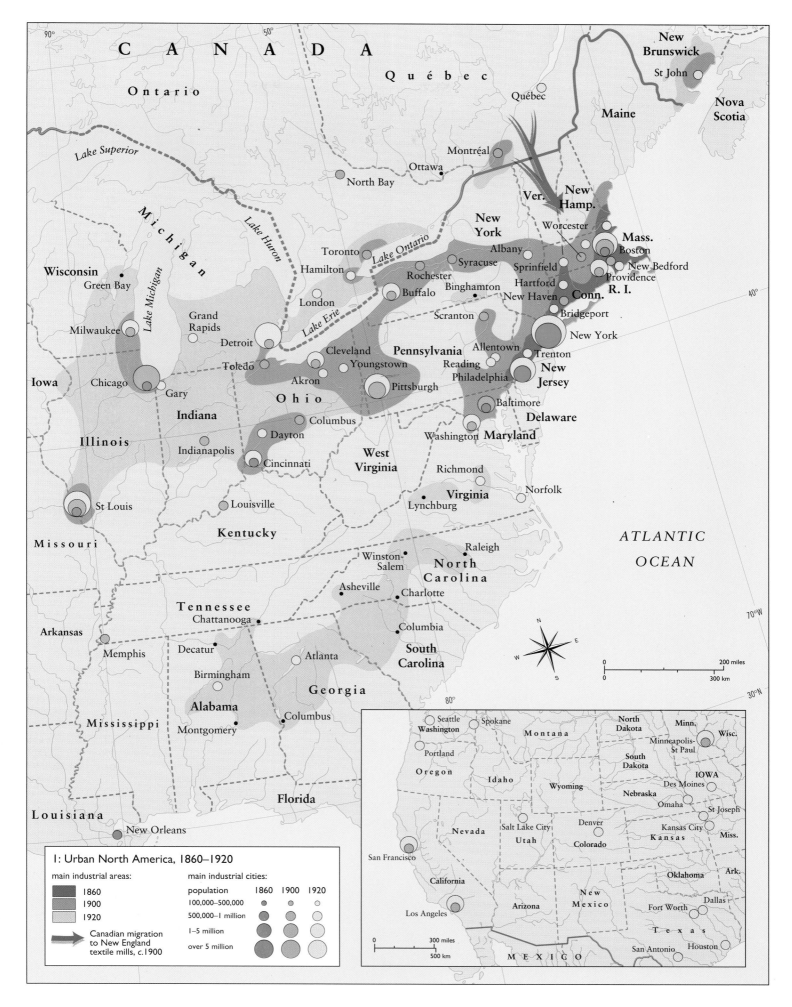

CANADA

Ontario

Québec

Québec

New Brunswick

St John

Lake Superior

North Bay

Ottawa

Montréal

Maine

Nova Scotia

Ver.

New Hamp.

New York

Worcester

Mass.

Boston

Toronto

Albany

Springfield

New Bedford

Providence

Wisconsin

Michigan

Hamilton

Syracuse

Hartford

R. I.

Green Bay

Rochester

Binghamton

New Haven

Conn.

London

Buffalo

Bridgeport

Milwaukee

Lake Ontario

Lake Huron

Lake Erie

Grand Rapids

Scranton

New York

Iowa

Lake Michigan

Detroit

Cleveland

Pennsylvania

Allentown

Trenton

New Jersey

Chicago

Toledo

Youngstown

Reading

Philadelphia

Illinois

Gary

Akron

Ohio

Pittsburgh

Baltimore

Delaware

Indiana

Columbus

Washington

Maryland

Dayton

Indianapolis

Cincinnati

West Virginia

Richmond

Missouri

St Louis

Louisville

Kentucky

Norfolk

Virginia

Lynchburg

ATLANTIC OCEAN

Raleigh

Winston-Salem

North Carolina

Asheville

Charlotte

Arkansas

Tennessee

Chattanooga

Columbia

South Carolina

Memphis

Decatur

Atlanta

Birmingham

Georgia

Alabama

Columbus

Mississippi

Montgomery

Louisiana

New Orleans

Florida

90° 50° 40° 70°W 80° 30°N

N
W E
S

0   200 miles
0   300 km

1: Urban North America, 1860–1920

main industrial areas:

▓	1860
▒	1900
░	1920

➤ Canadian migration to New England textile mills, c.1900

main industrial cities:

population	1860	1900	1920
100,000–500,000	●	●	○
500,000–1 million	●	●	○
1–5 million	●	●	○
over 5 million	●	●	○

Seattle Spokane

Washington

Montana

North Dakota

Minn.

Minneapolis-St Paul

Wisc.

Portland

Oregon

Idaho

South Dakota

IOWA

Des Moines

San Francisco

Nevada

Salt Lake City

Utah

Wyoming

Denver

Colorado

Nebraska

Omaha

St Joseph

Kansas City

Kansas

Miss.

California

Los Angeles

Arizona

New Mexico

Oklahoma

Ark.

Fort Worth

Dallas

T e x a s

San Antonio

Houston

MEXICO

0   300 miles
0   500 km

133

CHICAGO AND ITS PEOPLE

MIGRANT NEIGHBORHOODS IN CHICAGO, 1920

No city better reflected the richness and complexity of later 19th-century migration into the U. S. than Chicago.

Incorporated in 1833 immediately after the Indian land cession treaty, Chicago expanded rapidly: by 1930 it was the fifth largest urban area in the world, with a population approaching 3 million. Thousands came from Europe, the eastern U. S., the rural Midwest and, later, the South in search of jobs and a good life. In 1870, almost 30,000 residents called Chicago home: 20 years later, more than a million did. European migration contributed heavily to this growth. By 1890, almost 78 percent of residents were foreign-born or had foreign parents. Thirty percent of all Chicagoans were just a generation removed from Germany, 16 percent from Ireland. The various ethnic groups clustered in particular areas of the city, giving it a cultural patchwork that all Chicagoans understood. These neighborhoods were home to families from all over northwest Europe and North America.

Left: there were many Jews among those who migrated to Chicago from Poland, Russia, and Bohemia. Their Central European traditions lived on in Maxwell Street's lively market, photographed here at the beginning of the 20th century.

By the turn of the 20th century, immigrants from southern and eastern Europe began to arrive in large numbers. Poles surpassed the Germans as the city's largest national group, and immigrants from Russia, Sweden, and Italy outnumbered those from Ireland. Older immigrant groups abandoned their homes and regrouped in redefined ethnic communities further from the city center. Newer groups settled in these older areas and in new neighborhoods around the factories on the city's edges.

As World War I slowed this European migration, a higher proportion of Chicago's new migrants came from the south. Included in this migration were southerners of European heritage and a growing number of Mexicans, but the largest numbers were African-Americans. Unfortunately, Chicago, like the rest of America, had become less tolerant of new residents. A violent riot in 1919, triggered by a struggle over an invisible boundary between white and black Chicagoans, showed how little tolerance there was.

By 1920, Chicago's flood of European migrants had become a trickle. The ethnic neighborhoods that gave the city its distinctive social geography were increasingly populated by the children, grandchildren, and great-grandchildren of immigrants. A new geography was emerging based on the color of one's skin. The emerging migration patterns that were changing Chicago soon changed all of North America as well.

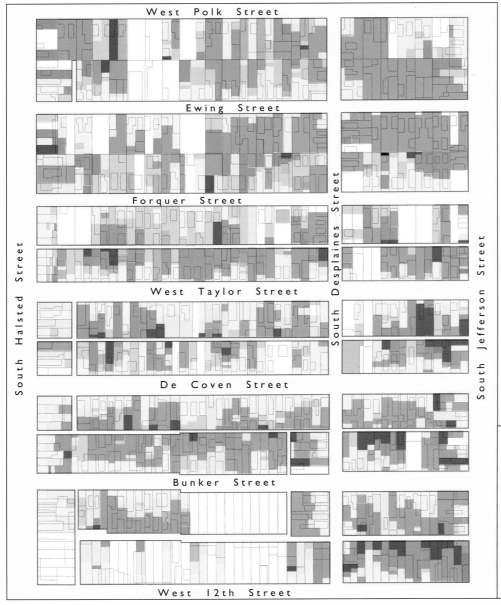

West Polk Street
Ewing Street
Forquer Street
West Taylor Street
De Coven Street
Bunker Street
West 12th Street

South Halsted Street
South Desplaines Street
South Jefferson Street

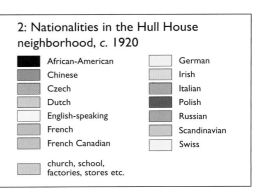

2: Nationalities in the Hull House neighborhood, c. 1920

African-American	German
Chinese	Irish
Czech	Italian
Dutch	Polish
English-speaking	Russian
French	Scandinavian
French Canadian	Swiss

church, school, factories, stores etc.

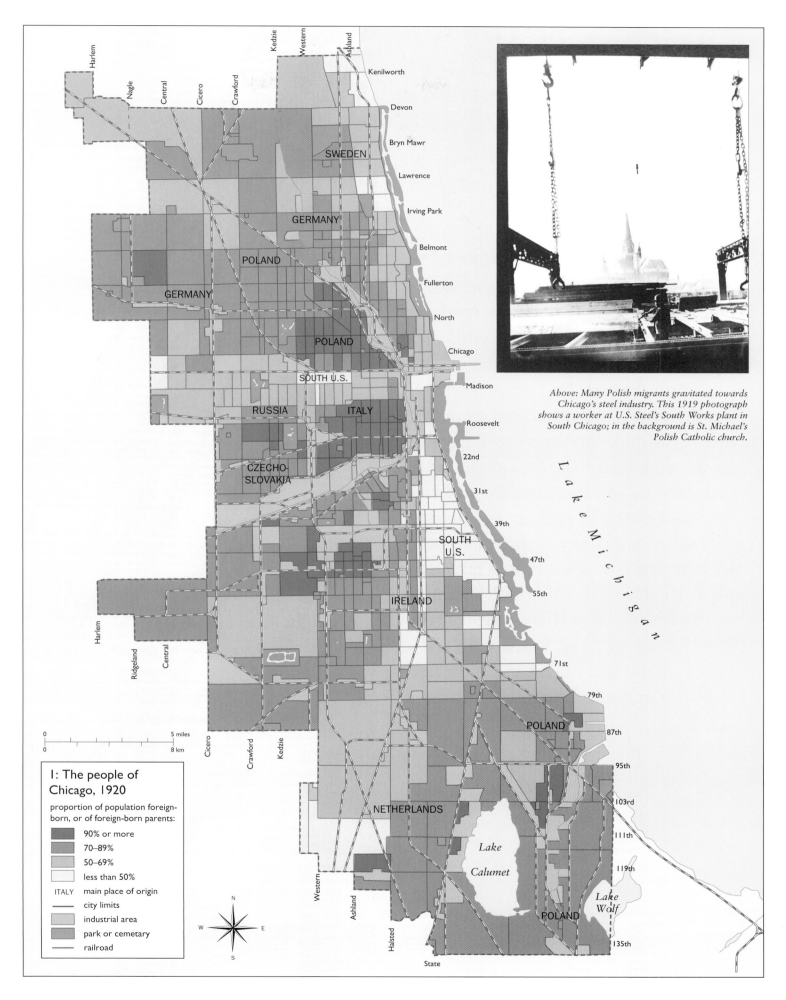

Harlem
Nagle
Central
Cicero
Crawford
Kedzie
Western
Ashland
Kenilworth
Devon
Bryn Mawr
Lawrence
Irving Park
Belmont
Fullerton
North
Chicago
Madison
Roosevelt
22nd
31st
39th
47th
55th
71st
79th
87th
95th
103rd
111th
119th
135th

SWEDEN
GERMANY
POLAND
GERMANY
POLAND
SOUTH U.S.
RUSSIA
ITALY
CZECHO-SLOVAKIA
SOUTH U.S.
IRELAND
POLAND
NETHERLANDS
POLAND
POLAND

Lake Michigan

Lake Calumet

Lake Wolf

Above: Many Polish migrants gravitated towards Chicago's steel industry. This 1919 photograph shows a worker at U.S. Steel's South Works plant in South Chicago; in the background is St. Michael's Polish Catholic church.

Harlem
Ridgeland
Central
Cicero
Crawford
Kedzie
Western
Ashland
Halsted
State

0   5 miles
0   8 km

1: The people of Chicago, 1920

proportion of population foreign-born, or of foreign-born parents:

- 90% or more
- 70–89%
- 50–69%
- less than 50%

ITALY   main place of origin
city limits
industrial area
park or cemetary
railroad

N
W   E
S

135

PART VI: PEOPLE ON THE MOVE

Introduction
by John H. Long

The period stretching from the end of World War I to the middle of the century was one of intense flux in North America. Advances in medicine and hygiene combined with mass migration to cause an explosion in the population of the continent, while harsh rural conditions and improved transportation brought people flocking to the cities. But the strained climate of the Depression fostered nativism and outright racism, resulting in exclusionary laws, quota systems, deportations, and even concentration camps. Reaction to this finally came in the form of the Brown decision of 1954, which ushered in the civil rights movement and began the concerted battle against discrimination in all walks of life

Right: A first view of New York City from the deck of the liner Mauritania *in 1950. Although air transport was becoming more common in the postwar years, many immigrants still made the epic journey by boat.*

Between 1915 and 1950 the population of North America increased by more than 50 percent. In the U. S., the total population topped 100 million between 1910 and 1920; in 1940, on the eve of American involvement in World War II, the federal census counted 131,669,275 persons, and in 1950 the total was 151,325,798. For Canada the comparable statistics are 8,787,949 in 1921, 11,506,655 in 1941, and 14,009,429 in 1951. Canada's territory increased in 1949 with the addition of Newfoundland, which until then had been an independent province; the Canadian census-takers counted just over 360,000 people there in 1951. Natural increase contributed more to this growth (e.g. an average of 1,518,000 per decade in Canada from 1921 to 1951) than immigration, even though newcomers continued to flow into both countries from Europe and Asia.

The contribution of natural increase to population growth in both Canada and the U. S. came despite the onset of the phenomenon known as the "demographic transition," where there is a decline in both fertility and mortality rates. In the United States this shift started between 1800 and 1810 with a drop in the birth rate; the death rate does not seem to have begun to fall until the 1870s. In Canada and Europe the shift started in the last half of the 1800s. Life expectancy at birth for Americans in 1920 was 57.4 years for whites and 47 years for blacks; in 1930 the figures were 60.8 for whites and 48.5 for blacks. According to the 1950 census, life expectancy in that year had risen to 69.1 years for whites and 60.8 for blacks. In Canada, the data for 1931 indicates a life expectancy of 60 years for men and 62.1 years for women—figures nearly identical with those for white Americans in 1930.

A significant factor in the demographic transition was the many improvements in public sanitation and health that were achieved in the early 20th century. At the end of the 19th century, as knowledge of pathogenic microorganisms grew and the "germ theory" of disease replaced previous ideas, states and cities began to take new public health measures. The pasteurization of milk and the purification of public water through filtration and treatment with chemicals such as chlorine greatly reduced the incidence of diarrhea, pneumonia, and bovine tuberculosis in infants and small children, as well as helping to prevent such scourges as cholera. The catastrophic 'flu epidemic of 1918-1919 that killed 50,000 people in Canada, 500,000 in the U. S., and at least 20 million worldwide (making it possibly the most devastating epidemic in history) not only had an immediate, devastating effect on population and settlement but also prompted a number of public health reforms that helped lower the death rate in subsequent decades.

Canada exhibited a net gain from immigration in the 1910s, 1920s, and 1940s, and lost only about 92,000 to emigration during the 1930s. The percentage of the Canadian population that was foreign-born rose very slowly from 22 percent in 1911 to 22.2 percent in 1931 and then fell to 17.5 percent in 1941 and to 14.7 percent in 1951. Canada's net gain from international migration can obscure the southward movement of a significant number of people, as Canada contributed substantially to the U. S. population before the Great Depression. U. S. authorities recorded the arrival of 742,185 people from Canada between 1911 and 1920, plus another 924,515 during the 1920s, but an average of only about 140,000 per decade in the 1930s and 1940s. United States immigration remained high until the Great Depression nearly halted it—almost 5.75 million in the 1910s, more than 4.1 million in the 1920s, but only 528,431 in the 1930s —and barely rose about 1 million in the 1940s.

The longstanding trend to urbanization continued without a break in this period, although it was almost brought to a standstill by the Great Depression (see below). The 1920 census in the United States reported that for the first time more Americans lived in cities and towns of at least 2,500 than lived in rural areas. Movement between cities and towns and between rural and metropolitan areas was facilitated by rail transport. In 1915 there were 1,260 American railroad companies operating trains over 391,142 miles of track; a decade and a half later, on the eve of the Depression in 1929, consolidation had reduced the number of companies to 809, while the trackage had increased to 429,054 miles. The next year, the extent of the railroad network reached its absolute maximum of 429,883 miles of track. By the time the U. S. entered the war at the end of 1941 the total trackage was down to about 400,000 miles, and it remained at that level into the 1950s.

The airplane had almost ceased to be a novelty by the eve of World War I. The new technology that provided the main competition for railroads was the automobile. In 1915 nearly 2,500,000 motor vehicles filled the streets (2,330,000 cars and about 160,000 trucks), and in 1929 just over 26,700,000 motorized vehicles were registered, of which 23,120,000 were cars, 34,000 were buses, and 3,550,000 were trucks. During most of the war, no cars or trucks were produced for civilian use, and when the pent-up demand was released in 1945, the industry took off. In 1955 there were almost 63 million vehicles registered, including more than 52 million cars, 10 million trucks, and a quarter of a million buses.

In the 19th century, steamboats and canals had increased the capacity of the transport system, but railroads became dominant because they not only had greater capacity but also could reach more places; in the 20th century the automobile, bus, and truck appeared to remove all the old limits on mobility. The effect of the motor vehicle on almost all facets of North American life has been remarkable . The isolation of rural farmers was broken by the automobile and the small truck, which brought not only the amenities of town life but quicker and easier access to medical care and educational facilities. The pattern of the modern city, with its business and commercial center ringed by an industrial belt and the whole surrounded by a residential suburban region is a product of the motor vehicle. Residential architecture has adapted itself to the ubiquitous car, as has the neighborhood in both city and suburb. Finally, the automobile industry was the core of a new kind of economy centered on consumer goods that emerged in the 1920s and has grown continuously to this day.

north as Canada. Americans whose lives were disrupted, especially farmers and their families in the middle and southern parts of the country, streamed westward, mainly to California, which received well over a million migrants. With the approach of World War II, farm conditions improved, but the growth of jobs in defense industries kept people moving to California. Most of those migrants never returned to their original homes. Canada suffered a similar fate; Saskatchewan was hit hardest of all provinces by the drought and over 120,000 people moved away, mostly to neighboring provinces.

Relief agencies everywhere were overwhelmed by the numbers of people who needed help, and in both Canada and the U. S. the hardships of the Depression aggravated relations between groups within society, especially between native-born and more recent immigrants. In Canada, the government gave in to pressure to help

Above: An illustration of the Wall Street Crash by Alfredo Ortelli. reproduced in the Italian journal Illustrazione del Popolo, *conveys the sense of panic and despair*

Left: Pandemonium breaks out on the streets of New York during the crash of October 24, 1929.

The Great Depression that began in 1929 and continued until World War II disrupted the lives of millions of people in North America and around the world. Farmers and workers who lost their jobs were hit hardest, and in many cases families split up as fathers left home in search of work. The drought that hit the great western farming areas of Canada and the U. S. simply added a natural agricultural catastrophe to the bitter results of a failed economy. In the U. S. the drought hit hardest around the panhandles of Oklahoma and Texas and nearby parts of Kansas, New Mexico, and Colorado, which earned the name of Dust Bowl. But the drought affected all of the Great Plains and hurt farmers as far

"Canadians First," and from 1929 to 1935 deported more than 17,000 individuals who needed public assistance. In both countries, migration from failed farm to industrial city was countered in part by movement out of the cities, as Depression-struck families headed for the countryside in the hope that there they could at least grow food enough to live on. This city-to-country flow was so great during the 1930s that it almost put a stop to the powerful, longterm urbanization trend: the growth of the urban population over the rural was a slim 0.4 percent. When the cycle of depression was finally broken, nearly all of those people returned to the cities.

The "Canadians First" movement that resulted in thousands of deportations during the Great Depression was just one example of the nativism widespread in both Canada and the U. S. Anti-Catholic sentiment, for example, had caused problems in the 19th century, and was still present. Governments sometimes fueled exclusionary feelings. In World War I, for example, the federal propaganda campaign against Germany was so successful that when the U.S. entered the war, almost anything German fell into disrepute—an irony considering that millions of German immigrants had helped to build the country throughout the previous century. German was no longer taught in schools, and the California state board of education labeled it a language of "brutality and hatred." Much anti-German activity, such as the decision not to play the music of German composers like Beethoven and the disappearance of pretzels and sauerkraut from restaurant menus, was superficial. More serious was the ostracism of people with a German background. The rise of patriotic vigilantism sometimes resulted in episodes of severe persecution and in often lethal attacks on people whose only crime was to have a German-sounding name.

The anti-communism and high patriotism that developed

Left: Under the heading "America and the Yellow Peril," a French illustrated newspaper supplement of January 1908 shows a family of Asian shopkeepers cowering as an angry crowd descends upon their San Francisco establishment during one of many attacks on immigrants of the time.

Above: An elderly woman prepares a meal at her hearth, in a typical sharecropper's home. Renting land and borrowing supplies in exchange for a share of the crop ensnared sharecroppers in a circle of debt and poverty that only ended with government reforms in the 1930s.

during World War I did not just evaporate after the war, and one group that exploited it fully was the Ku Klux Klan. The Klan had almost disappeared in the 1870s as a result of federal pressure and intervention, but it enjoyed a revival in the aftermath of World War I. In its new incarnation as a mainly urban organization, the Klan broadened the scope of its campaign of exclusionism, reflecting a widespread fear of new immigrants. After the war, this version of the Klan was not only against blacks; it was also against Catholics and Jews, labor unions, and radicals. A few Klansmen resorted to violence, but they were a small minority in an organization with a membership that reached 3 million in the 1920s and which favored marches, demonstrations, and political activity to press its platform. Late in the 1920s the Klan dwindled to almost nothing, and remained so until the civil rights movement and the anti-communist scares of the early 1950s provided new fuel for its fires.

In the aftermath of World War I, the nativism of earlier years, combined with the new fear of radicalism, especially communism, also affected immigration law in the

Above: The industrial district of Chattanooga in the Tennessee Valley, supplied with power from the Hales Bar Dam on the Tennessee River, one of the works of the Tennessee Valley Authority. The valley remained one of North America's poorest regions for many decades, but the TVA, created by Franklin D. Roosevelt in 1933, has become the largest power producer in the U. S., providing electricity for seven states, and encouraging industry to flock to the area.

U. S. One federal act in 1918 excluded foreign anarchists and anyone advocating the overthrow of government. Another, passed in 1920, provided for the deportation of foreign enemies and anarchists. As though building directly on the Chinese and Japanese exclusion treaties and agreements concluded around the turn of the century, Congress passed the first quota law in 1921. This limited the number of immigrants who could enter the U. S. each year to 3 percent of the total from their country already in the U. S., as determined in the 1910 census. There was also an overall maximum limit of 357,000. The National Origins Act of 1924 halved the maximum limit set in 1921 and restructured the calculation of quotas for individual countries. This new quota system was clearly slanted against Eastern and Southern Europe and in favor of more western countries such as Great Britain. Asians were almost completely excluded.

In 1948 the U. S. passed the Displaced Persons Act, a special law to provide for the immigration of people displaced from their homes in Europe by World War II and its aftermath. The McCarran–Walter Act of 1952 was a general immigration law that preserved the basic approach of the 1924 National Origins quota act, but eliminated the earlier prohibition against Asians and people from the Pacific. A number of new measures were also added by McCarran and Walter that were designed to keep subversives, particularly communists, out of the country. The quota system remains intact, although other details of the immigration law have changed.

Given the racial segregation and nativism that permeated immigration, the economy, and any number of other issues, it is no surprise that when World War II burst upon the U. S., the country's leaders merely reflected the prevalent attitudes, ideas, and beliefs of their time. They were certain that the loyalties of foreign-born Americans, particularly those with Japanese origins, would adhere to old radical and cultural lines, rather than citizenship by choice and other attachments that tied them to America. Canadians had similar difficulties in regarding their Japanese-American populations as anything but potential internal enemies. The result was the construction of concentration camps, equipped with small, poorly-built facilities, surrounded by barbed wire, and guarded by soldiers. Into those camps the U. S. and Canada poured residents and citizens of Japanese ancestry in a forced removal reminiscent of the Trail of Tears, when the Cherokee were uprooted from their homes over a century earlier. Of the 100,000 or so interned in the U. S., about 60,000 survive today; some have been able to recover some of their pre-war possessions, and all have been offered an apology and symbolic compensation.

According to official reports, the number of Native Indian and Inuit people in Canada grew moderately from 105,611 in 1911 to 165,607 in 1951. Their proportion of the total population held fairly steady at a little over 1 percent. In the U. S., the Census Bureau reported a total of 265,683 Indians in 1910, 244,437 in 1920, 332,397 in 1930, 333,969 in 1940, and 343,410 in 1950. In the absence of Indian immigration or a powerful epidemic, decade-to-decade variations in the figures for America are more irregular than might be expected. In fact, as Francis Paul Prucha has said, "Indians are difficult to count." Not only did the methods and procedures of the census-takers change over time, but there was also the problem of deciding what makes an Indian an Indian. The variations in number may have more to do with the different definitions used to generate the statistics than with actual changes in the numbers of people.

In Canada, statisticians divided the indigenous population into three categories: Indians (who live in southern Canada, often on reserves); Inuit (Eskimos living far to the north); and Metis (of mixed white and Indian/Inuit descent). The U. S. Census Bureau, through most of its history, has used far fewer categories; for a long time the distinctions were between white and non-white. By the early 20th century, people could be classified according to a long list of ethnic or national-origin labels (such as Irish, German, Chinese, English), but there was a single category for Indians and another for "Negroes."

The general approach of census-takers when classifying people by group origin is to ask them to identify themselves, but applying this standard to specific people in the field is often far from simple. The difficulty is perhaps best seen in the standards used by U.S. census-takers. In the 1910 census, "all persons of mixed white and Indian blood who have any appreciable amount of Indian blood are counted as Indians, even though the proportion of white blood may exceed that of Indian blood." In 1930, Indians were "not only those of full blood, but also those of mixed blood, except when the percentage of Indian blood was very small or when the person was regarded as a white person in the community. Persons of mixed Indian and black blood were counted as black unless Indian blood predominated and their status as Indians was generally accepted in their community." By 1950, the "Indian" included "fullblooded Indians, and persons of mixed white and Indian blood if they were enrolled on an Indian reservation or agency roll. Also included are persons of mixed Indian blood if the proportion of Indian blood is one-fourth or more, or if they are regarded as Indians in the community."

In 1950 the Census Bureau experimented with a more flexible and potentially more realistic classification system in an attempt "to identify persons of mixed white, Negro, and Indian ancestry living in certain communities in the eastern United States in a special category so they might be included in the categories 'Other races' and 'All other' rather than being classified white, Negro, or Indian." This was a category similar to the Canadians' "Metis." One unexpected result of this reform in the classification system was that what had long been recognized as a large concentration of Indians in Robeson County, North Carolina (unmistakable in both the preceding and following censuses), disappeared from the official maps and tables for 1950. In 1930, according to the official count, there were over 20,000 Indians in Robeson County, and in 1960 (without the special category) the number of Indians there came to 26,278. In 1950 Robeson County had 22,553 in the "Other races" category and virtually no "Indians."

Had the Census Bureau been a magician performing a parlor trick, the disappearance of Robeson County's Indians in one decade and their rematerialization in the next might be simply an odd and entertaining event, but it illustrates at least two important features of North American settlement history. First is the importance of understanding the foundation on which the data sets are constructed; to a very great extent our familiar classes of race and ethnicity are cultural creations of our own making, and it is not difficult to define a group in or out of existence. Second is the broad diversity that is a hallmark of the North American population. There has been so much mixing between racial, religious, and ethnic groups that, except in cases of original immigrants and their families, putting each person in one single category usually flies in the face of reality because there are very few people who are genetically pure descendants of just one group. Prucha's observation about the difficulty of counting Indians can be applied to any racial or ethnic group in North America.

Some scholars have pointed out that the advance of the white-man's frontier in America produced more frequent bloody clashes with Indians than in Canada, where there was relative peace between the two groups. Both countries tried to make treaties with the Indian tribes in which the Indians would give up their claims to land in return for reservations, gifts, or payments, and in some cases annuities. The Canadians are said to have succeeded in that approach partly because they could build on strong traditions of law and order established by the Hudson's Bay Company and the Northwest Mounted Police, and partly because there were large numbers of Metis who could and did serve as intermediaries between whites and Indians. Not to be overlooked, however, is the difference in the settlement histories of the two nations: chiefly, the fact that the non-Indian population of Canada did not grow as fast or exert as much pressure on Indian territory as it did in the U. S., thereby avoiding the persistent, intense conflict over land and its use that emerged early in America and inevitably led to bloodshed and war.

The number of people of African origins in Canada rose slightly from a total of 16,994 in 1911 to 18,202 in 1951; numbers which represent small percentages of the total population. In the U. S. the comparable numbers of blacks are 9,827,763 (about 10.6 percent of the total) in 1910 and 15,042,286 (9.9 percent of the total) in 1950. The decline in the percentage of the total population is due mostly to immigration of non-black African people. One of the two most remarkable developments for black people in this period was the "Great Migration," in which 400,000 blacks left the rural South for the industrial North to fill jobs during World War I. The movement hardly paused at the end of the war, however, and another 600,000 migrated northward during the 1920s. Not only were the settlement patterns and economy of the South disturbed by the departure of so many people, but there was an even more profound impact on Chicago, New York, and the other cities that were the destinations of this mass movement.

The second important development was the U.S. Supreme Court's ruling in Brown v. Board of Education of Topeka on May 17, 1954, which formally ended the federal acceptance of racial segregation and gave rise to the civil rights movement that has effected broad changes in employment, education, housing, and the patterns of everyday life. A related effect of the Brown decision has been the passage of laws prohibiting not only discrimination based on race, but also discrimination based on gender, religion, and ethnicity. Reforms in areas such as immigration law, labor law, housing practice, among others, can all be traced back to the revolutionary change brought about by the Brown decision in 1954.

Above left: The women's movement was given an unexpected boost by World War II, when industrial jobs created by wartime production drew 400,000 women into the labor force. Forced to leave the factories when the war ended, many women missed their work and the financial independence that it had allowed them.

Right: President Harry S. Truman surrounded by his congressional leaders at the 82nd Congress in 1951. Seen from left to right are: senators Ernest McFarland and Lyndon B. Johnson, President Truman, and representatives Percy Priest and John W. McCormack. In 1945, shortly after succeeding Roosevelt, the president issued the Truman Directive, which admitted 41,379 "Displaced Persons" to the U.S.

TIMELINE
1920–55

NORTH AMERICA	THE CARIBBEAN, CENTRAL & S. AMERICA	EUROPE, AFRICA, & ASIA
1920 Nov: Promising a "return to normalcy," Warren G. Harding wins landslide victory in presidential election	**1920** May: Obregón's forces capture Mexico City. Dec: Obregón becomes president of Mexico	**1920** Jan: Treaty of Versailles and League of Nations Pact come into force
1921 Some 800,000 immigrants arrive in U.S. May: Emergency Quota Act restricts immigration to 3 percent of each nationality present in U.S. in 1910. Dec: McKenzie King Canadian Prime Minister		**1921** Jan: British troops leave Ireland. Provisional government established at Dublin Castle
1922 Bursum Bill to legalize white squatters on Pueblo Indian lands is defeated	**1922** The Standard Oil Company obtains drilling concessions from Bolivian government	**1922** July: Soviet Union formally established. Oct: Mussolini takes power in Italy. Nov: Mustafa Kemal establishes secular regime in Turkey, ending Ottoman sultanate. Dec: Irish Free State established; Northern Ireland opts to remain in U.K.
1923 American Indian Defense Association formed. Aug: President Harding dies in office; Calvin Coolidge succeeds him	**1923** Jan: "Christ the King" movement attacks anti-clerical policies of Mexican government	**1923** Jan: French and Belgian troops occupy Ruhr valley of Germany in lieu of unpaid war reparations. March: Stalin succeeds Lenin as Communist Party General Secretary. Nov: Hitler stages unsuccessful putsch in Munich
1924 May: U.S. Immigration Act reduces quotas to 2 percent of each nationality already present in U.S. in 1890, and totally prohibits immigration from Japan	**1924** U.S. troops withdraw from Dominican Republic after 8 years. APRA (*Allianza Popular Revolucionaria Americana*) founded in Peru	**1924** Jan: Lenin dies. June: Murder of socialist deputy Matteotti begins persecution of anti-fascists in Italy
1926 June: Constitutional crisis in Canada as governor-general refuses to recognize Liberal election win	**1926** May: U.S. marines sent to Nicaragua to support regime of Adolfo Diaz against insurgents; they remain until 1933	
	1927 Marcus Garvey returns to Jamaica from the U.S. to establish political party. Dec: Mexican Congress overturns 1917 constitution and grants land rights to foreign companies	**1927** March: Chiang Kai-shek's forces take Shanghai. May: German economy collapses
1928 166,783 immigrants arrive in Canada. Nov: Herbert Hoover elected U.S. president	**1928** July: Mexican president Obregón assassinated	**1928** Jan: Trotsky sent into internal exile in Central Asia; Stalin in sole command of Soviet Union. Oct: Chiang Kai-shek becomes president of China
1929 July: Congress restricts immigration into U.S. to 150,000 per annum. Nov: Wall Street Crash wipes out $30 billion in stocks		
1930 4.5 million jobless in U.S. Hudson Bay Railway completed in Canada. Aug: Conservatives win Canadian election	**1930** Liberals take power in Colombia. Rafael Trujillo becomes dictator in Dominican Republic. Sept: military coup in Argentina	**1930** Effects of Wall Street Crash lead to unemployment throughout Europe. March: Gandhi begins civil disobedience campaign against British rule in India. Nov: Marshal Pilsudski forms right-wing government in Poland
1931 Drought and dust storms affect Canadian prairies and begin to move south		**1931** Sept: Japan invades Manchuria
1932 12 million jobless in U.S. Nov: F. D. Roosevelt elected U.S. president		
1933 March–June: Roosevelt announces "New Deal" to combat Depression; Tennessee Valley Authority begins construction of 9 large dams, which will continue until 1944	**1933** Jan: U.S. troops withdrawn from Nicaragua; Anastasio Somoza becomes dictator. Sept: Fulgencio Batista seizes power in Cuba	**1933** Jan: Adolf Hitler made Chancellor of Germany
1934 Indian Reorganization Act reverses policy of breaking up tribal governments by individual land allotments. May: windstorm blows 350 tons of topsoil from Montana, Wyoming, and the Dakotas		**1934** Youth Aliyah set up to get Jewish children out of Nazi Germany. Chinese communists split from Chiang Kai-shek and make "Long March" to establish separate state in north
1935 May: Works Progress Administration (WPA) begins to put U.S. unemployed to work on public projects. Aug: Social Security Act passed in U.S.	**1935** Cardeñas becomes president of Mexico. Begins land redistribution	**1935** Sept: Hitler's Nuremberg Laws deprive Jews of German citizenship. Oct: Italy invades Ethiopia
1936 Nov: President Roosevelt re-elected		**1936** July: Franco's rebellion begins Spanish Civil War. Hitler reoccupies the Rhineland
1937 May: U.S. Supreme Court rules that 1935 Social Security Act is constitutional		**1937** July: Japan invades China
	1938 March: Cardeñas nationalizes Mexico's oil and expropriates foreign-owned property. Riots throughout Caribbean in protest at Depression	**1938** March: Austria "united" with Germany after German troops go in to "preserve order" Sept: Munich agreement. Oct: Hitler annexes German-speaking Sudeten region of Czechoslovakia

NORTH AMERICA

THE CARIBBEAN, CENTRAL & S. AMERICA

EUROPE, AFRICA, & ASIA

1939 Sept: Canada enters World War II
Dec: First Canadian troops arrive in Britain

1940 Jan: Roosevelt submits defense budget.
May: Roosevelt asks Congress to appropriate money
for aircraft production. Nov: President Roosevelt
re-elected for third term

1941 Mar: Lend–Lease Act passed in U.S. Dec: Japan
bombs U.S. fleet in Pearl Harbor; U.S. enters war.
Leaders of Japanese community in U.S. interned

1942 110,000 Japanese-Americans sent to
internment camps

1944 National Congress of American Indians
organized in Denver, Colorado.
Nov: President Roosevelt re-elected for fourth term

1945 April: President Roosevelt dies; succeeded by
Harry S. Truman. Dec: Truman Directive admits
41,379 Displaced Persons to U. S.

1946 Nov: Canadian Close Relative Scheme allows
the admission of refugees nominated by a relative
already living in Canada, and Bulk Labor Scheme
admits those who meet specific labor shortages

1947 McKenzie King statement on long-term
immigration defines Canadian policy until 1962

1948 Court decree forces Arizona to give Indians right
to vote. April: U.S. Congress approves Marshall Plan.
Jun: U. S. Displaced Persons Act authorizes admission
of 205,000 DPs. Nov: President Truman re-elected

1949 March: Newfoundland joins Canada

1950 Senator Joseph McCarthy's "witchhunt"
against alleged communists.
Aug: U.N. establishes headquarters in New York

1951 USEP (U.S. Escapee Program) established. U.N.
High Commission for Refugees set up. Canadian
Indian Act gives Indians the right to vote

1952 Bureau of Indian Affairs relocates Indians to
cities. June: McCarran Act revises U.S. immigration
laws. Nov: Eisenhower elected U.S. president

1953 Aug: Refugee Relief Act provides U.S. visas for
55,000 Germans expelled from E. Europe

1954 May: U.S. Supreme Court declares segregation
in schools unconstitutional

1955 Bus boycott in Montgomery, Alabama, begins

1940 472 German Jews settle in Dominican
Republic. Trotsky assassinated in Mexico City

1942 Protocol of Rio de Janeiro: Ecuador loses vast
area of Amazonia to Peru

1944 Full adult suffrage introduced in Jamaica.
Batista steps down as Cuban president after election
defeat and retires to Florida

1946 Juan Peron becomes dictator in Argentina

1948 Assassination of liberal politician Jorge Eliecer
Gaitán leads to epidemic of political violence in
Colombia; 200,000 killed by 1953

1952 Mar: Batista seizes power in Cuba. Jun:
Agrarian reform in Guatemala; it will nationalize
400,000 acres of United Fruit Company land

1953 June: Coup d'etat in Colombia. July: Attack on
Moncada garrison begins Cuban Revolution

1954 June: U.S.-backed coup overthrows
Guatemalan government

1955 Sept: Juan Peron overthrown in Argentina.

1939 March: Hitler invades Czechoslovakia.
April: Italy invades Albania. Aug: Nazi-Soviet non-
aggression pact. Sept: Hitler invades Poland. Britain
and France declare war on Germany

1940 April: Germans invade Norway and Denmark.
May: Germans invade Belgium, Luxembourg, and the
Netherlands. June: France falls to Germany. Soviet
Union annexes Latvia, Lithuania, and Estonia

1941 April: Nazis occupy Yugoslavia and Greece
June: Hitler invades Soviet Union.
Dec: Germany and Italy declare war on U.S.

1942 June: Battle of Midway halts Japanese advance
in the Pacific; German offensive in Russia halted at
Stalingrad

1943 Feb: Germans abandon siege of Stalingrad
July: Tank battle at Kursk begins German expulsion
from Russia

1944 June: Allied troops land in Normandy

1945 Feb: Roosevelt, Churchill, and Stalin discuss
postwar settlement at Yalta. April: U.S. forces capture
Philippines; British troops discover concentration
camp at Belsen. May: Germany surrenders. Aug:
Atomic bombs dropped on Hiroshima and Nagasaki.
Potsdam Conference authorizes expulsion of ethnic
Germans from Eastern Europe; by the 1950s some 12
million have migrated. Sept: Japan surrenders

1945–48 Jewish migration from Europe to Palestine

1947 Jan: Soviet-backed regime takes power in
Poland. Dec: India becomes independent from Britain

1948 Feb: Soviet-backed regime takes power in
Czechoslovakia. May: State of Israel founded. June:
Russians blockade West Berlin; Berlin airlift begins

1949 Apr: NATO established. May: Soviet blockade
of Berlin lifted. Oct: People's Republic of China
established under Mao Tse-tung. Dec: Indonesia
achieves independence from the Netherlands

1950 June: U.S. air and naval forces sent to S. Korea

1951 Greece and Turkey become NATO members

1953 March: Stalin dies. June: Demonstrations and
strikes against communist rule in East Germany

1954 Algerian war for independence from France
begins. Dec: U.S. troops sent to Vietnam after French
defeat at Dien Bien Phu.

ENDINGS AND BEGINNINGS

NORTH AMERICA, 1920

In 1920, despite heavy immigration during the late 19th and early 20th century, most of North America's inhabitants were native born, with most of the recent arrivals concentrated in the industrial cities.

By 1920, the growing population of North American included 105,710,620 in the U. S. and 8,788,483 in Canada. Despite heavy immigration during the late 19th and early 20th century, North America in 1920 was inhabited principally by a native-born population. This is particularly evident in the eastern provinces of Canada, and in the part of the U. S. lying south of the Great Lakes from the Atlantic coast west through the middle west with the exception of the industrial zones. In Canada, the presence of a foreign-born population in Ontario draws attention to the countries with industrial cities, such as Toronto and Hamilton, and highlights the western provinces from Manitoba to the Pacific Coast. In the U. S., areas with more than 30 percent foreign-born population lie along the Mexican border as well as on the Canadian border in parts of Michigan, Minnesota, and North Dakota.

An exception to the general pattern of high foreign-born population in industrial cities and border areas is Sweetwater County in southern Wyoming, with a population of 13,640 that was 33.5 percent foreign-born white in 1920 but had been 44 percent in 1910. Sweetwater County's 4571 foreign-born white residents far exceeded the number in any of the other 20 counties in Wyoming, and even the combined total of the only two Wyoming towns of any size, Cheyenne and Casper. Situated on the Continental Divide, Sweetwater County was a region of oil drilling, mines, and sheep ranching in some sections of the mountain terrain. The largest contingent in the diverse foreign population were the 1833

from Greece, Italy, and Yugoslavia. Next were the 892 from the British Isles, 619 from Central Europe (Austria, Germany, Czechoslovakia, and Hungary), 507 from the Scandinavian countries (Finland, Sweden, Norway, and the Netherlands)—the majority Finnish, and 358 Mexicans. Also included in the country population were less than a hundred each from France, Poland, and Russia and other countries. In addition to the figures for native and foreign born white population, the county census showed 457 Asians and 164 Negroes.

Population growth in the U. S. during the 1910–1920 decade was 14 percent, in line with the 15 percent in Quebec, mainly in the suburbs of Montreal; and 13 percent for Ontario, principally in the suburbs of Toronto and Ottawa, and main cities near the U.S. border—Windsor, Hamilton, and Welland. Canada's Prairie Provinces grew much more by the 1921 decennial census: Alberta (36 percent), Saskatchewan (34 percent), Manitoba (24 percent), and British Columbia (25 percent). The Prairie Provinces also attracted many immigrants. Between 1910 and 1921, immigration almost doubled. In the peak year, 1913, 139,000 came from the U. S. and 150,000 from Great Britain.

By 1920, the Prairie Provinces had a diverse population in a measure reflecting the dislocations of World War I and the 1917 Russian Revolution. The main groups were Eastern Europeans from Poland, Galicia, the Ukraine, and Russia, along with a sizable number of Jewish immigrants from the former Austro-Hungarian empire and Russia. Also represented were Italians, Chinese, and other Asians. The smaller groups of immigrants were from Denmark, Belgium, the Netherlands, Norway, Sweden, and Finland, along with Assyrians and Bulgarians. The immigrant population formed enclaves in the western provinces or in the major cities; Montreal, Toronto, Winnipeg, and Vancouver.

People in both Canada and the U. S. expressed strong fears about the ultimate consequences of admitting so many foreigners into their respective countries. As a consequence, both governments passed legislation in the 1920s to restrict immigration. Many Americans considered immigrants a threat to "the American way of life." Legislation passed in the U. S. in 1921 and 1924 was designed to drastically reduce immigration from southern Europe and halt immigration from Asia. The exemption for people in the Western Hemisphere resulted in Mexicans becoming the largest group of immigrants coming into the U. S. in the 1920s. El Paso, Texas, became 50 percent Mexican during the decade.

The 1920 U. S. Census for the first time showed more than half the population living in cities or towns of over 2500 inhabitants rather then in rural areas. An increasing percentage of urban population was also evident in Ontario and Quebec; the division between rural and urban population was almost even in British Columbia. A slight edge toward rural population still remained in New Brunswick, Nova Scotia, Alberta, and Manitoba.

The ways of life for many North Americans changed during the 1920s, which was declared a "New Era." A constitutional amendment gave women the right to vote. The population became more mobile. Automobiles became affordable for middle class families, and highways with numbering systems were developed across the country. The increased use of electrical power, a replacement for steam, and development of water pump, changed kitchens and made possible the widespread introduction of indoor bathrooms. Radios and telephones created a first communications revolution, and "the movies" became a feature of North American life. Other changes followed the beginning of the prohibition era in January, 1920; the laws against selling alcoholic beverages were not repealed until 1933.

The affluence of the 1920s did not extend to all parts of the population. Although manufacturing output increased, jobs increased very little. After the expansive sales of the World War I years, farmers found their markets and incomes severely depressed and more than 3 million left agriculture during the decade. Although all Indians not previously enfranchised were finally declared U. S. citizens in 1924, contemporary investigations of the situation on reservations revealed the shocking prevalence of tuberculosis, eye disease, malnutrition, and government schools with little educational results.

Left: the 1920s witnessed the rapid growth of motorized transport: in 1920, 1.5 million cars were purchased; by 1929 the figure had risen to 5 million. Here, motorists queue at the toll gate of the Holland Tunnel connecting Manhattan Island to Hoboken. The tunnel was opened in 1927, and the tolls were used to finance other transport projects such as the George Washington Bridge, linking New York City with New Jersey.

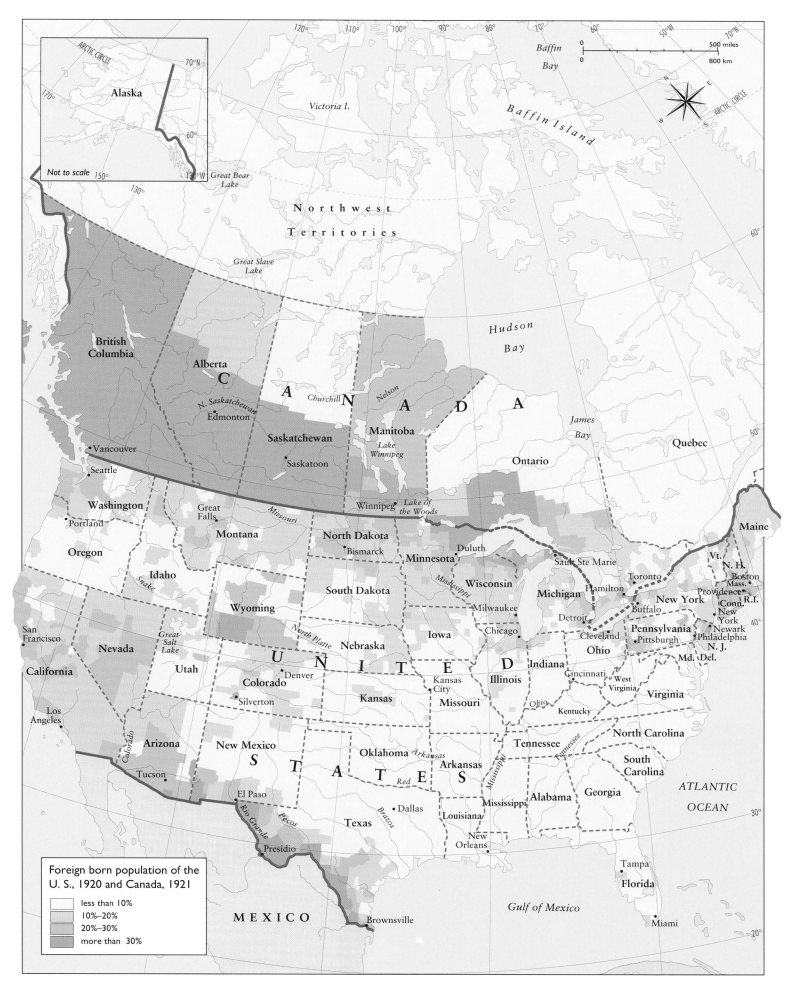

Foreign born population of the U. S., 1920 and Canada, 1921

- less than 10%
- 10%–20%
- 20%–30%
- more than 30%

THE GREAT MIGRATION
AFRICAN-AMERICANS MOVE NORTH, 1917–20

In the largest internal migration in North America's history, African-Americans leave the rural South in search of employment and freedom in the industrial cities of the North.

During the spring of 1917, the *Chicago Defender* gave a public face to one of the greatest population movements ever to occur within North America. Declaring May 15, 1917, the day of the Great Northern Drive, the paper urged African-Americans, the vast majority of whom lived in the rural South, to come to the industrializing North where job opportunities abounded and discrimination seemed somehow less oppressive.

The *Defender*'s call did not initiate this great migration—economic, social and political forces within the South led individuals and families to look for better lives outside the rural areas that, in 1900, were home to 77 percent of all African-Americans. In 1898, the boll weevil had begun its gradual spread east, destroying the cotton crops that had sustained many black families. Two years before, in the case of Plesey v. Ferguson, the Supreme Court had upheld the principle that segregation by race was legal in the U. S.. The result was a series of increasingly restrictive laws and practices, segregating black from white southerners and denying them equal access to services, jobs, education, and basic political rights such as voting and jury participation. Where laws failed to accomplish this segregation, lynchings and physical intimidation forced people to comply.

At first, African-American southerners looked toward the nearby cities that were easily accessible and offered employment. However, as World War I simultaneously created industrial jobs and restricted the European immigration that might fill them, northern cities became the ultimate destination. Attracted by reports of plentiful jobs, high wages and a freer society, men, women, and children boarded trains for what some even called the Promised Land. As the decade progressed, the stream of migrants became a mass migration that would not peak until after World War II. Some 450,000 African-

Americans left the South behind from 1913 to 1919. Virtually all went to a few cities in the North. By 1920, 73 percent of the migrants lived in the industrial districts around Indianapolis, Detroit, Cleveland, Kansas City, Pittsburgh, Cincinnati, St. Louis, Chicago, Philadelphia, and New York. There they created vibrant communities, enhancing the diverse cultural landscape that flourished in these urban environments.

The move northward was not without tension at both ends. Southern employers used legal and extra-legal means to keep African Americans at their jobs. Not satisfied with the results, they sent speakers north to explain why African-Americans belonged in the South. To the far north in Canada, a variety of groups tried to keep American blacks from migrating into the plains. In northern cities, groups and individuals worked actively to restrict the options available to these new residents. Often, these efforts turned violent. By 1910, race riots had erupted in several cities; the most notorious of these

Above: the move to the north has been commemorated in a series of paintings by the American artist Jacob Lawrence (born 1917), entitled The Migration of the Negro, *and painted during the 1940s.*

took place in Chicago and Washington D. C. in 1919. Nonetheless, the migration continued well into the 1960s as African-Americans sought better lives in the nation's cities. By then, they had become as urban as they had been rural when the century began. Whatever expectations the *Chicago Defender* may have had in 1917, the Great Northern Migration had surpassed them.

Oklahoma

Texas

■ El Paso

Left: this panel from Jacob Lawrence's series The Migration of the Negro *shows people queuing at a railroad for tickets to the industrial cities of the north. Their destinations—Chicago, New York, St Louis— are displayed above the ticket windows.*

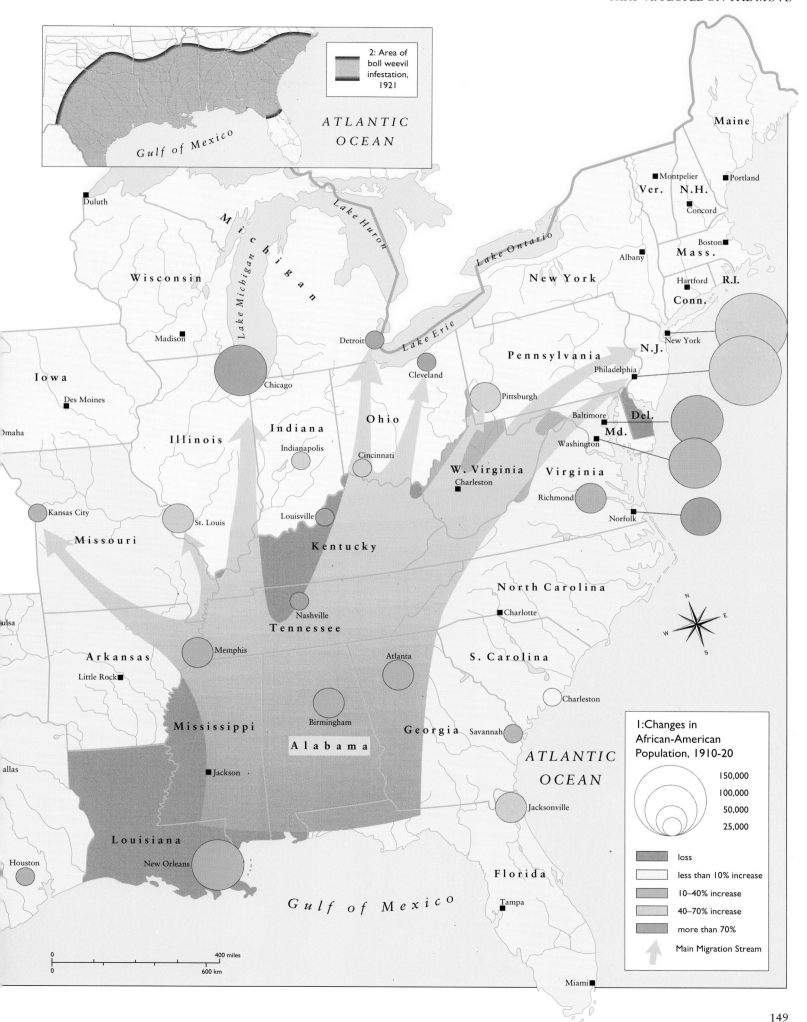

2: Area of boll weevil infestation, 1921

ATLANTIC OCEAN

Gulf of Mexico

Maine

Duluth

Michigan

Lake Huron

Lake Ontario

Montpelier   Portland

Ver.   N.H.

Concord

Albany   Boston

Mass.

Wisconsin

Lake Michigan

Lake Erie

New York

Hartford   R.I.

Conn.

Madison

Detroit

Cleveland

Pennsylvania

N.J.

New York

Iowa

Chicago

Philadelphia

Des Moines

Indiana   Ohio

Pittsburgh

Baltimore   Del.

Omaha

Illinois

Indianapolis

Cincinnati

Md.

Washington

Kansas City

St. Louis

Louisville

W. Virginia

Charleston

Virginia

Richmond

Missouri

Kentucky

Norfolk

Tulsa

Nashville

North Carolina

Charlotte

Tennessee

Arkansas

Memphis

Atlanta

S. Carolina

Little Rock

Charleston

Mississippi

Birmingham

Georgia   Savannah

Dallas

Alabama

ATLANTIC OCEAN

Jackson

Houston

Louisiana

New Orleans

Jacksonville

Florida

Tampa

Gulf of Mexico

Miami

1: Changes in African-American Population, 1910-20

150,000
100,000
50,000
25,000

loss

less than 10% increase

10–40% increase

40–70% increase

more than 70%

Main Migration Stream

0   400 miles
0   600 km

DEPRESSION AND DROUGHT

DUSTBOWL REFUGEES, 1931–39

The most notable internal migration of the 1930s was provoked by one of the biggest natural disasters in North America—a seemingly endless drought that destroyed crops from the plains of Saskatchewan to the plains of Texas.

The Great Depression of the 1930s fundamentally altered the lives of people around the world. Those in North America were no exception. In the worst years, unemployment averaged about 33 percent and climbed much higher in certain regions and for certain peoples. As a result, immigration to the continent slowed and return migration to Europe increased. The economic distress also affected migration trends within the continent. As the housing industry collapsed, suburbanization slowed. African-American migrants still worked their way north and west, but in lower numbers than in the decade before or after. Among the worst affected areas were the Appalachians. Almost a third of the population of Kentucky and Tennessee moved into Ohio, Indiana, Michigan, and California. By 1950, over 2.7 million people born in Kentucky lived in Ohio, and another 4 million were divided between the Upper Midwest and California.

Drought and soil erosion—brought on by over-farming of fragile prairie soils—turned the productive agricultural land of the Great Plains into what came to be known as the Dust Bowl. The timing and the severity of the drought varied, beginning with the Canadian provinces and northern American prairie states in 1931 and moving south by mid-decade. Strong winds exacerbated the effect of the severe lack of rain. On the morning of May 9, 1934, for example, one such windstorm blew some 350 tons of soil from Montana, Wyoming, and the Dakotas that, by evening, was falling like snow over Chicago.

Within two days, the once valuable topsoil had reached Boston, New York, Washington, and Atlanta and was being lost in the Atlantic.

As the soil blew east, the farmers, who depended on it and the rain that would not fall, began anxiously to look elsewhere for their livelihood. Families from all over the drought area moved to nearby locations, if jobs or other resources were available, or took to the road in search of opportunity in more distant locations. By far the most famous of these were the hundreds of thousands of people from the Dust Bowl region who migrated to California's cities and, particularly, agricultural valleys where they competed for jobs often left vacant by deported Mexican farm workers.

Feel-good advertising campaigns, such as this billboard image of 1937 (above), were designed to boost morale during the Depression, but their message often clashed with the harsh realities of 1930s life. Here, flood victims from Kentucky queuing for Red Cross relief offer an ironic perspective on an idealistic vision of American life which disregards the problems of poverty and unemployment. Below: a powerful image of conditions in the Dust Bowl, where the worst storms took place in the spring of 1935 following a February heatwave which saw temperatures soar to 75° fahrenheit. On April 14, a day which became known as "Black Sunday," clouds of blown topsoil engulfed western Kansas. Forced to abandon their farms by the relentless soil erosion, thousands of "Okies" loaded tents, mattresses, and cooking utensils onto trucks and cars and took to the road in the hope of finding agricultural work in California. Agencies were set up to help the vast numbers of unemployed. Right: a man makes enquiries at a field office of the Works Progress Administration (WPA), which made attempts to help the jobless.

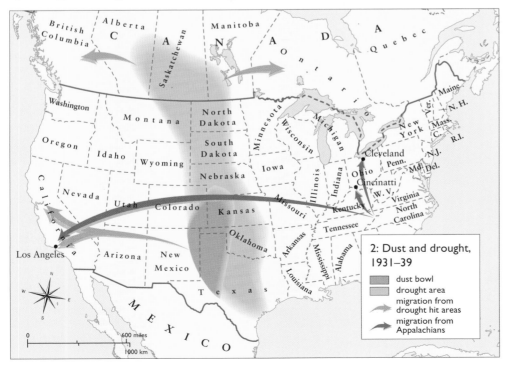

2: Dust and drought, 1931–39

- dust bowl
- drought area
- → migration from drought hit areas
- → migration from Appalachians

All we could do about it was just sit in our dusty chairs, gaze at each other through the fog that filled the room and watch the fog settle slowly and silently, covering everything—including ourselves—in a thick, brownish gray blanket. When we opened the door swirling whirlwinds of soil beat against us unmercifully… The door and windows were all shut tightly, yet those tiny particles seemed to seep through the very walls. It got into cupboards and clothes closets; our faces were as dirty as if we'd rolled in the dirt; our hair was gray and stiff and we ground dirt between our teeth.

A Garden City woman describes her experience of the Dust Bowl in the *Kansas City Times*, 1935

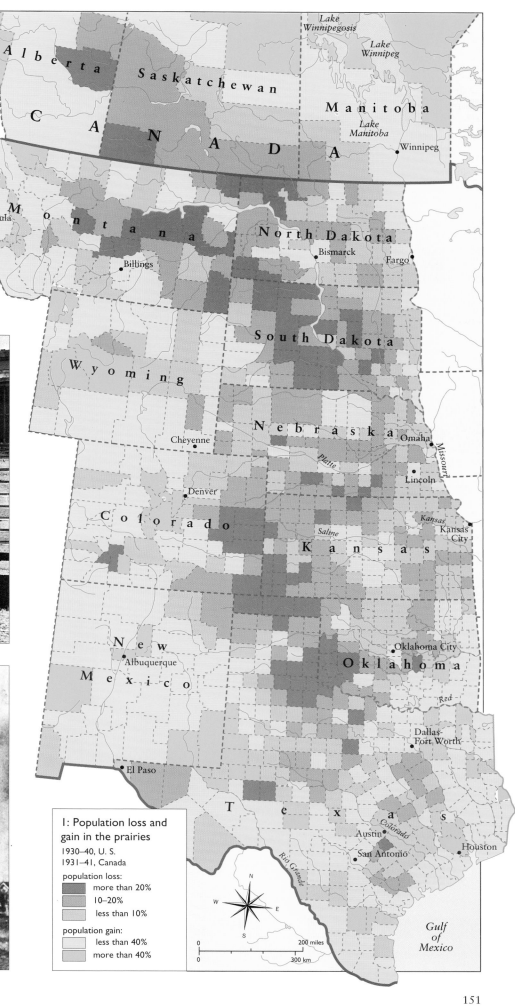

1: Population loss and gain in the prairies

1930–40, U. S.
1931–41, Canada

population loss:

more than 20%

10–20%

less than 10%

population gain:

less than 40%

more than 40%

0   200 miles

0   300 km

MOBILIZING THE PEOPLE FOR WAR
POPULATION CHANGES DURING WORLD WAR II, 1940–45

The production demands of World War II drew workers from the Appalachians and the South to the industrial cities and towns of the north, such as Cincinnati.

Situated on the middle course of the Ohio River, Cincinnati had developed as an industrial town between 1830 and 1880, when the population increase from 125,000 to 255,000 included many German-speaking people who came directly from Europe. In 1890, over a third of the population were foreign-born, chiefly from Austria-Hungary, Germany, Italy, and Great Britain. Cincinnati's importance as a destination for immigrants continued. In 1940, foreign-born whites and their children made up 40 percent of the city's population.

The 1930s had seen an influx of people from the Depression-hit Appalachian regions (> *pages 150–1*). African-Americans made up about 18 percent of the city's population in 1940. They came from Mississippi, Alabama, Georgia, and South Carolina. In Cincinnati, African-American and Appalachian families moved into different sections of the "Over the Rhine" district, occupied a century earlier by Germans. The African-Americans were concentrated in the West End and the lower Mill Creek basin, with additional settlements in South Avondale, parts of Mount Auburn and the riverside areas west of the city core. They also settled in Lincoln Heights, a northern industrial suburb where skilled and semi-skilled labor was in demand in the factories.

The migration to wartime defense industries including a second wave of African-Americans, many of whom achieved equal pay in defense industries. Between April 1940 and November 1943, employment increased almost 30 percent, from 289,370 to 362,960. Wartime employment peaked in November 1943, when the unemployment rate was only 1.4 percent. The additional 83,580 jobs were largely in manufacturing plants. Defense industry was located primarily in the Mill Creek corridor, where rail lines and intersecting roads linked related industries, and in the St Bernard-Oakley corridor, dominated by machine tool plants. Another growth area was Lockland, site of a large aircraft engine factory.

During the war, many industries adjusted their production lines. Distilleries produced industrial alcohol and special solvents. Pharmaceutical companies made drugs for medical units in combat zones. The manufacturer of safes changed to producing shields to protect crews operating anti-tank guns. Food processing plants developed packaged army rations for export, including special meat products for Russia. Clothing manufacturers turned to producing military uniforms. Across the Ohio River in Kentucky, the neighboring towns of Covington and Newport shared in the boom created by defense industry demands for steel products and small industries. Barge traffic on the Ohio River was also heavy.

In Cincinnati, the areas of most population growth were contiguous to the industrial development. The suburbs of Lockland, Reading, and Sharonville, and the city areas of Price Hill, Oakley, Bond Hill, and Kennedy Heights all showed increases of 100 percent or more. The surrounding areas, Middletown, Dayton, and Hamilton all contributed greatly to the war effort, and nearly doubled the population of the metropolitan area on the Ohio and Kentucky sides of the Ohio River to almost one million. The rise in the African-American population of Cincinnati continued in the years after World War II. The increased density of concentration in the Lower Mill Creek basin was evident in 1960, with the expansion into neighborhoods adjacent to the core area. In contrast, middle and upper class, predominantly white families occupied the surrounding hills and bluffs.

Cincinnati was just one of several cities in the industrial heartland of North America to be affected by the demands of wartime production. Appalachian and African-American families also went to Indianapolis and Gary, Indiana, to the converted automobile plants of the Detroit area and southeast Michigan, and to the steel mills of Youngstown, Cleveland, and Akron, Ohio. Canadian industrial towns also responded to wartime production demands, drawing their supplementary labor force from rural areas and the prairie provinces, accelerating a population movement that had begun during the drought years of the 1930s.

Below: this wartime poster issued by the Cincinnati soap giant Procter and Gamble explains the many wartime uses of their products. These included glycerine, which was used in high explosives.

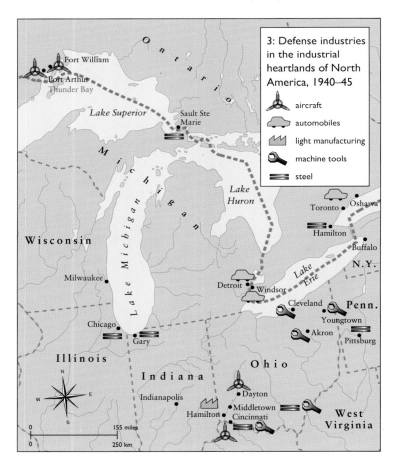

3: Defense industries in the industrial heartlands of North America, 1940–45

- aircraft
- automobiles
- light manufacturing
- machine tools
- steel

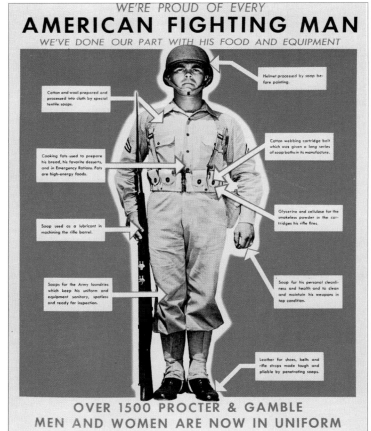

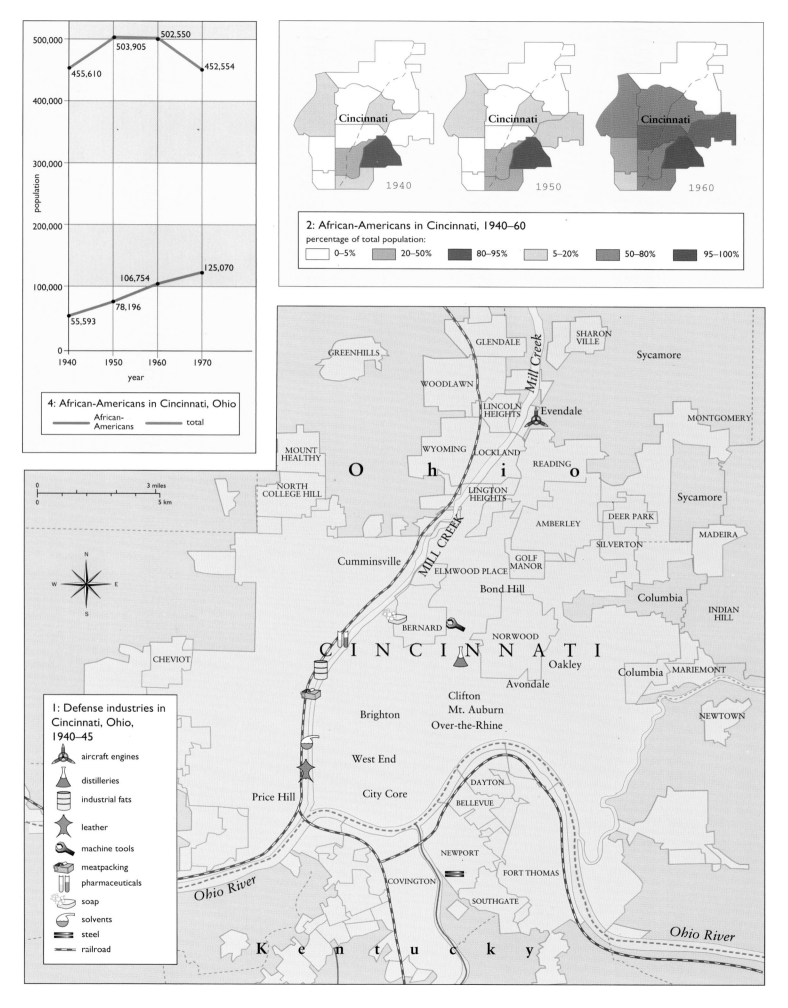

population / year

500,000 — 503,905 — 502,550

455,610

452,554

400,000

300,000

200,000

106,754 — 125,070

100,000

78,196

55,593

0

1940 1950 1960 1970

year

4: African-Americans in Cincinnati, Ohio

African-Americans — total

2: African-Americans in Cincinnati, 1940–60

percentage of total population:

0–5%   20–50%   80–95%   5–20%   50–80%   95–100%

Cincinnati 1940   Cincinnati 1950   Cincinnati 1960

0   3 miles
0   5 km

1: Defense industries in Cincinnati, Ohio, 1940–45

aircraft engines

distilleries

industrial fats

leather

machine tools

meatpacking

pharmaceuticals

soap

solvents

steel

railroad

GREENHILLS

GLENDALE

SHARON VILLE

Sycamore

Mill Creek

WOODLAWN

LINCOLN HEIGHTS

Evendale

MONTGOMERY

MOUNT HEALTHY

WYOMING

LOCKLAND

READING

O   h   i   o

NORTH COLLEGE HILL

LINGTON HEIGHTS

AMBERLEY

DEER PARK

Sycamore

SILVERTON

MADEIRA

Cumminsville

MILL CREEK

ELMWOOD PLACE

GOLF MANOR

Bond Hill

Columbia

INDIAN HILL

BERNARD

NORWOOD

CHEVIOT

C I N C I N N A T I

Oakley

Columbia

MARIEMONT

Avondale

Clifton

Mt. Auburn

NEWTOWN

Brighton

Over-the-Rhine

West End

DAYTON

City Core

BELLEVUE

Price Hill

NEWPORT

FORT THOMAS

COVINGTON

SOUTHGATE

Ohio River

K   e   n   t   u   c   k   y

Ohio River

153

CONFINED AND EVICTED
JAPANESE AND SIOUX INDIAN DISLOCATION, 1941–45

Over 100,000 people living along the west coast of the U. S. and Canada, and 1186 Indians in South Dakota, suffered harsh treatment as a result of government policies during World War II.

The Pacific coast was home to 88.5 percent of the U. S. mainland's 127,000 and 95.5 percent of Canada's 23,000 Japanese. The authorities insisted that these citizens and long-term resident aliens were a security risk, and decreed that they should be forced from their homes and jobs and relocated in internment camps. Within four days of the outbreak of war on December 7 1941, 1370 Japanese community leaders were taken into custody. The exclusion of Japanese from Military Zone 1, ordered on March 20 1942, was soon followed by a program for the internment of the entire Japanese-American population of the coastal area. The remaining 112,000 people were collected in 12 assembly centers in California, plus one each in Washington, Oregon, and Arizona. Two large assembly centers in California were race tracks at Tanforan in San Bruno and Santa Anita, where families were allocated individual horse stalls. The final step was distribution by the trainload to relocation camps. A contingent of 151 from Alaska ended up in Minidoka, Idaho. Ironically, the 150,000 Japanese living in the Hawaiian Islands were least affected as the government decided not to evacuate the islands.

In Canada, the authorities declared that all people of Japanese ancestry should be removed from the area west of the Cascade Mountains. They were concentrated in abandoned mining towns and camps, and many men were taken from their families to work on road crews. Some 5000 Japanese-Americans avoided internment by moving to more eastern cities such as Chicago, outside the exclusion zone, in the early years of the war, while 1200 volunteered for military service in Europe. Most, however, spent the war years as prisoners in ten isolated camps in the U. S. and 12 in Canada.

More than 3000 internees were subsequently transferred to Department of Justice internment camps. These so-called "dangerous" or "dissident" persons had protested against camp administrators in Manzanar and Posten, or gone on hunger strike at Tule Lake, where there was evidence of strong pro-Japanese sentiment. Manzanar, first of the camps, had a maximum of 10,000, but the largest concentration was at Tule Lake. All "potentially dangerous" evacuees were sent there, causing the population to top 18,000 for a time.

Exceptions and exemptions from regulations enabled some evacuees to leave the camps. By the end of 1942,

Above: immediately after Pearl Harbor, Japanese-American businessmen, editors, language teachers, and priests were taken to detention centers, loaded into trains in Los Angeles, Oakland, Seattle, and Portland, and sent to a detention camp in Missoula, Montana.

about 9000 evacuees had engaged in temporary agricultural work, principally in the sugar beet harvest in Oregon and other states, and for cotton growers in Arizona. About 250 college students were given leaves from camp to return to school in September 1943. Joining the army enabled 2355 men to leave the internment camps, and 161 women joined the WACS.

At the war's end in late August 1945, the 79,763 Japanese still in detention were allowed to return home, and between October 15 and December 5, all the centers except for Tule Lake were closed. For 5000 residents of the U. S. and 4000 of Canada, home meant Japan. For most of the American Japanese who stayed, it meant returning to the places they had been forced to leave: Los Angeles, Seattle, the fertile valleys of California, Oregon, and Washington. Canadian Japanese dispersed more widely, partly as a result of laws that prohibited them from returning to British Columbia until 1949. In both countries, those who had suffered began a long struggle for redress and to overturn a century of discrimination. Almost 50 years later, the U. S. government acknowledged it had been wrong, and offered symbolic payments to those who has spent the war years in internment camps.

In July 1942, five months after the order for Japanese internment, 125 extended families living on the Pine Ridge reservation in South Dakota received notices to vacate their homes within ten days. The U. S. government had decided to take over an area 43 miles long and 12.5 miles wide in the northwestern corner of the reservation for use as a gunnery range for aerial target practice. In 1956, when token recompense was paid by the government, 90 percent of the families were still homeless. The land was not returned to the Sioux until special legislation was enacted in 1968 and 1976.

Left: this 1942 painting, Making Our Mattress, by the Japanese-American artist Henry Sugimoto, depicts life in the relocation centers where they tried to recreate their lives.

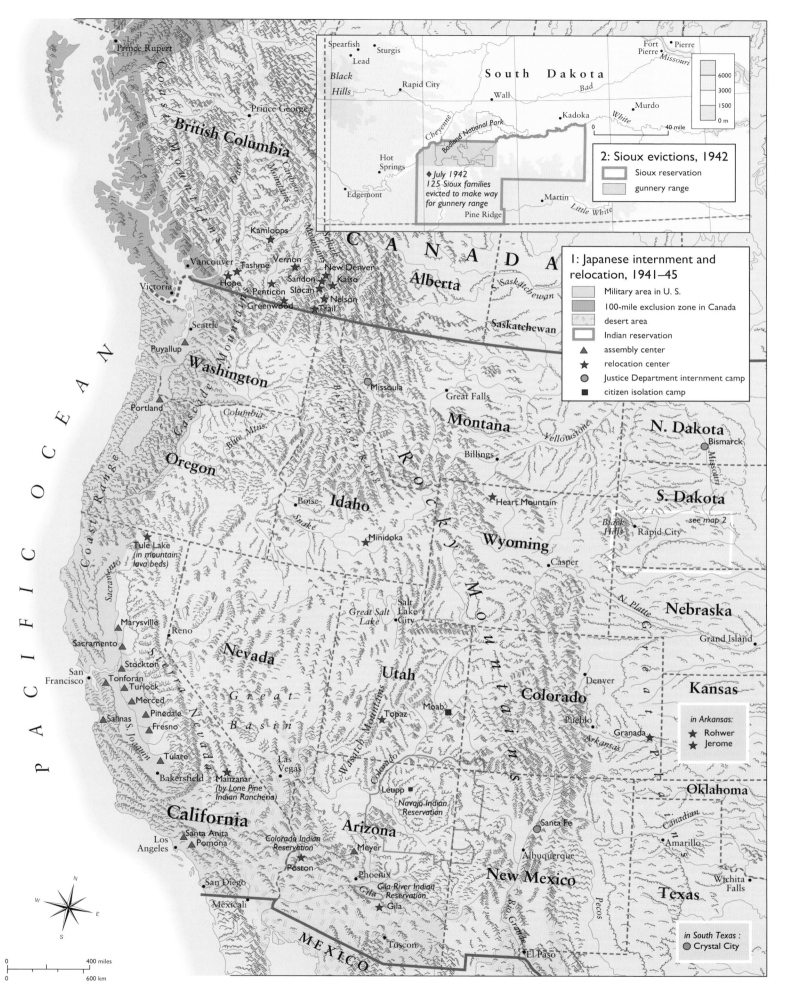

Inset map (upper): South Dakota

Spearfish • Sturgis • Fort Pierre • Pierre
Lead • Missouri
Black Hills
Rapid City • South Dakota
Wall • Bad
Kadoka • Murdo
White
Cheyenne
Badland National Park
Hot Springs
◆ *July 1942*
125 Sioux families evicted to make way for gunnery range
Edgemont
Martin
Little White
Pine Ridge

2: Sioux evictions, 1942
▢ Sioux reservation
▨ gunnery range

1: Japanese internment and relocation, 1941–45
▨ Military area in U. S.
▨ 100-mile exclusion zone in Canada
▨ desert area
▢ Indian reservation
▲ assembly center
★ relocation center
● Justice Department internment camp
■ citizen isolation camp

in Arkansas:
★ Rohwer
★ Jerome

in South Texas:
● Crystal City

PACIFIC OCEAN

Prince Rupert
British Columbia
Prince George
Kamloops
Vancouver • Tashme • Vernon • New Denver
Victoria • Hope • Sandon • Kaslo
Penticon • Slocan
Greenwood • Nelson
Trail
CANADA
Alberta
S. Saskatchewan
Saskatchewan
Seattle
Puyallup
Washington
Portland
Oregon
Columbia
Blue Mtns.
Missoula
Great Falls
Montana
Billings
Yellowstone
N. Dakota
Bismarck
Boise
Idaho
Snake
Heart Mountain
S. Dakota
Black Hills • Rapid City
see map 2
Minidoka
Wyoming
Casper
Tule Lake
(in mountain lava beds)
Great Salt Lake
Salt Lake City
N. Platte
Nebraska
Grand Island
Marysville
Reno
Sacramento
Stockton
San Francisco
Tonforan
Turlock
Merced
Salinas • Pinedale
Fresno
Nevada
Utah
Topaz
Moab
Colorado
Denver
Kansas
Pueblo
Granada
Arkansas
Tulare
Bakersfield
Manzanar
(by Lone Pine Indian Rancheria)
Las Vegas
Leupp
Navajo Indian Reservation
Oklahoma
Canadian
California
Santa Anita
Pomona
Los Angeles
Colorado Indian Reservation
Arizona
Meyer
Poston
Santa Fe
Albuquerque
New Mexico
Amarillo
San Diego
Phoenix
Gila River Indian Reservation
Gila
Texas
Wichita Falls
Mexicali
Tuscon
MEXICO
Rio Grande
Pecos
El Paso

0 — 400 miles
0 — 600 km

N W E S

155

THE HALF-OPEN DOOR
REFUGEES FROM HOT AND COLD WARS, 1933–79

Despite strict immigration quotas, many refugees from totalitarianism in Europe managed to reach North America during the troubled middle decades of the 20th century.

The millions of refugees created by World War I and its aftermath had little impact on North America. The 1921 Immigration Act had restricted immigration to 3 percent (reduced to 2 percent in 1924) of each national group in the U. S. in 1910. Since countries such as Poland and Czechoslovakia only became independent in 1918, their nationals were not eligible. Canada too restricted immigration in this period. Some 30,000 Russians fleeing the Bolshevik revolution reached the U. S. on League of Nations passports, but most found new homes in Europe.

Jews and anti-fascists began to leave Germany almost immediately Hitler came to power in January 1933. Between 1933 and 1938, some 102,000 German Jews fled to the U. S., and 6000 to Canada, but most settled elsewhere in Europe, particularly in Vienna, Paris, and Prague. When the Nazis annexed Austria and

the Sudetenland in 1938, however, the only safe haven lay across the Atlantic. Within the U. S., pressure grew to find a way around the immigration laws in order to save people from the Nazis. In 1940, a number of agencies were set up, including the National Refugee Service and

Above: the exodus of intellectuals from Germany after Hitler took power in 1933 has been described as the greatest migration of its kind since the fall of Constantinople in 1453. This triptych by Arthur Kaufman, entitled "Brain Drain," was begun in 1938 but not completed until 1965. It shows many of the German writers, artists, and scientists who found refuge in the U.S. In the foreground of the left-hand panel, on the far left, are the artist George Grosz and the composer Arnold Schoenberg; at the front of the center panel are Albert Einstein, Thomas Mann, and Erica Mann; to their right, in the next panel, is Kurt Weill.

the Emergency Rescue Committee. By early 1941 over 600 anti-fascist intellectuals had been rescued from Vichy France by the ERC, which got them across the Pyrenees to Lisbon, from where they sailed to New York. Among them were the novelist Heinrich Mann and the artists Marc Chagall and Marcel Duchamp. In 1944 a further 982 refugees, most of them Jews from Eastern Europe, were granted "temporary" admission by the Roosevelt administration.

The end of the war in Europe left some 20–30 million people homeless and stateless. Many, especially concentration camp survivors, were desperately ill. Resettlement in their country of origin was not a realistic option: 1000 Jews who tried to return to their homes in Poland were murdered by local people between the end of the war and the spring of 1947. Between 1945 and 1950, 72,000 concentration camp survivors were admitted to the U. S., and 16,000 to Canada. Displaced Persons camps were set up throughout

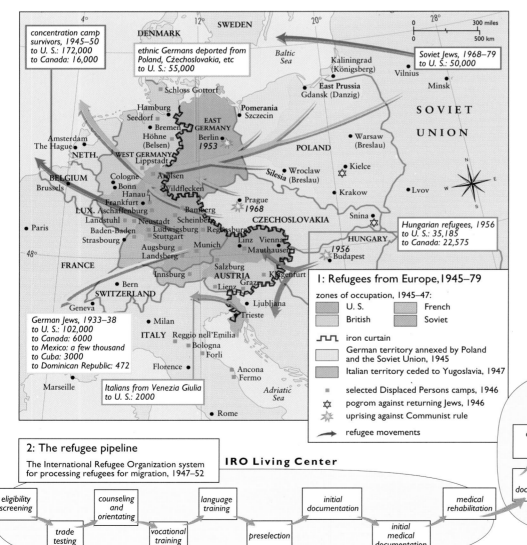

1: Refugees from Europe, 1945–79

concentration camp survivors, 1945–50 to U. S.: 172,000 to Canada: 16,000

ethnic Germans deported from Poland, Czechoslovakia, etc to U. S.: 55,000

Soviet Jews, 1968–79 to U. S.: 50,000

Hungarian refugees, 1956 to U. S.: 35,185 to Canada: 22,575

German Jews, 1933–38 to U. S.: 102,000 to Canada: 6000 to Mexico: a few thousand to Cuba: 3000 to Dominican Republic: 472

Italians from Venezia Giulia to U. S.: 2000

zones of occupation, 1945–47:
- U. S.
- British
- French
- Soviet

iron curtain

German territory annexed by Poland and the Soviet Union, 1945

Italian territory ceded to Yugoslavia, 1947

selected Displaced Persons camps, 1946

pogrom against returning Jews, 1946

uprising against Communist rule

refugee movements

2: The refugee pipeline

The International Refugee Organization system for processing refugees for migration, 1947–52

IRO Living Center

eligibility screening → trade testing → counseling and orientating → vocational training → language training → preselection → initial documentation → initial medical documentation → medical rehabilitation

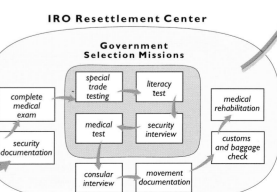

IRO Resettlement Center

Government Selection Missions

complete medical exam → special trade testing → literacy test → medical rehabilitation

security documentation → medical test → security interview → customs and baggage check

consular interview → movement documentation

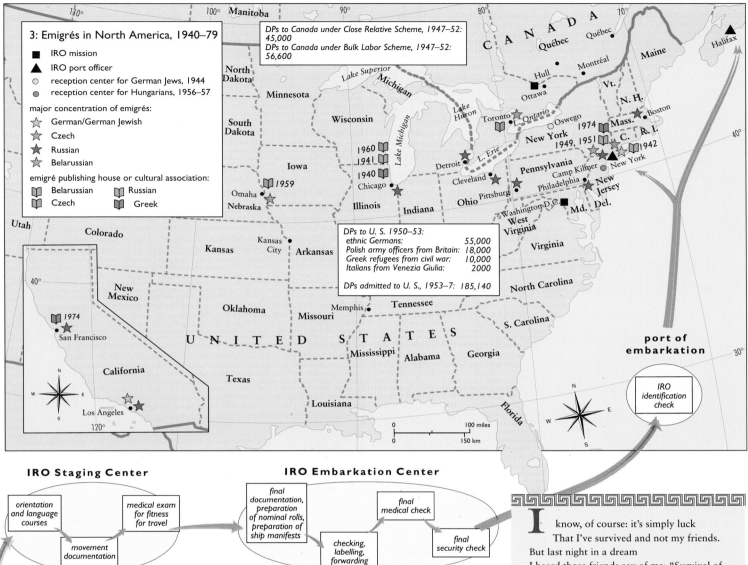

3: Emigrés in North America, 1940–79

■ IRO mission
▲ IRO port officer
○ reception center for German Jews, 1944
● reception center for Hungarians, 1956–57

major concentration of emigrés:
☆ German/German Jewish
☆ Czech
★ Russian
☆ Belarussian

emigré publishing house or cultural association:
📖 Belarussian   📖 Russian
📖 Czech   📖 Greek

DPs to Canada under Close Relative Scheme, 1947–52: 45,000
DPs to Canada under Bulk Labor Scheme, 1947–52: 56,600

DPs to U. S. 1950–53:
ethnic Germans:	55,000
Polish army officers from Britain:	18,000
Greek refugees from civil war:	10,000
Italians from Venezia Giulia:	2000

DPs admitted to U. S., 1953–7: 185,140

port of embarkation

IRO identification check

IRO Staging Center

orientation and language courses → movement documentation → medical exam for fitness for travel

IRO Embarkation Center

final documentation, preparation of nominal rolls, preparation of ship manifests → checking, labelling, forwarding of baggage → final medical check → final security check

---

Europe under the auspices of the United Nations Relief and Rehabilitation Administration (UNRRA). The Truman Directive of December 1945 gave DPs preference under the existing laws, thus admitting 41,379 refugees to U. S. In November 1946 Canada launched its Close Relative Scheme, which allowed the admission of refugees nominated by close relatives already living in Canada, and the Bulk Labor Scheme, to bring people who met specific labor shortages in Canada. The two schemes brought a total of 157,687 DPs to Canada by the end of 1951.

In addition, millions of *Volksdeutscher*—ethnic Germans—were expelled from Central and Eastern Europe, and in 1947 Italy was obliged to cede the Venezia Giulia region to Yugoslavia. (Some 2000 Italians from the area were eventually admitted to the U. S.) To cope with the scale of the problem, the United Nations set up the International Refugee Organization (IRO), which took over the running of the DP camps in July 1947. It provided medical care, job training, and language tuition for DPs, and arranged for their eventual resettlement. In 1948 the U. S. Displaced Persons Act authorized the admission of 205,000 DPs over two years; the Second Displaced Persons Act of 1950 raised the total to 400,000. Despite these efforts, the last of the camps was not closed until 1957.

From 1953 to 1963 about 190,000 refugees came to the U. S. from behind the Iron Curtain. When the Hungarian revolt was crushed by Soviet troops in December 1956, some 200,000 people—2 percent of the population—fled the country. Within six months, the UN High Commission for Refugees (which had replaced the IRO in 1952) found permanent asylum for most of them in 35 different countries. Of these, 35,185 went to the U. S. and 22,575 to Canada. Because the Hungarians were not eligible for visas under the national origins quotas, the Attorney General "paroled" them into the U. S. "in the public interest," a precedent later used to admit anti-Castro exiles from Cuba (> *pages 174–5*).

The Hungarians were temporarily housed at Camp Kilmer in New Jersey before being assigned sponsors. They settled in quickly. Most were young, male, and well-educated; about a quarter were craftsmen, the rest white-collar workers. By the end of 1957, over 65 percent had found employment. The Soviet invasion of Czechoslovakia in 1968 brought a further influx of refugees, possibly as many as 12,000, to the U. S. and Canada. The largest group of exiles from behind the Iron Curtain, however, were Soviet Jews. Most settled in Israel, but by 1979 there were 50,000 in the U. S.

I know, of course: it's simply luck
That I've survived and not my friends.
But last night in a dream
I heard those friends say of me: "Survival of the fittest"
And I hated myself.

Bertolt Brecht, "I, the Survivor"

The professional backgrounds of many of the refugees may actually have disadvantaged them when it came to adapting to life in a new country. It is one thing to learn a new language well enough to pursue a manual trade, but few could emulate the Russian novelist Vladimir Nabokov, who made a new career writing in English from the 1940s after settling in the U. S. For many, North America was not a new beginning but a place of exile, where they preserved their culture, social allegiances, and political disputes ready for the time when they could return to their homelands. Yet many did stay and make a lasting contribution to American cultural life, including the physicist Albert Einstein; Otto Klemperer, who became conductor of the Los Angeles Philharmonic; the composer Eric Wolfgang Korngold, who wrote scores for many Hollywood movies; and the film directors Fritz Lang, Otto Preminger, and Billy Wilder (German), Roman Polanski (Polish), and Miklos Forman (Czech).

PART VII:
CONTEMPORARY
NORTH AMERICA

Introduction
by Janice Reiff

The ethnic variety of North America's population has increased during the past half century, bringing the term "multiculture" into newspaper headlines and public affairs, particularly in the field of education. Immigrants and immigration are topics of lively debate as international population movements take on a political significance. Governments encourage or restrict emigration and immigration for reasons of national social policy and diplomatic strategy.

Right: throughout the 19th and early 20th centuries, New York City was the main port of entry for immigrants to the U. S. Even after the restrictive immigration laws of the 1920s, it had more foreign-born residents than any other U. S. city, and after the relaxation of the quota system in the 1960s it began to attract new communities from the Caribbean, including significant numbers of Cubans and Haitians.

Canada and the U. S. have followed nearly parallel policies with regard to immigration during the post World War II era. Yet since the sequence of legislation, and often specific objectives, have differed, the course of events in the two countries will be covered separately. Both nations have historic policies of preference for North European immigrants and exclusion of Asians. Relaxation of previous restrictions during the 1950s preceded radical changes in 1965 in the United States and 1967 in Canada when new laws were enacted.

As an initial step during World War II, the U. S. in 1943 repealed the 1882 Chinese exclusion law, finally permitting foreign-born Chinese to become citizens. But a quota of 105 per year made the law largely a symbolic victory, and previous legislation to exclude all other Asians remained in force until 1952. The War Brides Act of 1946 brought 200,000 alien wives and children into the United States, as well as a few hundred foreign husbands of women service personnel.

Special legislation for refugees commenced with the Displaced Persons Act of 1948 which enabled 220,000 people to settle permanently in the U. S.during the two following years, a quota later raised to 415,000. Displaced persons had to have sponsors who would be responsible for providing homes and jobs. Not until a revision in 1950 were provisions eliminated that discriminated against Jews and Catholics.

The atmosphere of the 1950s was humanitarian in reaction to the "Cold War," but also attentive to national security. Deportation of members of the Communist Party or organizations deemed to be "communist fronts" accompanied renewed suspicion of foreigners. The comprehensive Immigration and Nationality Act of 1952 (McCarran–Walter Act) set quotas granting about 85 percent to nations in northern and western Europe, but separating out immigrants from the British West Indies who could no longer be admitted under the British quota. The 1952 legislation set special preference categories for immigrants with academic and technical qualifications and other advanced training. It also enlarged the class of immigrants not subject to quotas, such as immediate relatives of naturalized newcomers and those in the class of permanent resident aliens.

The Hungarian Revolution in 1956, and the overthrow of the Batista regime in Cuba by Fidel Castro in 1959 both led to the admission of refugees. Quota limits were suspended to allow entry of 20,000 refugees in 1956 from Hungary and Yugoslavia. The following year, special arrangements were made for refugees from Dutch Indonesia. The 1960 World Refugee law aided people from Cuba and from China as well. By the 1960s, many people in the U. S. questioned the obviously discrimina-

Above: in 1959 Cuban revolutionaries led by Fidel Castro toppled the regime of Fulgencio Batista. Many supporters of the regime fled to Florida, where Batista himself had spent an earlier period of exile, forming the basis of a large Cuban population in Miami. Cold War politics meant that the Federal government gave support and encouragement to those escaping communist countries, although the welcome cooled somewhat after the 1980 Mariel boatlift.

tory "national origins" immigration law, while the nation claimed to be an asylum for the politically oppressed and a leader of the free.

Immigration law in the 1960s

More liberal immigration provisions were written into the Hart–Celler Act of 1965, which ended the system of quotas according to national origin and the restrictions on entry from Asia and the Pacific region. The limit for annual immigration was raised to 290,000 with 120,000 visas available for people in the western hemisphere and 170,000 from the eastern hemisphere, and a restricted number of visas available for refugees, though others could come under special circumstances.

The legislation of 1965, going into effect in 1968, brought significant changes to immigration patterns of the 1970s. For example, in 1975 close to 9,000 came from China, a country whose previous quota had been only 1000. From India, 14,000 arrived in 1975 in contrast to the 300 who came ten years earlier. The changes in geographic distribution are clearly demonstrated by comparing the percentages for the figures for the 1920 to 1960 era with these for 1975. During the earlier period of "national origins" quotas, 60 percent came from Europe, 35 percent came from Central and South America, and 3 percent from Asia. In contrast, in 1975 43 percent came from Central and South America, 34 percent from Asia, and only 19 percent from Europe. Although only about 6000 came to the U.S. from the Philippines in 1965, by 1979 the number passed 43,000.

The situation in Canada

During the same period that American immigration regulations were being revised, changes were being made in Canada's immigration laws and policies. Through the 1950s, the Canadian government encouraged sponsored immigrants, people whose relatives took the responsibility for housing and subsistence, at least on first arrival. This group, also called "family class" immigrants, made up 59 percent of total immigration into Canada in the peak year, 1959, but the average for the decade was closer to 37 percent. Many Canadians felt that this procedure increased the extended families of the South European immigrants who were principally unskilled laborers.

In 1952, the same year that the American Congress passed comprehensive new immigration laws, Canada passed an Immigration Act granting extreme discretionary powers to the minister and his subsidiary staff responsible for immigration. Regulations enacted four years later essentially prohibited immigration except for four categories arranged in order of the perceived desir-

Below: African-American parents and children demonstrate against school segregation in Saint Louis, Missouri, in the early 1960s.

ability as additions to Canadian society. At the top of the groups which were actually arranged according to national origin, were unsponsored British subjects from the United Kingdom and the white sector of the Commonwealth, along with immigrants of American or French origin. Second were unsponsored immigrants from selected western European nations; while the third rank included a broad range of sponsored relatives from Europe, America, and a few nations in the Middle East. The last category, essentially "other," was phrased to restrict Asians to the category of sponsored close relatives without openly stating the objective.

In the different spirit of the 1960s, the Act was amended in 1962, marking the first step toward ending overt racial discrimination in Canada's immigration policy. Admission to Canada in the future would be based on skills and means of support rather than national origin. With the expansion of Canada's economy and the boom years of the 1960s, Canada needed immigrants who were professionals, trained technicians, and laborers with special skills. These highly skilled workers were not available in Europe because they had jobs in the recovering post-war economy. Between 1946 and 1970, 278,000 immigrants with professional qualifications went to Canada.

A change of policy in Canada in 1967 inaugurated a policy known as "the point system" that appeared to ignore national origin or race. The prospective immigrants were given "points" based on their education, skills, available financial capital, and other resources. After 1967, immigration to Canada was no longer predominantly from Europe, but from Asia and from developing nations often grouped as the "Third World." By the mid-1970s, Canada's largest numbers of immigrants were coming from Asia and the Caribbean, followed by Latin America and Africa. This new pattern significantly increased the size of those ethnic groups.

New sources

Immigrants from India numbered 177 in 1954 and 8,672 in 1981. Substantial but not so dramatic was the change in Chinese immigration, which rose from 1930 in 1954 to 6681 in 1981. By contrast, German immigration decreased from 28,260 in 1954 to 1977 in 1981. Similarly, from Italy the number of immigrants in 1954 (24,420) fell to 2056 in 1981. The population influx that brought in highly skilled workers and professionals people from Asia and the Caribbean also created an unfavorable reaction and some resentment in Canada. Among the professional class were Sinhalese and others from Sri Lanka and India's mainland. Furthermore, the new labor demand seemed to require more working class families to join the industrial work force. Consequently, the next trend was to decrease the immigration of professionally competent people and augment the labor force with blue-collar workers from the Fiji Islands, Guyana (northwestern South America), and Trinidad. New government policy reduced South Asian immigration by two-thirds from 1975 to 1979. The percentage of professional immigrants from India fell from 42.6 percent in the period 1968–72 to 1.5 percent in 1983–84.

During the period that professional people from South Asia were arriving in large numbers in Canada, a similar trend was observable in the United States. Between 1965 and 1974, 75,000 foreign born physicians entered the country in response to an increased need for doctors in the Medicare system. Shortly after the new immigration law was published in 1965, an estimated 13,000 Korean medical personnel, the majority women nurses, entered

million annually, but some second and third generation undocumented Mexicans live in the U. S. Their numbers are small in Canada.

Refugees and retirees

New arrivals in North America are not all immigrants admitted according to the current policy of the national governments of Canada or the United States. Many are refugees whose destiny is also dependent upon international refugee and relief organizations. The United Nations and other intergovernmental and religious organizations direct the international movement of many refugee people. During the period 1952–70, the Intergovernmental Committee on European Migration dealt with 1,700,000 national migrants and refugees, planning for their resettlement. Since the end of World War II

Left: a U. S. Marine helps a Vietnamese woman across the deck of the amphibious ship USS Durham *after evacuation from South Vietnam by* Sea Knight *helicopter. Having withdrawn its troops in 1973 and reneged on its promises of military assistance, the U. S. left the South Vietnamese defenseless in the face of the final Communist onslaught of 1975.*

the United States. Between 1976 and 1986, the leading sources of immigration into the U. S. were the following groups: Canada and the United Kingdom, 280,000; Cuba, Jamaica, and the Dominican Republic, 670,000; China/Taiwan, Korea, the Philippines, and Vietnam, 1,798,000; Mexico, 720,000.

Mexican immigration has been a special problem in the U. S. given the fact that the two countries share a land border. Immigrants entering the country with official documents numbered about 38,000 in 1965; by 1978, the figyure had risen to 93,000. At the same time, perhaps as many as 8 million Mexicans have entered the country without documents. The Immigration and Naturalization Service apprehends and deports close to a

Canada, the United States, and Australia have taken in about 75 percent of the refugees. The numbers are: U. S., 1 million; Australia, 354,000; and Canada, 300,000.

The largest refugee group in the United States is the Cubans who have come in stages. After Fidel Castro came to power in 1959, the first group of educated and middle class Cubans established a base in Miami, though many settled in other parts of the country. In 1965, Castro permitted others to leave the island and an estimated 360,000 Cubans of diverse background came to Florida. The last contingent, often called the "Mariel group" of largely working class people, left in 1980–81. Many were brought across the water in small boats.

After 1965, a second source of refugees were the Vietnamese and other Southeast Asians including Chinese, Laotians, and Cambodians. During the next twenty years an estimated 700,000 entered the United States, some—like the Hmong—brought over with the help of churches and charitable organizations. The adjustment has been difficult particularly for the Laotians and Cambodians who once led agrarian lives.

Although the background for most of the maps in this part of the atlas is migration for economic gain, or because of intolerable social and political situations, there are also internal population trends of interest during the period of time from the end of World War II to the present. One population movement concerns the transfer of older and retired persons to southern living communities. A second internal migration map shows the migration to the cities of America's Indian population, a group of urban dwellers who nevertheless usually spend part of each year with kinfolk living in a reservation community.

Below: a Vietnamese man is punched in the face by an American official as he tries to board an airplane already overloaded with refugees attempting to flee from Nha Trang during the NVA's Final Offensive. The U. S. government offered protection to those fleeing regimes, but in practice the reception they received varied considerably according to fluctuations in Cold War politics and public opinion in the U. S.

TIMELINE
1955–95

NORTH AMERICA	THE CARIBBEAN, CENTRAL & S. AMERICA	EUROPE, AFRICA, & ASIA

1955–56 Bus boycott in Montgomery, Alabama

1957 Sept: Eisenhower signs Civil Rights Act. Arkansas National Guard attempts to exclude 9 black students from high school in Little Rock; Federal troops force them to withdraw and let students pass

1958 July: Alaska becomes 49th state of U.S. Aug: Hawaii becomes 50th state of U.S.

1959 Opening of the St Lawrence Seaway turns Toronto into a major seaport

1960 April: Civil Rights Bill. Nov: John F. Kennedy elected U.S. president. National Association for the Advancement of Colored People boycotts stores with segregated lunch counters

1961 Sept: "Freedom Riders" campaign against segregation on interstate buses

1963 Nov: John F. Kennedy assassinated. Vice President Lyndon B. Johnson succeeds him

1964 July: U.S. Civil Rights Act passed, prohibiting discrimination on the grounds of race or religion. Nov: Lyndon B. Johnson elected president

1965 Feb: Malcolm X assassinated. March: Civil Rights marches to Montgomery, Alabama. Aug: Voting Rights Act suspends literacy tests in areas where less than 50% of the population is registered to vote. Riots in Watts, Los Angeles, follow the arrest of a black motorist. Oct: Immigration Act amendments abolish nationality quotas for entry to U.S.

1966 July–Sept: Riots in Chicago, Cleveland, Brooklyn, and San Francisco

1967 June–July: Serious riots in many U.S. cities. French premier General de Gaulle declares "Vive Québec Libre" on visit to Canada. Sept: President Johnson puts forward Vietnam peace plan

1968 Parti Québecois founded by Rene Levesque (the beginning of the separatist movement). American Indian Movement (AIM) established. April: Dr Martin Luther King assassinated. June: Senator Robert Kennedy assassinated. June–July: Rioting in many U.S. cities. Nov: Richard M. Nixon becomes U.S. president

1969–71 American Indians occupy Alcatraz Island

1970 May: Four students shot by National Guard at Kent State University, Ohio, during demonstration against Vietnam War. Oct: Kidnap and murder of Cabinet Minister Pierre Laporte. War Measures Act imposed on Québec province

1971 President Nixon initiates policy of detente with USSR and China

1972 Feb: President Nixon visits China. May: Nixon visits Moscow and signs SALT I arms limitation treaty. June: Police arrest five members of the Campaign to Re-Elect the President in the act of burgling the Democrat campaign offices. Nov: President Nixon re-elected.

1956 Sept: Nicaraguan president Somoza assassinated

1957 Jamaica achieves cabinet government and full internal autonomy. Sept: François "Papa Doc" Duvalier elected president of Haiti

1959 Jan: Fidel Castro overthrows Batista government in Cuba

1960 April: Brasilia opened as new capital of Brazil

1961 April: 1500 U.S.-trained Cuban exiles fail to overthrow Castro in "Bay of Pigs" invasion. May: Rafael Trujillo, dictator in Dominican Republic since 1930, assassinated

1962 Aug: Jamaica and Trinidad and Tobago become independent from Britain

1964 March–April: Naval mutiny in Rio de Janeiro leads to the overthrow of Brazilian president Goulart and imposition of military regime

1965 April: U.S. sends marines into Dominican Republic to prevent Communists from taking power

1968 Hundreds of students killed when police open fire on a demonstration at the opening of Olympic Games in Mexico City. Oct: Military coup overthrows Brazilian president Belaunde

1970 Sept: Marxist Salvador Allende elected president of Chile

1971 April: Haitian president François "Papa Doc" Duvalier dies; succeeded by his 19-year-old son Jean-Claude ("Baby Doc")

1972–80 20,000–30,000 Haitians flee to U.S. Dec: Earthquake destroys Nicaraguan capital Managua

---

1956 Feb: Soviet leader Khruschev denounces Stalin at 20th Party Congress. Oct–Dec: Anglo-French invasion of Egypt fails (Suez Crisis). Nov: Uprising against Communist rule in Hungary crushed by Soviet tanks

1961 Increased U. S. involvement in Vietnam. Aug: Berlin Wall built

1962 June: French withdraw from Algeria. Oct: Cuban Missile Crisis brings threat of nuclear war

1964 Oct: Khruschev forced into retirement; Kosygin is Prime Minister but Leonid Brezhnev soon emerges as effective leader

1965 March: U.S. Marines land in Vietnam to protect USAF base at Da Nang

1966 Cultural Revolution begins in China

1967 April: Military coup in Greece. June: Six Day War between Israel and Arab States. Most of Poland's 30,000 remaining Jews emigrate as a result of government "anti-Zionist" campaign

1968 Jan: North Vietnamese launch Tet Offensive. Aug: Soviet troops invade Czechoslovakia and depose reform government of Alexander Dubcek. "Africanization" program in Kenya leads to mass exodus of Asian Indians

1970 April: U.S. troops sent into Cambodia

1971 15,000 Jews allowed to leave Soviet Union for Israel

1972 Jewish emigration from Soviet Union increases to 30,000 annually. Jan: "Bloody Sunday"—13 civilians shot by British troops during demonstrations in Derry, Northern Ireland. Aug: tens of thousands of Asian Indians expelled from Uganda; many go to Britain and Canada, about 1000 to U.S.

NORTH AMERICA

1973 Jan: Trial of Watergate burglars begins
Feb–May: 200 Oglala Sioux occupy site of Wounded
Knee massacre; two are killed. April: President Nixon
admits responsibility for cover-up of Watergate
break-in. Oct: Vice President Spiro Agnew pleads
guilty to tax fraud and resigns

1974 French adopted as the official language of
Québec. Aug: President Nixon resigns;
succeeded by Vice President Gerald Ford

1975 July: Congress extends 1965 Voting Rights Act
for 7 years and adds safeguards for Spanish-speaking
and other linguistic minorities

1976 Nov: Jimmy Carter wins U.S. presidential
election

1977 Sept: 29 Americans and 26 Cuban relatives
arrive in Florida as a result of repatriation agreement

1978 Nov: U.S. agrees to admit 47,000 "boat
people" fleeing Vietnam, Laos, and Cambodia

1980 Federal Census. Native American population of
U.S. is 1,418,195. Refugees Act gives statutory right
to protection in the U.S. to those at risk of
persecution. 125,000 Cuban "boat people" arrive
in Florida. Québec votes "non" to separatism.
Nov: Ronald Reagan wins U.S. presidential election

1982 Plebiscite in Northwest Territories of Canada
agrees establishment of a new, Inuit-governed
territory, Nanavut

1984 Nov: President Reagan re-elected

1988 Nov: George Bush wins U.S. presidential
election

1990 Struggle between Mohawk tribes and the
Sureté Québec police highlights issues of land
disputes and Indian rights in Canada. Census reveals
U.S. population to be 248,709,873—a 9.9 percent
increase since 1980

1992 April: Riots in Los Angeles follow the beating
of a black motorist by police.
Nov: Bill Clinton wins U. S. presidential election

1993 North America Free Trade Agreement
(NAFTA) signed by U.S., Mexico, and Canada

1995 June: U.S. Commission on Immigration Reform
recommends cutting immigration by one-third

THE CARIBBEAN, CENTRAL & S. AMERICA

1973 Former dictator Juan Peron elected president in
Argentina. Military coup overthrows Marxist
government of Salvador Allende in Chile

1976 March: Isabela Peron overthrown by military
junta; beginning of period of political terror in
Argentina

1977 Aug: U.S. and Cuba sign repatriation
agreement

1979 Nicaraguan dictator Anastasio Somoza overthrown by Sandinista rebels

1982 April–June: War between Britain and Argentina
over Falkland Islands (Malvinas)

1983 Oct: U.S. troops invade Grenada

1985 Sept: Earthquake in Mexico City

1986 Feb: Haitian president Jean-Claude Duvalier
deposed and exiled

1989 Jan: Panamanian dictator Manuel Noriega
surrenders to U.S. troops after they occupy the
country

1994 U.S. military intervention to restore
elected president Jean-Bertrand Aristide in Haiti.
Peasant uprising in Chiapas, Mexico

EUROPE, AFRICA, & ASIA

1973 Jan: Paris peace agreement—U.S. military to
withdraw from Vietnam in 60 days.
Oct: Israel defeats Arab states in Yom KippurWar

1974 July: Turkey invades Cyprus after attempted
union with Greece; Greek military junta collapses.
Sept: Frelimo government takes power in
Mozambique

1975 April: Final withdrawal of U.S. from Vietnam
as Communist forces overrun south. Nov: Spanish
dictator Franco dies; Juan Carlos proclaimed king

1976 Sept: Mao Tse-tung dies in China

1978 Sept: Presidents Sadat and Begin sign Camp
David peace accord between Egypt and Israel

1979 Jan: Shah flees from Iran. Feb: Ayatollah
Khomeini returns from Paris exile to establish Islamic
regime in Iran. June: President Carter and Soviet
leader Brezhnev sign SALT II arms limitation treaty.
Nov: Iranian students occupy U.S. embassy in
Teheran and take 90 diplomatic staff hostage. Soviet
Union invades Afghanistan

1980 April: U.S. rescue mission fails to release
hostages in Iran

1981 Jan: Teheran hostages released after 444 days
in captivity

1982 Soviet leader Leonid Brezhnev dies.
June: Israel invades Lebanon

1984 Britain signs agreement to transfer Hong Kong
to Chinese sovereignty in 1997

1985 Mikhael Gorbachev becomes Soviet leader.
Soviet troops withdraw from Afghanistan

1986 April: Nuclear accident at Chernobyl, Ukraine

1989 Autumn: Collapse of Communist regimes
throughout Eastern Europe. Nov: fall of Berlin Wall

1990 Aug: Iraqi troops invade Kuwait.
Oct: formal reunification of Germany

1991 Jan–Feb: Gulf War. May:Baltic republics
become independent from Soviet Union. June: Boris
Yeltsin wins first free elections for president of
Russian republic. Croatia and Slovenia declare
independence from Yugoslavia. Aug: Soviet hardliners
attempt coup against Gorbachev. Dec: Gorbachev
resigns; Soviet Union effectively ceases to exist

1993 Sept–Oct: Boris Yeltsin uses military force to
disband Russian parliament

1994 April: Free elections mark end of apartheid in
South Africa

SUBURBS AND SUN
JOB SEEKERS AND RETIREES MOVE SOUTH, 1950–90

Social changes after World War II meant that North Americans were no longer bound to remain where they were born or had settled. The young moved to find work, the elderly to retire; both chose smaller cities in warmer areas.

It started in 1950 with one young man's love of Southern California. He had been stationed there during the war, and knew this was where he wanted to live. After graduating from an Eastern university he packed his car, left his family and traveled some 3000 miles across the country to Los Angeles. He was followed a year later by his younger brother, then by his sister. Since his parents had already planned to retire somewhere warm, they made the trek from Pennsylvania to California in the spring of 1952, leaving family, friends, community, and all that was familiar.

This brief family history catches the beginning of a trend that was to continue for the next four decades as people in North America left the Rustbelt of the North and East for the Sunbelt of the South and West. As the workforce shifted away from traditional agricultural employment, the population moved to meet the changing demands for labor. During the first three decades after World War II, the largest population growth occurred in the West, followed closely by the South. Fertility patterns and family composition changed, transforming the patterns that had tied people to their locations. As war babies reached employment age, they formed a large element in the workforce that was young and geo-

graphically mobile. Crossing large distances was becoming less of an obstacle. Workers moved to places where jobs could be found, but where the state of the economy allowed them a choice, they showed a growing preference for sunny, low-density areas.

The 1950s also saw the beginning of a trend in residential communities that offered homes to those being displaced in a changing world. No longer tied to the places where they had lived and worked, more and more people retired to these specially created "single layer" communities in retirement villages and mobile home parks. Increased mobility and economic affordability allowed retirees some choice in selecting new homes. Elderly migrants showed the same preference as younger people for the sunny climates of the South and West, particularly the

Above: an elderly couple join in a game of bingo at Boot Kikkers in League City, Texas. Texas is a popular state for retired people seeking sunny climes in which to enjoy their leisure, and legal gambling is a prime leisure-time activity, and is now grossing in excess of $34.7 billion annually.

states of Florida, New Mexico, Texas, and California. The pattern of retirees migrating south and west has increased fairly consistently over the four decades from the 1950s to the 1990s. Between 1960 and 1970, the elderly population of small non-metropolitan areas in the U. S. increased by 46 percent; from 1970 to 1980, by 57 percent; and from 1980 to 1990 by a further 55 percent. The 1990s have also seen a growth in the popularity of states in the Northwest, such as Oregon, and the Northeast, such as Connecticut and New Jersey, as retire-

2: From Rustbelt to Sunbelt, 1990

— Rustbelt
— Sunbelt

source of new capital in Sunbelt areas:
- resort and retirement activities
- industry or energy production

What then? Shall we sit idly down and say
The night has come. It is no longer day?
No! Age is opportunity no less than Youth itself though in another dress,
And as the evening twilight fades away
The sky is filled with stars and worlds Invisible by day

Henry Wadsworth Longfellow

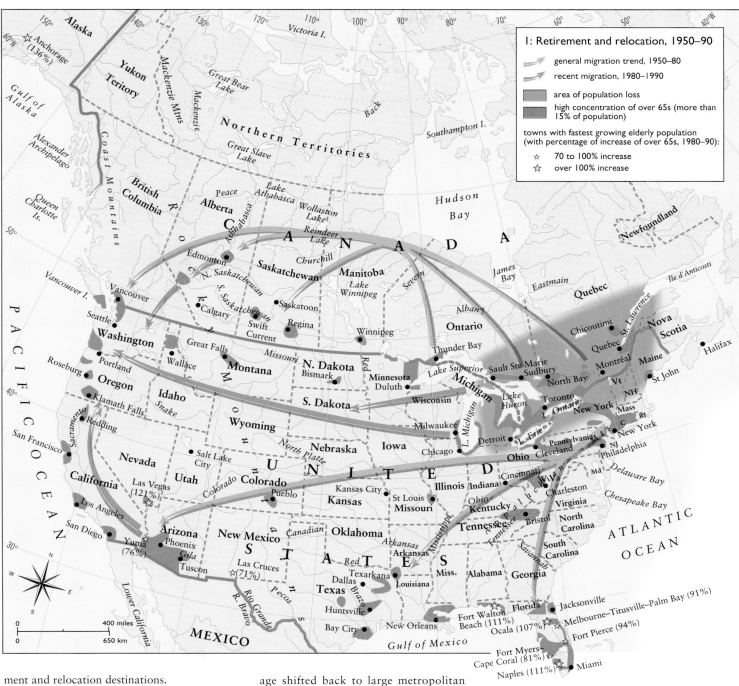

1: Retirement and relocation, 1950–90

- general migration trend, 1950–80
- recent migration, 1980–1990
- area of population loss
- high concentration of over 65s (more than 15% of population)

towns with fastest growing elderly population (with percentage of increase of over 65s, 1980–90):
- ☆ 70 to 100% increase
- ✪ over 100% increase

ment and relocation destinations.

By the end of the 1970s, enough people had moved to the Sunbelt to bring about a fundamental change in the economic geography of the U. S. The Rustbelt, with its great industrial cities such as Chicago, Cleveland, and Detroit, had been the economic powerhouse of the nation since the beginning of the 19th century, dominating all the other areas. But the fastest growing areas were now the South and West, creating a rising cycle of prosperity in those regions. People migrated there to find jobs—especially in the rapidly expanding computer industry—or to retire, and the new arrivals created a new demand for goods and services. In the late 70s and 80s, the trend appeared to go into reverse for a while as people of working age shifted back to large metropolitan areas. They did not return to the East however, but concentrated in the larger cities of the Sunbelt, such as Los Angeles, Houston, and Dallas. This left many small towns in the South and West with a predominantly elderly population during the 1980s and 90s.

Overall, the elderly population of both the U. S. and Canada is growing in all areas. People are also having fewer children, and as a result of these trends, a large part of the population has recently moved into the 65 or older category. The gradual but consistent migration of the elderly has redistributed them into smaller towns and rural areas in the West. Despite the steady increase in retirement migration however, large numbers of elderly people remain in the Northeast, particularly in the suburbs of the big cities of Pennsylvania, West Virginia, and Minnesota. Many had moved to the suburbs with their families after World War II; by the 1990s they had reached retirement age, while younger people had moved away— a phenomenon known as "aging-in-place."

The same general migration pattern can be found in Canada. People are moving west, away from big cities and into smaller metropolitan areas. The young leave one city for another, and more and more people with no connection to agriculture are choosing to live in rural areas. Many Canadians also like to retire to sunnier climates; some become "snowbirds," maintaining summer homes in Canada and winter homes in Florida, Arizona, California, or Hawaii.

BIG CITY INDIANS
THE URBAN RELOCATION PROJECT, 1950–70

Indian people moved into the big cities along with other Americans, both independently and as part of a government relocation program.

By 1960, there were approximately 166,000 Indians living in the big cities of the U. S. Out of that total, about 20,000 newcomers were there as a result of a government program to relocate Indians in urban areas with the ultimate goal of ending Indian reservations. Beginning in 1952, the Bureau of Indian Affairs offered one-way tickets, financial aid, and employment assistance to families and single men and women who agreed to leave their reservations. The first relocation offices were established in Chicago and Los Angeles. The program reached a peak in 1958 when 12 centers were operating between Cleveland, Ohio, and the West Coast.

By that time, however, it had become evident that few permanent jobs had materialized, and that Indian people had difficulty adjusting to the strange customs of urban life. Although the relocation program remained in place throughout the 1960s, it was allowed to lie dormant,

and many centers were closed. Finally, in 1970, the program was officially abandoned, along with the plan to terminate reservations.

Although the active period of the relocation program was over before 1960, eight centers remained open: Cleveland, Chicago, Denver, and Dallas as well as four in California at Los Angeles, San Francisco, Oakland, and San Jose. Of the 33,466 reservation Indians who participated in relocation, at least a third returned to their former homes. On the other hand, those who stayed provided bases for relatives and friends to come to look for work. Recruits for the relocation program were customarily moved long distances, to discourage them from returning to the reservations they had left behind. Alaskans usually came to Chicago; some Minnesota Ojibwa to Oakland, California, Sioux of South Dakota to Los Angeles, and Navajo to Chicago.

Indians also moved to the cities independent of the government relocation program. One of the early groups included Mohawks from the St Regis reservation in northern New York and the Kahnawake near Montreal. Their skill in bridge building was in demand for skyscraper con-

struction in New York City. The Mohawks established an enclave in Brooklyn, returning regularly to their reserves. During World War II, Bureau of Indian Affairs staff members urged Blackfeet and other western Indians to come to Seattle, Washington, to work in defense plants. By the 1970s, many Indian people had developed a pattern of moving back and forth between cities and reservations in both the U. S. and Canada.

The gathering of Indian people from many tribes in big cities created a new era of inter-tribal activity. The first big inter-tribal conference, bringing together 450 representatives of 90 Indian nations, took place in 1961 in Chicago, the first city to have a relocation center. The presence of many Indians in cities was also an important factor in creating the American Indian Movement (AIM), which was founded in Minneapolis in 1968.

Below: this 1983 painting, Reflections: Tribute to Our Iron Skywalkers, *by Arnold Jacobs (Onondaga) depicts one of the many Indian steelworkers who built the skyscrapers of New York City.*

the city
chases away
spirits from my hair
dreams from my reach
hope from my eyes
sirens kill the night
and i

mother drum
mother drum

Mark Turcotte,
"Mother Drum," 1995

Right: this 1955 photograph of an Ojibwa family watching TV in their new home in Oakland, California, projects the aim of the Relocation Program to absorb Indians into the "normal" urban population. It does not reflect the dislocation and loss experienced by many, or the lack of jobs to sustain the comfortable lifestyle depicted.

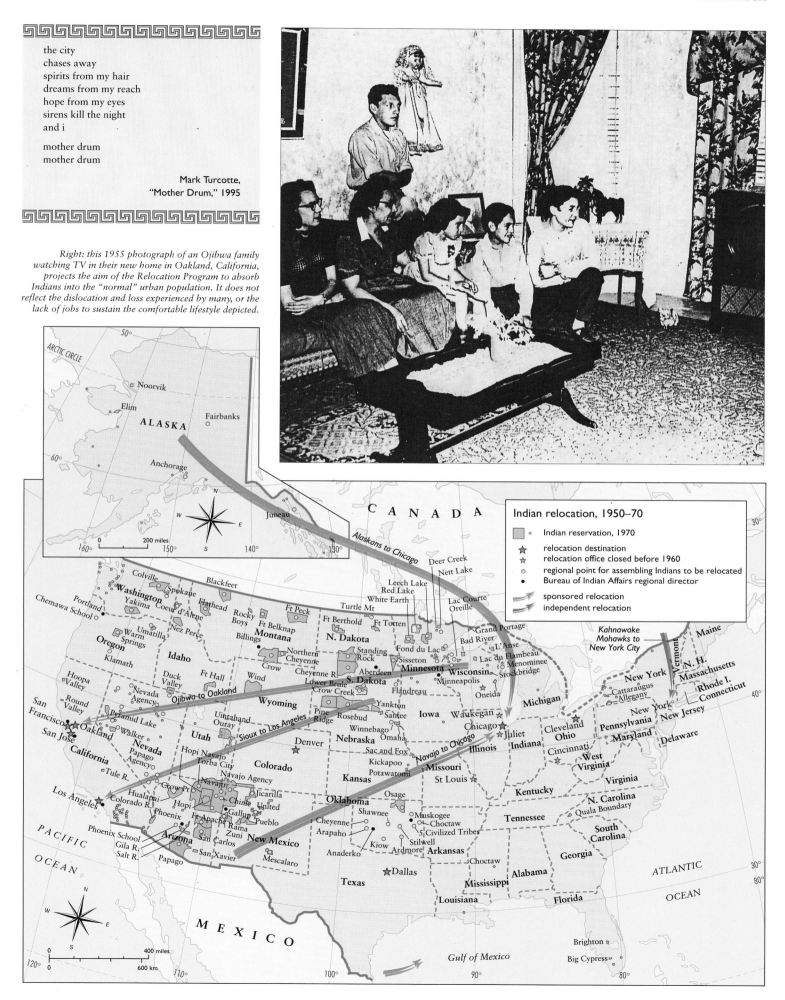

Indian relocation, 1950–70

- Indian reservation, 1970
- ☆ relocation destination
- ☆ relocation office closed before 1960
- ○ regional point for assembling Indians to be relocated
- ● Bureau of Indian Affairs regional director
- → sponsored relocation
- → independent relocation

FROM ISLAND TO MAINLAND
CARIBBEAN MIGRATION, 1952–95

Recent immigrants from the Caribbean Islands have settled on the North American mainland, seeking economic improvement or escaping political oppression.

Caribbean migrants to North America represent a diverse range of cultural traditions. They speak a variety of languages which include English (Jamaicans), French (Haitians), Spanish (Cubans, Dominicans, and Puerto Ricans), Yoruba (Haitians), and several creole languages. The immigrants' religions include Catholicism, several Protestant faiths, and the African-influenced *vodun* and *santería*.

The largest group of Caribbean immigrants in the U. S. came from Puerto Rico. There were three main periods of migration, the result of major changes in the island's economy. From 1870 to 1940, subsistence agriculture and the sharecropping of coffee was replaced by large-scale sugar production, which left much of the land in the hands of foreign-owned corporations. Many small farmers ousted from their land obtained contracts from labor recruiters

and migrated to Cuba, Hawaii, and Mexico. Travel restrictions to the U. S. were removed in 1917, when Puerto Ricans obtained U. S. citizenship. Operation Bootstrap (1947–65), a development program that offered tax exemptions to attract foreign corporations, industrialized the island but failed to provide enough jobs to offset the loss of agricultural work. As a result, many people emigrated in the 1940s, 50s and 60s, encouraged by the government and labor recruiters, and the availability of inexpensive airfares to the U. S. The most recent outmigration, which began in the 1960s and is still continuing, has been caused by the island's economic restructuring. Labor-intensive industries such as garment making have given way to capital-intensive ones (chemicals, machinery, and pharmaceuticals), and the number of jobs available has failed to match the increase in population.

Puerto Rican immigrants to the U. S. have traditionally found work in the service and garment industries of New York City, and in agriculture in Massachussetts, New Jersey, and New York. Since the late 1960s, however, this has begun to change; as a result of the decline of manufacturing in the northeastern cities, Puerto Ricans have begun to disperse throughout the U. S.

The first significant Jamaican migration to the U. S. took place between 1900 and 1930, and was composed of educated middle-class immigrants; they did not migrate to Canada in large

numbers until the 1950s. The flow of immigrants seeking economic opportunities in the U. S. and Canada increased after Britain restricted immigration in 1962. The "brain drain" of highly-educated professionals (teachers, nurses, and doctors) from Jamaica continued in the 1970s, as emigration increased and families were reunited in the U. S. and Canada. During the 1970s and 80s, Jamaican agricultural workers entered the U. S. temporarily under a guest worker program that supplied labor to Florida, Georgia, and the Carolinas.

Most immigration from Cuba was the result of political conflict. Exiles migrated to the U. S. in the late 19th century to organize Cuban independence, and again in the 1950s to plan the Cuban revolution. The largest migration, however, took place after the 1959 revolution, and was composed of Cubans opposed to Fidel Castro's government and attracted by economic opportunities in the U. S. Because of its political opposition to the Cuban government, the U. S. began to regard the Cubans as political refugees in 1960, and admitted them under the parole legislation previously applied to the Hungarian exiles of 1956 (> *pages 156–7*).

During the most intense periods of conflict with the U. S., the Cuban government restricted emigration. This broke the flow of immigration into three main waves, which took place between 1959 and 1962, from 1965 to 1973, and in 1980. While the immigrants who left

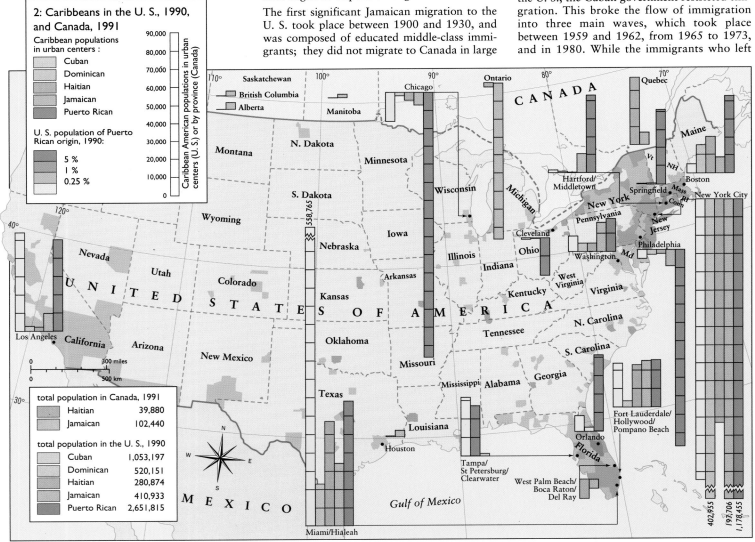

2: Caribbeans in the U. S., 1990, and Canada, 1991

Caribbean populations in urban centers:
- Cuban
- Dominican
- Haitian
- Jamaican
- Puerto Rican

U. S. population of Puerto Rican origin, 1990:
- 5 %
- 1 %
- 0.25 %

total population in Canada, 1991	
Haitian	39,880
Jamaican	102,440

total population in the U. S., 1990	
Cuban	1,053,197
Dominican	520,151
Haitian	280,874
Jamaican	410,933
Puerto Rican	2,651,815

before 1959 were predominantly upper and middle class "white" Cubans, the 1980 immigrants included many Afro-Cubans. The deterioration of Cuba's economy in the 1980s and 90s is as likely a motive for recent emigrants as opposition to the government.

Large-scale emigration from the Dominican Republic began in 1961, when Rafael Trujillo, the island's dictator since 1930, was assassinated. Trujillo's obsession with security had severely restricted emigration. Economic opportunities in the U. S. drew mostly urban, middle-class immigrants to big cities such as New York and Miami. Most obtained working-class jobs in the service sector, such as restaurant and child-care work, or in the garment trade or other light manufacturing industries. Dominicans also migrated to Puerto Rico, where many joined the stream of Puerto Ricans entering the U. S.

Haitian immigration surged during the brutal dictatorships of François "Papa Doc" Duvalier (1958–71) and his son Jean-Claude ("Baby Doc," 1971–86). At first, urban middle-class professionals migrated by plane. Later, in the 1980s and 90s, poorer immigrants escaped to Florida in flimsy boats. The U. S., concerned to maintain its diplomatic ties with the Haitian government, denied them refugee status and deported them. Critics maintained that this policy was racist, because it deported the Haitians, who were predominantly of African descent, while welcoming Cubans, who were mostly of European origin. After a military coup deposed the democratically-elected president Jean-Bertrand Aristide in 1991, U. S. policy changed from deporting to detaining Haitian refugees After the 1994 U. S. intervention to restore Aristide to power, the detained refugees were repatriated to Haiti.

Above: many recent immigrants from the Caribbean have settled in New York City, particularly in the boroughs of Brooklyn and the Bronx (> pages 176–7). In Brooklyn the annual West India Day parade has become a well-established event in the city's calendar.

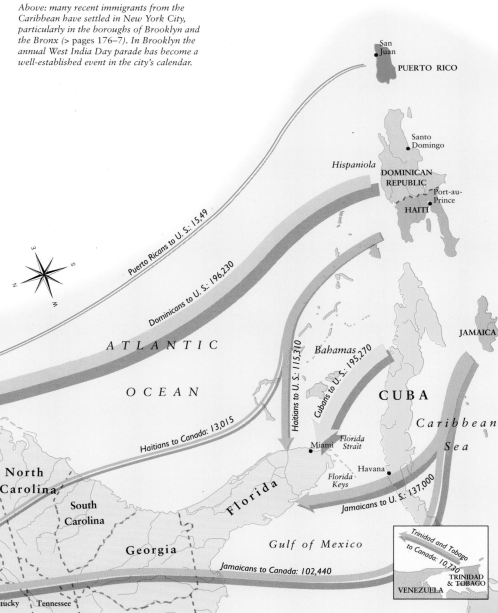

1: Caribbean migration to the U. S., 1980–90, and Canada, 1981–91

main emigrant streams:

⇨ Cuban	⇨ Jamaican
⇨ Dominican	⇨ Puerto Rican
⇨ Haitian	⇨ Trinidadian and Tobagan

0 — 200 miles
0 — 300 km

Puerto Ricans to U. S.: 15,49

Dominicans to U. S.: 196,230

Haitians to U. S.: 115,310

Cubans to U. S.: 195,270

Haitians to Canada: 13,015

Jamaicans to U. S.: 137,000

Jamaicans to Canada: 102,440

Trinidad and Tobago to Canada: 10,730

EL NORTE
SPANISH-SPEAKING AMERICANS COME NORTH, 1910–95

Throughout the 20th century, Mexicans have come north in search of work. In recent decades they have been joined by Central Americans fleeing persecution and war.

Mexican immigration has traditionally been fueled by the U. S. need for labor. During the 19th century, Arizona mines, south Texas farms, and national railroad construction projects attracted Mexican workers. In the early 20th century, increasing industrialization and the development of agribusiness created a need for more labor throughout the Southwest and Midwest. When Asian workers were excluded by the immigration laws of 1882 and 1908, it was Mexicans who replaced them. Labor shortages during the world wars and economic expansion also increased immigration.

Mexico's efforts to modernize its economy in the 1870s by promoting technology and encouraging foreign investment strengthened its ties to the U. S. The U. S. became Mexico's major foreign investor in mining and railroads, and a market for its agricultural produce and minerals. In Mexico, railroad development drove land prices up. Large landowners responded by buying property from small landholders, transforming them into landless workers. The mechanization of agriculture, mining, and transportation, and the introduction of U. S. manufactured

Above: a Mexican worker crosses a tomato field in the southern U. S. Under the Bracero Program (1942–1964), which was begun in response to the labor shortages of World War II, workers were recruited in Mexico and provided with seasonal contracts in agricultural work and railroad construction.

goods displaced Mexican workers and artisans. Mexican railroad development brought labor recruiters into Mexico to contract workers for agricultural, railroad, and assembly-line jobs in the U. S., and decreased the cost of travel. Spurred on by falling wages and unemployment in Mexico, workers migrated by rail to Mexican cities, from where they traveled to the U. S. The political turmoil of the Mexican Revolution (1910–17) helped accelerate this immigration.

The U. S. adopted a "revolving door" policy towards Mexican immigration in which Mexican workers were allowed to enter the U. S. during labor shortages but forced to depart during recessions and periods of widespread anti-immigrant sentiment. Official deportations of Mexicans (including some American citizens) occurred during the 1920–22 recession, the Great Depression (1930s), and the post-Korean War recession (1953–55). These periods are characterized by resentment against immigrants who are blamed for the economic crises. The threat of deportation allowed U. S. employers to benefit by keeping wages low and restricting labor organizing. This policy provided employers in the Southwest with low-wage labor but appeased restrictionist sentiments by denying citizenship to workers.

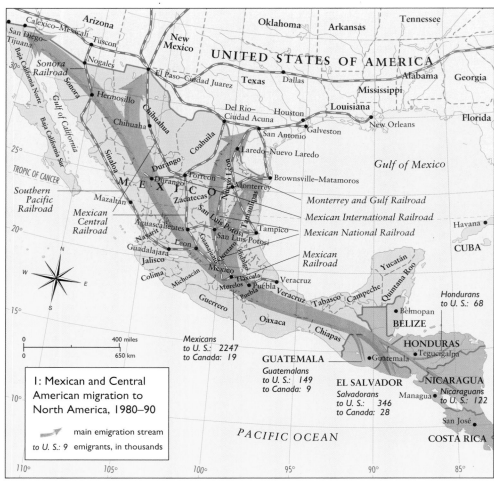

I: Mexican and Central American migration to North America, 1980–90

main emigration stream
to U. S.: 9 emigrants, in thousands

Mexicans
to U. S.: 2247
to Canada: 19

Guatemalans
to U. S.: 149
to Canada: 9

Salvadorans
to U. S.: 346
to Canada: 28

Hondurans
to U. S.: 68

Nicaraguans
to U. S.: 122

Sonora Railroad
Southern Pacific Railroad
Mexican Central Railroad
Monterrey and Gulf Railroad
Mexican International Railroad
Mexican National Railroad
Mexican Railroad

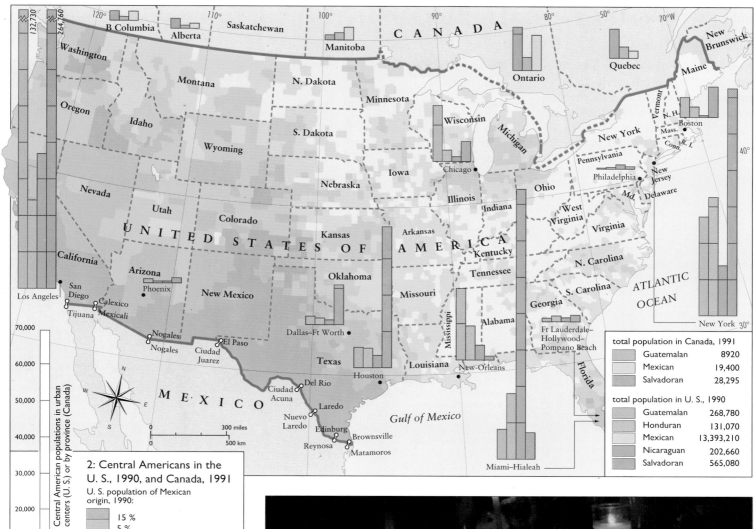

2: Central Americans in the U. S., 1990, and Canada, 1991

U. S. population of Mexican origin, 1990:

- 15 %
- 5 %
- 1 %
- 0.25 %

∞ cross–border twin cities

Central American populations in urban centers (U. S.) or by province (Canada)

total population in Canada, 1991	
Guatemalan	8920
Mexican	19,400
Salvadoran	28,295

total population in U. S., 1990	
Guatemalan	268,780
Honduran	131,070
Mexican	13,393,210
Nicaraguan	202,660
Salvadoran	565,080

During the 1960s, the immigrant workers began to shift from rural to urban jobs in the construction, garment, and service industries. Many were employed on the U. S. side of cross-border twin cities such as San Diego-Tijuana or El Paso-Ciudad Juarez, commuting across the international boundary twice a day. But the Mexicans did not find employment only in the border regions; the ease of transportation and the increased variety of jobs helped them to disperse throughout the U. S.

Toward the end of the 1970s, the Mexican immigrants were joined by large numbers of Central Americans. Escaping from civil wars, political persecution, and economic displacement in their home countries, they crossed into Mexico and made their way to "El Norte"—the north—in the hope of crossing the Rio Grande into the U. S. As with the refugees from Cuba and Haiti (> *pages 174–5*), their admission depended on political considerations. The Carter administration gave "extended voluntary departure" status to some 20,000 Nicaraguans living in the U. S. when the Sandinistas took power in 1979; those seeking refuge from right-wing governments were less fortunate. The 1980 Refugee Act reaffirmed the U. S. policy of giving priority

to those fleeing Communist countries. That year, some 12,000 Salvadorans were detained in camps in the U. S. before being deported. In 1981, only two out of 5510 Salvadoran applicants were granted refugee status; between 300 and 500 were deported each month.

In Guatemala, the government waged a relentless "counter-insurgency" campaign on the Indian population. Some 200–300 people a week fled across the border into Mexico in the early 1980s, until the Mexican authorities began to exclude them. Many went on to enter the U. S. By 1982, there were some 300,000–500,000 Salvadorans, and a few tens of thousands of Guatemalans, in the U. S. Most were

Above: All Souls' Day, 1988, a young Mexican girl lights candles before Our Lady of Mount Carmel, sculpted c.1838 by Rafael Aragon and combining both Spanish and Central American influences.

liable to be deported to countries where they believed their lives to be in danger. The situation gave rise to what became known as the Sanctuary Movement. Many church congregations in the U. S., both Catholic and Protestant, considered it their obligation to shelter those in flight from oppression, and hid refugees from El Salvador and Guatemala in their homes and churches. Despite the widespread publicity it attracted, the campaign had little influence on government policy in Central America.

173

THE WORLD'S METROPOLIS

NEW YORK CITY, 1980–90

New York, for so long the first port of entry for new arrivals to the U. S., continues to be the city with the most diverse population in North America despite the effect of immigration controls during the 20th century.

By the end of the 19th century, when Jacob Riis wrote his influential books *The Children of the Poor* and *How the Other Half Lives*, New York City was characterized by its enclaves of Italians, Jews, Chinese, Irish, and African-Americans. The restrictive Immigration Acts of 1921 and 1924 had the effect of making this most cosmopolitan of cities slightly less cosmopolitan. Earlier generations of immigrants became assimilated or moved out to the suburbs, and were not replaced by new arrivals. Although the immigrant population of New York remained between three or four times the level for the U. S. as a whole, their numbers were declining in line with figures for the rest of the country.

When the Hart-Celler Act of 1965 abolished the discriminatory quota system, New York once again assumed its traditional role as the world's metropolis. By this time many of the older immigrant communities had moved out of the city center; the new ones came from parts of the world that had not been strongly represented in the city before, especially from the Caribbean (> *pages 172–3*). More than 45 percent of immigrants to New York in the period 1983 to 1989 came from the Caribbean. During the 1980s, some 40,000 Dominicans settled in New York. From its original nucleus in Washington Heights, the Dominican community has expanded across the Harlem River into the West Bronx. Haitians, Jamaicans, and Guyanese have settled in Crown Heights, Flatbush/Midwood, and East Flatbush. In 1980 they made up 9 percent of the city's Hispanic population; by 1990 the figure had increased to 19 percent. Puerto Ricans have long been established in the city, although in the early 1990s more left than arrived. Puerto Rican migration has always been circular to some extent; as U. S. citizens, Puerto Ricans could enter freely, and were therefore able to come to the mainland, earn some money, and then return to the island. Other recent Hispanic arrivals include Ecuadorians and Colombians.

Some of the old communities have continued to attract new arrivals. New York's Chinatown dates back to the 1890s, when it was centered on a small area around Mott Street on Lower East Side. The late 1980s saw a new wave of Chinese immigrants—26,000 from 1983 to 1989—who have spread out from this historic center into East Village and across the East River into Brooklyn. More than half still live in Manhattan, however. Chinese now equals Italian as the third most widely spoken language in New York, after English and Spanish. Other Asians who have settled in the city include Koreans and South Asians. Both groups have tended to congregate in North Queens, particularly around Flushing, Elmhurst, and Jackson Heights.

Recent immigrants have concentrated in the northern and southern ends of Manhattan. More than half the population of Washington Heights and Inwood, for example, were foreign-born by 1990. In the Bronx, where half the population now speak another language than English at home, the number of foreign-born residents in several districts has risen by between 55 and 79 percent. Many recent arrivals have also settled in Queens, where they represent more than a third of the total population. In Brooklyn, the percentage of foreign-born residents grew from just under 24 percent in 1980 to just over 29 percent in 1990. Staten Island, in contrast, has less than 12 percent.

There were over 1.6 million immigrants in New York City in 1980, and over 2 million in 1990—28 percent of the total population. The numbers of people moving out of New York City during the 1980s just outstripped the numbers moving in: 1.5 million as opposed to 1.4 million. Of those who left, 70,000 went to the western U. S., 51,000 to the Midwest, 117,000 to Florida, and 112,000 to the rest of the South. The movement of people in both directions has altered the social composition of the city. The new arrivals have mostly been young: 40 percent of them are between the ages of 25 and 40, compared to 29 percent of the general population. But they have not matched the outmigration of people of working age, and as a result New York had more young children and elderly people in 1990 than in 1980.

New York remains almost unique among great world cities in retaining large residential enclaves within its commercial and business core, Manhattan Island. A short walk from the upmarket shopping of Madison Avenue (above) leads to areas such as the Lower East Side, which are largely populated by recent arrivals to the U. S.

3: Settlement of Chinese immigrants, 1983-89

total number of Chinese immigrants:

- 10,000 and over
- 5000-9999
- 2000-4999
- 1000 and over

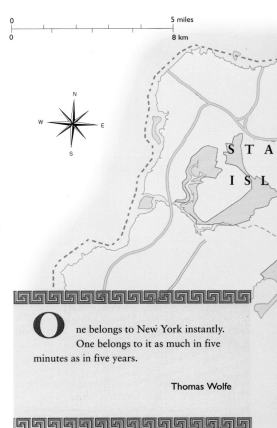

O ne belongs to New York instantly. One belongs to it as much in five minutes as in five years.

Thomas Wolfe

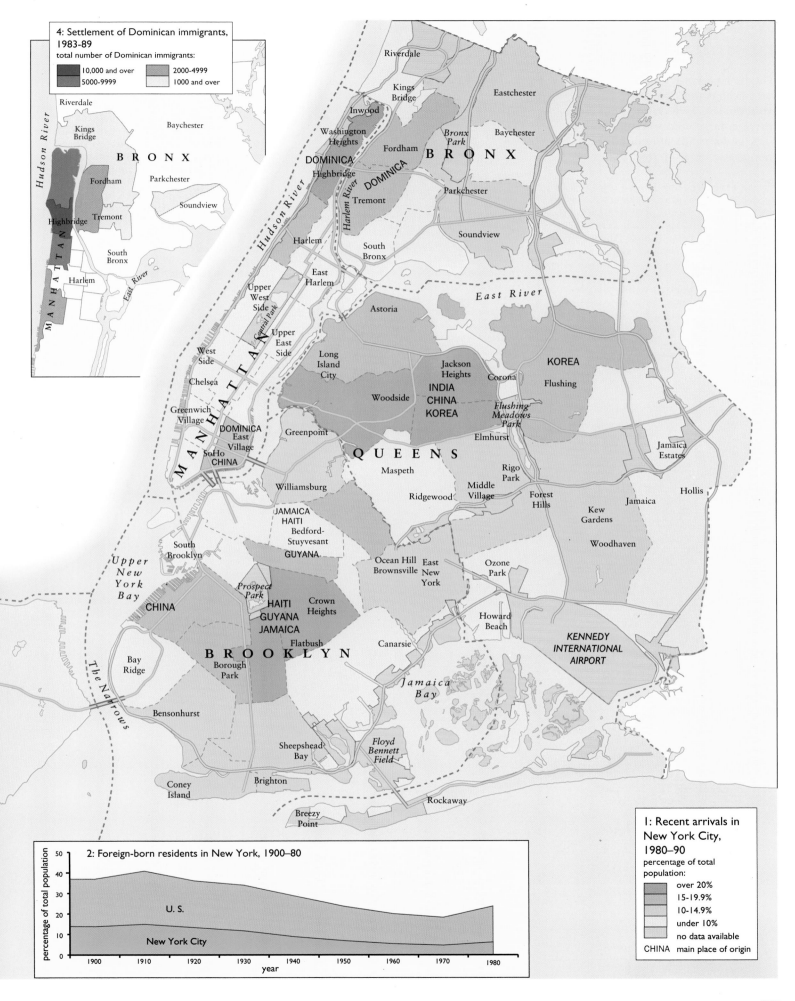

4: Settlement of Dominican immigrants, 1983-89

total number of Dominican immigrants:

- 10,000 and over
- 5000-9999
- 2000-4999
- 1000 and over

2: Foreign-born residents in New York, 1900-80

percentage of total population

U.S.

New York City

year

1: Recent arrivals in New York City, 1980-90

percentage of total population:

- over 20%
- 15-19.9%
- 10-14.9%
- under 10%
- no data available

CHINA main place of origin

A CONTINUOUS JOURNEY
IMMIGRANTS FROM SOUTH ASIA AND THE MIDDLE EAST, 1900–91

Middle Easterners and South Asians have been coming to North America since the late 19th century, but did not arrive in large numbers until both the U. S. and Canada liberalized their immigration laws in the 1960s.

The area broadly defined as the "Middle East" is predominantly the Arab world, in which Islam is the dominant religion. The area encompasses Jordan, Lebanon, Syria, Iraq, Palestine, Saudi Arabia, Egypt, Sudan, Libya, Algeria, Tunisia, and Morocco, as well as non-Arab Muslim countries such as Turkey and Iran. The geographical definition, however, also embraces the Jewish state of Israel, as well as the substantial Christian populations and smaller sects in Syria and Lebanon, and in large cities of other countries. Christian Syrians and Lebanese, though they speak Arabic, do not usually classify themselves as "Arabs" because the term is so closely associated with Islam.

Most Turks and Iranians, on the other hand, are Muslims but not Arabs. South Asia is virtually a separate sub-continent, which encompasses India, Sri Lanka, Bangladesh, Pakistan, Nepal, and the Maldives. Much of it is Islamic, but there are very sizable areas in which other religions, such as Hinduism and Buddhism, predominate.

The earliest Middle Eastern immigrants were Christians from Syria, then a province of the Ottoman Empire that dominated the eastern Mediterranean for a 400-year period ending in 1918. Most came from the mountainous coastal area between the port cities of Tripoli and Beirut (now in Lebanon, which did not become a separate republic until 1946.) The Syrian experience illustrates the immigrant networks that sent new people by stages clear across the U. S. Syrians became peddlers, starting in the port communities of New York and penetrating the entire nation, including the South where there were few immigrants. Suppliers became important people who developed other businesses, particularly dry goods and grocery stores.

The largest Arab population in the U. S. today is located around Detroit, Michigan, including Wayne, Oakland, and Macomb counties, where the estimated number is close to 40,000. This is about 10,000 above the Arab populations of New York and Los Angeles. The center of activity is South Dearborn, Michigan. Other pockets of Middle Easterners have developed around the country. Since the 1960s, Egyptians who are largely Coptic Christians have established a large community in Jersey City as well as Los Angeles. The largest Jordanian and Palestinian settlements have been in the Chicago area, followed by Detroit and New York state which has a thriving community in Yonkers. Yemeni immigrants have mostly become farm workers in California.

Recent immigration from the Middle East has included a large student population, as well as refugees in 1978 and 1979. At the same time, tourist and temporary visas have increased the numbers living within the U. S. In 1979–80, 19,000 Iranians were admitted as immigrants; while the previous year—a peak year— 116,000 visas were issued to Iranian nationals,

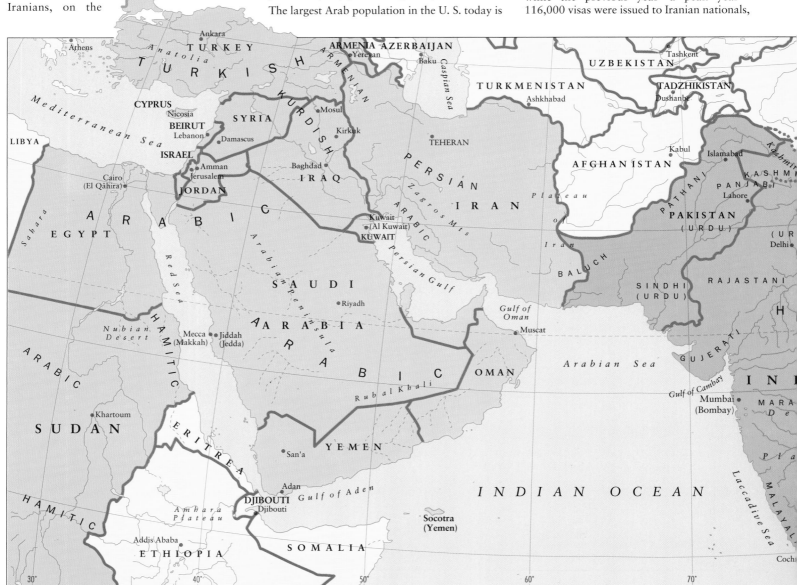

Above: the first Middle Easterners to arrive in North America were Syrians, though many of them came from areas now in Lebanon. By the 1890s, when this drawing was made, they had already formed a substantial enclave around Washington Street in New York.

I: Asia and The Middle East

TAMIL language group

including over 33,000 for students and 71,000 for tourists. During the academic year 1979–80, 51,000 Iranian students—usually prefering engineering and other technical studies—were the largest foreign student contingent in America. Their presence raises the Iranian population percentage in the communities where they study, such as Oklahoma State University in Stillwater, the University of Oklahoma in Norman, Southern Illinois University in Carbondale, the University of Kansas in Lawrence, University of Los Angeles at Davis, University of Tennessee at Martin, Louisiana Technical University at Rushton, Alabama A and M University in Normal, Pittsburgh State University in Kansas. The student population accounted for 41 percent of the 123,000 Iranians in the U. S. Turks have also been prominent in American academic circles, as students, educators, and intellectuals; there were 2500 studying in American universities in 1980.

In the 20 years prior to 1980, more than 67,000 people, mostly Jews, arrived in the U. S. from the state of Israel. Close to 60,000 have stayed. Some are Arab Muslims who would probably identify themselves as Palestinians, and others are Christians including Armenians. Three-quarters are Ashkenazi Jews, predominantly of European origin. But the population also includes Sephardic Jews from Africa and parts of the Middle East, whose language is Arabic. Like prior immigrants, many planned to return and had support from the Israeli government in achieving this objective.

The largest Israeli enclave is in New York City and western Long Island, residence for probably 15,000 of their number. Los Angeles has its separate community, with more than 1000 in Chicago and around Silver Springs, Maryland, a suburb of Washington, D.C. In percentages of county population, Israelis number about 25 percent in suburban Rockland County, New York, 19 percent around Silver Springs, Maryland, and 16 percent around Hackensack, New Jersey.

The numbers of Middle Easterners in North America include, not only naturalized citizens, but also permanent residents, students, visitors, and long-term—perhaps second and third gener-

177

ation—residents who did not enter through regular immigration procedures. For this reason, population estimates are flexible. There are probably well over 100,000 who identify themselves as Turks, born in the Ottoman Empire before 1923 or in the Turkish Republic after that date, whose home language is Turkish and religion is Muslim. Armenians, whose homeland has been part of Turkey and the USSR, are a Middle Eastern people with a long history in the U. S. Many have worked in carpet factories and in sales of rugs, but most started by working in New England factories. Workers have spread principally by satellite communities that have fanned out from an early base in Worcester, Massachusetts, establishing a network with allied centers in Watertown as well as in Providence and Pawtucket, Rhode Island, where they worked in rubber, silk, and paint factories. Outlying settlements were established successfully near silk mills at Pattersone and other cities in New Jersey, around Rensselaer near Albany, New York where men worked in a steam locomotive plant in Schenectady and the women worked at home doing finishing work on making shirts.

A different route of migration brought Russian Armenians to California by way of Canada, beginning a chain migration from Russia to industrial jobs in Riverside. Other Armenians moved from eastern cities to work in the vineyards around Fresno in California's San Fernando Valley. Using accumulated savings, a number became owners of fig and raisin producing acreage. This westward migration resulted in Fresno becoming the second largest

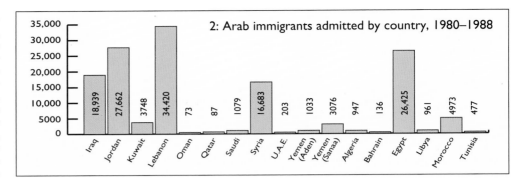

2: Arab immigrants admitted by country, 1980–1988

Armenian community within the U. S. By 1980, California had become home for 42 percent of the American population of Armenian descent, enlarged by the arrival of 14,000 Armenians that the Soviet Union permitted to emigrate beginning in 1976. Armenians in California are not a cohesive group; within the Los Angeles area, their choices of different neighborhoods reflect earlier residence in the San Fernando Valley, Soviet Armenia, Iran, Syria, or Lebanon.

Asian Indians, sometimes identified as South Asians, have mostly settled in Canada, as a result of British Commonwealth connections. The 40,000 South Asians now living in Canada have not become a single community, but represent many heritages and streams of migration passing through other parts of the world. For many, coming to Canada was a second or third step in long overseas journeys by way of the West Indies, Great Britain, South or East Africa, or the Fiji Islands. The majority have settled in Ontario and provinces further west. They have

formed more than 250 voluntary associations.

The original South Asian settlement consisted of 10 men who came to British Columbia in 1903, and established a base that by 1908 had expanded to a population of 5000, principally Sikhs from the Punjab. Prejudice against Asians produced legislation that effectively curtailed further immigration until wives and other family members were allowed to enter Canada after World War I. The base community developed practically in isolation until a quota system was established in the 1950s permitting relatives of earlier settlers to immigrate, as well as people from other parts of South Asia.

Ontario rather than British Columbia became the destination of most of the new wave of South Asian migration, which included Bengalis, Tamils, Sinhalese, and Punjabis. Still, this group numbered only 1000 by 1961. The less restrictive immigration laws of 1967 brought in 60,000 South Asians by 1971. About half went to Ontario, but newcomers

3: Asian Indian population in the U. S., 1990

- 0-500
- 500-1,000
- 1,000-1,000,000

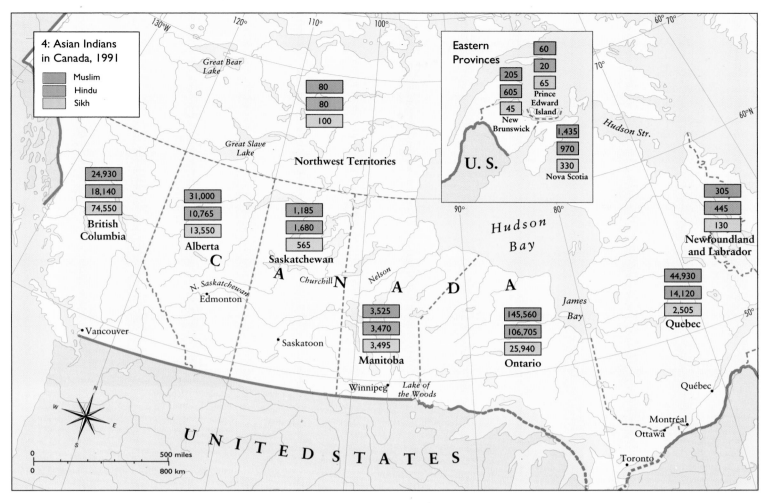

4: Asian Indians in Canada, 1991

- Muslim
- Hindu
- Sikh

Northwest Territories: 80 / 80 / 100

British Columbia: 24,930 / 18,140 / 74,550

Alberta: 31,000 / 10,765 / 13,550

Saskatchewan: 1,185 / 1,680 / 565

Manitoba: 3,525 / 3,470 / 3,495

Ontario: 145,560 / 106,705 / 25,940

Quebec: 44,930 / 14,120 / 2,505

Newfoundland and Labrador: 305 / 445 / 130

Eastern Provinces

New Brunswick: 205 / 605 / 45
Prince Edward Island: 60 / 20 / 65
Nova Scotia: 1,435 / 970 / 330

were distributed to every province. Diversity increased in the 1970s with the arrival of 6000 of the South Asians expelled from Uganda in 1972. They included Ismailis, Hindus, and Sunni Muslim Gujaratis.

Canada's South Asians include many professional people and educators who hold professorships in Canadian universities. Tamils have also taken jobs as schoolteachers. On the other hand, many South Asian women have worked in the garment industry and low paying service and cleaning jobs. The largest Muslim and Hindu populations are in Ontario, although Alberta has an important representation. The first mosque in Canada was built in Alberta in 1938. Edmonton today has significant groups of both Muslims and Hindus; the latter remain closely in touch with their religious gurus. New immigration has brought the number of Punjabis in Vancouver to 40,000 (out of a total population of 4,722,000). The traditional unity of the Sikh community is affected by recent immigration and the addition of non-Asian converts, called *goras*. Canada's South Asian population is expected to surpass 600,000 by the beginning of the 21st century.

Far fewer South Asians have arrived in the U. S., although there are more than 106,000 spread broadly through the New York metropolitan areas: 57,000 in Queens County, New York, 15,000 in Brooklyn, 7400 in Manhattan, 11,000 in the Bronx, and 4100 on Staten Island, with an additional 12,000 in Nassau County on western Long Island. Another 40,000 are in New Jersey in the area of New Brunswick,

Jersey City, and Hackensack. Chicago's Asian Indian population is 39,000 with an additional 14,000 in suburban Du Page County, a distant second place. Houston, Texas, has more than 21,000 Asian Indians, while there are 10,000 in Dallas and only 4500 in Fort Worth. In the vicinity of Washington, D.C., there are 13,300 in Montgomery County, Maryland, almost

10,000 in Fairfax County, Virginia, and 6100 in Prince Georges County, Maryland. Forming a network unrevealed by census data, some Asian Indians in the U. S. have undertaken the operation of small local motels across the country. This special type of business venture by Asian Indians has been portrayed in the film *Mississippi Masala*, (1991).

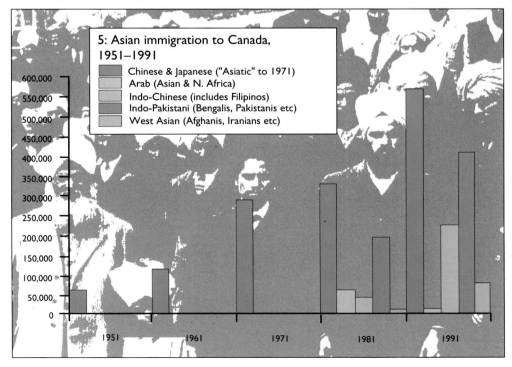

5: Asian immigration to Canada, 1951–1991

- Chinese & Japanese ("Asiatic" to 1971)
- Arab (Asian & N. Africa)
- Indo-Chinese (includes Filipinos)
- Indo-Pakistani (Bengalis, Pakistanis etc)
- West Asian (Afghanis, Iranians etc)

MOVING EAST
PACIFIC MIGRATIONS, 1965–9

Asians in North America have become more visible during the past 20 years, creating neighborhoods not only in the large metropolitan areas, but also in suburbs and smaller cities.

The total number of Asians and Pacific Islanders, including Hawaiians, was about 7,274,000 in the 1990 census, constituting 2.9 percent of the total population of the mainland U. S. There are 69 counties in 23 of the 48 mainland states with total Asian populations above 15,000; and 19 of those counties are in California. America's recent Asian immigrants live principally in states on the Pacific Coast, and Arizona, Nevada, and Utah; along the Atlantic seaboard, in the upper Midwest, and in Texas. High Asian populations are found in the counties around Los Angeles, San Francisco, and Fresno in the southern Central Valley. New York's metropolitan area naturally also has high numbers, but particular Asian groups have concentrated in other cities.

An interesting variant on the general Asian population distribution is the Hmong people from the hill country on the borders of Vietnam, Thailand, and Laos. Since they were recruited to support the American military effort in Vietnam, they have been brought to America as refugees. In the Minneapolis-St Paul area of Minnesota, there are more than 16,000 Hmong people, rivaling the 18,000 in Fresno, California. A second center of Hmong activities is Milwaukee, Wisconsin, which reports 3350, a concentrated settlement that is sending groups to other towns in Wisconsin. The estimated 2000 in Wausau are close to 10 percent of the town's population. Sheboygan and Eau Claire also have significant Hmong refugees. The folk art of the Hmong people, demonstrating skilled reverse applique, embroidery, and sewing techniques, is featured in art shows and provides a major source of income for Hmong women.

Other people from Southeast Asia are broadly distributed across the country. In Texas, Houston has a Vietnamese population of 31,000, while there are 18,000 more in the Dallas–Fort Worth region. Over 12,000 live in the commercial and residential area of Fairfax County, Virginia, across the Potomac River from Washington, D.C. On the other hand, the largest Cambodian community is in Massachusetts; 9000 are settled in Cambridge and other Boston suburbs, but very few in Boston itself. Similar numbers are on the West Coast where 8400 are in the Seattle–Tacoma vicinity. Providence, Rhode Island, has populations of 3600 Cambodians and 2500 from Laos. Philadelphia is home to about 4000 Cambodians. Thai people are more evenly distributed. The largest county population, the 3400 in Cook County, Illinois, covers Chicago. Smaller Thai populations of between 1000 and 2000 are found in Seattle, Dallas, Houston, Las Vegas (Nevada), Virginia's Fairfax County and Maryland's Montgomery County—both suburbs of Washington, D.C.

The 49,000 Koreans in the Queens district of western Long Island, New York, are clearly the largest group in the country, except for Los Angeles. The Korean community in the New York area includes another 6100 on Manhattan, 600 in Brooklyn, and 2900 on Staten Island making the total close to 62,000. The second largest community is in Chicago with 30,000. Koreans are prominent in Fairfax County, Virginia (18,000), and Montgomery County, Maryland (12,000), but also have 16,000 in Bergen County, New Jersey, where Hackensack is the principal city. Koreans have specialized in operating small grocery stores. The largest Filipino community outside California is in Chicago and Cook County, Illinois, where there are 45,000 augmented by another 9000 in suburban Du Page County. Virginia Beach on the Atlantic shore in southeast Virginia is home for more than 13,000 Filipinos, while St Georges County, Maryland has 7100. Las Vegas, Nevada, has attracted 7900. Jersey City has

Above: the Chinese are oldest and largest of the Asian communities in North America. "Chinatowns" can be found in several major cities;the one in New York's Lower East Side dates back to the late 19th century and is still attracting new arrivals.

more than 13,000 Filipinos, while nearby Newark, New Jersey, has 5600.

Aside from the well-known "Chinatowns" in California, New York, and Chicago, significant Chinese populations can also be found in Seattle and Houston (each 25,000); Montgomery County, Maryland (17,500); Boston and Cambridge, Massachusetts including suburbs (45,000); New Brunswick, New Jersey (11,000); Philadelphia, Pennsylvania, (12,000); and Phoenix, Arizona (9600). While central New York City has 71,000 Chinese, the Japanese population is only 10,000; although there are 16,000 around Hackensack, New Jersey; and 9000 in Westchester County, New York. Other large Japanese settlements outside California are: Seattle, 20,000 (5000 less than the Chinese); Chicago, 15,000. Smaller cities have 1000–3000 Japanese residents. Japanese have always been prominent in Seattle, Vancouver, and other Pacific Coast communities.

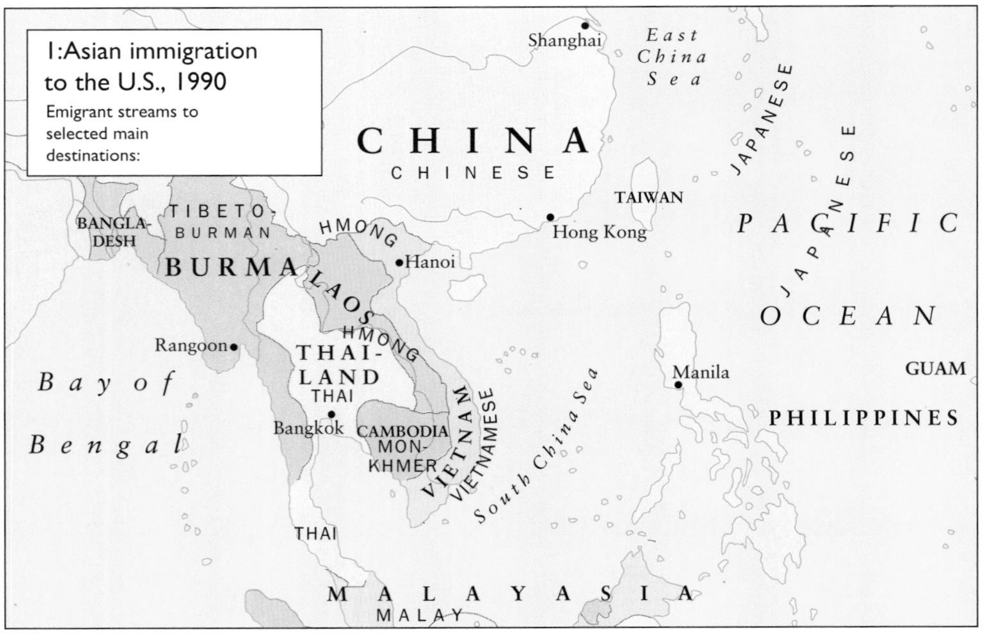

1: Asian immigration to the U.S., 1990

Emigrant streams to selected main destinations:

(Map showing China, Southeast Asia, and the Pacific Ocean with labels: Shanghai, East China Sea, CHINA, CHINESE, TAIWAN, Hong Kong, JAPANESE, PACIFIC OCEAN, GUAM, Manila, PHILIPPINES, BANGLA-DESH, TIBETO-BURMAN, BURMA, HMONG, Hanoi, LAOS, Rangoon, THAILAND, THAI, Bangkok, CAMBODIA, MON-KHMER, VIETNAM, VIETNAMESE, South China Sea, Bay of Bengal, MALAYASIA, MALAY)

2: Asians in the U. S., 1990

Chinese	1,645,000	0.7%
Filipinos	1,407,000	0.6%
Japanese	847,600	0.3%
Asian Indian	815,400	0.3%
Korean	798,800	0.3%
Vietnamese	614,500	0.2%
Hawaiian	211,000	
Laotian	149,000	
Cambodian	147,000	
Hmong	90,000	
Samoan	63,000	
Guamanian	49,000	

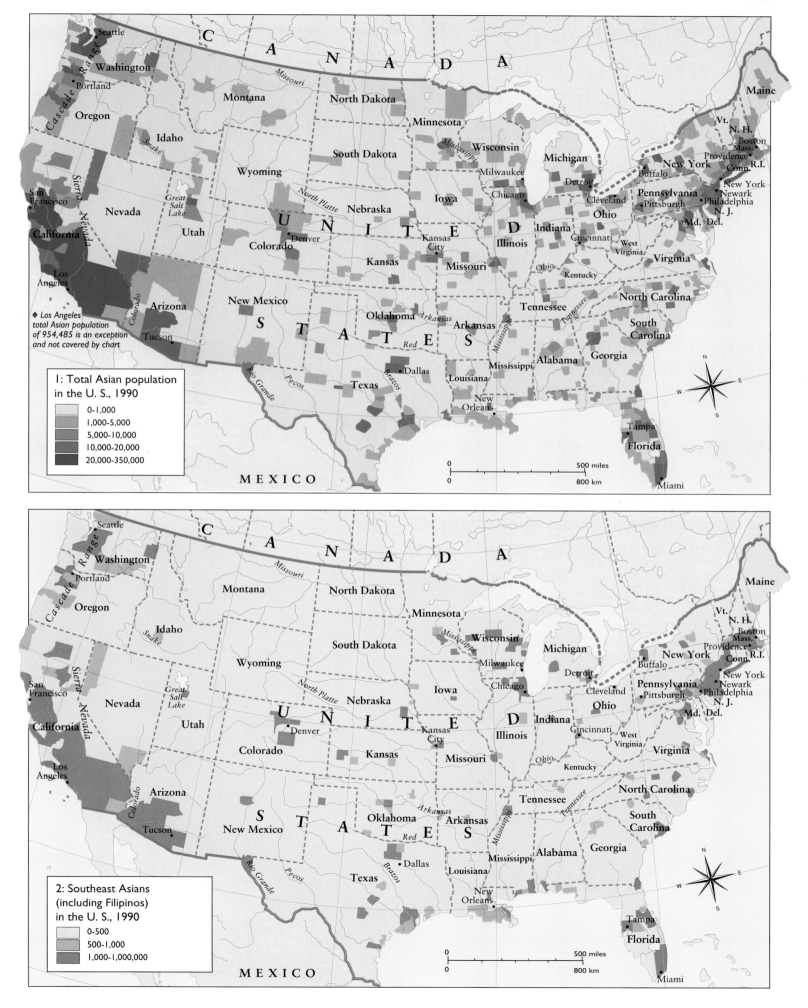

1: Total Asian population in the U. S., 1990

◆ Los Angeles total Asian population of 954,485 is an exception and not covered by chart

- 0–1,000
- 1,000–5,000
- 5,000–10,000
- 10,000–20,000
- 20,000–350,000

2: Southeast Asians (including Filipinos) in the U. S., 1990

- 0–500
- 500–1,000
- 1,000–1,000,000

181

PART VIII: NORTH AMERICA AFTER FOUR CENTURIES OF IMMIGRATION

Introduction
by Helen Hornbeck Tanner

Contemporary North America is characterized by great cultural vibrancy and diversity, created in large part by the interaction of its many ethnic groups. While racial issues remain at the forefront of the modern social debate, and while the tendency to conformism continues to foster prejudice and the restriction of social freedom, there are signs that tolerance may be increasing among North America's people

Right: the bright lights and ceaseless bustle of the continent's great metropolitan areas have served as a magnet for immigrants chasing the American dream. Located on sites formerly occupied by Indian tribes, the cities will perhaps one day themselves be the object of archaeological investigation

The contemporary maps of North American cities in this concluding section are the climax of the series designed to portray successive stages in the settling of North America. The results of more than 300 years of foreign settlement, migration, and immigration are accumulated in the urban areas across the continent. At a time closer to the period of mass migration at the turn of the century, people spoke of America as a "melting pot," but the incoming and already resident populations never completely mixed and homogenized. Now the more realistic figure of speech describing the ethnic patterns of modern cities is "cultural mosaic."

Neighborhoods in large cities can be readily distinguished by the languages of the signs over shops and in shop windows, particularly the pharmacies, grocery stores, and restaurants. One distinctive element of the neighborhoods, the food, has spilled out to other parts of cities. An increasing variety of regional and ethnic cuisine is advertised in the commercial and popular dining areas of big cities. On the streets, a casual and totally unscientific indication of the newest immigration trends is the national origin of taxi drivers, as this is an occupation often taken up by recent arrivals.

The timespan of this atlas, at least 15,000 years archaeologically and far longer speculatively, is too long to be covered in only 55 map spreads. The earlier millennia, for which much less data is available, are covered maps which are widely spaced chronologically. It seems apparent from the archaeological and geological record that for many millennia in North America the people changed very little. Their numbers increased, and climates varied. Then, about 4000–5000 years ago, population movements and localized innovations spurred more rapid change in the way in which some of the people lived and in the groups that they formed.

In the modern era, the arrival of settlers from Europe in the early 17th century inaugurated the era of accelerated population growth. The overseas population increased in complexity, too, with the arrival of Africans. At the same time, the population of the original inhabitants, who became known as Indians, began to decline precipitously. The first European settlers came to a continent that was already fully occupied. In the Chesapeake Bay region, coastal Algonquian communities were being pressed on by Siouan people advancing from the Appalachian foothills. In other parts of the woodlands, wars were in progress over hunting grounds. The unique computer-generated map of 21,000 pre-1800 archaeological sites in Arkansas in the Part I introduction shows how completely the land area of that particular state had been utilized before white settlement was appreciable. (Comparable information is not available for any other state.) On the

basis of environmental studies, it seems possible that habitable parts of North America had reached the carrying capacity of the land, considering the existing ways of life before the arrival of Europeans.

The original people had identified the best places to live, where they had food, water, and firewood. The densely inhabited sections of North America today are areas of former concentrations of Indian people. Most of the cities and towns of North America today are situated on the same sites selected by the earlier inhabitants, and the archaeological record will always be incomplete, for many are as yet unrevealed and others remain inaccessible. For example, an automobile plant in South Bend, Indiana, was built on the site of an ancient village established on the portage between the St Joseph and Kankakee rivers. In Peoria, Illinois, a factory was likewise constructed on an old village site. An accidental mudslide revealed an ancient village on the Pacific Coast in Washington. Most archaeological investigation in North America is carried out by amateurs, and new discoveries which help to fill in the story of past inhabitants are regularly reported.

The principal European nations which colonized North America—Spain, France, and England—each brought along attitudes that reflected their previous experience in dealing with people of different customs and religions. The Catholic monarchs of Spain had spent centuries driving the Muslim Arabs from the Iberian peninsula; the goal of the "expulsion of the Moors" was only accomplished in 1492. The same religious zeal and military methods were used to advance the Spanish colonial frontier in North America with missions and presidios. From experience with revolts organized in the Netherlands, the Spanish were strongly prejudiced against Protestants.

Before the French entered the Indian trade in Canada, they had instructive experience in dealing with Indian people in Brazil, in connection with the dye wood trade. French administrators knew the importance of adopting Indian protocol in councils and the achievement of agreements through discussion, confirmed by the exchange of gifts. The French learned that to maintain an alliance, the gifts should be given annually. In Brazil, too, they found that the intermarriage of French traders and Indian women facilitated trade. They did not compose incomprehensible written treaties, as the English did, for which the signatures rather than the mutual understandings were important.

Militantly Protestant English arrived in North America imprinted by their experience of conquering predominantly Catholic Ireland in the 1560s. They had brutally driven Irish people, whom they called "savages," from their homes and confined them to reservations in order to acquire their land. The English in North America made use of the same procedure and justification to acquire the lands of Indian people. The prejudice against the Irish and against Catholics in general, was part of Boston's English heritage long before Irish refugees from the potato famine arrived in the 1840s.

The maps of the first settlements show communities clinging to shorelines while most of the continent still consisted of Indian homelands. The French were the first to penetrate the interior of the country, but the expansion of people transcontinentally was an American accomplishment. The westward movement was not steady or orderly, but came in bursts of thousands of people, beginning with the 80,000 who went down the Ohio River to Kentucky in the Revolutionary War era, and the 300,000 who followed the "Wilderness Road" toward the Mississippi. A big population surge into the upper Middle West followed the opening of the Erie Canal in 1825. The Gold Rush of 1849 precipitated a veritable avalanche of people to California.

Mapping North America's incoming population begins with the settlers from Northern Europe and the people who were brought from West Africa. Subsequent maps show the additional sectors of the globe that successively contributed to the streams of migration to North America. Not until the late 19th century did South European immigration become significant. The single colonizing expedition from the Mediterranean to British Florida in the 18th century is the subject of a special map. Immigration to North America was one part of the worldwide population movements that were in progress throughout the 19th century.

Although many of America's original settlers considered themselves refugees, the big waves of refugees and the later "displaced persons" were the consequences of successive periods of warfare in Europe, Africa, and Asia. Immigration to North America seems to be one of the repercussions of wars all over the world. The people already living in North America have responded much as the Indian people did when Europeans began to arrive. A limited number of people can be welcomed as guests, but when the numbers become large, the reaction becomes "stay out." The wariness, distrust, and fear of foreigners was first expressed in immigration acts in the U. S. and Canada in the 1920s. Yet when numbers of unfortunate people in wartorn areas became a matter for international concern in the 1960s, both the U. S. and Canada reacted by liberalizing their immigration laws. These legislative changes, bringing in new immigration, also changed the population patterns and increased the ethnic variety of cities and even of smaller towns away from metropolitan areas. In the aftermath of the Vietnam War, refugees from an entirely new sector of Asia came to North America. With the addition of new waves of refugees and displaced persons from the Middle East, particularly professional people, the U. S. and Canada are again taking stock of their capacity to accommodate new immigration. An immigration board in Canada has been criticized for being too lenient in the handling of appeals from rejected immigrants and refugees. In the U. S., a recent congressional report has recommended that the immigration quota, which was elevated 30 years ago, be reduced by one third.

Cities are the focal points of discussions about relationships between the different kinds of people who have come to live in North America. The variety is seen in the number of languages spoken at home by children in public schools. Celebrations of holidays and festivals are held according to different calendars. To some people, this is disturbing. There is a strong urge toward conformity in North America's heritage, but a slender thread of great tensile strength asserts the early Quaker insistence on individual freedom and tolerance that seems necessary for greater tranquillity in the cities. Prejudice may be gradually subsiding. North Americans of European heritage look to the future, believing in the line of progress and growth that leads to a better future.

A different view of the course of human events is held by many Indian people. Philosophers of Indian heritage have a circular view of time, believing in cycles of human existence. The continued presence of Indian people in their homeland is demonstrated in the map showing some of the sites of contemporary Indian pow wows and major celebrations. To philosophic Indians, the few centuries of immigration are a brief interval of time in the current cycle. After another few thousand years, the great cities may be just archaeological sites in a continent with a different distribution of a population of unknown size in another cycle of time.

THE CULTURAL MOSAIC
SIX NORTH AMERICAN CITIES, 1990

Above: the coastline of Miami, Florida, where tourism and retirement migration boosted postwar development

Few North American locations represent its diverse population as well as its cities. Their street names, parks, and monuments attest to the presence of virtually every group of peoples that ever lived within their boundaries. Their churches, clubs, markets, and neighborhoods provide living testimony of the vitality of their many cultures. Often these cultures have blended: sometimes quietly, in families that describe themselves as Irish-Polish-German Canadians or Vietnamese-African-Native-Americans, other times more visibly, in restaurants that advertise Chinese-Italian-American food or in grade school classes where students speak 14 different languages. In this mix of imported and hybrid culture, the six cities that appear on these pages—Miami, Toronto, Chicago, Regina, Los Angeles, and Honolulu—illustrate the amazing diversity that characterizes both the U. S. and Canada.

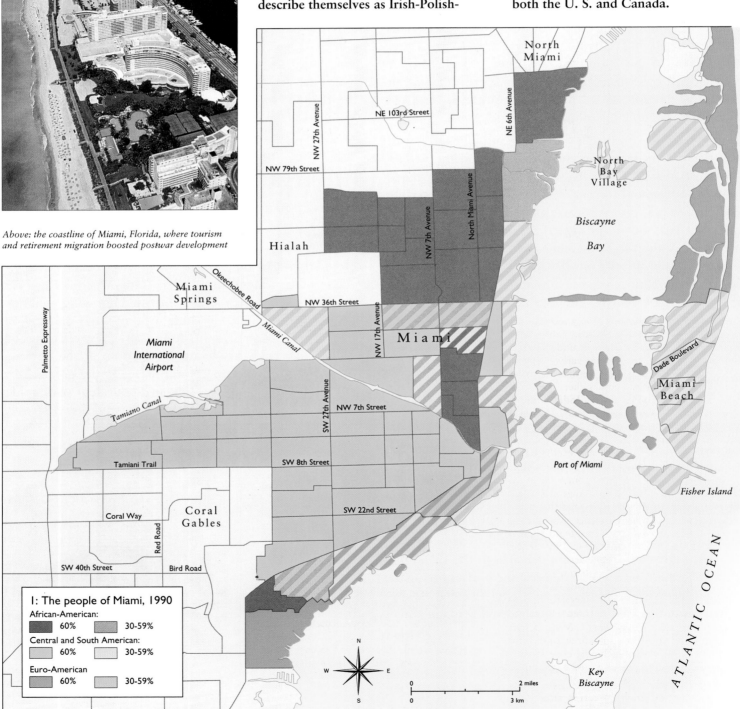

1: The people of Miami, 1990

African-American:
- 60%
- 30-59%

Central and South American:
- 60%
- 30-59%

Euro-American
- 60%
- 30-59%

2: The people of Toronto, 1990

Afro-Canadians
60% 30-59%

Asian
60% 30-59%

Euro-American
60% 30-59%

Miami

The development of Miami is very recent, even by North American standards. Early land grants, made while Florida was under British and Spanish rule in the 18th and early 19th centuries, failed to establish any permanent settlement; by the late 19th century there was little more than a post office and an Indian trading post. In 1896, however, an energetic landowner, Mrs Julia B. Tuttle, encouraged the construction of the Florida East Coast Railroad, and opened a hotel. The Spanish-American War of 1898 gave the new city a boost as 7500 U. S. troops were stationed there. The first real boom came in the early 1920s, with plans to encourage retirement migration. Land was in such demand that deeds were sold on the streets (a practice subsequently declared illegal). The city's population grew from 30,000 in 1920 to 85,000 in 1925. Then, in September 1926, a hurricane destroyed many of the new buildings, and the boom collapsed. Much of the infrastructure—roads, highways, railroads, and civic amenities—survived, however. These formed the basis of a more sustained development after World War II. Much of this was based on tourism and retirement-related industries and services, including construction, but recent decades have also seen a growth in electronics and information technology.

The city's biggest growth occurred after 1959, when Fidel Castro came to power in Cuba. The U. S. granted political asylum to those fleeing the new regime (> *pages 172–3*). Most of these were relatively well-to-do Cubans, who formed a substantial exile community in the city. By 1980, however, the welcome had cooled. That summer, 125,000 exiles set out in small boats from the harbor of Mariel in Cuba for Florida. At first they were greeted as a "freedom flotilla," but soon they were being blamed for crime throughout the Greater Miami area. Haitian boat people received less encouragement from the federal government since the Duvalier dictatorship from which they were escaping was not communist.

By 1990 the population of Miami had reached 358,648. The city and metropolitan area have been boosted by African-American migration from rural areas, mostly in the south, and by white Americans and Canadians—"sunbirds"—fleeing harsh winters (> *pages 168–9*). Many of the latter have settled in Miami Beach, a fact reflected in the 1990 Census: the non-Hispanic white percentage in Miami–Hileah area stood at 30.2 percent; in Miami City it was 12.2 percent; and in Miami Beach 48.3 percent.

In 1993, of the 21,561 documented immigrants to Miami, 27.9 percent were Cuban, 10.2 percent Nicaraguan, 7.8 percent Haitian, 6.1 percent Columbian, and 5.2 percent from the Dominican Republic.

Toronto

Toronto began its life in 1793 when the British established the city as the capital of the new province of Upper Canada, on a site recently purchased from the Mississauga Indians. By 1797, when the legislature first met, the settlement had been renamed York, only reverting to its original name in 1834, when it was incorporated as a city. By then, immigration had built up the population to over 9000. This continued after the Canadian Confederation of 1867, when Toronto became the capital of the province of Ontario. It soon established itself as an industrial and financial center, a position strengthened when the opening of the St Lawrence Seaway in 1959 turned the city into a major seaport.

Until World War II, the population was largely of British origin, but after the war a steady influx of immigrants from other European countries (> *pages 156–7*) have given the city strong Italian, Jewish, and Czech communities. The city's links within the British Commonwealth—particularly with Hong Kong, India, Jamaica, and Bermuda—have also enhanced its cosmopolitan character. Among 3.9 million residents of greater Toronto in 1991, nearly 1.5 were immigrants from elsewhere; some 860,000 of these had arrived since 1971. They are clustered in one of five Chinatowns, in the Corso Italia and Little Italy, Little India, Portugal Village, Korean Town, and in Caribbean pockets. There are, however, relatively few Latin Americans from outside the Caribbean.

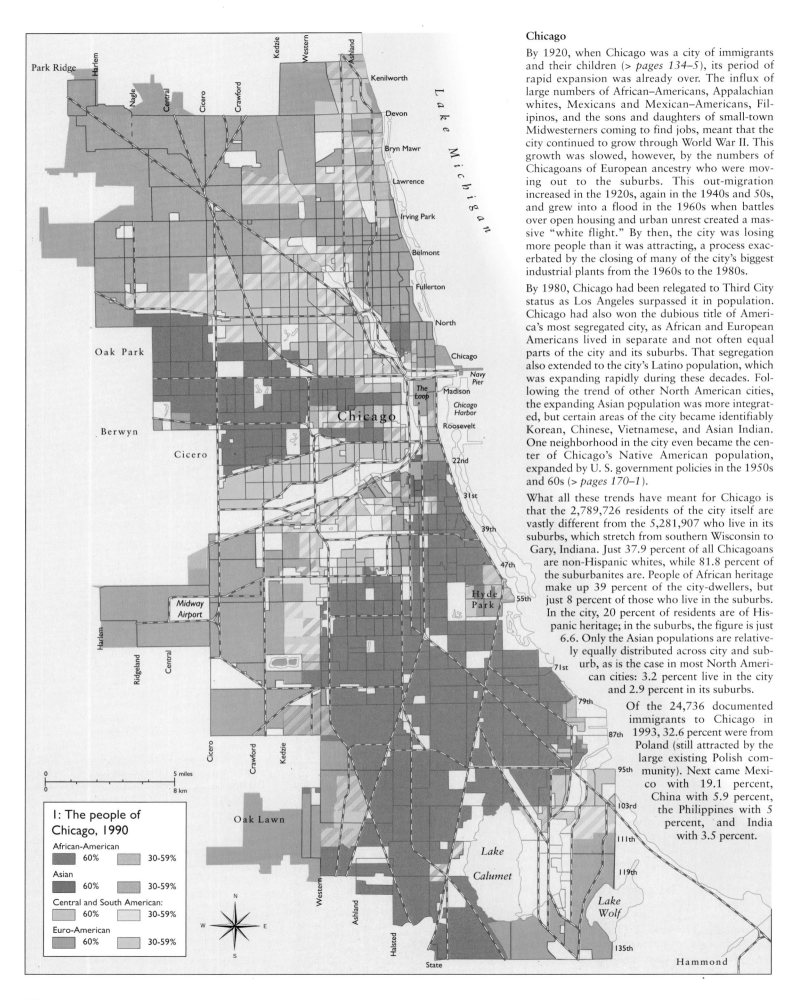

I: The people of Chicago, 1990

African-American
60%   30-59%

Asian
60%   30-59%

Central and South American:
60%   30-59%

Euro-American
60%   30-59%

0 ——————— 5 miles
0 ——————— 8 km

Chicago

By 1920, when Chicago was a city of immigrants and their children (> *pages 134–5*), its period of rapid expansion was already over. The influx of large numbers of African–Americans, Appalachian whites, Mexicans and Mexican–Americans, Filipinos, and the sons and daughters of small-town Midwesterners coming to find jobs, meant that the city continued to grow through World War II. This growth was slowed, however, by the numbers of Chicagoans of European ancestry who were moving out to the suburbs. This out-migration increased in the 1920s, again in the 1940s and 50s, and grew into a flood in the 1960s when battles over open housing and urban unrest created a massive "white flight." By then, the city was losing more people than it was attracting, a process exacerbated by the closing of many of the city's biggest industrial plants from the 1960s to the 1980s.

By 1980, Chicago had been relegated to Third City status as Los Angeles surpassed it in population. Chicago had also won the dubious title of America's most segregated city, as African and European Americans lived in separate and not often equal parts of the city and its suburbs. That segregation also extended to the city's Latino population, which was expanding rapidly during these decades. Following the trend of other North American cities, the expanding Asian population was more integrated, but certain areas of the city became identifiably Korean, Chinese, Vietnamese, and Asian Indian. One neighborhood in the city even became the center of Chicago's Native American population, expanded by U. S. government policies in the 1950s and 60s (> *pages 170–1*).

What all these trends have meant for Chicago is that the 2,789,726 residents of the city itself are vastly different from the 5,281,907 who live in its suburbs, which stretch from southern Wisconsin to Gary, Indiana. Just 37.9 percent of all Chicagoans are non-Hispanic whites, while 81.8 percent of the suburbanites are. People of African heritage make up 39 percent of the city-dwellers, but just 8 percent of those who live in the suburbs. In the city, 20 percent of residents are of Hispanic heritage; in the suburbs, the figure is just 6.6. Only the Asian populations are relatively equally distributed across city and suburb, as is the case in most North American cities: 3.2 percent live in the city and 2.9 percent in its suburbs.

Of the 24,736 documented immigrants to Chicago in 1993, 32.6 percent were from Poland (still attracted by the large existing Polish community). Next came Mexico with 19.1 percent, China with 5.9 percent, the Philippines with 5 percent, and India with 3.5 percent.

Regina

Standing in stark contrast to Chicago is the fourth city, Regina, Saskatchewan. The smallest city considered here, it is also the most European in its heritage. Founded in 1822 as Pile O'Bones, due to the stacks of buffalo bones found along the creek, it began to expand after the construction of the Canadian Pacific Railway. The settlement became the capital of Northwest Territory in 1882 (when it was given its present name in honor of Britain's Queen Victoria), and of the new province of Saskatchewan in 1905. After World War II the city expanded rapidly as a manufacturing center, with oil refineries, auto plants, meatpacking and a steel works. It also became a major distribution center for the agricultural produce of the prairies. By 1961 its population had reached 112,141, rising to 191,127 by 1966.

Of Regina's 191,692 residents in 1991, 91 percent were born in Canada. Some 5 percent of those identify themselves as First Nations. Only 3 percent of its people were born on any continent other than Europe or North America. Nonetheless, the city reflects the ethnic diversity of the Canadian plains from which it draws. Although more people claim British origin than any other single ethnic origin, German ethnicity is a close second. The city also has substantial numbers of residents who claim Ukrainian, Polish, and Hungarian heritage. A long-standing Chinese community has been enlarged by newer immigrants. More recently, Asian Indians have found a home in Regina, and a small community of Vietnamese has emerged.

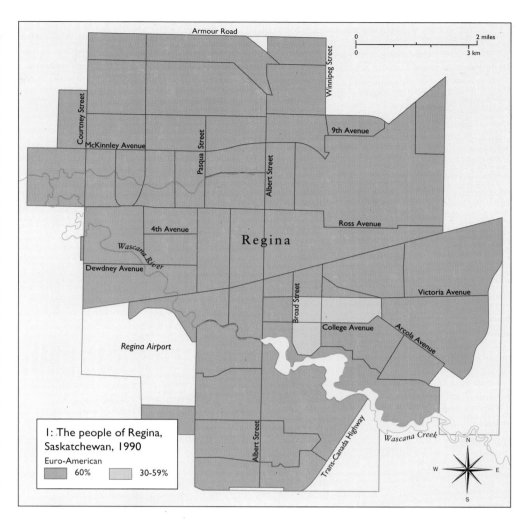

1: The people of Regina, Saskatchewan, 1990

Euro-American

60% 30-59%

Los Angeles

The next most westerly city, Los Angeles, California, is America's second largest. In its unending, centerless sprawl, it provides a model of the future of North American cities. It looks across the Pacific in terms of population and business; but it also looks south to Mexico and Latin America, and northeast to the rest of North America. The population statistics for 1990 reflect its location at the confluence of three important migration streams. Of the 8,863,164 persons in Los Angeles County, 40.8 percent are whites of non-Hispanic origin, 10.5 percent are blacks of non-Hispanic origin, 10.5 percent are of Asian heritage, and 37.8 percent are Latinos, primarily of Mexican heritage.

The city's origins date back to 1781, when El Pueblo de Nuestra Señora de los Angeles de Porciuncula was established (> *pages 76–7*). For its first 65 years, Californios and local Indians dominated. After 1846, when U. S. forces captured the city from Mexico, the European-American component expanded, although L. A. remained, at best, a sleepy town in the 25 years following its incorporation as an American city in 1850, the year of California's statehood. After the completion of major railroad connections in the

Left: a lively street festival takes place against the modernistic skyline of the Euro-American dominated Loop area of Chicago. Chicago is a strongly segregated city, where ethnic minorities are concentrated mainly in the city itself, while non-Hispanic whites predominate in the suburban surrounds.

1870s and 1880s, the population was swelled by American-born settlers looking for a better life in the west, and steady streams of migrants from Asia and from Mexico. By the turn of the century, some 100,000 persons lived in Los Angeles while only 325,000 lived in all of southern California.

The 1920s brought about Los Angeles' first great population boom as oil and movies led the industrial growth of the region and hundreds of thousands left "back east" to come to the city of the Angels. Iowa and Ohio clubs sprang up throughout the L.A. basin, and members of the city's growing Jewish population were identified, not only by their German, Polish, or Russian origins, but also by whether they were from Chicago or New York. In addition, the migration of African-Americans made Los Angeles the largest center of African-Americans on the west coast. The political revolution in Mexico and a shortage of workers in Los Angeles during that decade also brought about a three-fold increase in the size of the region's Mexican population. Filipinos, at that time American nationals, were also recruited as workers. Many of these workers were "repatriated" during the Depression of the 1930s, leaving openings for the dust bowl refugees and other migrants who arrived from throughout America during that decade (> pages 150–1). By 1940, the population of the region had climbed to 3.7 million.

Los Angeles' biggest growth came, however, during and after World War II. A center of military production and activity, the city attracted large numbers of war-workers, both white and black. Businesses once again recruited large numbers of Mexicans to fill critical labor shortages, some left by the Japanese who had all been forced to leave L. A. for the internment camps (> pages 154–5). Following the war, the immigration expanded. Soldiers who had seen southern California decided they would return there. The Asian population increased as the Japanese returned home, and immigrants and refugees from a number of countries came to what was arguably the Asian capital of North America. Mexicans continued to come north. Immigrants from Europe, the Middle East, and the Indian sub-continent joined them. By the mid-1960s, Los Angeles had become one of America's most culturally diverse cities, a trend that increased after the passage of the 1965 Immigration Act. Moreover, the newest waves of immigrants from Southeast Asia and Central America have diversified the city's Asian and Latin American populations. Little Saigon has joined Little Tokyo in the Los Angeles metropolitan landscape, and immigrants from Central America now outnumber those from Mexico.

Honolulu

The most westerly of the cities, Honolulu, can only be claimed as a North American city in a political sense: it is the capital of America's 49th state. Perhaps as a result, its population is one of the most diverse and distinctive in the U. S. For over a thousand years, until Captain James

Above: Toronto has seen an influx of European refugees, and the city is known for its cosmopolitan character

Cook arrived in 1778, Hawaii, and Honolulu, was the home of the Hawaiian people, descendants of Polynesian travelers who arrived there around AD 750. Slowly for the first 40 years, and more rapidly after 1820, Euro-Americans and Europeans came to the islands in search of sandalwood, souls, and sugar. By 1845, Honolulu had become the capital of both the

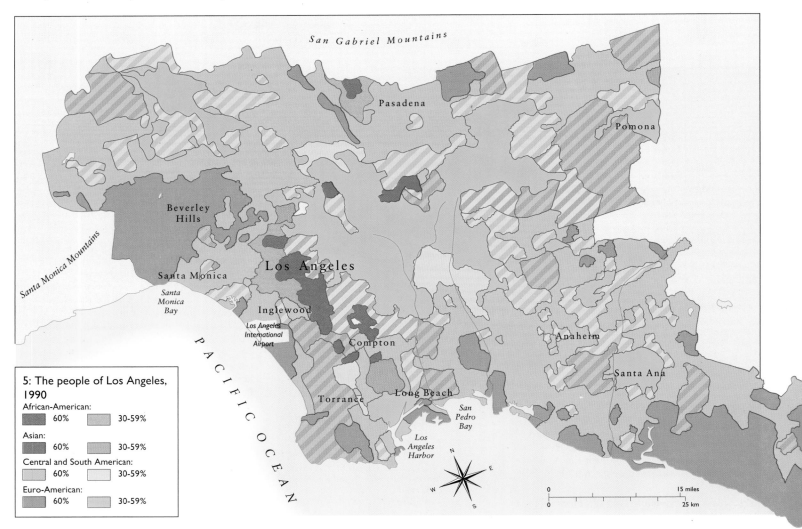

5: The people of Los Angeles, 1990

African-American:
60%   30-59%

Asian:
60%   30-59%

Central and South American:
60%   30-59%

Euro-American:
60%   30-59%

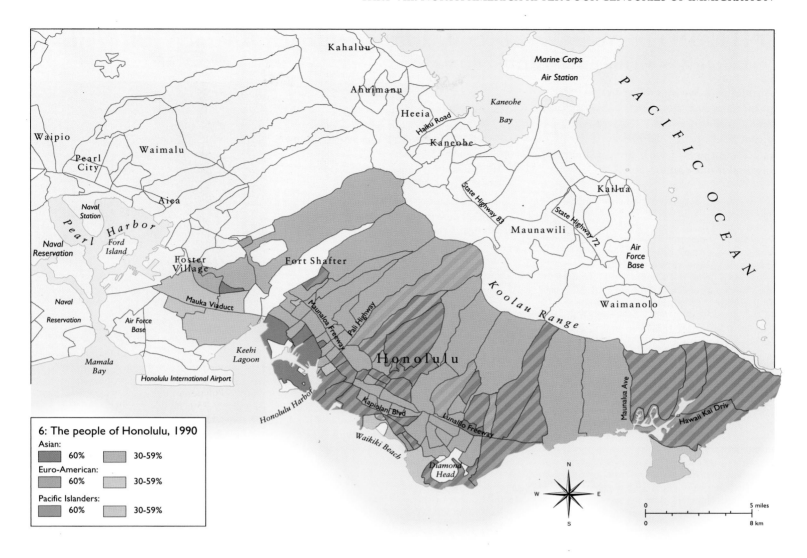

6: The people of Honolulu, 1990

Asian:
60% | 30-59%

Euro-American:
60% | 30-59%

Pacific Islanders:
60% | 30-59%

Hawaiian monarchy and the American business community, and home to a rising population of Americans of European descent and a native population that had been badly reduced by diseases brought by the newcomers. From 1852, a desperate need for workers to tend the sugar cane led businessmen to recruit workers from China. As the Chinese population grew and moved out of the sugar fields and into the cities, new recruits were sought first in Japan and then in the Philippines and Korea, after the Hawaiian monarchy was overthrown and the islands annexed to the U. S. in 1898. Those newer migrants also gradually moved away from agriculture into Honolulu, where they joined the earlier residents and smaller settlements of German, Portuguese, and Puerto Rican immigrants. By 1937, when the U.S. Congress defeated an attempt for Hawaiian statehood, in part because of its population composition, Honolulu was already a city whose population was dominated by people of Asian heritage. The degree to which these Hawaiians were an integral part of the city's economic, social, and cultural life was visible during World War II when those of Japanese descent were not interned, as was the case on the mainland (> pages 154–5).

In the years after statehood (1959), Honolulu's Asian heritage population increased even more. The growth of the Japanese economy led to increasing Japanese investment in Honolulu property and business. At the same time, Honolulu's distance from the North American mainland decreased the likelihood of the migration of Americans of African descent, and those from Mexico and other Latin American countries as it had deterred European migrants in the 19th century. As a result, by 1990, 60 percent of Honolulu's population of 365,272 identified themselves as being of Asian origin. Of those, 29 percent described themselves as of Japanese descent, 12.3 percent as Chinese, and another 12.3 percent as Filipino. People of European descent accounted for almost 27 percent of the population. Only 8 percent of the population were native Hawaiians and another 2.5 percent hailed from other Pacific Islands. Less than 5 percent identified themselves as being of Hispanic origin and 1.3 percent as being of African origin.

Right: peopled originally by Polynesian travelers, ancestors of today's Hawaiian population, Honolulu has become home to a wide diversity of peoples since Captain Cook arrived on its sunny shores in 1778.

THE POW WOW CIRCUIT
AMERICA'S FIRST PEOPLES TODAY

Annual pow wows are held every year in more than a thousand reserves, cities, and communities across North America, a reminder and a celebration of the continuing presence of the continent's original inhabitants.

"Pow wow" is derived from the Algonquin word for medicine men or spiritual leaders, "pau wau." Early European settlers thought it referred to the events at which they officiated, and the usage stuck. Modern pow wows feature dance, song, and drumming; though they are often seen by non-Indians as entertainment, they form an important link with the American Indian past. Many Indians travel hundreds of miles to attend these gatherings, which provide an opportunity for reflection and celebration, and to meet family and friends.

At least 2000 pow wows are held each year throughout Canada and the U. S., from Nova Scotia to California, including even Alaska and Hawaii. Before the 1970s, there were probably only about 20 or 30 big annual pow wows, but the numbers of these events have been growing steadily. Dance contests, a prominent feature of contemporary pow wows, began in the 1920s. Now the prize money draws skilled dancers and audiences that include an increasing number of non-Indians who enjoy the performances as well as the chance to buy art work and handicrafts. Non-Indians are invited to join in the Friendship and Inter-tribal dances. Through this experience, they begin to learn more about Indian ways of life. Foreign travelers are more apt to seek out Indian pow wows than North American tourists.

N ow for a short time the drums are yours. Beat them loudly and clumsily with your youth. For youth has always given them reason to dance in pure delight.

Beat them tenderly and possessively with the cautious flings of middle age. For there are long years between childhood and manhood…

With all your energy for their final song, beat the drums lovingly, extracting only the finest notes with all the skill of learned musicians.

Anna Lee Walters,
"Come My Sons," 1974

Modern pow wows have their origin in celebrations that took place on reservations. Gallup, New Mexico has been the site of pow wows for 70 years. In New York City, the pow wow tradition at one community center has been continuous since 1963. Local pow wows are being organized throughout the country, accompanied variously by fairs, markets, Indian princess contests, rodeos, and family camping. Among the largest events are the "Gathering of Nations" in Albuquerque, New Mexico, the Red Earth pow wow in Oklahoma City, and the Crow Fair near Billings, Montana.

The largest events are usually organized by the leaders of federally recognized tribes. Not all pow wows are big commercial events, however. The more traditional pow wows have names such as "Honor the Earth," or include references to "elders" or "veterans," two groups always given special respect in Indian country. A pow wow with a title in an Indian language rather than English is probably a more traditional celebration. But some pow wows are promoted by cultural organizations and people of goodwill who may or may not have Indian heritage. Examples are the campus sponsored pow wow at Stanford University in Palo Alto, California, and the summer gathering held by the Minnitrista Cultural Center in Muncie, Indiana.

The vigorous tradition of pow wows is evidence of the persuasive presence of the descendants of the Original People of North America after 15,000 years of habitation and 400 hundred years of adjusting to immigration. Indian people give North America its distinctive identity, and differentiate it from all other continents of the world.

The color and movement of dance competitions (above) are an important element in modern pow wows such as this one, held in Milwaukee in 1992. The jingle dresses worn by the women and children (left) reflect a 20th-century Indian tradition. The idea originated in the 1920s, when a dancer on an Ojibwa reservation in Minnesota dreamt that the jingles would be good medicine. In recent years, jingle dresses have enjoyed a revival with Indian dancers of all ages.

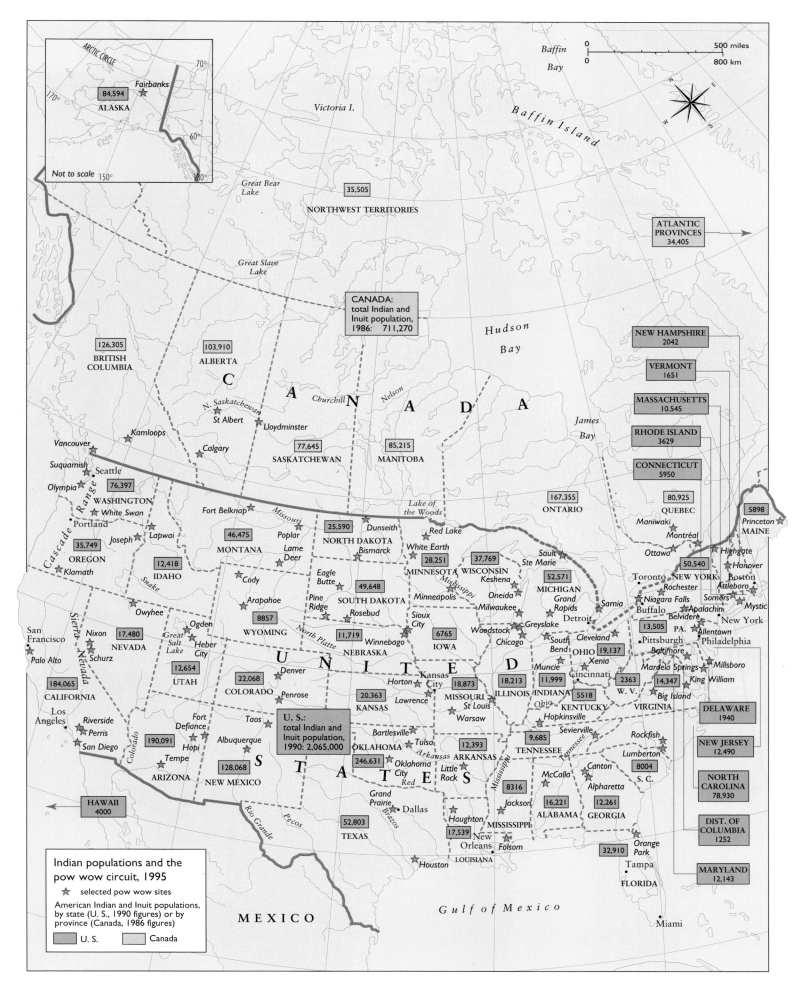

ARCTIC CIRCLE

84,594
ALASKA

Fairbanks

Not to scale

Baffin
Bay

500 miles
800 km

Victoria I.

Baffin Island

Great Bear
Lake

35,505
NORTHWEST TERRITORIES

Great Slave
Lake

CANADA:
total Indian and
Inuit population,
1986: 711,270

Hudson
Bay

James
Bay

NEW HAMPSHIRE
2042

126,305
BRITISH
COLUMBIA

103,910
ALBERTA

C

A

N

A

D

A

VERMONT
1651

MASSACHUSETTS
10,545

N. Saskatchewan
St Albert
Lloydminster

Churchill

Nelson

RHODE ISLAND
3629

Kamloops

Calgary

77,645
SASKATCHEWAN

85,215
MANITOBA

CONNECTICUT
5950

Vancouver

Suquamish
Seattle

Olympia

76,397
WASHINGTON
White Swan
Portland

Lapwai

35,749
OREGON
Joseph

Klamath

Snake

Cascade Range

Fort Belknap

46,475
MONTANA
Poplar
Lame
Deer

25,590
NORTH DAKOTA
Bismarck

Dunseith

167,355
ONTARIO

80,925
QUEBEC

Maniwaki

Montréal

Ottawa

50,540

5898
Princeton
MAINE

Highgate

Hanover

Missouri

Red Lake

White Earth

28,251

37,769
WISCONSIN
Keshena

Sault
Ste Marie

52,571
MICHIGAN
Grand
Rapids
Detroit

Toronto

NEW YORK
Rochester

Sarnia

Niagara Falls
Buffalo

Boston
Attleboro

Somers

Mystic

Belvidere

Apalachin

New York

12,418
IDAHO

Cody

Eagle
Butte

MINNESOTA
Bismarck

Minneapolis

Oneida

Milwaukee

Greyslake

Chicago

Woodstock

South
Bend

13,505
PA.
Pittsburgh

Allentown
Philadelphia

Owyhee

Arapahoe

49,648
SOUTH DAKOTA
Rosebud

Mississippi

Sioux
City

Cleveland

Xenia

19,137
OHIO

Cincinnati

Baltimore

Mardela Springs

Millsboro

King William

Nixon

17,480
NEVADA
Schurz

Ogden

8857
WYOMING

Pine
Ridge

11,719

6765
IOWA

Muncie

18,213
ILLINOIS

11,999
INDIANA
Ohio

2363
W. VA.

14,347

Big Island

San
Francisco

Palo Alto

Sierra Nevada

Great
Salt
Lake
Heber
City

12,654
UTAH

Denver

22,068
COLORADO
Penrose

North Platte

Winnebago

Kansas
City

Horton

18,873
MISSOURI
St Louis

Warsaw

Kansas
City

Hopkinsville

5518
KENTUCKY

Sevierville

VIRGINIA

Rockfish

DELAWARE
1940

NEW JERSEY
12,490

Los
Angeles

Riverside
Perris

San Diego

Colorado

Fort
Defiance

190,091
Hopi
Tempe

128,068
NEW MEXICO

Taos

Albuquerque

S

U

N

I

T

20,363
KANSAS

Lawrence

Bartlesville

Tulsa

E

D

246,631
OKLAHOMA
Oklahoma
City
Red

Little
Rock

Arkansas

12,393
ARKANSAS

9,685
TENNESSEE

Tennessee

S

T

A

T

E

8004
S. C.

Canton

Alpharetta

Lumberton

NORTH
CAROLINA
78,930

HAWAII
4000

Rio Grande

Pecos

52,803
TEXAS

Grand
Prairie
Brazos

Dallas

Houston

8316
Jackson

17,539
MISSISSIPPI

Haughton

New
Orleans

LOUISIANA

Folsom

McCalla

16,221
ALABAMA

12,261
GEORGIA

32,910

Orange
Park

Tampa

FLORIDA

DIST. OF
COLUMBIA
1252

MARYLAND
12,143

184,065
CALIFORNIA

12,654
UTAH

ARIZONA

MEXICO

Gulf of Mexico

Miami

Indian populations and the
pow wow circuit, 1995

⭐ selected pow wow sites

American Indian and Inuit populations,
by state (U. S., 1990 figures) or by
province (Canada, 1986 figures)

U.S.   Canada

U.S.:
total Indian and
Inuit population,
1990: 2,065,000

Lake of
the Woods

VIEWED FROM A DISTANT LOOKOUT
THE SATELLITE IMAGE OF NORTH AMERICA, 1995

Four centuries of immigration have totally altered the face of the North American continent, as can be seen from space in this satellite photograph.

The contrast between the world image at the opening of this volume and this night view is thought provoking. The world without people shows the dramatic differences in terrain: the mountains, lakes, and rivers; the dense forests, broad plains, white glacial ice, and bright colored deserts and canyons. The animals and their homes are not apparent in a distant view. In a portrait, the world without people appears more static and tranquil than it ever was.

But there were probably few times that bright light would be visible from afar, and the light would always be fire or lightning. Volcanoes intermittently belched fire and flames into the air. Lightning set the forests ablaze, and strong winds might carry a conflagration across many miles for days and nights. Lightning could also start fires that burned across open prairies until stopped by broad rivers. But these events were occasional, and the night sky remained black except for pale reflected light.

The satellite picture taken at night presents a radically different picture of the continent. Almost everywhere, the works of human settlers are in evidence in the bright patches of light that mark their cities, their highways, their oil refineries, dams, power plants, and other industrial sites. Today, the night sky is never black in cities and towns, though there are thinly-inhabited areas where solitary lights scarcely cast an outward beam. The brilliance of the illumination reflects the density of population, clearly pointing out the concentrations of settlement all over North America.

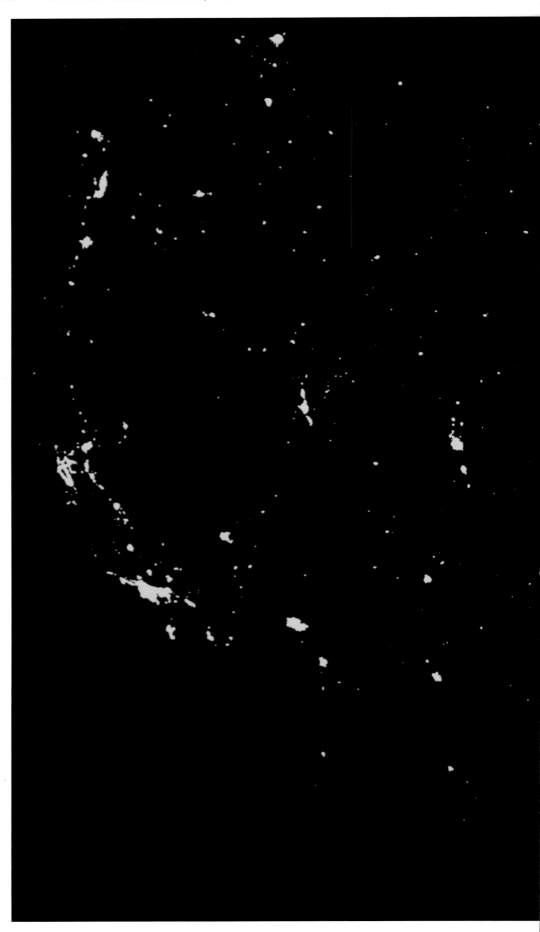

Right: viewed from space, at night, the pattern of settlement is clearly visible in the city lights. While the eastern seaboard, Midwest, and California coasts are brightly illuminated, the Rockies and desert Southwest remain in almost total darkness. In Canada, the lights burn bright along the St Lawrence River and in the southern prairie cities; but the far north remains sparsely inhabited.

SELECTED BIBLIOGRAPHY

ATLASES

Allen, James P., Turner, Eugene, J., *We The People: An Atlas of America's Ethnic Diversity* (1st ed.), Macmillan, New York 1988.

Brown, S. Kent, et al., eds., *Historical Atlas of Mormonism*, New York 1994.

Burpee, Lawrence J., ed., *An Historical Atlas of Canada*, Thomas Nelson & Sons, Toronto 1927.

Clay, James W., et al., eds., *North Carolina Atlas: Portrait of a Changing Southern State*, p.14, Figure 1.2, Chapel Hill 1975.

Coe, Michael, Dean Snow, and Elizabeth Benson, *Atlas of Ancient America*, Facts On File, New York 1986.

Department of the Interior, *Atlas of Canada*, ed. James White, The Toronto Lithographing Company, Toronto 1906.

Droysen G., ed., *Allgemeiner Historischer Handatlas*, Velhagen & Klasing, Bielefeld 1886.

Edwards, Ruth Dudley, *An Atlas of Irish History* (2nd ed.), Methuen, London and New York 1981.

Fox, Edward W. ed., *Atlas of American History*, Oxford University Press, New York 1964.

Gentilcore, R. Louis, Head, C. Grant, *Ontario's History in Maps,* University of Toronto Press, Toronto 1984.

Gilbert, Martin, *Atlas of American History* (2nd rev. ed.), Dorset Press, London 1985.

Gustafson, Bengt Y., *Atlas till Historien* (4th ed.), Sweden, Nacka 1981.

Hans-Erich Stier et al., eds., (8th ed.), *Großer Atlas Zur Weltgeschichte*, Westermann, Braunschweig 1972.

Harris R. Cole, et al., eds., 3 vols., *Historical Atlas of Canada*, University of Toronto Press, Toronto 1987–1993.

Hilliard, Sam Bowers, *Atlas of Antebellum Southern Agriculture*, Baton Rouge, Louisiana 1989.

Homberger, Eric, *The Historical Atlas of New York City*, Henry Holt and Co., New York 1994)

Hornbeck, David, *California Patterns: A Geographical and Historical Atlas*, Mayfield, Palo Alto 1983.

Jackson, Kenneth T., ed., (2nd. ed.), *Atlas of American History*, Scribner's Sons, New York 1978.

Kagan, Hilde H., ed., *The American Heritage Pictorial Atlas of United States History,* American Heritage Publishing Co., New York 1966.

Kerr, Donald, *A Historical Atlas of Canada* (2nd ed.), Nelson & Sons, Don Mills, Ontario 1966.

Lord, Clifford L., Lord, Elizabeth H., *Historical Atlas of the United States* (2nd rev. ed.), Henry Holt and Co., New York 1953.

Miller, Theodore R., *Graphic History of the Americas*, John Wiley & Sons, New York 1969.

Mitchell, R. D. and Groves, P. A., *North America: The Historical Geography of a Changing Continent*, Hutchinson, London 1987.

Modelski, Andrew M., *Railroad Maps of North America: The First Hundred Years*, Library of Congress, Washington, D.C: 1984.

Oxford Regional Economic Atlas. The United States and Canada (2nd ed.), Oxford University Press, Oxford 1975.

Paullin, Charles O., *Atlas of the Historical Geography of the United States,* Washington, D.C. Carnegie Institution, New York, American Geographical Society of New York, 1932.

Preston, Ralph N., *Early Washington Atlas* (2nd. ed.), Binford & Mort, Portland, Oregon 1981.

Prucha, Francis P., *Atlas of American Indian Affairs*, University of Nebraska Press, Lincoln 1990.

Rooney John F., et al., eds., *This Remarkable Continent: An Atlas of United States and Canadian Society and Cultures*, Texas A & M University Press, College Station 1982.

Scott, James W., DeLorme, Ronald L., *Historical Atlas of Washington*, University of Oklahoma Press, Norman 1988.

Segal, Aaron, *An Atlas of International Migration*, Hans Zell Publ., London 1993.

Tanner, Helen H., ed., *Atlas of Great Lakes, Indian History*, University of Oklahoma Press, Norman 1987.

Weissbach, Lee Shai, *Map Studies of New England Settlements*, Manuscripts, Harvard University, 1977.

Wilkie, Richard W. and Jack Tager, eds., *Historical Atlas of Massachusetts*, 20, 17, Amherst 1991.

Zentralinstitut für Geschichte der Akademie der Wissenschaften der DDR, (2nd ed.), *Atlas Zur Geschichtel I*, VEB Hermann Haack, Gotha 1976.

BOOKS AND PERIODICALS

Abbott, *Historical Aspects of the Immigration Problem,* Arno, New York 1969.

Acuña, Rodolfo. *Occupied America: A History of Chicanos*, 3rd ed., Harper & Row, New York 1988.

Adovasio, J.M., J. Donahue, and R. Stuckenrath, "The Meadowcroft Rockshelter Radiocarbon Chronology 1975–90," *American Antiquity*, Vol. 55, No. 2, pp 348–354, April 1990.

Alverd, C.W., Lee Bidgood, eds., *The First Explorations of the Trans-Allegheny Region by the Virginians 1650–1674*, A.H. Clark & Co., Cleveland 1912.

Anderson, Alan B., and James S. Frideres, *Ethnicity in Canada. Theoretical Perspectives*, Toronto 1981.

Appleyard, Reginald T., "International Migration in Asia and the Pacific" pp. 89–167 in same ed., *International Migration Today*, 2 vols., Unesco Paris 1988.

Archdeacon, Thomas J., *Becoming American. An Ethnic History*, New York 1983.

Au'aukawhi, Confeseón de Canito, Causas Criminales G19, 14 de Setiembre de 1686, Parral Archive.

Avery, Donald, *"Dangerous Foreigners." European Immigrant Workers and Labor Radicalism in Canada, 1896–1932*, Toronto 1979.

Bade, Klaus, "German Emigration to the United States and Continental Immigration to Germany, 1879–1914," *Central European History*, 13 (1980), 348–377.

Bade, Klaus J., ed., *Deutsche im Ausland – Fremde in Deutschland. Migration in Geschichte und Gegenwart*, Beck München 1992.

Bade, Klaus, ed., *Population, Labor and Migration in 19th and 20th Century Germany*, New York 1986.

Bahr, Erhard and See, Carolyn, *Literary Exiles & Refugees in Los Angeles*, University of California, 1988.

Baily, Samuel L., "The Adjustment of Italian Immigrants in Buenos Aires and New York, 1870—1914", *American Historical Review* 82 (1983), 281–305.

Bailyn, Bernard, *The Peopling of British North America: An Introduction*, New York 1986.

Bailyn, Bernard, *Voyagers to the West: A Passage in the Peopling of America on the Eve of the Revolution*, New York 1986.

Barkan, Elliott R., *Asian and Pacific Islander Migration to the United States. A Model of New Global Patterns*, Westport, Ct. 1992.

Barnett, Homer G., *The Coast Salish of British Columbia*, University of Oregon Press, Eugene 1955.

Barrat, John, "Clovis people dug oldest well in North America," *Smithsonian Runner* 94–2, March–April 1994, 1, 8.

Baugh, Timothy G., Charles W. Terrell, "An Analysis of Obsidian Debitage and Protohistoric Exchange Sytems in the Southern Plains as Viewed from the Edwards I Site (34BK2), *Plains Anthropologist* 27–95, Feb., 1982.

Beals, Ralph L., *The Comparative Ethnology of Northern Mexico Before 1750*, Ibero-Americana 2, University of California, Berkeley 1932.

Beals, Ralph L., *The Aboriginal Culture of the Cahita Indians*, Ibero-Americana 19, University of California, Berkeley 1943.

Bean, L.J., "Cahuilla," pp. 575–87 in *California, Volume 8*, edited by R.F. Heizer, in *HONAI*, gen. ed., W.C. Sturtevant, Smithsonian Institute, Washington, D.C. 1978.

Bean, L.J., "Gabrielino," pp. 538–49 in *California, Volume 8*, edited by R.F. Heizer, in *HONAI*, gen. ed., W.C. Sturtevant, Smithsonian Institute, Washington, D.C. 1978.

Berend, T. Ivan, and Gyorgi Ranki, *The European Periphery and Industrialization, 1780–1914* New York 1982.

Biesele, Rudolph, *History of the German Settlements in Texas 1831–1861*, Austin, Texas.

Birkit-Smith, Kaj, Frederica de Laguna, *The Eyak Indians of the Copper River Delta*, Levin and Munksgaard, Copenhagen 1938.

Blake, William P., "New Locality of the Green Turquois known as Chalchulte, and on the Identity of Turquois with the Callais or Callaina of Pliny," *American Journal of Science*, 3rd ser., 25, 1883.

Boas, Franz, "Tsimshian Mythology," pp. 27–1037 in *Twenty-First Annual Report of the Bureau of American Ethnology 1909–1910*, Government Printing Office, Washington 1916.

Bobinska, Celina, and Andrzej Pilch, eds., *Employment-Seeking Emigrations of the Poles World Wide, XIXc and XXc*, Krakow 1975.

Bodnar, John, *The Transplanted. A History of Immigrants in Urban America*, Bloomington, Ind. 1985.

Brasser, Ted J., *Riding on the Frontier's Crest*, Mercury Series Ethnology Division Paper 13, National Museum of Canada, Ottawa 1974.

Breton, Raymond, "Institutional Completeness of Ethnic Communities and the Personal Relations of Immigrants", *American Journal of Sociology* 70 (1964), 193–205.

Breton, Raymond, et al., *Ethnic Identity and Equality. Varities of Experience in a Canadian City*, Toronto 1990.

Bretos, Miguel A. *Cuba & Florida: Exploration of an Historic Connection, 1539–1991*, Historical Association of Southern Florida, Miami 1991.

Brettell, Caroline, *Men Who Migrate, Women Who Wait*, Princeton 1987.

Brooks, George R., ed., *The Southwest Expedition of Jedediah S. Smith*, A.H. Clark Co., Glendale, 1977.

Brown, Wallace, and Hereward Senior, *Victorious in Defeat: The Loyalists in Canada*, New York 1984.

Buchignani, Norman, Doreen M. Indra, with Ram Srivastava, *Continuous Journey. A Social History of South Asians in Canada*, McClelland and Stewart Ltd., in association with the Multiculturalism Directorate, Department of the Secretary of State and the Canadian Government Publishing Centre, Supply and Services, Canada 1985.

Burch, Ernest S. Jr., "War and Trade," pp. 227–40 in *Crossroads of Continents*, edited by W.W. Fitzhugh and Aron Crowell, Smithsonian Institute, Washington, D.C. 1988.

Burnet, Jean R. with Howard Palmer, *"Coming Canadians." An Introduction to a History of Canada's Peoples*, Toronto 1988.

Burrus, Ernest S.J., ed., *Kino and Manje*, Jesuit Historical Institute, Rome 1971.

Burt, Larry W., *Roots of the Native American Urban Experience: Relocation Policy in the 1950s*, Paper presented at meeting of the Organization of American Historians, Minneapolis, Minnesota, April 1985.

Campbell, Persia Crawford, *Chinese Coolie Emigration to Countries within the British Empire*, London 1923.

Cardich A., "Recent Excavations at Lauricocha (Central Andes) and Los Toldos (Patagonia)," in *Early Man in America from a Circum-Pacific Perspective*, edited by A.L. Bryan, University of Alberta, Edmonton 1978.

Casey-Leininger, Charles R,. "Making the Second Ghetto," in Henry L. Taylor, *Race and the City*, University of Illinois Press, Urbana 1993.

Catlin, George, *North American Indians*, Leary, Stuart & Co., Philadelphia 1920.

Caywood, Louis R., Edward H. Spicer, "Tuzigoot, A Prehistoric Pueblo of the Upper Verde," *Museum Notes* 6:9, March 1934.

Caywood, Louis R., *Tuzigoot*, National Park Service, Berkeley 1935.

Cheng, Lucie, and Edna Bonacich, eds., *Labor Migration Under Capitalism: Asian Workers in the United States Before World War II*, Berkeley, 1984.

"Cincinnati Goes To War," *The Queen City Heritage Journal of the Cincinnati Historical Society*, Vol. 49, No. 1 Spring, 1991, pp. 21–80.

Cincinnati City Planning Commission, *The Economy of the Cincinnati Metropolitan Area*, City Planning Commission of Cincinnati, 1946.

Cincinnati City Planning Commission, *Industrial Land Use, Past and Present*, City Planning Commission of Cincinnati, 1946.

Cockcroft, James D. *Outlaws in the Promised Land: Mexican Immigrant Workers and America's Future*, Grover Press, New York 1986.

Conzen, Kathleen N., *Immigrant Milwaukee, 1836–1860: Accommodation and Community in a Frontier City*, Harvard University Press, Cambridge, Mass. 1976.

Cooper, Dereck W. "Migration from Jamaica in the 1970s: Political Protest or Economic Pull?," in *International Migration Review* 19(4): 728–745.

Curtin, Philip D., *The Rise and Fall of the Plantation Complex. Essays in Atlantic History*, Cambridge 1990.

Daniels, Roger, *Asian Americans: Chinese and Japanese in the United States since 1850*, Seattle 1988.

Daniels, Roger, *Coming to America. A History of Immigration and Ethnicity in American Life*, New York 1990.

Data on New Netherland Settlements, 1620–1664, Manuscripts, Harvard University 1980–1993.

Debouzy, Marianne, ed., *In the Shadow of the Statue of Liberty*, Paris 1988.

de Laguna, Frederica, "Tlingit: People of the Wolf and Raven," pp. 58–63 in *Crossroads of Continents*, edited by W.W. Fitzhugh and Aron Crowell, Smithsonian Institute, Washington, D.C. 1988.

De Lange, Nicholas, *Atlas of the Jewish World*, Phaidon, Oxford 1984.

DePlatter, Chester B., Charles Hudson, and M.T. Smith, "The Route of Juan Pardo's Explorations in the Interior Southeast, 1566–1568," *Florida Historical Quarterly* 62, 1983, pp.125–58.

Díaz-Briquets, Sergio and Sidney Wintraub, ed. *Determinants of Emigration from Mexico, Central America, and the Caribbean*, Westview Press, Boulder 1991.

Dickason, Olive Patricia, *Canada's First Nations: A History of Founding Peoples from Earliest Times*, University of Oklahoma Press, Norman 1992.

Dickinson, Joan Younger, *The Role of the Immigrant Women in the U. S. Labor Force, 1890–1910* reprint, New York 1980.

Dillehay, T.D., "A Late Ice-Age Settlement in Southern Chile," *Scientific American* 251:4, 1984, pp.100–17.

Dillehay, T.D., "The Cultural Relationships of Monte Verde: a Late Pleistocene Settlement Site in the Subantarctic Forest of South-central Chile," in *New Evidence for the Pleistocene Peopling of the Americas*, edited by A.L. Bryan, University of Maine, Center for the Study of Early Man, Orono 1986.

Dixon, E. James, *Quest for the Origins of the First Americans*, University of New Mexico Press, Albuquerque 1993.

Dobyns, Henry F., "Trade Centers: The Concept and a Rancherian Culture Area Example," *American Indian Culture and Research Journal* 8:1, 1984, pp.23–35.

Doherty, J. E. and Hickey, D. J., *A Chronology of Irish History since 1500*, Gill and Macmillan, Dublin 1989.

Drucker, Phillip, *The Northern and Central Nootkan Tribes*, Bureau of American Ethnology, Bull, 144, Government Printing Office, Washington, D.C. 1941.

Dusenbery, Verne A., "Canadian Ideology and Public Policy: The Impact on Vancouver Sikh Ethnic and Religious Adaptation," *Canadian Ethnic Studies*, Vol. XIII, No. 3, 1981.

Ekholm, Gordon, F., *Excavations at Guasave, Sinaloa, Mexico*, Anthropological Papers, Vol. 39, Pt. 2, American Museum of Natural History, New York 1942.

Emmons, George T., *The Chilkat Blanket*, Memoir, Vol. 3, American Museum of Natural History, New York 1907.

Emmons, George T., "An Account of the Metting of La Pérouse and the Tlingit," *American Anthropologist* 10, 1911.

Emmons, George T., *Jade in British Columbia and Alaska and its use by the Natives*, Museum of the American Indian, Indian Notes and Monographs, No. 35, Heye Foundation, New York 1923.

Erickson, Charlotte, *Invisible Immigrants*, Miami 1972.

Escobar, Francisco de, "Diary," pp. 1012–31 in Pt. 2, *Don Juan de Onate Colonizer of New Mexico, 1595–1628*, translated by G.P. Hammond and Agapito Rey, University of New Mexico Press, Albuquerque 1953.

Espinosa, J.M., translator, *First Expedition of Vargas into New Mexico, 1692*, University of New Mexico Press, Albuquerque 1940.

Ewers, John C., "The Indian Trade of the Upper Missouri Before Lewis and Clark: An Interpretation," *Missouri Historical Society Bulletin* 10:4, 1954.

Fagan, Brian M., *The Great Journey: The Peopling of Ancient America*, Thames & Hudson, New York 1987.

Fairbanks, R.G., "A 17,000-Year Glacio-eustatic Sea Level Record: Influence of Glacial Melting Rates on the Younger Dryas Event and Deep-Ocean Circulation," *Nature* 342:637–42.

Fitzhugh, William W., and Aron Crowell, *Crossroads of Continents: Cultures of Siberia and Alaska*, color map pp. 237–37, Smithsonian Institute, Washington, D.C. 1988.

Fladmark, Knut R., "Routes: Alternative migration corridors for Early Man in North America," *American Antiquity* 44, 1979, pp.55–69.

Fladmark, Knut R., *British Columbia Prehistory*, National Museum of Man, Canadian Prehistory Series, Toronto 1986.

Forde, C. Daryl, *Ethnography of the Yuma Indians*, Publications in American Archaeology and Ethnology, Vol. 28, No. 4, University of California, Berkeley 1931.

Friis, Herman R. *Series of Population Maps of the Colonies and the United States, 1625–1790*, Rev. ed., American Geographical Society, New York 1968.

Gabaccia, Donna R., *Militants and Migrants. Rural Sicilians Become American Workers*, New Brunswick 1988.

Gabaccia, Donna, *Immigrant Women in the United States: A Selectively Annotated Multidisciplinary Bibliography*, Westport 1989.

Garis, Roy L., *Immigration Restriction*, New York 1927.

George, M.V., *Internal Migration in Canada*, The Queen's Printer, Ottawa 1970.

Gibson, James R., "The Maritime Trade of the North Pacific Coast," pp. 375–90 in *History of Indian–White Relations*, Vol. 4, edited by W.E. Washburn in *Handbook of North American Indians*, gen. ed., W.C. Sturtevant, Smithsonian Institute, Washington, D.C. 1988.

Gilbert, Martin, *Atlas of the Holocaust*, Michael Joseph, London 1982.

Gjerde, Jon, *From Peasants to Farmers: The Migration from Balestrand, Norway, to the Upper Middle West*, Cambridge 1985.

Glazer, Nathan, and Daniel P. Moynihan, *Beyond the Melting Pot: the Negroes, Puerto Ricans, Jews, Italians, and Irish of New York City*, Cambridge, Mass. 1963.

Glazier, Ira, and Luigi de Rosa, eds., *Migration across Time and Nations. Population Mobility in Historical Context*, New York 1986.

Glenn, Susan A., *Daughters of the Shtetl: Life and Labor in the Immigrant Generation*, Ithaca, 1990.

Goa, David J., Harold G. Coward, and Ronald Neufeldt, "Hindus in Alberta: A Study in Religious Continuity and Change," *Canadian Ethnic Studies*, Vol. XVI, No. 1, 1984.

Colovin, P.N. *The End of Russian America: Captain P.N. Golovin's Last Report, 1862*, Portland, Oregon 1979.

Gordon, Milton M., *Assimilation in American Life. The Role of Race, Religion, and National Origins*, New York 1964.

Gould, J. D., "European Inter-Continental Emigration, 1815–1914: Patterns and Causes," *Journal of European Economic History*, 8 (1979), 593–679.

Gould, J. D., "European Inter-Continental Emigration. The Road Home: Return Migration from U. S. A.," *Journal of European Economic History*, 9 (1980), 71–112.

Greenwood, Michael J., *Migration and Economic Growth in the United States*, Academic Press, New York 1981.

Griffin, Patricia C., *Mullet on the Beach*, El Escribano, St Augustine Journal of History, Vol. 27, 1990, St. Augustine, Florida.

Gruhn, Ruth, "Linguistic Evidence in Support of the Coastal Route of Earliest Entry in the New World," *Man* n.s. 23:1, 1988, pp. 77–100. Reprinted pp. 51–63 in *The First Ones: Readings in Indian/Native Studies*, edited by David R. Miller, et al. Saskatchewan Indian Federated College Press, Craven 1992.

Guerin-Gonzales, Camille, and Carl Strikwerda, eds., *The Politics of Immigrant Workers. Labor Activism and Migration in the World Economy since 1830*, New York 1993.

Gutiérrez, David G. *Walls and Mirrors: Mexican Americans, Mexican Immigrants, and the Politics of Ethnicity*. University of California Press, Berkeley 1995.

Gutman, Herbert G., *Work, Culture, and Society in Industrializing America*, New York 1976.

Hackett, Charles, W., ed., *Historical Documents Relating to New Mexico, Nueva Vizcaya, and Approaches Thereto, to 1773*, Carnegie Institution of Washington, Vol. III, Washington, D.C. 1937.

Haeberlin, H.K., J.A. Teit, H.H. Roberts, and F. Boas, "Coiled Basketry in British Columbia and Surrounding Region," pp. 119–484 in *Forty-First Annual Report of the Bureau of American Ethnology 1919–24*, Government Printing Office, Washington, D.C. 1928.

Hall, Gwendolyn Midlo, *Africans in Colonial Louisiana: The Development of Afro-Creole Culture in the Eighteenth Century*, Louisiana State University Press, Baton Rouge 1992.

Handbook of North American Indians, William C. Sturtevant, gen. ed., 9 vols. Smithsonian Institute, Washington 1978.

Handbook of Texas, eds. Walter Prescott Webb et al., 3 vols., Austin, Texas 1952–1976.

Harzig, Christiane, and Dirk Hoerder, eds., *The Press of Labor Migrants in Europe and North America, 1880s to 1930s*, Bremen 1985.

Hawkins, Freda, *Canada and Immigration : Public Policy and Public Concern*, McGill–Queen's University Press, Montreal and London 1972.

Haynes, C.V. Jr., Geoarchaeological and Paleohydrological Evidence for a Clovis-Age Drought in North America and its Bearing on Extinction," *Quaternary Research* 35:438–50.

Henri, Florette, *Black Migration: The Movement North, 1900-1920*, Garden City, N. Y. 1976.

Herberg, Edward N., *Ethnic Groups in Canada. Adaptations and Transitions*, Scarborough 1989.

Herrmann, Augustine, *The Rare Map of Virginia and Maryland, 1673*, Washington, D.C. 1911.

Higham, John, *Strangers in the Land: Patterns of American Nativism, 1860–1925*, New York 1963.

Hinshalwood, Sophia G., *The Dutch Cultural Area of the Mid-Hudson Valley*, p.27, Figure 5, PhD, Rutgers, 1981

Hoerder, Dirk, ed., *American Labor and Immigration History, 1877–1920s: Recent European Research*, Urbana, Ill. 1983.

Hoerder, Dirk, ed., *Labor Migration in the Atlantic Economies. The European and North American Working Classes During the Period of Industrialization*, Westport, Ct. 1985.

Hoerder, Dirk, *People on the Move. Migration, Acculturation, and Ethnic Interaction in Europe and North America*, German Historical Institute, Washington, D.C., Annual Lecture Series No. 6, Berg, Providence 1993.

Hoerder, Dirk, ed., *"Struggle a Hard Battle" – Essays on Working Class Immigrants*, DeKalb, Ill. 1986.

Hoerder, Dirk, and Horst Rößler, eds., *Distant Magnets. Expectations and Realities in the Immigrant Experience*, New York 1993.

Hoerder, Dirk, et al., eds., *Roots of the Transplanted*, 2 vols., New York 1994.

Holborn, Louise W., *The International Refugee Organization*, Oxford University Press 1956.

Hoxie, Frederick E., ed., *Indians in American History*, Harlan Davidson, Inc., Arlington Heights, Illinois 1988.

Huggins, Nathan I., *Black Odyssey*, New York 1979.

Hunt, George T., *The Wars of the Iroquois*, University of Wisconsin Press, Madison 1940.

Hutchinson, E. P., *Legislative History of American Immigration Policy, 1798–1965*, Philadelphia 1981.

Isajiw, Wsevolod W., *Ethnic Identity Retention*, Center for Urban and Community Studies, Toronto 1981.

Israel, Milton, "South Asia in Ontario," *Polyphony: The Journal of the Multicultural History Society of Ontario*, Special Issue, Vol. 12, Toronto 1990.

Jackson, James H., Jr., and Leslie Page Moch, "Migration and the Social History of Modern Europe", *Historical Methods* 22 (1989), 27–36.

Jennings, Francis, *The Founders of America*, New York.

Jennings, Jesse D., *Prehistory of North America*, 3rd ed., Mayfield Pub. Co., Mountain View, CA. 1989.

Jensen, Joan M., *Passage from India. Asian Indian Immigrants in North America*, New Haven 1988.

Jimenez, Alfredo, editor. *Handbook of Hispanic Cultures in the United States: History.*, Arte Público Press, Houston, Texas 1994.

Johnston, Hugh, "The Development of the Punjabi Community in Vancouver since 1961," *Canadian Ethnic Studies*, Vol. XX, No. 2, 1988.

Kamphoefner, Walter D., *The Westfalians: From Germany to Missouri*, Princeton 1987.

Kamphoefner, Walter D., Wolfgang Helbich, and Ulrike Sommer, eds., *News from the Land of Freedom. German Immigrants Write Home*, Ithaca, N.Y. 1991 – German original: Munich 1988.

Kanellos, Nicolas, ed. *Hispanic-American Almanac.* Gale Research, Detriot 1994.

Kanungo, Rabindra N., *South Asians in the Canadian Mosaic*, Kala Bharati, Montreal 1984.

Karni, Michael, ed., *The Finnish Experience in the Western Great Lakes Region: New Perspectives*, Vammala 1975.

Keegan, Gerald, *Famine Diary*, ed. J. J. Mangan FSC, Wolfhound, Dublin 1991.

Kehoe, Thomas F., and Alice B. Kehoe, "Stones, Solistices and Sun Dance Structures," *Plains Anthropologist*, Vol. 22, No. 76, Pt. 1, pp. 85–95, 1977.

Kehoe, Thomas F., and Alice B. Kehoe, *Solstice – Aligned Boulder Configurations in Saskatchewan*, Mercuries, No. 48, Canadian Ethnology Service, Museum of Man, Ottawa 1978.

Keil, Hartmut, and John B. Jentz, eds., *German Workers in Industrial Chicago, 1850–1910: A Comparative Perspective*, DeKalb 1983.

Kelley, J. Charles, *Jumano and Patarabueye: Relations at La Junta de Los Rios*, Museum of Anthropology, Anthropological Papers No. 77, University of Michigan, Ann Arbor 1986.

Kelly, Isabel, *Excavations at Culiacán, Sinaloa*, Ibero-Americana 25, University of California, Berkeley 1945.

Kennedy, Roger C., *Hidden Cities: The Discovery and Loss of Ancient North American Civilization*, The Free Press, New York and Toronto 1994.

Kino, Eusebio F., *Kino's Historical Memoir of Pimeria Alta*, translated by H.E. Bolton, A.H. Clark, Cleveland 1919.

Knight, Vernon J. Jr., "Late Prehistoric Adaption in the Mobile Bay Region," pp. 198–215 in *Perspectives on Gulf Coast Prehistory*, edited by D.D. Davis, University Presses of Florida, Gainesville 1984.

Laming-Emperaire, A., "Missions archéologiques franco-brésiliennes de Lagoa Santa, Minas Gerair, Brésil–le Gran Abri de Lapa Vermalha, P.L., *Rev. Pre-Hist.*, 1979, pp. 53–89.

Loescher, Gil and Scanlan, John A., *Calculated Kindness: Refugees and America's Half-Open Door, 1945–The Present*, Collier Macmillan, London 1986.

Lorant, Stefan, *The New World*, Duell, Sloan & Pierce, New York 1945.

Loss, Allan, and Art Wolfe, *Indian Baskets of the Pacific Northwest and Alaska*, Portland, Oregon.

Luomala, Katherine, "Tipai-Ipai," pp. 592–609 in *California Volume 8*, edited by R.F. Heizer in *HONAI*, gen. ed., W.C. Sturtevant, Smithsonian Institute, Washington, D.C. 1978.

Marrus, Michael R., *The Unwanted: European Refugees in the Twentieth Century*, Oxford University Press 1985.

Martellone, Anna Maria, "Italian Mass Emigration to the United States, 1876–1930: A Historical Survey," *Perspectives in American History*. n.s. 1 (1984), 379–423.

McClellan, Catharine, *Part of the Land, Part of the Water: A History of the Yukon Indians*, Douglas & McIntyre, Vancouver and Toronto 1987.

McNeish, R.S., "The Early Man Remains for Pikimachay Cave, Ayacucho Basin, Highland Peru," pp. 1–48 in *Pre-Liano Cultures of the Americas: Paradoxes and Possibilities*, edited by R.L. Humphrey and Dennis Stanford Anthropological Society of Washington, Washington, D.C. 1979.

McNeish, R.S., "The Stratigraphy of Pikimachay, AD 100," in *Prehistory of the Ayacucho Basin, Peru, Vol. II: Excavations and Chronology*, University of Michigan Press, Ann Arbor 1981.

Mendizádal, Miguel O de, "Influencia de la sal en la distribución geográfica de los grupos indigenas de México," pp. 93–100 in Proceedings of the *Twenty-Third International Congress of Americanists Held at New York, 1928*, Science Press Printing Co., New York 1930.

Mendoza, Antonio de, April 17, 1540, "Letter to the King," translated by G.P. Winship, pp. 547–51 in *Fourteenth Annual Report of the Bureau of Ethnology*, Government Printing Office, Washington 1896.

Millar, J.F.V., *The Gray Site: An Early Plains Burial Ground*, Vol. 1, Manuscript Report No. 304, Ottawa Parks Canada.

Miller, Kerby, *Emigrants and Exiles: Ireland and the Irish. Exodus to North America*, New York 1985.

Mitchell, Christopher, ed. *Western Hemisphere Immigration and United States Foreign Policy*, Pennsylvania State University Press, University Park 1992.

Moch, Leslie Page, *Moving Europeans: Migration in Western Europe since 1650*, Bloomington 1992.

Morales Carrión, Arturo. *Puerto Rico: A Political and Cultural History*, W.W. Norton, New York 1983.

Morawska, Ewa, "Labor Migrations of Poles in the Atlantic World Economy, 1880—1914", *Comparative Studies in Society and History* 31 (1989), 237–72.

Myer, W.E., "Indian Trails of the Southeast," edited by J.R. Swanton, pp. 727–857 in *Forty-Second Annual Report of the Bureau of American Ethnology 1924–1925*, Government Printing Office, Washington 1928.

Navarro Garcia, Luis, *Sonora y Sinaloa en el Siglo XVII*. Sevilla: Escuela de Estudios Hispano-Americanos, CLXXVI, 1967.

Neils, Elaine M., *Reservation to City: Indian Migration and Federal Relocation*, University of Chicago Geography Department, Chicago, Illinois 1971.

Nelson, O.N., ed., *History of the Scandinavians and Successful Scandinavians in the United States*, vol. 1, Haskell, New York 1969.

Norman, Hans, and Harald Runblom, *From Sweden to America: A History of the Migration*, Minneapolis 1976.

North-Eastern Approaches, Newsletter, 1, No. 2, 1977 (pre-1700 settlements N.H. and Maine).

Nugent, Walter, *Crossings. The Great Transatlantic Migrations, 1870–1914*, Bloomington, Ind. 1992.

Ostergren, Robert C., *A Community Transplanted: The Trans-Atlantic Experience of a Swedish Immigrant Settlement in the Upper Midwest, 1835–1915*, Madison 1988.

Packard, Vance, *A Nation of Strangers*, David McKay Company, Inc., New York 1972.

Palmer, Ransford W., ed. *In Search of a Better Life: Perspectives on Migration from the Caribbean*, Praeger, New York 1990.

Rodman, Paul, *Mining Frontiers of the Far West, 1848–1880*, New York 1963.

Phillips, Philip, and James A. Brown, et.al., *Pre-Columbian Shell Engravings from the Craig Mound at Spiro, Oklahoma*, Peabody Museum of Archaeology and Ethnology, Pt. 1, Vol. 1, Harvard University, Cambridge, Mass. 1978.

Piore, Michael J., *Birds of Passage: Migrant Labor and Industrial Societies*, New York 1979.

Portes, Alejandro and Rubén G. Rumbaut. *Immigrant America: A Portrait*, University of California Press, Berkeley 1990.

Potter, Stephen R., *Commoners, Tribute, and Chiefs: The Development of Algonquian Culture in the Potomac Valley*, University Press of Virginia, Charlottesville and London 1993.

Puskas, Julianna, *From Hungary to the United States, 1880–1914*, Budapest 1982.

Ray, Arthur J., "The Hudson's Bay Company and Native People," pp. 335–350 in *History of Indian–White Relations*, Vol. 4, edited by W.E. Washburn, in *Handbook of North American Indians*, gen. ed., W.C. Sturtevant, Smtihsonian Institute, Washington, D.C. 1988.

Reddy, Marlita J., ed., *Statistical Record of Native North Americans*, Gale Research, Detroit 1993.

Richmond, Anthony, *Global Apartheid: Refugees, Racism and the New World Order*, Oxford U.P., Toronto, Canada 1994.

Riley, Carol L., "Las Casas and the Golden Cities," *Ethnohistory* 23:1, Winter 1976.

Riley, Carol L., *The Frontier People: The Greater Southwest in the Protohistoric Period*, University of New Mexico Press, Albuquerque 1987.

Riley, Thomas J., Gregory R. Walz, Charles J. Bareis, Andrew C. Fortier, and Katherine Parker, "Accelerator Mass Spectrometry (AMS) Dates Confirm Early Zea Mays in the Mississippi River Valley," *American Antiquity*, Vol. 59, No. 3, July 1994.

Robertson, James A., translator, *True Relation of the Hardships Suffered by Governor Fernando de Soto & Certain Portuguese Gentlemen During the Discovery of the Province of Florida*, Florida State Historical Society, Deland 1933.

Rogers, Andrei, ed., *Elderly Migration and Population Redistribution*, Belhaven Press, London 1992.

Rosoli, Gianfausto, ed., *Un Secolo di Emigrazione Italiana, 1876–1976*, Rome 1980.

Rountree, Helen C., ed., *Powhatan Foreign Relations, 1500–1722*, University Press of Virginia, Charlottesville and London 1993.

Ruby, Robert H., and John A. Brown, *Myron Eells and the Puget Sound Indians*, Superior Pub. Co., Seattle 1976.

Sánchez, George J. *Becoming Mexican American: Ethnicity, Culture and Identity in Chicano Los Angeles, 1900–1945*, Oxford University Press, New York 1993.

Sánchez Korrol, Virginia. *From Colonia to Community: The History of Puerto Ricans in New York City, 1917–1948*. Greenwood Press, Westport, Conn. 1983.

Sauer, Carl, *The Road to Cibola*, Ibero-Americana 3, University of California, Berkeley 1932.

Saunders, Joe W., and Thurman Allen, "Hedgepath Mounds, an Archaic Mound Complex in North-Central Louisiana, *American Antiquity* 59 (3), pp. 471–489, 1994.

Schlesier, Karl H., ed., *Plains, Indians, AD 500–1500: The Archaeological Past of Historic Groups*, University of Oklahoma Press, Norman and London 1994.

Sedelmayr, Jakob, "Sedelmayr's Relación of 1746," translated by Ronald L. Ives, pp. 99–117 in *Anthropological Papers*, Bureau of American Ethnology, Bull, 123, Government Printing Office, Washington, D.C. 1939.

Seller, Maxine Schwartz, *To Seek America: A History of Ethnic Life in the United States*, Englewood Cliffs 1988.

Sheehan, Michael S., "Cultural Responses to the Altithermal: The Role of Aquifer-Related Water Sources," *Geoarchaeology: An International Journal*, Vol. 9, No. 2, pp. 113–137, 1994.

Shergold, Peter R., *Working-Class Life: The "American Standard" in Comparative Perspective, 1899–1913*, Pittsburgh 1982.

Simon, Rita J., and Caroline B. Brettell, *International Migration: The Female Experience*, Totowa, N. J. 1986.

Sowter, T.W.E., "Indian Trade, Travel, and Transportation," *Archaeological Report*, Ontario Provincial Museum, 1916.

Spier, Leslie, *Klamath Ethnography*, Publications in American Archaeology and Ethnology, Vol. 30, University of California, Berkeley 1930.

Steward, Julian H., *Basin-Plateau Aboriginal Sociopolitical Groups*, Bureau of American Ethnology, Bull, 120, Government Printing Office, Washington, D.C. 1938.

Swagerty, William R., "Indian Trade in the Trans-Mississippi West to 1870," pp. 351, in *History of Indian–White Relations*, edited by W.E. Washburn in *Handbook of North American Indians*, Vol. 4, gen. ed., W.C. Sturtevant, Smithsonian Institute, Washington 1988.

Swan, James G., *The Indians of Cape Flattery at the Entrance of the Strait of Fuca*, Washington Territory, Smithsonian Contributions to Knowledge, Vol. 16, No. 8, 1870.

Swierenga, Robert P., *They Came to Stay: Essays on Dutch Immigration*, New Brunswick 1988.

Teague, George A., "The Nonflaked Stone Artifacts from Las Colinas," pp. 102–47 in *The 1968 Excavations at Mound 8 Las Colinas*, edited by Laurens C. Hammack and Alan P. Sullivan, Arizona State Museum Archaeological Series No.154, University of Arizona, Tucson 1981.

Takaki, Ronald, *Strangers from a Different Shore: A History of Asian Americans*, Boston 1989.

Tanner, Helen Hornbeck, *Zespedes in East Florida, 1784–1790*, University of Miami Press, Coral Gables 1963. Rev. ed., University of Florida Press, Gainesville 1989.

Tanner, Helen Hornbeck, "The Career of Joseph LaFrance, Coureur de Bois in the Upper Great Lakes," in Jennifer S.H. Brown, W.J. Eccles, and Donald P. Heldman, eds. *The Fur Trade Revisited: Selected Papers of the Sixth North American Fur Trade Conference, Mackinac Island, Michigan 1991*, Michigan State University Press/Mackinac State Historic Parks, East Lansing/Mackinac Island 1994.

Taylor Henry L., *Race and the City: Work, Community, and Protest in Cincinnati, 1820–1970*, ed. Henry Louis Taylor, Jr., University of Illinois Press, Urbana 1993.

Taylor, Philip, *The Distant Magnet. European Emigration to the U.S.A.*, New York 1971.

Teit, James A., *The Lillooet Indians*, American Museum of Natural History, Memoir, Vol. 4, No. x, New York 1906.

Teit, James A., *The Shuswap Indians*, American Museum of Natural History, Memoir, Vol. 4, New York 1909.

Thernstrom, Stephen, ed. *Harvard Encyclopedia of American Ethnic Groups*, Belknap Press of Harvard University Press, Cambridge, Mass. 1980.

Thistlethwaite, Frank, "Migration from Europe Overseas in the 19th and 20th Centuries," *XIe Congrès International des Sciences Historiques, Rapports*, Vol. 5, Uppsala 1960.

Thomas, William I., and Florian Znaniecki, *The Polish Peasant in Europe and America*, 5 vols. (Chicago, Bosten, 1918–1920, repr. in several different editions).

Tilly, Charles, "Migration in Modern European History," in William H. McNeill and Ruth S. Adams, eds., *Human Migration. Patterns and Politics*, 48–72 Bloomington 1978.

Tinker, Hugh, *A New System of Slavery. The Export of Indian Labour Overseas 1830–1920*, London 1974.

Tower, Donald B., *The Use of Marne Mollusca and Their Value in Reconstructing Prehistoric Trade Routes in the American Southwest*, Excavators' Club, Papers Vol. 2, No. 3, Cambridge 1945.

Trigger, Bruce G., *The Children of Aataentsic II: A History of the Huron People to 1660*, McGill–Queen's University Press, Montreal 1976.

Udall, Stewart L., *To the Inland Empire: Coronado and Our Spanish Legacy*, Doubleday & Co., Garden City 1987.

Upham, Steadman, *Politics and Power*, Academic Press, New York 1982.

Vecoli, Rudolph J., and Suzanne M. Sinke, eds., (1991). *A Century of European Migrations, 1830–1930* Urbana, Ill. 1991.

Velarde, Luis, "Velarde's Description of Pimeria Alta," pp. 622–675 in *Kino and Manje*, edited by E.J. Burrus, Jesuit Historical Institute, Rome 1971.

Walker, James W. St.G. *The West Indians in Canada*, Canadian Historical Association, Ottawa 1984.

Warren, A.H., "Geological and Mineral Resources of the Cochiti Reservoir Area," pp. 46–58 in *Archaeological Investigations in Cochiti Reservoir, New Mexico*, Vol. 4, edited by J.V. Biella and R.C. Chapman, University of New Mexico Department of Anthropology Office of Contract Archaeology, Albuquerque 1979.

Webb, Clarence H., "The Poverty Point Culture," *Geoscience and Map*, Vol. 17, School of Geoscience, Louisiana State University, Baton Rouge 1977.

Weber, David J. *The Spanish Frontier in North America*, Yale University Press, New York and London 1992.

Weinberg, Sydney Stahl, *The World of Our Mothers: The Lives of Jewish Immigrant Women*, New York 1988.

Willcox, Walter F., and Imre Ferenczi, *International Migrations*, 2 vols., New York 1929, 1931.

Winzerlins, Oscar W., *Acadian*, Odyssey, Baton Rouge 1955.

Wolf, Eric R., *Europe and the People without History*, Berkeley, CA. 1982.

Wood, Peter H., Gregory A. Waselkov, and M. Thomas Hatley, eds., *Powhatan's Mantle: Indians in the Colonial Southeast*, University of Nebraska Press, Lincoln and London 1989.

Wood, W. Raymond, "Plains Trade in Prehistory and Protohistoric Intertribal Relations," pp. 98–109 in *Anthropology on the Great Plains*, edited by W. Raymond Wood and Margot Liberty, University of Nebraska Press, Lincoln 1980.

Wright, James V., The Ontario Iroquois Tradition, National Museum of Canada, Bull 210, Ottawa 1966.

Wyman, Mark, *DP: Europe's Displaced Persons, 1945–1951*, Balch Institute Press, Philadelphia 1989.

Wyman, Mark, *Round-Trip to America: The Immigrants Return to Europe, 1880–1930*, Ithaca: Cornell 1993.

Yans-McLaughlin, Virginia, *Family and Community: Italian Immigrants in Buffalo, 1880–1930*, Ithaca 1977.

Zogby, John, *Arab America Today*, Arab America Institute, Washington, D.C. 1990.

We made extensive use of information published by Statistics Canada and its predecessor agencies, dominion and provincial, and by the U.S. Bureau of the Census.

INDEX

The items shown below in **bold** type refer to picture captions or map pages.

Items in *italic* type indicate references in quotes.

ACKNOWLEDGEMENTS

A project of this scope has called for the cooperation and assistance of many people in Canada, England, Germany, Poland, and the United States. John S. Aubrey, Gabriele Scardellato, and Chris Schüler handled more research than their identification as map contributors would indicate. Henry R. Drewal reviewed parts of both maps and text. Assistance with research queries was generously given by: Alice B. Kehoe, Nancy O. Lurie, David R. Miller, Byron Moldafski, Brian S. Osborne, Raymond D. Fogelson, Charles Hudson, Lee Davis, Gwendolyn Midlo Hall, Jon T. Gibson, Hiram F. Gregory, Robert J. Surtees, William R. Swagerty, Tom Dillehay, Raymond J. DeMallie, Douglas Parks, Patricia C. Griffin, Heather Jones, Denys Delage, André Caissy, Dee Ann Story, Roger Thompson, Catharine McClellan, Robert Karrow, Patrick Morris, James Ackerman, James Grossman, Olive Patricia Dickason, Roger Walke, Sabine Kirschenhoffer, Joan Johnson, and David Pedlar.

For Indian locations on Bernard Bailyn's map of the English colonies, Robert S. Grumet was particularly helpful. Other anthropologists, archaeologists, and historians who supplied data for specific areas were: David Ghere, Colin Calloway, Dean Snow, William N. Fenton, Kevin McBride, Eric Johnson, Jean O'Brien Kehoe, Kathleen Bragdon, Paul A. Robinson, Charlotte Taylor, Marshall Becker, Thomas Davidson, Helen Rountree, Stephen R. Potter, and David Phelps.

Special aid in securing illustrative material was provided by John F. Hornbeck, Joe Holbach, Pamela Steele, John Magill, Edward Dahl, Mary Holt, Jami J. Lockhart, Dee Marvin, Kimberly Miller, and Page Edwards.